EYEWITNESS TRAVEL

FLORENCE & TUSCANY

MAIN CONTRIBUTOR: CHRISTOPHER CATLING

LONDON, NEW YORK,
MELBOURNE, MUNICH AND DELHI
www.dk.com

PROJECT EDITOR Shirin Patel
ART EDITOR Pippa Hurst
EDITORS Maggie Crowley,
Tom Fraser, Sasha Heseltine
DESIGNERS Claire Edwards,
Emma Hutton, Marisa Renzullo
MAP CO-ORDINATORS Simon Farbrother, David Pugh

CONTRIBUTORS
Anthony Brierley, Kerry Fisher,
Tim Jepson, Carolyn Pyrah

MAPS
Jan Clark, James Mills-Hicks
(Dorling Kindersley Cartography)

PHOTOGRAPHERS
Philip Enticknap,
John Heseltine, Kim Sayer

ILLUSTRATORS
Stephen Conlin, Donati Giudici Associati srl,
Richard Draper, Robbie Polley

Reproduced by Colourscan, Singapore
Printed and bound by South China Printing Co. Ltd., China

First published in Great Britain in 1994
by Dorling Kindersley Limited
80 Strand, London WC2R 0RL

**Reprinted with revisions 1994 (twice), 1996,
1997, 1999, 2000, 2001, 2002, 2003, 2004, 2005, 2006**

Copyright 1994, 2006
© Dorling Kindersley Limited, London
A Penguin Company

A CIP CATALOGUE RECORD IS AVAILABLE FROM THE BRITISH LIBRARY.

ISBN 1-40531-087-1
ISBN 978-14053-1-087-1

FLOORS ARE REFERRED TO THROUGHOUT IN ACCORDANCE WITH EUROPEAN
USAGE; IE THE "FIRST FLOOR" IS THE FLOOR ABOVE GROUND LEVEL

Front cover main image: Santa Maria del Fiore, Florence

**The information in this
DK Eyewitness Travel Guide is checked annually.**
Every effort has been made to ensure that this book is as up-to-date
as possible at the time of going to press. Some details, however,
such as telephone numbers, opening hours, prices, gallery hanging
arrangements and travel information are liable to change. The
publishers cannot accept responsibility for any consequences arising
from the use of this book, nor for any material on third party
websites, and cannot guarantee that any website address in this
book will be a suitable source of travel information. We value the
views and suggestions of our readers very highly. Please write to:
Publisher, DK Eyewitness Travel Guides, Dorling Kindersley,
80 Strand, London, WC2R 0RL.

CONTENTS

HOW TO USE THIS
GUIDE 6

Putto in Palazzo Vecchio

INTRODUCING FLORENCE AND TUSCANY

FOUR GREAT DAYS IN
FLORENCE AND
TUSCANY 10

PUTTING FLORENCE
AND TUSCANY
ON THE MAP 12

A PORTRAIT OF
TUSCANY 18

FLORENCE AND
TUSCANY THROUGH
THE YEAR 34

THE HISTORY
OF FLORENCE AND
TUSCANY 40

Flag from Siena's Palio

A Tuscan country scene in the Crete

FLORENCE AREA BY AREA

FLORENCE AT A GLANCE **58**

CITY CENTRE EAST **60**

CITY CENTRE NORTH **84**

CITY CENTRE WEST **100**

OLTRARNO **114**

Cheese seller in Siena

FOUR GUIDED WALKS **128**

FLORENCE STREET FINDER **138**

TUSCANY AREA BY AREA

TUSCANY AT A GLANCE **150**

WESTERN TUSCANY **152**

NORTHERN TUSCANY **168**

EASTERN TUSCANY **190**

CENTRAL TUSCANY **206**

SOUTHERN TUSCANY **230**

TRAVELLERS' NEEDS

WHERE TO STAY **244**

RESTAURANTS, CAFES AND BARS **264**

SHOPS AND MARKETS **284**

ENTERTAINMENT **290**

SPECIALIST HOLIDAYS AND OUTDOOR ACTIVITIES **292**

SURVIVAL GUIDE

PRACTICAL INFORMATION **296**

Fresco in Santa Maria Novella

TRAVEL INFORMATION **306**

GENERAL INDEX **316**

PHRASE BOOK **335**

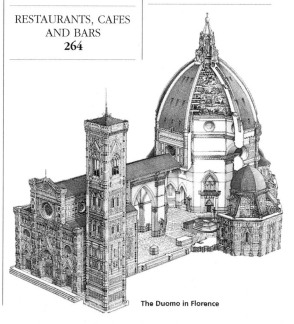
The Duomo in Florence

HOW TO USE THIS GUIDE

This guide helps you get the most from your stay in Florence and Tuscany. It provides both expert recommendations and detailed practical information. *Introducing Florence and Tuscany* maps the region and sets it in its historical and cultural context. *Florence Area by Area and Tuscany Area by Area* describe the important sights, with maps, pictures and detailed illustrations. Suggestions for food, drink, accommodation and shopping are in *Travellers' Needs*, and the *Survival Guide* has tips on everything from the Italian telephone system to getting to Tuscany and travelling around the region.

FLORENCE AREA BY AREA

The historic centre of the city has been divided into four sightseeing areas. Each has its own chapter, which opens with a list of the sights described. All the sights are numbered and plotted on an *Area Map*. The detailed information for each sight is presented in numerical order, making it easy to locate within the chapter.

Sights at a Glance lists the chapter's sights by category: Churches; Museums and Galleries; Historic Buildings, Streets and Piazzas.

All pages relating to Florence have red thumb tabs.

A locator map shows where you are in relation to other areas of the city centre.

1 Area Map
For easy reference, the sights are numbered and located on a map. The sights are also shown on the Florence Street Finder *on pages 140–47.*

2 Street-by-Street Map
This gives a bird's eye view of the heart of each sightseeing area.

A suggested route for a walk covers the more interesting streets in the area.

Stars indicate the sights that no visitor should miss.

3 Detailed information on each sight
All the sights in Florence are described individually. Addresses, telephone numbers, opening hours and information on admission charges and wheelchair access are also provided.

TUSCANY AREA BY AREA   445

CENTRAL TUSCANY

1 Introduction

The landscape, history and character of each region is described here, showing how the area has developed over the centuries and what it offers to the visitor today.

TUSCANY AREA BY AREA

In this book, Tuscany has been divided into five regions, each of which has a separate chapter. The most interesting sights to visit have been numbered on a *Regional Map*.

Each area of Tuscany can be quickly identified by its colour coding.

2 Regional Map

This shows the road network and gives an illustrated overview of the whole region. All the sights are numbered and there are also useful tips on getting around the region by car, bus and train.

3 Detailed information on each sight

All the important towns and other places to visit are described individually. They are listed in order, following the numbering on the Regional Map. Within each town or city, there is detailed information on important buildings and other sights.

Stars indicate the best features and works of art.

For all the top sights, a Visitors' Checklist provides the practical information you will need to plan your visit.

4 The top sights

These are given two or more full pages. Historic buildings are dissected to reveal their interiors; museums and galleries have colour-coded floorplans to help you locate the most interesting exhibits.

INTRODUCING FLORENCE AND TUSCANY

FOUR GREAT DAYS IN FLORENCE
AND TUSCANY 10–11

PUTTING FLORENCE AND
TUSCANY ON THE MAP 12–17

A PORTRAIT OF TUSCANY 18–33

FLORENCE AND TUSCANY
THROUGH THE YEAR 34–39

THE HISTORY OF FLORENCE
AND TUSCANY 40–57

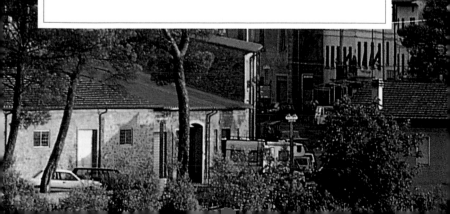

FOUR GREAT DAYS IN FLORENCE AND TUSCANY

There is something for just about everyone in Florence and Tuscany: from viewing some of the world's greatest Renaissance art to wandering around designer boutiques; and from exploring the surrounding countryside with its historic hilltowns, wine and charming restaurants to visiting one of the many spa towns. Each of these itineraries has a theme, but they can be tailored to suit your needs. Apart from the day of art in Florence, which can be done on foot, parts of the family day may be easier by bus or taxi while the other days do require a car. The price guides include the cost of travel, food and admission fees.

Shoes with style at the Ferragamo Shoe Museum, Florence

RENAISSANCE ART AND SHOPPING

• **The magnificent Duomo and Brunelleschi's dome**
• **Michelangelo's David**
• **Renaissance art in the Uffizi**
• **Stylish shoes and chic shops**

TWO ADULTS allow at least €75

Morning
Start the day at Brunelleschi's glorious church of **San Lorenzo** *(see pp90–91)*, with its unfinished, rough-hewn façade. The adjacent **Medici Tombs** *(see p91)*, designed by Michelangelo as a mausoleum for the Medici family, are gloomy yet impressive. Just a five-minute walk from here is the breathtaking **Duomo** *(see pp64–5)* with its vast dome also by Brunelleschi. Opposite it is the **Baptistry** with its ornate East Doors *(see p66)*, and the Campanile with fine views of the dome and the city below. Pause for a lively, cheap lunch at **Da Mario** *(see p270)*.

Afternoon
Stroll across to **Piazza della Signoria** *(see pp76–7)*, where a copy of Michelangelo's celebrated *David* stands outside the **Palazzo Vecchio** *(see pp78–9)*. The real one is in the **Galleria dell'Accademia** *(see p94–5)*. Just round the corner is the **Uffizi** *(see pp80–3)*, with its unrivalled collection of Renaissance art. At least half a day is needed to appreciate its wonderful treasures so you may wish to return another day to spend more time here. Head to the **Ponte Vecchio** *(see pp106–7)*, taking in the jeweller's shops and old workshops that line the bridge.
Afterwards walk to **Via de' Tornabuoni** *(see p105)* with its chic boutiques for a spot of shopping. For anyone interested in footwear, Ferragamo's Shoe Museum is also here. Finish with a chilled glass of *prosecco* at **Procacci** *(see p283)*.

A FAMILY DAY OUT IN FLORENCE

• **Gory waxworks**
• **Picnic in the Boboli Gardens**
• **Explore the Palazzo Vecchio**
• **Ride around town in a horse-drawn carriage**

FAMILY OF 4 allow at least €120

Morning
First thing, if it is a fine day, go to the **Mercato Centrale** *(see p88)* to stock up on goodies for a picnic. Then, head over to the Oltrarno and the **Museo "La Specola"** *(see p119)*, an unusual zoological museum with a rather gory display of 18th-century anatomical waxworks (parental discretion may be required for young children).
The **Boboli Gardens** *(see pp124–5)* makes a great spot for a picnic lunch and a run around. If it's raining, try one of the many eateries near **Piazza di Santo Spirito** *(see p118)*. In either case, lunch should be followed by a

A nightmarish scene at the Waxworks at La Specola

gelato (ice cream) from **Café Ricchi** *(see p272)* in the same square.

Afternoon
On a warm day, take the kids for a swim at the outdoor pool at **Bellariva** *(see p293)*, open Jun–mid-Sep. If cool, a visit to **Palazzo Vecchio** *(see p78)* is a good bet; tours of secret passages and other activities (also in English) geared to all ages are organized within the palazzo museum. End the day with a leisurely ride around the *centro storico* in one of the horse-drawn carriages that stand in Piazza Signoria, before going for a pizza.

MEDIEVAL HISTORY, ART AND CULTURE

- A dramatic hilltown
- Siena's striped Duomo
- Sienese art in the Pinacoteca Nazionale
- An aperitivo in the Piazza del Campo

TWO ADULTS allow at least €135

Morning
Arrive by car early in **San Gimignano** *(see pp212–15)*, arguably Tuscany's most famous hilltown. Must-see sights here are the 13th-century towers, the frescoes in the Collegiata church, and the art in the Museo Civico. You might like to buy a bottle of the local Vernaccia wine and have a coffee in Piazza della Cisterna before setting off to **Siena** *(see pp216–19)*.

Head straight for theatrical Piazza del Campo where the energetic can climb the Torre del Mangia, while others can visit the medieval state rooms in the Palazzo Pubblico. Don't miss Lorenzetti's frescoes of the *Allegory of Good and Bad Government*. Take a break for lunch at the **Osteria Le Logge** *(see p280)*.

Afternoon
Visit the striped Gothic **Duomo** *(see pp220–21)*, then pop into the **Pinacoteca**

Archway view of Siena's Piazza del Campo at dusk

Nazionale *(see p219)* to see its 12th-15th century Sienese masters. Or you could wander the streets on the lookout for signs, which represent the 17 *contrade* (or districts), such as ceramic animal plaques and fountains. End the day with an *aperitivo* at one of the bars on Piazza del Campo.

TUSCAN HILL TOWN TOUR

- Montepulciano and its Vino Nobile wines
- A leisurely lunch in Pienza
- Frescoes in Sant'Anna
- A soak in the thermal pools at Bagno Vignoni

TWO ADULTS allow at least €75

Morning
Drive to **Montepulciano** *(see p227)*, one of Tuscany's highest hilltop towns and

famous for its Vino Nobile wines. Visit the Duomo and Sangallo's Temple of San Biagio just outside the town. About 5 km (3 miles) to the southeast, the tiny medieval village of **Monticchiello** *(see p209)*, set in an idyllic landscape, is a wonderful place to stop for a coffee break. Its 13th-century church is worth a visit too. Move on to **Pienza** *(see p226)*, Pope Pius II's ideal Renaissance town, where you will find charming cobbled streets and panoramic ramparts to explore. Buy some local *pecorino* (sheep's cheese) before lunching at **La Pergola** *(see p279)*.

Afternoon
From Pienza, the road winds through glorious countryside. Take a detour to the remote monastery of **Sant'Anna in Camprena** (where part of *The English Patient* was filmed) with its refectory frescoes by Sodoma *(see p226)*. Once you get to **San Quirico d'Orcia** *(see p225)*, visit the beautiful 12th-century Collegiata, with three Romanesque doorways carved in local travertine. There is also a pretty 16th-century Italianate garden, the Horti Leonini. Finish the day with a soak in the outdoor 37 °C (98.6 °F) pools at the Hotel Posta Marcucci in the medieval spa village of **Bagno Vignoni** *(see p226)*. You will find several good restaurants for dinner.

Tall cypress trees, in the timeless landcape of southern Tuscany

Putting Florence and Tuscany on the Map

Tuscany lies in Central Italy, bordered by the regions of Emilia-Romagna, Marche, Umbria and Lazio. Along with Elba, several islands in the Ligurian Sea also form part of Tuscany. A region of rolling hills, mountains and rugged Mediterranean coastlines, Tuscany covers an area of 22,992 sq km (8,875 sq miles), and has a population of over 3.5 million. There are international airports at Pisa and Florence. Florence is about 2½ hours by train from Rome, and about 3 hours from Milan.

München (Munich)

GERMANY

LIECHTENSTEIN Innst

FRANCE

Genève (Geneva)

SWITZERLAND

St Moritz

Rhône

L. Maggiore

EUROPE

NORWAY FINLAND

SWEDEN

ESTONIA RUSSIAN FEDERATION

DENMARK LATVIA

LITHUANIA

REP OF IRELAND UNITED KINGDOM

NETHERLAND BELORUSSIA

BELGIUM GERMANY POLAND

LUXEMBOURG

CZECH REP.

SLOVAKIA

FRANCE AUSTRIA

SWITZERLAND HUNGARY

SLOVENIA ROMANIA

ITALY CROATIA

BOSNIA SERBIA AND

AND MONTENEGRO

SPAIN HERZEGOVINA BULGARIA

Firenze MACEDONIA

(Florence) ALBANIA

GREECE

L. di Garda

Bergamo

Milano (Milan)

Po

Genova (Genoa)

See inside back cover

Bolog

La Spezia

Lucca FIRENZI (FLORE

Nice Pisa Arn

Livorno TOSCANA (TUSCANY) Are

Toulon Siena

Ligurian Sea

Piombino

Elba

Calvi Bastia

Porto S. Stéfano

CORSICA Civitavecchia

Tyrrhenian Sea

KEY

☐ Tuscany

⚓ Ferry port

✈ Airport

▬ Motorway

▬ Major road

— Railway line

Olbia

SARDINIA

| 0 kilometres | 100 |
| 0 miles | 100 |

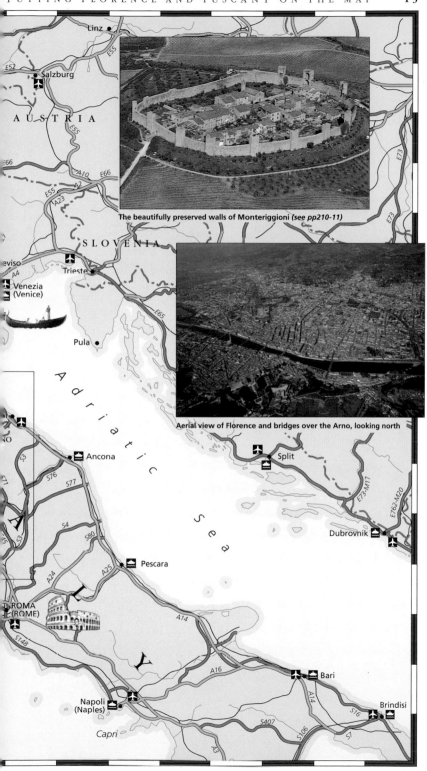

The beautifully preserved walls of Monteriggioni *(see pp210-11)*

Aerial view of Florence and bridges over the Arno, looking north

Greater Florence

S65 ↑ Bologna

↑ Faenza
S302

VIA DELLE MASSE

VIA BOLOGNESE

Mugnone

VIA FAENTINA

Terzolle

Pian
di S.
Bartolo

rpiolle

Trespiano

Pian di
Mugnone

VIA DEI BOSCONI

MONTE
MUSCOLI

VIA DI VINCIGLIATA

Careggi

La Lastra

FIESOLE

VIA DELLA COLLINA

Le
nche

VIA BOLOGNESE

La Pietra

Lapo

Ponte alla
Badia

S. Domenico

MONTE
CECERI

Mensola

Montebeni

redi

Camerata

Maiano

V.D. SELVA

Il Salviatino

Settignano

San
Gervasio

Poggio
Gherardo

Stazione di
Campo
di Marte

Campo
di Marte

Coverciano

Ponte a
Mensola

Stazione Centrale
di Santa Maria Novella

Filarocca

San Salvi

Pontassieve

E N Z E

VIA ARETINA S67

te
Carraia

Madonnone

Varlungo

S. Iacopo
al Girone

Ponte
Vecchio

Ponte alle
Grazie

Ponte S.
Niccolò

Ponte G. da
Verrazzano

VIA GENERALE DALLA CHIESA

Ponte di
Varlungo

Ricorboli

VIA DI VILLAMAGNA

VIA DI VILLAMAGNA

obolino

MONTE
ALLE
CROCI

Gavinana

Nave a
Rovezzano

Rimaggio

VIALE   EUROPA

Gamberaia

Sorgane

**BAGNO
A RIPOLI**

oggio
periale

Arcetri

Piazza
Calda

Pian Dei
Giullari

Ponte
a Ema

Ema

Stazione di
Firenze Sud

S. Piero
a Ema

A1 (E35)

ONTE
CCIOLI

AUTOSTRADA DEL SOLE

MILANO-ROMA

VIA DELL'ANTELLA

MONTE
FATTUCCHIA

S. Gersole

Grassina

S222

↑ Greve in
Chianti

Florence City Centre

Florence's best sights are encompassed within such a compact area that the city seems to reveal its treasures at every step. The sights described in this book are grouped within four areas, each of which can be easily explored on foot. In the centre is the massive Duomo, providing a historical as well as geographical focus to the city. Santa Croce to the east and San Marco to the north, with Santa Maria Novella to the west and the Palazzo Pitti in Oltrarno, mark the outlying areas.

City Centre West *(see pp100–13)*: Ponte Santa Trinità, with Ponte Vecchio behind

Oltrarno *(see pp114–27)*: taking a break in Piazza di Santo Spirito

KEY

▦	Major sight
FS	Railway station
▦	Bus terminus
▦	Coach terminus
P	Parking
ⓘ	Tourist information
✚	Hospital with casualty unit
▦	Police station
✝	Church
✡	Synagogue

City Centre North *(see pp84–99)*: fountain in Piazza della Santissima Annunziata

City Centre East *(see pp60–83)*: main entrance to Palazzo Vecchio

0 metres 500

0 yards 500

A PORTRAIT OF TUSCANY

Tuscany is renowned throughout the world for its art, history and beautiful landscape. Here the past merges with the present to a remarkable degree, for its people pride themselves on their heritage. Independent and combative, for centuries they have preserved their surroundings and traditions, in which must lie much of Tuscany's eternal fascination for the outsider.

The people of Tuscany are fiercely proud of their ancestry, which they trace back to the Etruscans. Geneticists have even discovered gene segments that are uniquely Tuscan: there are strong similarities between the faces carved on Etruscan cremation urns *(see pp42–3)* and those of the people on the streets of modern Tuscany.

A classic Tuscan face captured by Botticelli

Florence and its surroundings were occupied by the Germans during World War II, and memories of the disgrace suffered under Fascism are still strong. As a result, people in this area have a fierce love of democracy and a strong sense of obligation to vote and participate in politics, even at grass-roots levels, through referendums on such issues as whether to ban traffic from the centre of Florence, for example. Florentines will, however, take the law into their own hands, as they did when they fought the police in 1990 to prevent the closure of San Lorenzo market.

The Tuscan love of home has resulted in a strong *campanilismo*: parochialism defined by the sound of the local church bell (in the campanile or belltower). Social anthropologists see in it a survival of medieval inter-city conflicts. It can be observed at many a Tuscan festival when, beneath the pageantry, there is a serious rivalry between a city's different quarters.

A timeless view and way of life: peaceful old age in Casole d'Elsa

◁ Brilliant, medieval-style pageantry before Siena's Palio *(see p222)*

A rare sight today – farming with oxen near Pienza

Even the working day of many Tuscans echoes that of their ancestors centuries ago. For people who work out in the fields, the day begins at sunrise, as early as 4:30am in summer. Farm and vineyard labourers will have completed a day's work by noon, when they retire indoors to eat and rest.

Until the 1950s, most Tuscans were familiar with this pattern of life: the region still relied on a feudal system, *mezzadria*, whereby peasants working on the land without payment took a share of the crops as their reward. Today, agricultural produce remains an important ingredient in the Tuscan economy, but

A cheese stall in Florence

only 20 per cent of Tuscans now work in agriculture. Many farming families left the land in favour of a stable income and a shorter working day as factory hands. Town dwellers have a much easier way of life, but the old rhythms prevail: the *siesta* period is still observed, so that almost everything closes for a few hours in the afternoon. Wise travellers soon learn that it pays to follow the same pattern, rising early to join the café throng, before heading out to study ancient frescoes in peace. In the middle of Florence there are several lively early morning markets where you can buy fresh, local produce *(see p287)*. Bargain hunters and food-loving Tuscans frequent them, but by 2pm the stallholders will have packed up.

Churches open at 8am, and, except on Sunday when mass is held, there will be few other people to disturb your thoughts if you stray into one. Today, very few Tuscans go regularly to church and Sunday is spent visiting friends, watching sport or enjoying

Clerics in conversation, Colle di Val d'Elsa

family lunch. After the burst of activity that marks the beginning of the day, Tuscan towns adopt a more sedate pace. New building is prohibited inside their walls, so that very many people of school or working age travel out, by bus or car, to schools, offices or factories in the suburbs, leaving the old centres to visitors.

The grape harvest in Chianti

Some of the larger towns, particularly Pisa, Lucca, Florence and Siena, have resisted this tide, determined not to become museum cities given over entirely to tourism. They have thriving

The hour for relaxing in Cortona

service sectors, testimony to the same Tuscan flair for banking, insurance and accountancy that made the Medici family and the "Merchant of Prato" (see p188) some of the richest people in their time. It is, however, the lucky few who work in such beautiful towns. They practise as lawyers, architects, conservationists or designers and are often graduates of the renowned local universities: Pisa, Siena and Florence. For the great majority of Tuscans, however, the working day is spent in purpose-built suburbs, such as the one linking Prato to the Firenze Nuova (New Florence) suburbs west of the city. The Tuscan economy, however, still remains firmly rooted in craft traditions. Top designers from Milan use the textile factories of Prato and Florence for the execution of their designs. Gold-working is not confined to the Ponte Vecchio workshops in Florence – Arezzo produces jewellery which is sold throughout Europe.

THRIVING EXPORTS

Glass, marble and motorcycles are among Tuscany's most important industrial products, while its olive oil and wine are exported worldwide. This explains why Livorno, Tuscany's port, is the second busiest in Italy, while Pisa's Galileo Galilei airport is rapidly becoming a major air-freight distribution centre.

Individual Tuscan artistry can best be admired in the heart of any Tuscan town during the evening promenade – the *passeggiata*. One moment the streets are empty, the next they are filled with elegant people strolling and chatting. The skill of *fare bella figura* ("looking good") is so prized that visitors will be judged by the same standard. It is an opportunity for you to join in the inherently Tuscan aspiration to create a civilized world.

Italian chic, or *bella figura*

A Tuscan Town Square

Town bell in the campanile

The main square or piazza of nearly every Tuscan town is the focus for much of the town's activities. It is here that the townsfolk gather around 6–7pm for the daily *passeggiata*, the traditional evening stroll, or to participate in local festivals and rallies. In most towns there are certain religious and civic buildings that are usually grouped around the piazza. Many of these buildings, you will notice, have standard features, such as the campanile, the *cortile* or the loggia, each of which fulfils a specific function. And often you will find that many of these buildings are still in use today, performing the same function for which they were originally built during the 13th–16th centuries.

Wellhead
Water was a valuable resource that was protected by strict laws to prevent pollution.

Marble or hard sandstone paving

A palazzo is any town house of stature. It is usually named after its owner.

Cortile
The arcaded court-yard, or cortile, of a palazzo served as an entrance hall shielded from the outside; it also provided a cool retreat.

There are three floors in most palazzi. Public reception rooms were on the middle floor, the *piano nobile*.

The ground floor was used for storage and workshops. Today many ground floors are let to businesses, while the owners live above.

Baptismal font

Stemmae
Stone-carved coats-of-arms, belonging to citizens who served as councillors and magistrates, are often seen on public buildings.

The Baptistry, usually octagonal, was a separate building to the west of the church. After baptism, the infant was carried ceremoniously into the church for the first time.

Festival in the Piazza
The prestigious buildings of the main piazza often form an appropriate backdrop to costumed tournaments involving jousting, archery and horsemanship, recalling the medieval arts of war.

Fishtail battlements

Loggia
Many loggias, built to provide shelter from the sun or rain, now harbour colourful street markets.

The Palazzo del Comune (town hall) often houses the Museo Civico (town museum) and the Pinacoteca (art gallery).

Wide central nave, with narrower side aisles

Loggia or colonnade

The campanile rose high so that the town bells could be heard far and wide. The bells were rung to announce public meetings or mass, to sound the curfew, or, when rung furiously *(a stormo)*, to warn of impending danger.

The Duomo (from Latin *Domus Dei* or House of God) is the cathedral, the focal point of the piazza. A smaller parish church is called a *pieve*.

Side Chapel
Wealthy patrons paid for ornate tombs, paintings and frescoes in their own private chapels to commemorate their dead.

Understanding Architecture in Tuscany

Romanesque capital

The survival of so many fine Gothic and Renaissance buildings is part of Tuscany's immense appeal. Whole streets and squares, such as the Piazza dei Priori in Volterra *(see p167)* and the streets around the Mercato Nuovo in Florence, and even towns such as San Gimignano, have scarcely changed since the 16th century. Simple clues, such as the shape of arches, windows and doorways, reveal the style of the building and when it was built.

Gothic palazzi in Cortona

ROMANESQUE (5TH TO MID-13TH CENTURIES)

The Tuscan Romanesque style developed from late Roman architecture. Early Tuscan churches, such as Sant'Antimo *(see pp44–5)*, have round arches, Roman-style columns and arcades. Profuse surface decoration was introduced in the 12th century, resulting in the jewel-like church façades of Pisa and Lucca.

A twisted knot

Interlace and knots are typical motifs.

Capitals are carved with animal and human heads.

Gables often have three tiers of arcading.

The central portal is flanked by smaller side doors.

Pisa's San Paolo a Ripa d'Arno (see p161), *begun in 1210, has restrained geometric patterns on the lower façade and exuberant arcades above.*

Marble patterning on stonework

GOTHIC (13TH TO MID-15TH CENTURIES)

Pointed arches are the key feature of Gothic architecture. The style was introduced to Tuscany by French Cistercian monks who built the abbey of San Galgano in 1218 *(see p224)*. Siena then made this style her own, using it for the city's Duomo, palazzi and civic buildings such as Palazzo Pubblico *(see pp218–23)*.

The crockets are shaped like leaves and flowers.

Santa Maria della Spina *(1230–1323), with its pointed gables and spikey pinnacles* (see p161), *is a typical example of Pisan Gothic architecture.*

Pinnacles, like miniature spires, bristle from the roofline.

Pointed gables

Gabled niches, sheltering statues of saints or Apostles, are a Gothic innovation.

St Luke, from Orsanmichele

RENAISSANCE (15TH AND 16TH CENTURIES)

Brunelleschi, the father of Renaissance architecture, was inspired by the purity and simplicity of Classical Roman buildings. This style is reflected in his first true Renaissance work, the loggia of the Spedale degli Innocenti in Florence (1419–24) *(see p95)*, with its elegant lines and simple arched bays. The style he created was adopted with enthusiasm by his fellow Florentines, who saw their city as the "new" Rome.

Arch with tear-drop keystone

Courtyard, Spedale degli Innocenti

Classical cornices are moulded in Roman style.

String courses define each floor.

Wedge-shaped masonry around semi-circular window arches is characteristic of Renaissance buildings.

Palazzo Strozzi
(see p105) *is typical of many Tuscan Renaissance buildings. The rusticated stonework gives an impression of strength and stability.*

BAROQUE (LATE-16TH AND 17TH CENTURIES)

The theatrical Baroque style, much favoured by the popes in Rome, largely passed Tuscany by. Although a few churches in Florence were given new façades in the 17th century, the Florentine version of the Baroque style is very Classical in spirit and not as bold or as exuberant as elsewhere in Italy.

Santo Stefano dei Cavalieri (see p156) *has columns and pilasters on its Baroque façade, which give the illusion of depth.*

Curved pediments are typical of the Baroque style.

Baroque architects liked to use intricate mouldings.

Scroll

Swag

Cartouche with swags and scrolls

Window surrounds are highly ornamented.

Deliberate interplay of curvaceous forms and straight lines features in Baroque architecture.

Understanding Art in Tuscany

Tuscany was the scene of one of the most influential and sustained artistic revolutions in history. Its masterpieces record the transition from the stylized charm of medieval art to the Classical beauty and richness of the High Renaissance.

No detailed setting or background

Idealized figures

MEDIEVAL ART

Medieval art served as an aid to prayer and contemplation. The Virgin, patron saint of many Tuscan cities, including Siena, was often depicted as the Queen of Heaven, surrounded by adoring angels and saints.

Gold, symbolizing purity, was used lavishly.

Lack of spatial depth

Unifying flow of drapery

Maestà *(1308–11)*
The stylized figures in this detail from Duccio's huge altarpiece for Siena cathedral are painted with great delicacy.

The figures form a triangle, symbolizing the Holy Trinity. The viewer's eye is drawn upwards to the figures of Christ and God the Father at the apex.

The Virgin and St John are depicted as real people, rather than idealized figures.

Lorenzo Lenzi, Masaccio's patron, kneels opposite his wife.

RENAISSANCE ART

The artistic revolution known as the Renaissance, which spread throughout Europe from the 15th century onwards, had its roots in Tuscany. Inspired by ancient Roman art, sculptors and painters brought about a "rebirth" of Classical ideals.

They were supported by wealthy and cultured patrons, themselves fascinated by the works of such Classical authors as Plato and Cicero. Nudes, landscapes, portraits, and scenes from mythology

The Trinity *(c.1427)*
Masaccio pioneered perspective in painting, using architectural illusion to create a three-dimensional effect (see p110).

TIMELINE OF GREAT TUSCAN ARTISTS

1200	1250	1300	1350
	1260–1319 Duccio di Buoninsegna	**1267–1337** Giotto di Bondone	
			1377–1455 Filippo Brunelleschi
1245–1315 Giovanni Pisano			
		1270–1348 Andrea Pisano	**1374–1438** Jacopo della Quercia
	1245–1302 Arnolfo di Cambio		
		1319–47 Ambrogio Lorenzetti	**1378–1455** Lorenzo Ghiberti
	1240–1302 Cimabue	**1283–1344** Simone Martini	
			1386–1460 Donatell·
1223–84 Nicola Pisano			

☐ **Medieval Artists**

MANNERIST ART

Mannerist artists used "hot" colours, elongated forms and deliberately contorted poses, often within complicated, large-scale compositions.

The twisted pose and vivid colours of Michelangelo's *Holy Family (see p81)* established the key features of the style. Few artists could match the monumental scale of his work, but Bronzino, Pontormo and Rosso Fiorentino brought new life to traditional biblical subjects by their skilful and dramatic composition.

Statues of Roman gods reflect a direct debt to Classical art.

Writhing figures create a sense of dramatic tension.

Flesh and musculature are painted in subtle gradations of light and shade.

The Martyrdom of St Lawrence *(1569)*
With Mannerist bravura, Bronzino shows the human body in numerous poses (see p90).

and everyday life became legitimate subjects for art.

Rejecting the stylized art of the medieval era, Renaissance artists studied anatomy in order to portray the human body more realistically, and strove to develop innovations to please their patrons. They learned how to apply the mathematics of linear perspective to their art, to create the illusion of spatial depth. Painters set figures against recognizable landscapes or city backgrounds, and flattered their patrons by including them as onlookers or protagonists of the scene.

La Maddalena (1438), by Donatello

The greatest Renaissance artists also added another dimension, that of psychological realism. It is evident in Donatello's sculpture *La Maddalena*, which vividly conveys the former prostitute's grief and penitence. Even when painting traditional subjects, they often tried to express the complexities of human character and emotion. The religious elements of the Virgin and Child theme gave way, for example, to an exploration of the mother-child relationship, as in the *Madonna and Child* (c.1455) by Fra Filippo Lippi *(see p82)*.

Pallas, symbolizing wisdom, tames the centaur, representing brute animal impulse.

Pallas and the Centaur
Botticelli's allegory (1485) typifies the Renaissance interest in pagan myth.

1400	1450	1500	1550
1400–82 Luca della Robbia	1449–94 Ghirlandaio	1483–1520 Raphael	
1401–28 Masaccio	1452–1519 Leonardo		1511–92 Bartolomeo Ammannati
1406–69 Fra Filippo Lippi	1457–1504 Filippino Lippi	1486–1531 Andrea del Sarto	
1410–92 Piero della Francesca			1524–1608 Giambologna
1397–1475 Paolo Uccello	1445–1510 Botticelli	1477–1549 Sodoma	1511–74 Giorgio Vasari
1396–1472 Michelozzo	1435–88 Verrocchio	1475–1564 Michelangelo	1503–72 Agnolo Bronzino
c.1395–1455 Fra Angelico	1421–97 Benozzo Gozzoli	1494–1556 Jacopo Pontormo	1500–71 Benvenuto Cellini
			1495–1540 Rosso Fiorentino

☐ Renaissance Artists   ☐ Mannerist Artists

Renaissance Frescoes

Frescoes decorate the walls of churches, public
buildings and private palaces throughout Tuscany.
Renaissance artists, in particular, favoured the medium
of fresco painting for decorating new buildings. The
word *fresco*, meaning "fresh", refers to the technique of
painting on to a thin layer of damp, freshly laid plaster.
Pigments are drawn into the plaster by surface tension
and the colour becomes fixed as the plaster dries. The
pigments react with the lime in the plaster to produce
very strong, vivid colours. As the colours do not lie on
the surface, restorers are able to remove the superficial
soot and grime that have accumulated over the years
to reveal the original, embedded colours *(see pp56–7).*

Chiaroscuro
*This is a subtle method of
contrasting light and dark
for dramatic effect.*

Jewel-like Colours
*Artists used rare, costly minerals to
create bright, striking pigments. The blue
of Mary's robe in Piero della Francesca's*
Madonna del Parto *(c.1460) (see p197)
is made from lapis lazuli.*

Earth colours such as reds and
browns came from clay-based
paints containing iron.

White pigment was
used for important
highlights because it
reflects light.

Use of Sinopia
*The outlines of the fresco
were drawn on to the plaster
undercoat using a red pigment called* sinopia. *This
layer was visible through the
final plaster coat, guiding
the artist as he painted in
the details (see p156).*

The Giornato
Once the final plaster coat was applied, artists had to work quickly before it dried. This meant painting a small area of plaster each day (the giornato, *or daily portion). Joins between the sections were often concealed in borders, columns and frames.*

Masons left the bare wall surface uneven.

The bare wall was covered with coarse plaster, called *arriccio*, made of clay, hair, sand and lime.

The artist either sketched his design on to the *arriccio* using the pigment *sinopia*, and then painted directly on to the plaster, or he prepared a charcoal drawing on paper which was copied onto the wall.

The final fresco was painted on to a top coat of fine, lime-based plaster called *intonaco*.

Workshops
The master artist worked in tandem with apprentices employed in his workshop. The master concentrated on important features, such as faces and expressive gestures.

Apprentices
While learning their trade, apprentices painted drapery, backgrounds and architectural details in the style of their master.

What to Buy in Tuscany

As a centre for high fashion and quality antiques, Florence is expensive but hard to beat. Bargains also abound, especially in leather goods and shoes. For food lovers there is a wide variety of wines, olive oils and preserves. Away from Florence, small farm estates in Tuscany sell their produce, such as honeys, liqueurs and wines, direct to the public, while many Tuscan towns have their own craft and food specialities. *(See also pp284–9.)*

Desk tidy made of traditional hand-marbled paper

Marbled-paper notebook and box of pencils

Colourful Stationery

Marbled paper is a Florentine speciality. You can buy it in sheets and notebooks, or shaped into carnival masks and even birds and flowers.

Soap made to an ancient recipe

Flower-scented air freshener

Greetings Cards

Beautifully illustrated cards are sold at bookshops and museums.

Hand-made Perfumes and Toiletries

The products in Florentine pharmacies have often been made to ancient formulas by monks and nuns.

Terracotta and ceramic bowl

Hand-painted majolica

Ceramics and Reproductions

*Tuscan potters produce highly decorative pieces, from modern originals (*artistiche*) and Renaissance copies (*reproduzioni*) to attractive kitchenware. You can also buy copies of your favourite sculptures.*

Alabaster figurine from Volterra

Reproductions of Renaissance ceramics

Woven leatherwork
handbag

Elegant document case

Small coin purse

Quality Leather Goods
*Fine leather handbags, wallets and jackets are all
remarkably good value, but fake designer brands
are also sold by street traders and market stalls.*

Belt with distinctive Gucci buckle

Hand-crafted men's footwear

Beautifully
made lady's shoe

Luxury charm bracelet

Designer
silk scarf

Fashionable Footwear
*Even Hollywood filmstars come to
Florence to buy shoes from
boutiques such as Ferragamos.*

Fashion Accessories
*Florence has all the top names in
fashion, including homegrown
couturiers like Gucci.*

Sunflower honey
from Montalcino

Chocolate and biscuit cake

Red wine vinegar
and fine olive oil

Tuscan Delicacies
*Lovers of good food will
want to visit an* alimentari
*(grocer's) to choose from the
fascinating range of stock
available. Tuscan products
to sample and take back
home include bottled
antipasti, fruity olive oils,
delicious honeys and a wide
variety of confectionery.*

Artichoke hearts with
peppers and olives

Sun-dried tomatoes
in sunflower oil

Peppers preserved
in olive oil

The Landscape of Tuscany

Tuscany is rich in wildlife, especially flowers and the insects that feed on them, including bees, crickets, cicadas and grasshoppers, whose song is heard during the summer months. For years Tuscan farmers were too poor to afford modern intensive agricultural methods, so the region was, until recently, still farmed by traditional methods. As a result, rural areas have remained relatively unspoiled, a safe haven for many species of flora and fauna – with the exception of the songbird, which has fallen victim to the Tuscan passion for hunting.

Cypress Trees
The flame-shaped cypress is often planted as a windbreak in fields and along roadsides.

Building on hilltops ensures a cooling wind in summer.

The Crete
The clay landscape south of Siena is one of bare hillocks and ravines, denuded of topsoil by heavy rain.

Terracing
The steep hillsides are farmed by cutting terraces and holding the soil in place with stone walls.

TUSCAN FARMLAND
A typical Tuscan farm will combine olive groves and vineyards with fields of maize and barley to feed the cattle and chickens.

Garfagnana Landscape
Much of this region is an unspoilt national park where deer, boar, martens and eagles are protected.

Viticulture
*Many families make their
own wine and every spare
plot is planted with vines.*

Olives
*The olive tree with its silver-
backed leaves is widely
cultivated. Many farms sell
home-produced olive oil.*

TUSCAN WILDLIFE

The best time to see the Tuscan countryside is in May and
June when all the flowers are in bloom. Autumn rains
bring a second burst of flowering later in the year, and
then cyclamen carpet the woodland floors. Even winter
has its flowers, such as hellebores and snowdrops.

Animals, Birds and Insects

Hummingbird *hawk moths
hover in front of brightly
coloured flowers, feeding
with their long tongues.*

Swifts perform
*aerial acrobatics at dusk,
flying high above the city
rooftops and towers.*

The green lizard *feeds on
grasshoppers and basks on
walls in the sunlight.*

Wild boars *are abundant
but very shy as they are
hunted for their tasty meat.*

Wayside Flowers

The blue chicory *plant
flowers all summer and is
used as animal fodder.*

Pink, white and red
*flowering mallows are a
valuable food plant for bees.*

The blood-red poppy *often
grows alongside bright white
oxeye daisies.*

The almond-scented *bind-
weed attracts a variety of
different insects.*

FLORENCE AND TUSCANY
THROUGH THE YEAR

Tuscany is most beautiful in May when meadows and waysides are carpeted with the same bright flowers that Botticelli's Flora blithely scatters in *Primavera*, his celebration of spring *(see p82)*. Autumn is equally colourful, when the beech and chestnut woods turn a glorious blaze of seasonal red and gold.

A July harvest, medieval-style

The best months for escaping the heat and the crowds are May, September and October. Easter should be avoided, as also July and August, because of the long queues outside major museums. During August, when Tuscans head for the sea, you will find shops, bars and restaurants closed. To see traditional festivities like the Palio in Siena or Arezzo's Joust of the Saracen, you will need to book accommodation a year ahead, but there are many other local festivals to enjoy. For information, enquire at main tourist offices *(see p297)*.

SPRING

Tuscany begins to wake from winter as Easter approaches. The hillsides are vibrant with the soft green of new leaves and the scent of fresh growth. Even in the cities there is a sense of renewal as hanging baskets and window boxes are displayed outside from April onwards, and wisteria and iris bloom in the public gardens.

Instead of winter's heavy game dishes, asparagus, a speciality of the Lucca area, begins to feature on restaurant menus, along with tender young beans, usually served in lemon juice and oil.

Except at Easter time, the streets and main sights are rarely overcrowded, but the weather can be unpredictable and unseasonably wet.

A window box in bloom: the first sign of spring in Cortona

"Explosion of the Carriage" festival

MARCH

Carnevale *(four Sundays leading to Lent and Shrove Tuesday)*, Viareggio *(see p38)*.
Scoppio del Carro, or the Explosion of the Carriage *(Easter Sunday)*, Piazza del Duomo, Florence. An 18th-century gilded cart is pulled to the cathedral doors by white oxen, and a dove-shaped rocket swoops down a wire from above the High Altar inside to ignite fireworks in the cart. Ostensibly a celebration of the Resurrection, the ceremony has roots in pagan fertility rites. Many Tuscans still believe that a successful firework display means a good harvest.
Festa degli Aquiloni, or Kite Festival *(first Sunday after Easter)*, San Miniato *(see p163)*. Kite lovers perform aerial acrobatics on the Prato della Rocca, the grassy common above San Miniato.

APRIL

Sagra Musicale Lucchese, *(April– early July)* Lucca *(see pp178–9)*. This extensive festival of sacred music is held in the city's numerous Romanesque churches.
Mostra Mercato Internazionale dell'Artigianato, or Exhibition of Crafts *(last week)*, Fortezza da Basso, Florence. An important European exhibition of the work of artists and artisans.

MAY

Maggio Musicale, Florence. This is the city's major arts festival and it now lasts until late June, with concerts by the Orchestra Regionale Toscana, directed by Zubin Mehta, and other international performers. The festival has been extended to include dance (from classical ballet to experimental work) and fringe events.
Festa del Grillo, or the Cricket Festival *(first Sunday after Ascension Thursday)*, Le Cascine, Florence. The huge park to the west of Florence, where Shelley wrote *Ode to the West Wind*, is the setting for this event, a celebration of the joys of spring. Stallholders used to sell live crickets, which were then released to bring good luck. These days the festival is celebrated with handmade crickets.
Balestro del Girifalco, or Falcon Contest *(first Sunday after 20 May)*, Massa Marittima *(see p39)*.

AVERAGE DAILY HOURS OF SUNSHINE

Sunshine Chart
Tuscany has been praised for its light, which has a clear golden quality most noticeable when the intensely sunny days of high summer begin to shorten. Spring and autumn days are still warm, with plenty of hours of sunshine to enjoy.

SUMMER

From June onwards, Tuscany's festive calendar becomes increasingly crowded. There are with scores of small town festivals, many of them taking place around Midsummer Day, the feast of John the Baptist, on 24 June. These provide an opportunity to sample local food and wine and join in the atmosphere, or to seek out some of the bigger set-piece festivals.

JUNE

Calcio in Costume, or Football in Costume *(24 June and two other days in June)*, Florence *(see p38)*.
Estate Fiesolana, or Fiesole Summer *(mid-June to end August)*, Fiesole *(see p132)*. Festival of music, arts, drama, dance and film. Many events are staged in the amphitheatre.
Regata di San Ranieri *(17 June)*, Pisa *(see p156)*. Boat

A glorious crop of sunflowers in high summer

races in costume and processions of colourfully decorated boats on the river Arno. After dark, its bankside buildings are illuminated by tens of thousands of flaming torches.
Gioco del Ponte or Game of the Bridge *(last Sunday in June)*, Pisa. A ritual battle played out on a bridge *(see p38)*.

JULY

Corsa del Palio *(2 July and 16 August)*, Siena. Tuscany's most famous event *(see p222)*.
Pistoia Blues *(early July)*, Piazza del Duomo, Pistoia *(see pp186–7)*. Famous international festival of blues music, lasting for a week.
Settimana Musicale Senese *(dates vary)*, Siena *(see pp218–19)*. Throughout this "Musical Week", chamber music and classical concerts are performed in splendid settings, such as the Palazzo Chigi-Saraceni.

Celebrating a local saint's day on the streets of Siena

Italian ice cream, a feast for all ages

AUGUST

Festival Pucciniano *(late July–all August)*, Torre del Lago Puccini *(see p175)*. Performances of the composer's operas in an open-air theatre by the lake where he lived.
Rodeo della Rosa *(15 August)*, Alberese. Cowboys of the Maremma *(see pp236–7)* demonstrate cattle herding.
Cantiere Internazionale d'Arte *(late July–early August)*, Montepulciano *(see p227)*. Directed by the composer Hans Werner Henze, this is an important festival of new work by leading composers, dramatists and choreographers.
Festa della Bistecca *(15 August)*, Cortona *(see pp204–5)*. The Festival of the Beefsteak – a local speciality.
Il Baccanale *(penultimate Saturday)*, Montepulciano *(see p227)*. Feast of wine, food and song to celebrate the local Vino Nobile *(see p268)*.

AVERAGE MONTHLY RAINFALL

Rainfall Chart
Autumn is the wettest time in Tuscany, with heavy downpours which can last for days, especially late in the season. Late summer storms often bring relief from the intense heat. Winter and spring usually have fairly low rainfall.

AUTUMN

Autumn is the season of the *vendemmia*, the grape harvest. Visitors should watch for public notices of the many *sagre*, or festivals, that take place throughout the region. These are family-oriented events which typically feature a single local speciality which is in season, such as *funghi porcini* (porcini mushrooms). The first frosts will occur any time from the end of October, and at this point the great tracts of woodland all over Tuscany begin to turn brilliant shades of red and gold.

Autumn in the Val d'Orcia, in southern Tuscany

Grape-picking by hand in a Chianti vineyard

SEPTEMBER

Giostra del Saraceno or the Joust of the Saracen *(first Sunday)*, Arezzo *(see p39)*.
Festa della Rificolona *(7 September)*, Piazza della Santissima Annunziata,

Florence. Children from all over the city carry candle-lit paper lanterns to honour the eve of the birth of the Virgin.
Palio della Balestra or Crossbow Festival *(second Sunday)*, Sansepolcro *(see pp196–7)*. Costume parades and flag throwing accompany a crossbow competition between Sansepolcro and the Umbrian town of Gubbio.
Luminara di Santa Croce *(13 September)*, Lucca *(see pp178–9)*. The city's famous relic, the *Volto Santo*, a wooden statue of Christ, is paraded around by torchlight.
Rassegna del Chianti Classico *(second week)*, Greve in Chianti. The biggest Tuscan celebration of local wines.
Mostra Mercato Internazionale dell'Antiquariato *(Sep–Oct, in odd-numbered years)*, Florence. A major biennial antiques fair.

OCTOBER

Amici della Musica *(Oct–Apr)*, Florence. The "Friends of Music" concert season begins.
Sagra del Tordo or Festival of the Thrush *(last Sunday)*, Montalcino *(see p39)*.

Participant in the Joust of the Saracen festival in Arezzo

AVERAGE MONTHLY TEMPERATURE

Temperature Chart
July is the hottest, driest month, with June and August only marginally less so. These are the least comfortable months for sightseeing. Choose late spring or early autumn for this, when you can also sit outside until late.

NOVEMBER

Festival dei Popoli *(Nov– Dec)*, in venues throughout Florence. Tuscany's most important film festival. Open to everyone, it shows films in their original language with Italian subtitles.

WINTER

This can be a good time to visit Florence and enjoy the city's museums and churches in tranquillity. It can be bitterly cold, but the skies are blue and the city is often bathed in golden sunlight, making this many photographers' favourite season. All over Tuscany, town squares are filled with the aroma of roasting chestnuts, and in December, the last of the olive crop is being harvested in the southernmost parts.

DECEMBER

Fiaccole di Natale, or Festival of Christmas Torches *(Christmas Eve)*, Abbadia di San Salvatore, near Montalcino *(see p224)*. Carols and torchlight processions in memory of the shepherds from the first Christmas Eve.

JANUARY

Capodanno. New Year's Day is celebrated with gusto all over Tuscany. There are firework displays, and volleys from hunters firing into the air, and from exploding firecrackers: all are part of a ritual to frighten away the ghosts and spirits of the old year and welcome in the new.

Roasting chestnuts, Montalcino

Pitti Immagine Uomo *(throughout January)*, Fortezza da Basso, Florence. At this prestigious fashion show, Italian designers and international couturiers gather to present their spring and summer collections for men. Children's collections (Pitti Bimbo) are sometimes presented in January too.

FEBRUARY

Carnevale *(Sundays before Lent, Shrove Tuesday)*, Viareggio *(see p175)*. A festive event renowned for its parades, competitions and amusing floats, often inspired by topical themes *(see p38)*.

There are many other opportunities to enjoy pre-Lent celebrations, such as the equally splendid carnival festivities that take place in San Gimignano and Arezzo.

PUBLIC HOLIDAYS

New Year's Day (1 Jan)
Epiphany (6 Jan)
Easter Monday
Liberation Day (25 Apr)
Labour Day (1 May)
Ferragosto (15 Aug)
All Saints' Day (1 Nov)
Immaculate Conception (8 Dec)
Christmas Day (25 Dec)
Santo Stefano (26 Dec)

Florence's Piazza di Santo Spirito in winter – serene and free of crowds

Festivals in Tuscany

Many Tuscan festivals celebrate battles and historical events that took place centuries ago; others have their origins in medieval tournaments. Yet they are not merely a pastiche of history, put on for the benefit of tourists. They are living festivals, mounted with an amazing degree of skill and commitment to authenticity and perfection. This can be seen in such details as the embroidery on the costumes worn by the participants and in the exhilarating displays of horsemanship, jousting or archery. Here is a selection of Tuscany's best.

Pisa's Game of the Bridge

Football in Costume at fever pitch

FLORENCE

Calcio in Costume, or Football in Costume (a festival held over three days in June, with the final taking place on 24 June), is a combination of football and rugby. Each of the four medieval quarters of the city (Santo Spirito, Santa Croce, San Giovanni and Santa Maria Novella) fields a team of 27 men. The games are usually held in Piazza Santa Croce, and always attract a lively crowd. There is fierce rivalry among the teams, and play can be quite violent. The final prize is a live cow. Before the game, the players and other characters in sumptuous 14th-century dress parade through the city.

The final coincides with the feast of John the Baptist, the patron saint of the city. These events are cele-brated by a firework display, best seen from the north bank of the Arno, between Ponte Vecchio and Ponte alle Grazie, or from Fiesole.

WESTERN TUSCANY

The last Sunday in June is the occasion for the Gioco del Ponte, or Game of the Bridge, in Pisa *(see pp156–7)*. This battle, in Renaissance costume, takes place between the Pisans who live north of the river Arno and those who live south. Arranged into teams, they attempt to push a seven-tonne carriage over the historic Ponte di Mezzo (literally, the Middle Bridge), which divides the city. On the actual day, the river's banks are crowded with thousands of onlookers. This event probably has its roots in pre-Renaissance times, when there was no regular army and all citizens had to be trained and ready for war.

Some of the participants wear suits of antique armour which date from the 15th and 16th centuries, and their shields bear the colours of the city's different districts. This regalia is kept in the Museo Nazionale di San Matteo *(see p157)* when it is not in use.

NORTHERN TUSCANY

Carnevale (Carnival) in Viareggio *(see p175)*, on Shrove Tuesday and the four Sundays leading to it, is famous for its imaginative floats. These carry elaborate satirical models of politicians and other public figures. After courting contro-versy in recent years, however, this celebration is now more of a family event, but there is still an abundance of pointed visual jokes that can be app-reciated by those in the know.

The designers of the floats enjoy much flattery and prestige, and their creations remain on view all year. As elsewhere, the occasion is one of merrymaking, and it combines ancient pagan rituals and Christian values.

One of the spectacular floats from the Viareggio Carnival

Knights waiting to charge at the Joust of the Saracen in Arezzo

The festival is essentially an excuse for gastronomic over-indulgence, and a celebration of its thriving local economy, which is based on olive oil and wine production. Brunello is widely regarded as one of the finest of Italian wines.

Visitors are welcome to participate, and more conventional specialities, such as *porchetta* (roast suckling pig), are available for those who prefer not to eat songbirds. Archery competitions are also held in Montalcino during August to mark the beginning of the hunting season

SOUTHERN TUSCANY

Balestro del Girifalco, or the Falcon Contest, takes place in Massa Marittima *(see p234)* on the first Sunday after the feast of San Bernardino (20 May) and again on the second Sunday in August. It is preceded by a long procession through the town of people in dazzling Renaissance costume, accompanied by flag-waving and music. The contest itself is a test of ancient battle skills and the teams represent the town's three traditional historic divisions, which are known as *terzieri* or thirds. Marksmen come forward and try to shoot down a mechanical falcon, tethered on a wire, with their crossbows. Great precision is required to hit the target and the whole contest is imbued with intense *terzieri* rivalry.

EASTERN TUSCANY

The Piazza Grande in Arezzo *(see pp198–9)* is the scene of the Giostra del Saracino, or Joust of the Saracen. Held on the first Sunday in September, this tournament dates back to the Crusades in the Middle Ages, when all Christendom dedicated itself to driving the North African Arabs (the Moors) out of Europe.

There are lively and colourful processions to precede the event, in which eight costumed knights charge towards a wooden effigy of the Saracen. The aim is to try to hit the Saracen's shield with lances and then avoid a cat-of-three-tails swinging back and unseating them. Each pair of knights represents one of Arezzo's four rival *contrade* (districts), and their supporters occupy a side each of Piazza Grande. They are quiet when

their own *contrada* knights are jousting, but make as much noise as is possible to distract the opposition. The winner receives a gold lance.

CENTRAL TUSCANY

The most important festival in this region is Siena's Palio *(see p222)*, but the Sagra del Tordo, or Festival of the Thrush, is also a great attraction. It takes place in Montalcino *(see pp224–5)* on the last Sunday in October. The 14th-century Fortezza (castle) is the setting for an archery contest which is fought in traditional costume by members of the town's four *contrade*. This is accompanied by considerable consumption of the local red Brunello wine and, much to the horror of many bird-lovers, of charcoal-grilled thrush.

Archery at the Festival of the Thrush in Montalcino

Renaissance finery at the Falcon Contest in Massa Marittima

THE HISTORY OF FLORENCE AND TUSCANY

Tuscany is rich in historical monuments. Etruscan walls encircle many of the region's hilltop towns and the streets within are lined with medieval and Renaissance palazzi, town halls testifying to the ideals of democracy and self-government, and churches built on the ruins of ancient pagan temples. The countryside, too, is dotted with castles and fortified villages, symbols of the violence and intercommunal strife that tore Tuscany apart for so many years during the medieval period. Typical of these is the hilltop town of San Gimignano *(see pp212–15)*, with its defensive towers.

The Marzocco lion, emblem of Florence

Some of the most imposing castles, such as the Fortezza Medicea in Arezzo *(see p198),* bear the name of the Medici family. Their coat of arms, found all over Tuscany, is a reminder of the role they played in the region's history. They presided over the simultaneous birth of Humanism and the Renaissance and, later, when they were Grand Dukes of Tuscany, patronized eminent scientists and engineers such as Galileo. Tuscany has also played a part in wider events: Napoleon was exiled to Elba, and Florence served briefly as capital of the newly united Italy (1865–71).

Much damage was done to Tuscany's art and monuments by World War II bombing and the floods of 1966. However, major restoration projects undertaken as a result have stimulated research into up-to-date scientific methods. In this way, Tuscany's artistic heritage continues to inspire contemporary life – something it has always done for the many creative people who live and work here and for its endless trail of admiring visitors.

16th-century map of Italy, showing Pisa and the river Arno leading to Florence

◁ San Gimignano, held by its patron saint, and little changed since Taddeo di Bartolo (1362 –1422) painted it

Etruscan and Roman Tuscany

The Etruscans migrated to Italy from Asia Minor around 900 BC, attracted to the area they called Etruria (now in Tuscany, Lazio and Umbria) by its mineral wealth. This they exploited to produce weapons, armour, tools and jewellery to trade with Greece. After a fierce war with Rome in 395 BC, the Etruscan civilization was eclipsed by Roman rule. Many aspects of Roman religion can be attributed to the Etruscans, including animal sacrifice and divination – reading the will of the gods in animal entrails or cloud patterns. Everyday Etruscan life and the preoccupation with the afterlife are reflected in detailed carved cremation urns and tombs like those at Volterra (*see pp166–7*).

Etruscan earrings worked in gold

Wax writing tablets were used to keep household accounts.

A covered wagon carved on the urn shows the Etruscans were skilled at carpentry.

Bronze Chimera (*4th-century BC*)
The wounded chimera (part goat, lion and serpent) is a dramatic example of Etruscan bronze casting.

Athletic Games
Tomb paintings depicting chariot races, dancing and athletics suggest that the Etruscans had festivals similar to the Olympic Games of the ancient Greeks.

ETRUSCAN CREMATION URN

Much of what is known about the Etruscans comes from studying the contents of their tombs. This 1st-century BC terracotta cremation urn from Volterra is carved with scenes from Etruscan domestic life.

The relief depicts the last journey of the deceased into the underworld.

TIMELINE

900 BC	800	700	600	500	400
9th century BC Earliest evidence of Etruscans on Elba		**508 BC** Lars Porsena, Etruscan ruler of Chiusi, leads an unsuccessful attack on Rome			**474 BC** Etruscans defeated in Asia Minor by their commercial rivals; trade with Greece suffers and Etruscan ports such as Populonia begin to decline
	7th century BC Beginning of extensive maritime trade with Greece and the Near East		**6th century BC** Founding of the Dodecapolis, a confederation of the 12 most powerful Etruscan cities	*Coin from Populonia*	**395 BC** Rome captures Veii in Lazio, signalling the end of Etruscan independence

Circular Chandelier
Sixteen oil lamps decorate the rim of this bronze chandelier, made around 300 BC.

The family of the deceased watches the funeral cortège.

Statue of Venus
Under Roman rule, the Etruscans adopted new deities like Venus, goddess of beauty.

Lead Tablet
Etruscan priests recorded details of their prayers and religious rites on lead tablets. However, their language has not yet been fully deciphered, and many of their beliefs and traditions are not yet understood.

WHERE TO SEE ANCIENT TUSCANY

The famous bronzes of the *Chimera* and the *Orator* are in Florence's Museo Archeologico *(see p99)*. Good museum collections are in Fiesole *(pp132–3)*, Volterra *(p166)*, Chiusi *(p228)*, Cortona *(p204)* and Grosseto *(p238)*. There are tombs at Vetulonia *(p238)* and Sovana *(p238)*, and the ruins of an Etruscan town have been excavated near Roselle *(p238)*.

Etruscan Rock-cut Tomb
The tombs in Sovana date from the 3rd century BC (p238).

Roman Theatre
The bath and theatre complex excavated in Volterra was built after Rome conquered the city in the 4th century BC (p167).

5 BC All Tuscany now under Roman control; e Etruscans forced to pay tribute in bronze, grain and iron

90 BC Etruscans granted Roman citizenship, marking the end of their existence as a distinct culture

AD 250 Christianity brought to Florence by Eastern merchants; St Minias martyred in the city

AD 313 Constantine grants official status to Christianity

| 200 | 100 | AD 1 | 100 | 200 | 300 | 400 |

Bronze of a Roman Orator c. 300 BC

20 BC Military colony of Saena (Siena) founded

59 BC Florentia (Florence) founded as a town for retired Roman army veterans

AD 405 Flavius Stilicho defeats the Ostrogoths besieging Florence

Early Medieval Tuscany

Medieval carved stone lion

The church kept the flame of learning alive during the dark years when Tuscany was under attack from Teutonic tribes such as the Goths and Lombards. Charlemagne, responding to the pope's request for help, drove the Lombards out of Tuscany in the 8th century. He was crowned Holy Roman Emperor as his reward, but this was soon to spark off a long conflict between church and emperor about who should rule Italy.

Early church have simple wooden jois...

Mosaic Madonna

A 12th-century mosaic of the Virgin from Cortona (see p204) is typical of the Byzantine-influenced art of the early medieval period.

The capitals are carved with biblical scenes.

Knight on Horseback

This 11th-century carving from Sovana's cathedral symbolizes the conflict between pope and emperor over control of the church.

Priests' quarters

Chapel of Sant'Agata

Like most early churches in Tuscany, the 12th-century octagonal brick chapel in Pisa, with its pyramid-shaped roof, was built on the grave of a Christian saint martyred by the Romans (see p156).

Semi-circular chapels with limpet-shell roofs are a typical feature of the period.

TIMELINE

552 Totila the Goth attacks Florence

570 Lombards conquer northern Italy

Carts used by Charlemagne's army in battle

500	600	700	800

774 Charlemagne, King of the Franks, begins a campaign to subjugate the Lombards

7th-century Lombardic gold crown in the Bargello Museum, Florence (see pp68–9)

800 Charlemagne crowned Holy Roman Emperor

The bells in the campanile were rung to call the village to church and prayer.

Countess Matilda
Matilda, the last of the Margraves, ruled Tuscany in the 11th century and built many churches in the area.

Baptismal Font
Scenes taken from the lives of Moses and Christ adorn the 12th-century font at San Frediano, Lucca (see pp178–9).

SANT'ANTIMO *(see p228)*

Founded, according to legend, by Charlemagne in 781, the shape of the church demonstrates the influence of the Roman *basilica* (law court) on the design of early churches; the altar occupies the position of the magistrate's chair.

The ambulatory ran behind the altar and was used for processions.

WHERE TO SEE EARLY MEDIEVAL TUSCANY

Well-preserved early medieval churches are found throughout Tuscany: in San Piero a Grado *(see p161)*; Barga *(p174)*; Lucca *(pp178–9)*; San Quirico d'Orcia *(p225)*; Massa Marittima *(p234)*; Sovana *(p238)*; San Miniato al Monte in Florence *(p130)*; and in Fiesole *(p132)*.

Castello di Romena
The 11th-century tower near Bibbiena was built by the Guidi family, who dominated the area.

Santi Apostoli in Florence
Founded in 786, the church includes columns from ancient Roman baths (p109).

	1062 Pisa captures Sicily and becomes the foremost Mediterranean port	1152 Frederick Barbarossa is crowned Holy Roman Emperor and invades Italy	1186 Siena cathedral begun
900	1000	1100	1200

c.1025–30 Guido d'Arezzo invents a form of musical notation

1063 Pisa cathedral begun

1115 Countess Matilda dies

1125 Florence captures and destroys Fiesole

12th-century Tuscan School Crucifixion

Late Medieval Tuscany

During the 13th century Tuscany grew rich on textile manufacturing and trade. Commercial contact with the Arab world led the Pisan mathematician Fibonacci to introduce Arabic numerals to the West; a new under-standing of geometry followed and Tuscan architects began to build ambitious new buildings. At the same time, Tuscan bankers developed the book-keeping principles that still underlie modern accountancy and banking practice. It was also an age of conflict. Cities and factions fought ruthlessly and incessantly to secure wealth and power.

Defensive towers protected the city.

Contented citizens had time for leisure.

Condottieri (mercenaries) were hired to settle conflicts.

Dante's Inferno
Dante (in blue) was caught in the Guelph-Ghibelline conflict and was exiled from Florence in 1302. He took revenge in his poetry, describing his enemies' torments in Hell.

Petrarch and Boccaccio
Petrarch and Boccaccio (top and bottom left), like Dante, wrote in the Tuscan dialect, not Latin. Petrarch's sonnets and Boccaccio's tales were very popular.

GOOD GOVERNMENT

Ambrogio Lorenzetti's early 14th-century allegorical fresco in Siena's Palazzo Pubblico *(see pp218–19)* shows thriving shops, fine buildings and dancing citizens, symbolizing the benefits of good government. Another fresco, *Bad Government*, shows rape, murder, robbery and ruin.

TIMELINE

1215 Start of conflict between Guelph supporters of the pope and Ghibelline supporters of the Holy Roman Emperor

1252 First gold florin minted

1260 Siena defeats Florence at Montaperti

1278 Campo Santo begun in Pisa

1200	1220	1240	1260	1

1220 Frederick II of Germany is crowned Holy Roman Emperor and lays claim to Italy

1224 St Francis receives the "stigmata" (the wounds of Christ) at La Verna

1284 Pisan navy defeated by Genoa; the beginning Pisa's decline as a po

Florin stamped with the lily of Florence

Wool Traders' Emblem
Luca della Robbia's roundel depicts the Lamb of God, symbol of the Calimala (wool importers), whose trade guild was the most powerful in Florence.

A building boom resulted from increased prosperity.

St Francis (1181–1226)
From monasteries founded in Tuscany by St Francis, the Franciscans brought about a major religious revival in reaction to the excesses of the church.

WHERE TO SEE LATE MEDIEVAL TUSCANY

San Gimignano's spectacular towers *(see pp212–15)* show what most Tuscan cities must have looked like during the Middle Ages. Siena has the best surviving late medieval town hall *(pp218–19)*, and Pisa's Leaning Tower, Duomo and Baptistry *(pp158–60)* reflect the willingness of architects of this period to experiment with new styles.

Medieval building techniques
Circular putlock holes show where medieval builders placed their scaffolding timbers.

Lucignano
Some of Tuscany's best-preserved medieval architecture, including several defensive towers, can be seen in Lucignano (p203).

Bankers in Siena
Tuscan banks provided loans to popes, monarchs and merchants. Many bankers were ruined when Edward III of England defaulted on his debts in 1342.

94 Work begins on ●rence's cathedral

1300 Giovanni Pisano carves pulpit for Pisa's cathedral

1350 Pisa's Leaning Tower completed; Boccaccio begins writing *The Decameron*

1377 Sir John Hawkwood appointed Captain General of Florence

1300	1320	1340		1380

1302 Dante begins writing *The Divine Comedy*

1345 Work begins on Florence's Ponte Vecchio

1348–93 Black Death carries off half the Tuscan population

1299 Work begins on Palazzo Vecchio in Florence

Sir John Hawkwood, English mercenary

1374 Death of Petrarch

The Renaissance

Della Robbia roundel from the Cappella de' Pazzi (1430)

Under astute Medici leadership, Florence enjoyed a period of peace and prosperity. Rich bankers and merchants invested in fine palaces to replace their cramped tower houses, and paid for the adornment of churches. The result was an outpouring of art and architecture, remarkable for its break with the Gothic past and its conscious attempt to give "rebirth" to Classical values. The rediscovery of works by ancient philosophers like Cicero and Plato profoundly influenced the intellectual preoccupations of the day. Their ideas inspired the Humanists, who emphasized the role of knowledge and reason in human affairs.

Textile Market
The thriving Florentine textiles industry allowed the textile guilds and merchants like the dye importer Rucellai (see p104) to become patrons of the arts.

Terracotta roundels of babies in swaddling bands, added by Andrea della Robbia in 1487, reflect the building's function as an orphanage.

Classical arches illustrate the Florentine passion for ancient Roman architecture.

Battle of San Romano *(1456)*
Florence hired condottieri *(mercenaries) to fight its battles. Its citizens were therefore free to concentrate on making the city wealthy. Uccello's striking depiction of the Florentine victory over Siena in 1432 is an early attempt to master perspective.*

SPEDALE DEGLI INNOCENTI

The archetypal Renaissance building, Brunelleschi's colonnade (1419–26) for the *Spedale degli Innocenti* (see p95) is a masterpiece of restrained Classical design. Europe's first orphanage, the *Spedale* is also a major social monument.

TIMELINE

1402 Florence Baptistry doors competition *(see p66)*

1416 Donatello completes his *St George (see p67)*

1425–7 Masaccio paints *The Life of St Peter* frescoes in Santa Maria del Carmine *(see pp126–7)*

1436 Brunelleschi completes dome for Florence cathedral *(see pp64–5)*. Work starts on San Marco *(see pp96–7)*

| 1400 | 1410 | 1420 | | 1440 |

1406 Pisa falls to Florence

1419 Work begins on the Spedale degli Innocenti

Cosimo il Vecchio

1434 Cosimo il Vecchio returns from exile

Grey sandstone
and white
plaster contrasts
radically with
the rich surface
ornamentation
of late medieval
architecture.

Classical
Corinthian
capital

Humanist Scholars
By studying a broad range of subjects, from art to politics, the Humanists fostered the idea of Renaissance man, equally skilled in many activities.

WHERE TO SEE RENAISSANCE TUSCANY
Most of Florence was rebuilt during the Renaissance. Highlights include San Lorenzo *(see pp90–91)*, Masaccio's frescoes in the Brancacci Chapel *(pp126–7)*, many paintings in the Uffizi *(pp80–83)* and the sculptures at the Bargello *(pp68–9)*.

Pienza Duomo *(1459)*
Pope Pius II's plans for a model Renaissance city at Pienza (p226) were never fully realized.

David *(1475)*
A favourite Florentine subject (see p77), Verrocchio's bronze emphasizes David's youth and vulnerability.

Pazzi Family Emblem
The wealthy Pazzi were disgraced after trying to assassinate Lorenzo the Magnificent and seize control of Florence in 1478.

San Marco Cloister *(1437)*
Cosimo il Vecchio paid for Michelozzo's cloister (pp96–7) and used it as a retreat.

1454–66 Piero della Francesca's *The Legend of the True Cross (see pp200–1)*

Lorenzo the Magnificent

1480 Botticelli's *Primavera*. The villa at Poggio a Caiano begun *(see p165)*

1450	1460	1470	1480	1490

1464 Death of Cosimo il Vecchio

1469 Lorenzo the Magnificent comes to power

1478 Pazzi conspiracy

1485 Botticelli's *The Birth of Venus*

1492 Death of Lorenzo the Magnificent

The Medici of Florence

Medici coat
of arms,
San Lorenzo

The Medici family held power in Florence almost continuously from 1434 until 1743. Their rule began discreetly enough with Cosimo il Vecchio, son of a self-made man, Giovanni di Bicci. For years, Cosimo and his descendants directed policy with popular support, but without ever being voted into office. Later generations gained titles and power but ruled by force. Two were elected pope and, after the Republic *(see pp52–3)*, the decadent Alessandro took the title Duke of Florence. From him control passed to Cosimo I, who was crowned Grand Duke of Tuscany.

Giovanni di Bicci
An astute merchant banker, he founded the Medici fortune.

Giovanni di Bicc
(1360–1429)

① Cosimo il Vecchio
(1389–1464)

② Piero the Gouty
(1416–69)

③ Lorenzo the
Magnificent
(1449–92)

Giuliano
(1453–78)

Giulio, Pope Clement
(1478–1534)

④ Piero
(1472–1503)

⑤ Giovanni,
Pope Leo X
(1475–1521)

⑦ Giuliano,
Duke of Nemours
(1479–1516)

⑥ Lorenzo,
Duke of Urbino
(1492–1519)

⑧ Alessandro, Duke of Flore
(1511–37: parentage uncert

Lorenzo the Magnificent
A poet and statesman, Lorenzo was the model Renaissance man. One of his greatest achievements was to negotiate peace among the cities of northern Italy.

Catherine, Duchess of
Urbino *m* Henry II of
France (1519–89)

Catherine of France
Catherine married Henri II of France in 1533. She is shown with two of her sons, who both became French kings: Charles IX and Henri III. Yet another son became Francis II of France.

Pope Leo X
Elected pope when only 38, Leo's corrup plans to fund the rebuilding of St Peter's Rome triggered a furious reaction that le to the birth of the Protestant movement.

MEDICI PATRONAGE

As one of the most powerful families in Florence, the Medici were responsible for commissioning some of the greatest works of the Renaissance. Many artists flattered their patrons by placing them prominently in the foreground of their paintings. In Botticelli's *Adoration of the Magi* (1475), the grey-haired king who is pictured kneeling at the feet of the Virgin is Cosimo il Vecchio. The kneeling figure in the white robe is his grandson, Giuliano. The young man holding a sword, on the far left of the painting, is thought to be a rather idealized portrait of Lorenzo the Magnificent, Cosimo's other grandson.

Adoration of the Magi (1475) by Botticelli

Lorenzo
(1394–1440)

Pierfrancesco
(1431–77)

Lorenzo
(1463–1503)

Giovanni
(1467–1514)

Pierfrancesco
(1487–1525)

Giovanni delle
Bande Nere
(1498–1526)

⑨ Cosimo I
m Eleonora of Toledo
(1519–74)

eonora of Toledo
*onora, pictured with
e of her children, was
e daughter of Don
dro, Spanish
ceroy at Naples.*

Francesco I
m Joanna of Austria
(1541–87)

⑩ Ferdinando I
(1549–1609)

Cosimo I
*The architect of a strong
and prosperous Tuscany,
Cosimo I established
efficient government
throughout the region.*

Maria
m Henry IV of France
(1575–1642)

⑪ Cosimo II
(1590–1621)

Anna Maria Lodovica
*The last of the Medici,
Anna Maria left her
estate to the
people of
Florence in
perpetuity.*

Louis XIII of France
(1601–43)

Henrietta Maria
m Charles I of
England
(1609–69)

Elisabetta
m Philip IV of
Spain
(1692–1766)

⑫ Ferdinando II
(1610–70)

⑬ Cosimo III
(1642–1723)

KEY

- ☐ Born in 14th century
- ☐ Born in 15th century
- ☐ Born in 16th century
- ☐ Born in 17th century
- ① Succession of rule

Gian Gastone
(1671–1737)

Anna Maria Lodovica
(1667–1743)

The Florentine Republic

Savonarola (1452–98)

In 1494, when Piero de' Medici abandoned Florence to the invading troops of Charles VIII of France, the city was declared a Republic. Under the leadership of the religious fundamentalist, Girolamo Savonarola, the people were encouraged to believe that God was their only ruler. After his execution in 1498, the Republic survived 32 years of constant attack. Finally, in 1530, the Medici Pope, Clement VII, and the Holy Roman Emperor, Charles V of Spain, combined forces and returned the city to Medici rule.

Palazzo Vecchio Frieze
The inscription, "Christ is King", on this Republican frieze implies that no mortal ruler has absolute power.

Present-day Boboli Gardens

Charles VIII Enters Siena
When the French invaded Tuscan cities in 1494, Savonarola claimed it was God's punishment for the Tuscan obsession with profane books and art. He ordered such objects burned in bonfires of "vanity".

Judith and Holofernes
Donatello's statue of the virtuous Judith slaying the tyrant Holofernes was placed in front of the Palazzo Vecchio in 1494 to symbolize the end of Medici rule.

THE SIEGE OF FLORENCE *(1529–30)*
Besieged by 40,000 papal and imperial troops, the citizens of Florence held out for ten months before starvation and disease led to their surrender. Vasari's fresco in the Palazzo Vecchio shows the full extent of the city's defences and the scale of the enemy assault.

TIMELINE

1498 Savonarola burnt at the stake

1504 Michelangelo completes *David* (see p77)

1512 Florence besieged by Cardinal Giovanni de' Medici

1495	1505	1510

1494 Charles VIII attacks Florence. Savonarola seizes power from Medici family

1502 Soderini elected first chancellor of the Republic

1509 Pope Julius II begins driving the French from Italian soil

Chancellor Soderini

1513 Giovanni de' Medici crowned Pope Leo X

Execution of Savonarola

Savonarola was an inspirational orator who commanded great popular support. His political enemies had him executed for heresy in 1498.

All roads out of Florence were blocked.

Artillery platform

Troops camped to the south.

Niccolò Machiavelli

The author of The Prince, a treatise on the ruthless skills required to be a successful politician, was the last Republican chancellor.

WHERE TO SEE REPUBLICAN TUSCANY

A plaque in Piazza della Signoria *(see pp76–7)* marks the spot where Savonarola was executed; his cell can be seen in San Marco *(pp96–7)*. Michelangelo's *David (p94)* symbolizes the victory of the youthful Republic over tyranny. The Republican council met in the Salone dei Cinquecento *(p76)*.

Tower of San Miniato
This was reinforced in 1530 as a gun platform (pp130–31).

Michelangelo's Sketches
During the siege of 1530, Michelangelo worked in the safety of the Cappelle Medicee (pp90–91).

Crystal casket belonging to Pope Clement VII

1527 Florentine Republic reconstituted when Rome is sacked by imperial troops

1531 Alessandro de' Medici becomes first Duke of Florence

1525

1530

1520 Michelangelo begins work on Medici tombs *(see p91)*

1521 Giulio de' Medici crowned Pope Clement VII and Medici rule restored in Florence

1530 Siege of Florence by combined forces of pope and emperor

1532 Posthumous publication of Machiavelli's *The Prince*

The Grand Duchy

Cosimo I was created Grand Duke of Tuscany in 1570, having forced Tuscany into a state of political unity for the first time. A period of prosperity followed, in spite of the corrupt and debauched nature of Cosimo's heirs. When the Medici line ended in 1737, the Grand Duchy was inherited by the Austrian Dukes of Lorraine. They were removed from power in 1860 during the Risorgimento, when the Italian people joined forces to overthrow their foreign rulers. From 1865–70, Florence was the nation's capital. With the final unification of Italy in 1870, however, the centre of power returned to Rome.

The Church
rejected Galileo's discoveries.

Galileo explains
his theory of gravity.

Leopoldo and Family
Leopoldo I, later Emperor Leopold II of Austria, introduced many reforms, including abolition of the death penalty

Livorno Harbour
Livorno became a free port in 1608: ships from every nation were granted equal docking rights, and the resulting influx of Jewish and Moorish refugees contributed to the city's prosperity.

The Old Market
Florence's Old Market was knocked down in 1865, when the city was briefly the Italian capital. In its place is the triumphal arch of the Piazza della Repubblica (see p112).

THE AGE OF SCIENCE

Galileo was one of several brilliant scientists who benefited from Medici patronage during the 17th century, making Tuscany a centre of scientific innovation. His experiments and astronomical observations laid the foundations for modern empirical science, but led to his persecution for contradicting the teachings of the Roman Catholic Church.

TIMELINE

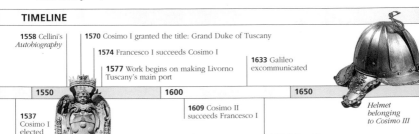

1558 Cellini's *Autobiography*

1570 Cosimo I granted the title: Grand Duke of Tuscany

1574 Francesco I succeeds Cosimo I

1577 Work begins on making Livorno Tuscany's main port

1633 Galileo excommunicated

1550	1600	1650

1537 Cosimo I elected Duke of Florence

Emblem of the Medici dukes

1609 Cosimo II succeeds Francesco I

1642 Galileo dies under house arrest at Arcetri, near Florence

Helmet belonging to Cosimo III

The Grand Tour

It became fashionable for wealthy 18th-century European aristocrats to visit Tuscany. This detail from Zoffani's Tribuna *(1770) shows a tour of the Uffizi.*

Galileo conducted his experiments using specially designed equipment *(see p74)*.

Cosimo II gave refuge to Galileo after the Church accused him of heresy.

National Rule

Florence ran up huge debts while serving as the Italian capital. This cartoon shows a protest against the seat of power (the Palazzo Vecchio) being transferred to Rome.

WHERE TO SEE GRAND DUCHY TUSCANY

The Uffizi art collection *(see pp80–83)* was assembled by the Medici at this time, along with the collections in the Palazzo Pitti *(pp120–23)*, the building from which the Grand Dukes ruled Tuscany for over 300 years. The story of Galileo and his contemporaries is told in the Museo di Storia della Scienza in Florence *(p74)*. The frescoes of the Sala del Risorgimento, in the Palazzo Pubblico, Siena *(p218)*, depict the events that preceded the final unification of Italy.

Palazzo dei Cavalieri
Francavilla's statue of Cosimo I (1596) marks the entrance to Vasari's ornate Palazzo (p156).

Napoleon's Bathroom
Napoleon never used this bathroom (1790–99), built for him at the Palazzo Pitti (pp120–23).

1765 Grand Duke Leopoldo I introduces many social reforms

1796 Napoleon's first Italian campaign

1799 France defeats Austria: Tuscany ruled by Louis de Bourbon, then by Napoleon's sister, Elisa Baciocchi

1815 Napoleon defeated at Waterloo

1822 Shelley drowns near Livorno

1840 Ruskin visits Florence

1750	1800	1850

1743 Death of Anna Maria Lodovica, last of the Medici

1737 End of Medici dynasty; rule passes to Austrian House of Lorraine

1814 Napoleon exiled to Elba

John Ruskin (1819–1900), who revived critical interest in the Renaissance

1865 Florence chosen as capital of new Italian state

1871 Italian capital returns to Rome

The Modern Era

The 20th century has seen many threats to Florence's fragile artistic heritage. The city's historic bridges, except for the Ponte Vecchio, were destroyed during World War II, and worse was to come in 1966 from devastating floods. Traffic and pollution have also taken their toll, leading to tough environmental controls aimed at preserving the historic city centre. Fortunately, the city has energetically risen to these challenges. It continues to thrive both on its proud heritage as a tourist destination and as a living, working city with a robust commercial and industrial base.

Traffic Control
In 1988 Florence banned cars from the city centre.

La Bohème *(1896)*
This popular opera by Puccini, Tuscany's greatest composer, often features in the region's music festivals (see p35).

Firenze Nuova
Florentine commerce and industry are moving to the suburb of "New Florence", leaving the city centre free for cultural and creative enterprises.

ART RESTORATION

Great pride is taken in Tuscany's artistic heritage, and modern scientific methods are used to analyse frescoes before restoration, such as *The Procession of the Magi (see p89)*. These methods include computer-aided mapping of the pigments and plotting any structural damage.

TIMELINE

Domenico Tiburzi, folk hero and notorious Maremman bandit

1896 First performance of Puccini's *La Bohème*

1922 Mussolini heads Italy's first Fascist government

1940 Italy enters World War II

1943 Fall of the Fascists

1890	1900	1910	1920	1940

1915 Italy enters World War I on the side of the Allies (France, Britain and Russia)

1896 Domenico Tiburzi is caught and shot after 24 years on the run

1944 Many historic structures in Tuscany are damaged by Allied bombing or retreating Nazis

The 1966 Floods

On 4 November, floodwater from the Arno rose to 6 m (19.5 ft) above street level. Many art treasures were ruined; some are still in restoration.

WHERE TO SEE MODERN FLORENCE

The shops of Via de' Tornabuoni and Via della Vigna Nuova *(see p105)* sell the best in Florentine fashion. Exhibitions of photographs at the Museo Alinari *(p104)* illustrate the city as it has developed during the 20th century. Cimabue's ruined *Crucifixion (p72)*, in the museum of Santa Croce, is displayed as a reminder of the 1966 floods.

A scanned image lets restorers trace existing outlines and reconstruct damaged areas.

Fashion

Many Florentine designers have become house-hold names. These include Pucci, who invented the "Palazzo Pyjamas", Gucci, Ferragamo (see p266) and, more recently, rising stars like Daelli and Coveri.

Commands for operating the computer program

Railway station *(1935)*
The Functionalist station is one of the city centre's few notable modern buildings (see p113).

San Giovanni Battista *(1964)*
Giovanni Michelucci's modern church stands near Amerigo Vespucci airport.

Tourism

Florence and Tuscany have long been popular destinations for tourists (see p55). Florence now receives some 5 million visitors each year.

1966 Floods in Florence

1957–65 Italian industrial boom

1987 The Sorpasso: Italian economy outstrips that of France and the UK

| 50 | **1960** | **1970** | | **1990** | **2000** |

Italy becomes a ...lic

1993 The Uffizi damaged in a terrorist explosion

1999 Italy joins the single European currency

Bomb damage at the Uffizi

FLORENCE AREA
BY AREA

CITY CENTRE EAST 60–83

CITY CENTRE NORTH 84–99

CITY CENTRE WEST 100–113

OLTRARNO 114–127

FOUR GUIDED WALKS 128–137

FLORENCE STREET FINDER 138–147

CITY CENTRE EAST

The dominant building in this part of Florence is the magnificent Duomo, the first place most people will visit when they arrive in the city. Traffic is now banned in the Piazza del Duomo, which makes it easier to appreciate the immensity

Duomo clock, decorated in 1443 by Paolo Uccello

of this great building. It is, in fact, so large that a comprehensive view is impossible from such close quarters. As you wander the streets to the south you will continually catch glimpses of its multi-coloured marble cladding.

The area's other major church, Santa Croce, containing the tombs and monuments of many great Florentines, sits at the centre of the traditional artisans' quarter. These streets have few prestigious palaces, but there is a lively and attractive sense of community. It is here that you will find characterful neighbourhood shops and restoration workshops where specialists continue to repair the many books and works of art damaged in the 1966 floods *(see pp56–7)*.

SIGHTS AT A GLANCE

Museums and Galleries
The Bargello pp68–9 **6**
Casa Buonarroti **10**
Casa di Dante **4**
Museo di Firenze com'era **8**
Museo Horne **12**
Museo dell'Opera del Duomo **2**
Museo di Storia della Scienza **13**
Palazzo Nonfinito **7**
Palazzo Vecchio pp78–9 **17**
The Uffizi pp80–83 **18**

Churches
Badia Fiorentina **5**
Duomo, Campanile and Baptistry pp64–5 **1**
Orsanmichele **3**
Santa Croce pp72–3 **11**
Santo Stefano al Ponte **14**

Historic Streets and Piazzas
Piazza della Signoria pp76–7 **16**

Shops
Erboristeria **15**

Ice-Cream Parlours
Bar Vivoli Gelateria **9**

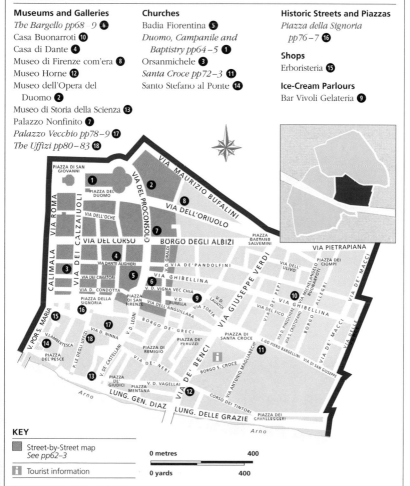

KEY

	Street-by-Street map See pp62–3
i	Tourist information

0 metres 400
0 yards 400

◁ **Michelangelo's** *David* **in Piazza della Signoria**

Street-by-Street: Around the Duomo

Statue on Orsanmichele façade

Much of Florence was rebuilt during the Renaissance, but the eastern part of the city retains a distinctly medieval feel. With its confusing maze of tiny alleyways and hidden lanes, it would still be recognizable to Dante. His house, the Casa di Dante, still stands near the parish church where he first glimpsed his beloved, Beatrice Portinari *(see p70)*. He would also recognize the Bargello and, of course, the Baptistry. One of the oldest streets is the Borgo degli Albizi. Now lined with Renaissance palaces, it follows the line of the ancient Roman road to Rome.

The dome, completed in 1436, was designed by Brunelleschi to dwarf even the great buildings of ancient Greece and Rome.

★ **Duomo, Campanile and Baptistry**
The vast Duomo holds up to 20,000 people. It is elegantly partnered by Giotto's campanile and the Baptistry, whose doors demonstrate the artistic ideas that led to the Renaissance ❶

PIAZZA DI SAN GIOVANNI

PIAZZA DEL DUOMO

VIA DELL' OCHE

VIA S. ELISABETTA

VIA DE' MEDICI

VIA ROMA

VIA D. SPEZIALI

VIA DE' CALZAIUOLI

VIA DE' CER

V.D. TAVOLINI

V.D. CIMATORI

VIA

The Loggia del Bigallo was built for the Misericordia by Alberto Arnoldi in 1358. During the 15th century, abandoned children were displayed here for three days. If, after this time, their parents had not claimed them, they were sent to foster homes.

V. DE' LAMBERTI

CALIMALA

VIA PORTA ROSSA

★ **Orsanmichele**
The carvings on the walls of this Gothic church depict the activities and patron saints of the city's trade guilds, such as the Masons and Carpenters ❸

Via dei Calzaiuoli, lined with smart shops, is the focus of the *passeggiata*, the traditional evening stroll.

★ Museo dell'Opera del Duomo
Works removed from the Duomo, Campanile and Baptistry, like this panel by Verrocchio, are displayed here ❷

LOCATOR MAP
See Florence Street Finder map 6

Palazzo Nonfinito
This is now the anthropological museum ❼

Pegna, a mini-supermarket tucked away in the Via della Studio, sells a range of gourmet treats including chocolate, honey, wine, balsamic vinegar and olive oil *(see p285)*.

Palazzo Salviati, now the head office of the Banca Toscana, has 14th-century frescoes in the main banking hall.

Santa Margherita de' Cerchi is where Dante married Gemma Donati in 1285.

★ The Bargello
The city's old prison is home to a rich collection of applied arts and sculpture, like this figure by Cellini (1500–71) ❻

Badia Fiorentina
The Badia's bell regulated daily life in medieval Florence ❺

STAR SIGHTS

★ Duomo, Campanile and Baptistry

★ The Bargello

★ Museo dell'Opera del Duomo

★ Orsanmichele

Casa di Dante
This medieval house is a museum devoted to Dante's life and work ❹

KEY

– – – Suggested route

0 metres   100

0 yards   100

Duomo, Campanile and Baptistry ❶

Set in the heart of Florence, Santa Maria del Fiore – the Duomo, or cathedral, of Florence – dominates the city with its enormous dome. Its sheer size was typical of Florentine determination to lead in all things, and to this day, no other building stands taller in the city. The Baptistry with its celebrated doors (see p66) is one of Florence's oldest buildings, dating perhaps to the 4th century. In his capacity as city architect, Giotto designed the Campanile in 1334; it was completed in 1359, 22 years after his death.

The Campanile
At 85 m (276 ft), the Campanile is 6 m (20 ft) shorter than the dome. It is clad in white, green and pink Tuscan marble.

Gothic windows

The Neo-Gothic marble façade echoes the style of Giotto's Campanile, but was only added in 1871–87.

★ Baptistry Ceiling
Colourful 13th-century mosaics illustrating the Last Judgment are set above the large octagonal font where many famous Florentines, including Dante, were baptized.

Main entrance

The terracotta panels with bas-reliefs are by Andrea Pisano.

South Doors

Steps to Santa Reparata
The crypt contains the remains of the 4th-century church of Santa Reparata, demolished in 1296 to make way for the cathedral.

STAR FEATURES

★ Brunelleschi's Dome

★ Baptistry Ceiling

For hotels and restaurants in this region see pp250–56 and pp270–73

The top of the dome offers spectacular views over the city.

★ **Brunclleschi's Dome**
Brunelleschi's revolutionary achievement was to build the largest dome of its time without scaffolding. As you climb the 463 steps to the top, you can see how an inner shell provides a platform for the timbers that support the outer shell.

Bricks of varying size were set in a self-supporting hcrringbonc pattcrn – a technique Brunelleschi copied from the Pantheon in Rome.

Last Judgment **frescoes by Vasari**

VISITORS' CHECKLIST

Piazza del Duomo. **Map** 2 D5 (6 D2). 🚌 *1, 6, 14, 17, 23.* **Duomo Tel** *055 230 28 85.* **Open** *10am–5pm Mon–Sat (to 3:30 Thu, to 4:45 Sat), 1:30–4:45pm Sun.* 🕇 *7:30am, 8:30am, 9am, 9:30am, 6:30pm Mon–Sat; 5pm (English) Sat; 7:30am, 9am, 10:30am, noon, 6pm Sun.* 🎫 ♿ 🎫 **Dome Open** *8:30am–7pm Mon–Sat (to 5:40 Sat).* **Crypt Open** *10am–5pm daily (to 4:45 Sat, from 1:30 Sun; to 4pm Thu Oct–Jun).* **Campanile Open** *8:30am–7:30pm daily.* 📷 **Baptistry Open** *noon–7pm Mon–Sat, 8:30am–2pm Sun.* 🕇 📷 🎫 **All closed** *1 Jan, 15 Aug & relig hols.* **Adm charge.** **www**.operaduomo.firenze.it

Chapels at the East End
The three apses house five chapels each and are crowned by a miniature copy of the dome. The 15th-century stained glass is by Lorenzo Ghiberti and other artists.

The octagonal marble sanctuary around the High Altar was decorated by Baccio Bandinelli.

Entrance to steps to the dome

Marble Pavement
As you climb up to the dome, you can see that the 16th-century marble pavement is laid out as a maze.

TIMELINE

Panel from South Doors

4th–5th centuries Thc Baptistry and Santa Reparata church built	**1403–24** Ghiberti's North Doors added	**1425–52** Ghiberti's East Doors, the "Gate of Paradise", added
	1338 Andrea Pisano's South Doors added	**1887** Long-delayed completion of the cathedral façade

400	600	800	1000	1200	1400	1600	1800

897 First documented record of the Baptistry

1209 Zodiac pavement laid in Baptistry

1436 Dome completed

1359 Giotto's Campanile completed

11th–13th centuries Baptistry re-clad in green and white marble

1271 *The Last Judgment* completed on Baptistry ceiling

1296 Arnolfo di Cambio begins the new cathedral on the site of Santa Reparata

The East Doors of the Baptistry

Lorenzo Ghiberti

Lorenzo Ghiberti's celebrated doors were commissioned in 1401 to mark Florence's deliverance from the plague. Ghiberti was chosen after a competition involving seven leading artists, including Donatello and Brunelleschi. Ghiberti's and Brunelleschi's trial panels (*see p69*) are so different from Florentine Gothic art of the time that they are often regarded as the first products of the Renaissance.

Ghiberti's winning panel

The "Gate of Paradise"

Having spent 21 years on the North Doors, Ghiberti worked on the East Doors from 1424 to 1452. Michelangelo enthusiastically dubbed them the "Gate of Paradise". The original panels are in the Museo dell'Opera del Duomo; those on the Baptistry are copies.

The jagged rocks, symbolizing Abraham's pain, are carefully arranged to emphasize the sacrificial act.

Abraham and the Sacrifice of Isaac

Architecture is used to create the illusion of spatial depth. Ghiberti was a master of perspective.

Joseph Sold into Slavery and Recognized by his Brothers

KEY TO THE EAST DOORS

1	2
3	4
5	6
7	8
9	10

1 Adam and Eve are Expelled from Eden
2 Cain Murders his Brother, Abel
3 The Drunkenness of Noah and his Sacrifice
4 Abraham and the Sacrifice of Isaac
5 Esau and Jacob
6 Joseph Sold into Slavery
7 Moses Receives the Ten Commandments
8 The Fall of Jericho
9 The Battle with the Philistines
10 Solomon and the Queen of Sheba

Duomo, Campanile and Baptistry ❶

See pp64–5.

Museo dell'Opera del Duomo ❷

Piazza del Duomo 9. **Map** 2 D5 (6 E2). **Tel** 055 230 28 85. **Open** 9am–7:30pm Mon–Sat; 9am–1:30pm Sun & public hols. **Closed** 1 Jan, Easter Sun, 25 Dec. **Adm charge.** 📷 📓 🚻 ♿

The museum has recently opened after extensive remodelling. Parts of the museum have been replanned, and there are now a series of rooms dedicated to the history of the Duomo. Information about the renovation is available in English and Italian.

From the ticket booth, the main room is reached through open spaces containing Etruscan and Roman reliefs, carvings and sarcophagi.

The main ground floor room contains statues from the workshop of Arnolfo di Cambio, which were once placed in the cathedral's niches. Some are by Arnolfo himself, including the Gothic *Madonna of the Glass Eyes*.

Nearby are found Nanni di Banco's *St Luke*, Bernardo Ciuffagni's *St Matthew* and, most striking of all, Donatello's *St John*. The three were carved between 1408 and 1415. A newly-added side room contains 14th–15th century religious paintings and a number of reliquaries, one of which contains the finger of San Giovanni.

Michelangelo's *Pietà* has pride of place on the staircase. The hooded figure of Nicodemus is widely believed to be a self-portrait. That Mary Magdalene is the inferior work of a pupil is strikingly obvious.

The first room on the upper floor is dominated by two choir lofts, dating to the 1430s, by Donatello and Luca della Robbia. Carved in crisp white

Carving from della Robbia's choir loft in the Museo dell'Opera del Duomo

marble and decorated with coloured glass and mosaic, both depict children playing musical instruments and dancing. But while della Robbia's figures seem innocent, Donatello's look like frenzied participants in some primitive ritual.

Among a number of works by Donatello in this room are his statue of *La Maddalena* (1455) *(see p27)* and several Old Testament figures, including the prophet Abakuk (1423–5), affectionately known by Florentines as *lo zuccone* (marrow-head).

The room to the left contains an exhibition of the tablets which used to decorate the bell tower, some by Andrea Pisano and della Robbia.

Leaving this room, visitors descend to a lower level housing examples of the tools used by Brunelleschi's workmen, and a copy of di Cambio's original cathedral façade. Visitors then ascend to a courtyard, where one finds some of the original panels of doors of the baptistry, as well as the exit.

Orsanmichele ❸

Via dell'Arte della Lana. **Map** 3 C1 (6 D3). **Tel** 055 28 49 44. **Open** 9am–noon (to 1pm Sat & Sun) & 4–6pm daily. **Closed** 1st & last Mon of each month; 1 Jan, 1 May, 25 Dec. 📷

The name is a corruption of *Orto di San Michele*, a former monastic garden. Orsanmichele was built in 1337 as a grain market, but was soon turned into a church. The open arcades became windows, and though these are now bricked in, the original Gothic tracery can still be seen. The outside walls have 14 niches, each holding a statue of the patron saint of one of Florence's major *Arti* (guilds). The interior has two parallel naves. To the right is an extraordinary 1350s altar by Andrea Orcagna. It is covered in cherubs and carved reliefs and encrusted with coloured marble and glass. Close by is Bernardo Daddi's *Virgin and Child* (1348), its frame beautifully carved with angels. Orsanmichele is temporarily closed. Call ahead of your visit.

St George on the façade of Orsanmichele

They used to ...ld Brunel-...chi's dome

The Bargello ❻

Built in 1255 as the city's town hall, the Bargello is the oldest seat of government surviving in Florence. In the 16th century it was the residence of the chief of police and a prison: executions took place here until 1786. After extensive renovation, it became one of Italy's first national museums in 1865. The Bargello houses a superb collection of Florentine Renaissance sculpture, with rooms dedicated to the work of Michelangelo, Donatello, Verrocchio, Giambologna and Cellini, as well as a collection of Mannerist bronzes and examples from the decorative arts.

Arms and Armour Collection

Ivory Collection

Mercury
Giambologna's famous 1564 bronze shows an athletic youth poised for flight.

Magdalen Chapel

Carrand Collection

GALLERY GUIDE

To the right of the entrance hall, the Michelangelo Room is presided over by his Bacchus (1497). The courtyard staircase leads up to the Upper Loggia, filled with statues of birds by Giambologna. To the right is the Donatello Room, which contains the panels for the Baptistry doors competition of 1401. The Magdalen Chapel and Islamic Collection are also on the first floor. The Verrocchio Room, the Andrea and Giovanni della Robbia rooms, the Arms and Armour Collection and the Room of the Small Bronzes are on the second floor.

The courtyard was once the place of execution.

★ Bacchus
The Roman god of wine with a small satyr was Michelangelo's first major work (1497). The modelling is Classical, but the unsteady, drunken posture mocks the poise of ancient works.

KEY

☐	Ground floor
☐	First floor
☐	Second floor
☐	Temporary exhibitions
☐	Non-exhibition space

Michelangelo Room

The tower dates to the 12th century.

Entrance

Lady with a Posy
This bust (1474), attributed to Andrea Verrocchio (1435–88), may have been done in collaboration with Leonardo da Vinci.

VISITORS' CHECKLIST

Via del Proconsolo 4. **Map** 4 D1 (6 E3). **Tel** 055 238 86 06; bookings: 055 294 883. ▦ 14, A. **Open** 8:30am–1:50pm daily. **Closed** 1 Jan, 1 May, 25 Dec, 2nd & 4th Mon & 1st, 3rd & 5th Sun of each month. **Adm charge**. ⌀ ₠ ♿ ▯

Room of the Small Bronzes

Ivory Saddle
Made for the Medici, this saddle inlaid with ivory was used during jousts in 15th-century Florence.

Upper Loggia

★ David
This famous bronze by Donatello (1450) was the first nude statue by a Western artist since Classical times (see pp46–7).

Donatello Room

Islamic Collection

★ Baptistry Doors Competition Panel
Brunelleschi's bronze panel depicting Abraham about to slay Isaac was made in 1401 for the Baptistry doors competition (see p66).

The Bargello has a daunting and heavily fortified façade.

STAR EXHIBITS

* ★ Baptistry Doors Competition Panel
* ★ David by Donatello
* ★ Bacchus by Michelangelo

BARGELLO PRISON

Among the notorious figures executed here was Bernardo Baroncelli. He went to the gallows in 1478 for his part in the failed attempt to assassinate Lorenzo the Magnificent in the Pazzi conspiracy *(see p49)*. Baroncelli's body, hanging from a window in the Bargello as a warning to other anti-Medici conspirators, was sketched by Leonardo da Vinci.

Casa di Dante ❹

Via Santa Margherita 1. **Map** 4 D1 (6 E3). **Tel** 055 21 94 16. **Open** Call tourist office for opening hours.

It is uncertain whether the poet Dante Alighieri (1265–1321) was actually born here, but at least the house looks the part. In 1911, the remains of a 13th-century tower house were restored to give the building its rambling appearance.

Just a short stroll north of the house is the parish church of Santa Margherita de' Cerchi, built during the 11th century. It is here that Dante is said to have first caught sight of Beatrice Portinari, whom he idolized in his poetry. The church, which is often used for Baroque chamber music and organ recitals, contains a fine altarpiece by Neri di Bicci (1418–91).

Bust of Dante on the façade of Casa di Dante

Badia Fiorentina ❺

Via del Proconsolo. **Map** 4 D1 (6 E3). **Tel** 055 23 44 545. **Open** 4:30–6:30pm Mon–Fri; 10:30–11:30am Sun & public hols. ✍

The abbey, one of Florence's oldest churches, was founded in 978 by Willa, the widow of Count Uberto of Tuscany. Their son, Count Ugo, was buried inside the church in 1001. His splendid tomb was carved by Mino da Fiesole and dates from 1469–81. Mino also carved the altarpiece and, in the right transept, the tomb of Bernardo Giugni, the Florentine statesman, with its fine effigy of Justice.

Filippino Lippi's *The Virgin Appearing to St Bernard* (1485) also enlivens an otherwise drab and solemn interior. Its remarkable detail, particularly in the landscape, makes it one of the most artistically significant works of the 15th century.

The peaceful Chiostro degli Aranci ("cloister of the orange trees") is a little hard to find. Look for a door to the right of the altar. Sadly, the orange trees that the monks used to cultivate here are no longer present. The two-tier cloister, built by Rossellino in 1435–40, has a well-preserved fresco cycle showing scenes from the life of St Benedict. Dating from the 15th century, it was restored as recently as 1973.

An early fresco by Bronzino (1503–72) can also be seen in the north walkway. Excellent views of the hexagonal campanile, which gets mentioned by Dante in the *Paradiso* section of *The Divine Comedy*, can be enjoyed from the cloister.

In the 14th century, a series of readings and lectures devoted to Dante's work were given at the Badia by the poet Boccaccio. In keeping with the spirit of these meetings, the abbey is today often used for talks and concerts.

The Bargello ❻

See pp68–9.

Palazzo Nonfinito ❼

Via del Proconsolo 12. **Map** 2 D5 (6 E2). **Tel** 055 239 64 49. **Open** 9am–1pm Thu–Tue (to 5pm Sat). **Closed** 1 Jan, 25 Apr, Easter Sun, 1 May, 24 Jun, 15 Aug, 8 Dec, 25–26 Dec, 31 Dec. ✍

The Palazzo Nonfinito (Unfinished Palace) was begun by Buontalenti in 1593 and was still incomplete when it became Italy's first museum of anthropology and ethnology in 1869. The most striking architectural feature is an imposing inner courtyard usually attributed to Cigoli (1559–1613).

The museum's opening hours are severely restricted. However, it's worth setting aside some time to see the collection of art from Italy's former African colonies, and material carried away by Captain Cook, the 18th-century British explorer, on the last of his Pacific voyages.

The Virgin Appearing to St Bernard (1485) by Filippino Lippi

19th-century copy of the *Pianta della Catena*, showing Florence's cityscape

Museo di Firenze com'era ❽

Via dell'Oriuolo 24. **Map** 2 D5 (6 F2).
Tel 055 261 65 45. **Open** 9am–2pm
Fri–Wed (last adm: 30 mins before
closing). **Closed** 1 Jan, Easter Sun,
1 May, 15 Aug, 25 Dec. **Adm charge**.

The museum traces the
development of the city
through drawings, plans and
paintings. One of the most
fascinating exhibits is the
Pianta della Catena, a 19th-
century copy of a woodcut
made around 1470. The title
refers to the chain-like border
that surrounds the whole image, which shows Florence at
the height of the Renaissance.
Some buildings, for instance
the Palazzo Pitti, can be seen.

The Palazzo Pitti features
again in the delightful
sequence of lunettes made by
the Flemish artist Giusto Utens
in 1599. They show all the
Medici villas and gardens,
with fascinating vignettes of
rural life (*see pp121 and 165*).

One room is devoted to a
scheme devised by Giuseppe
Poggi, the city architect
involved in remodelling
much of central Florence
during its brief stint as the
capital of Italy in 1865–71.
If the scheme had been
implemented, large parts of
the centre would have been
destroyed. The scheme was
halted after an international

outcry, but not before buildings
had been cleared for the new
Piazza della Repubblica (*see
p112*) and the 14th-century
walls had been torn down.

Bar Vivoli Gelateria ❾

Via Isola delle Stinche 7r. **Map** 4 D1
(6 F3). **Tel** 055 29 23 34. **Open**
Mar– Oct: 7:30am–1am Tue–Sat,
9:30am– 1am Sun; Nov–Feb:
7:30am–midnight Tue–Sat,
9:30am–midnight Sun. **Closed** 1st
20 days of Jan & last 20 days of Aug.

Bar Vivoli Gelateria

This tiny ice-cream parlour
attracts large crowds and long
queues for its rich iced
concoctions. Vivoli claims to
make the "best ice cream in
the world", and the walls of
the bar are covered in press

clippings from ice-cream
connoisseurs that strongly
support this view.

The bar stands at the heart
of the colourful Santa Croce
district, with its narrow alleys
and tiny squares. Here, you
will find small shops that
serve the local community,
rather than cater for tourists,
and scores of little workshops
where craftsmen make picture
frames or mend furniture. Via
Torta is typical of the area.

Casa Buonarroti ❿

Via Ghibellina 70. **Map** 4 E1.
Tel 055 24 17 52. **Open** 9:30am–
2pm Wed–Mon. **Closed** 1 Jan,
Easter Sun, 25 Apr, 1 May, 15 Aug,
25 Dec. **Adm charge**. ⬜ ♿

Michelangelo (whose
surname was Buonarroti)
lived briefly in this group
of three houses which he
bought as an investment in
1508. Subsequent generations
of his descendants added what
they could to a significant
collection of his works.

Among these is his earliest
known work, the *Madonna
della Scala*, a marble
tavoletta, or rectangular relief,
carved in 1490–92. There is
also a relief from 1492,
showing *The Battle of the
Centaurs*, and the design,
never used, for the façade of
San Lorenzo, shown in a
wooden model.

Santa Croce ⓫

The magnificent Gothic church of Santa Croce (1294)
contains the tombs of many famous Florentines,
including Michelangelo and Galileo. The spacious, airy
interior is enhanced by the radiant frescoes of Giotto and
his gifted pupil, Taddeo Gaddi, painted early in the 14th
century. The Arnolfo and Brunelleschi Cloisters provide
visitors with fine examples of Renaissance architectural
precision, and a moment of peace and tranquillity during
their tour. The rest of the monastic buildings ranged
around the cloister form a museum
of religious painting and sculpture.

The façade was reclad with
coloured marble in 1863 paid
for by an English benefactor,
Francis Sloane.

Lorenzo Ghiberti
(1378–1455), creator
of the magnificent
doors of Florence's
Baptistry, is buried
here, along with his
sons and assistants,
Vittorio and Lorenzo.

Machiavelli *(see p53)* was buried
here in 1527. His monument, by
Innocenzo Spinazzi, was
erected in 1787.

Ticket booth →

Galileo's Tomb
*Condemned by the church in
1616, Galileo was denied a
Christian burial until 1737,
when this tomb by Giulio
Foggini was erected.*

Entrance

Michelangelo's Tomb
*Michelangelo never completed
the* Pietà *he planned for his own
tomb (see p67). This monument
was designed in 1570 by
Vasari. The figures are
Painting, Architecture
and Sculpture.*

Exit

Tree of Life
by Taddeo
Gaddi

★ Cimabue's Crucifixion
*This ruined 13th-century
masterpiece still expresses the
grandeur of Cimabue's artistry.*

Refectory /

STAR FEATURES

★ Cappella de' Pazzi

★ Cimabue's
Crucifixion

★ Fresco by Gaddi in
Baroncelli Chapel

Donatello's Crucifix (1425) is found in the Bardi di Vernio Chapel. The perfect balance in its form and its subtle play of light and shadow fill it with drama and realism. It is one of the most beautiful works of Florentine humanism.

In the Bardi and Peruzzi Chapels, Giotto's frescoes depict scenes from the lives of St Francis, St John the Baptist and St John the Evangelist.

The Neo-Gothic campanile was added in 1842, after the original was destroyed in 1512 by lightning.

VISITORS' CHECKLIST

Piazza di Santa Croce. **Map** 4 E1 (6 F4). **Tel** 055 24 66 105. ▭ C, 14, 23. **Open** 9:30am–5:30pm daily (from 1pm Sun). Ticket office closes at 5pm. No visits during mass. ♦ 8am, 9am (not Aug), 6pm Mon–Sat; 8am, 9:30am, 11am, noon, 6pm Sun and relig hols. **Adm charge.** ⌀ 🅱 🛈

★ Fresco by Gaddi in Baroncelli Chapel
This image of an angel appearing to sleeping shepherds (1338) was the first true night scene depicted in fresco.

Sacristy

Tomb of Leonardo Bruni
Rossellino's effigy (1447) of the great Humanist, depicted in serene old age, is a triumph of realistic portraiture.

This second cloister was designed by Brunelleschi, and offers a peaceful spot to absorb the atmosphere.

★ Cappella de' Pazzi
Brunelleschi designed this domed chapel in 1430. Delicate grey stonework frames white plaster inset with Luca della Robbia's terracotta roundels of the Apostles.

Museo Horne

Santa Croce ⓫

See pp72–3.

Museo Horne ⓬

Via de' Benci 6. **Map** 4 D1 (6 F4).
Tel 055 24 46 61. **Open** 9am–1pm
Mon–Sat. **Closed** 1 Jan, Easter Sun,
Easter Mon, 25 Apr, 1 May, 15 Aug,
1 Nov, 25–26 Dec. **Adm charge.** ⓘ

The museum's small collection
of paintings, sculpture and
decorative arts was left to the
city by Herbert Percy Horne
(1844–1916), the English art
historian. It is housed in a
splendid example of a Renaissance *palazzino* (small town
house), built in 1489 for the
wealthy Alberti family.

The arrangement of rooms,
with a working and storage
area at ground level and
grander apartments above, is
typical of many Renaissance
houses. The Alberti family,
who grew wealthy from the
city's thriving cloth trade, had
wool-dyeing vats in the
basement and drying
racks in the courtyard.

Most of the museum's major
artifacts, for instance a
number of important 17th-
and 18th-century drawings,
are now housed in the Uffizi.
However, the collection still
boasts at least one major
exhibit: Giotto's 13th-century
St Stephen polyptych (an
altarpiece with more than
three panels). There is also
a *Madonna and Child*
attributed to Simone Martini
(1283–1344) and *Madonna* by
Bernardo Daddi (c.1312–48).

The kitchen, which was built
on the top floor to stop fumes
passing through the entire
house, now contains Horne's
collection of Renaissance pots
and cooking utensils.

Museo di Storia della Scienza ⓭

Piazza de' Giudici 1. **Map** 4 D1 (6 E4).
Tel 055 265 311. ▦ B, 23. **Open**
winter: 9:30am–5pm Mon–Sat (to
1pm Tue), 10am–1pm second Sun of
the month; summer: 9:30am–5pm
Mon–Sat (to 1pm Tue & Sat). **Closed**
1 Jan, 25 Apr, 1 May, 24 Jun, 15 Aug,
8, 25 & 26 Dec. **Adm charge.** ⓘ ♿

This small museum is something of a shrine to the Pisa-
born scientist Galileo Galilei
(1564–1642). Exhibits include
his telescopes and the lens
he used to discover the
largest moons of Jupiter.

The museum also features
large-scale reconstructions of
his experiments into motion,
weight, velocity and acceler-
ation. These are sometimes
demonstrated by the attendants.

In memory of Galileo, in
1657 Florence founded the
world's first-ever scientific
institution, the Accademia
del Cimento (Academy for
Experimentation). Some of the
academy's inventions, such
as early thermometers,
hygrometers and
barometers

are on show here. Of equal
interest are the huge globes
made during the 16th and
17th centuries to illustrate the
motion of the planets and stars.

Also look out for Lopo
Homem's map of the world,
dating to 1554, and the nautical
instruments invented by Sir
Robert Dudley, the Elizabethan
marine engineer. He was
employed by the Medici dukes
to build the harbour at Livorno
from 1607–21 *(see p162).*

**Galileo Galilei (1564–1642), court
mathematician to the Medici**

Santo Stefano al Ponte ⓮

Piazza Santo Stefano al Ponte.
Map 3 C1 (6 D4). **Tel** 055 22 58 43.
Phone to check opening times.

St Stephen "by the bridge",
dating to 969, is so called
because of its close
proximity to the
Ponte Vecchio.

Armillary sphere of 1564, used to map the stars and planets

MAPPING THE WORLD

The same preoccupation with space that made Florentine artists such masters of perspective also made them excellent navigators and mapmakers. Florentine cartographers based their maps on the observations and navigational records of early explorers. That is how America came to be named after the Florentine Amerigo Vespucci rather than Christopher Columbus. When Columbus returned from his transatlantic voyage, King Ferdinand of Spain hired Vespucci, an expert navigator, to check whether Columbus really had discovered a new route to the Indies. Vespucci was the first to realize that Columbus had discovered a new continent and he described his own voyage in a series of letters to Piero de' Medici. As soon as the letters were made public, Florentine cartographers rushed out revised maps of the world based on Vespucci's account. Out of loyalty to a fellow Florentine, they named the New World Amerigo, which was later corrupted to America.

Tip of South America still unmapped

Argentina mapped for the first time

Africa and Arabia well-mapped thanks to centuries of trading

The Antipodes were yet to be "discovered"

16th-century map by the Portuguese cartographer Lopo Homem, in the Museo di Storia della Scienza

The Romanesque façade, dating to 1233, is its most important architectural feature. Florentines, however, know the church better as a venue for some top-quality orchestral concerts.

Erboristeria ⑮

Spezieria–Erboristeria Palazzo Vecchio. Via Vacchereccia 9r.
Map 3 C1 (6 D3). **Tel** 055 239 60 55.
Open 9am–7:30pm Mon–Sat, first & last Sun of month. **Closed** 1 Jan, 1 May, 25 & 26 Dec.

This ancient herbalist's shop, known as Palazzo Vecchio, is hidden among the pavement cafés lining Via Vacchereccia, off Piazza della Signoria. It has a lovely frescoed interior. Several such shops in Florence sell a range of herbal soaps, pot pourri, cosmetics and fragrances made to ancient recipes by monks and nuns in various parts of Tuscany. Another *erboristeria* is just around the corner at Calimala 4r. Called the Erboristeria della Antica Farmacia del Cinghiale (Herbalist at the Old Boar Pharmacy), it takes its name from the famous bronze boar statue in the Mercato Nuovo opposite *(see p112)*.

Piazza della Signoria ⑯

See pp76–7.

Palazzo Vecchio ⑰

See pp78–9.

The Uffizi ⑱

See pp80–83.

Arno façade of the Uffizi with the Vasari Corridor (pp106–7) above

Piazza della Signoria ⑯

The piazza is a unique outdoor sculpture gallery and, with the Palazzo Vecchio *(see pp78–9)*, has been at the heart of Florentine politics since the 14th century. Citizens gathered here when called to a *parlamento* (a public meeting) by the Palazzo's great bell. The statues, some copies, commemorate major events in the city's history. Many are linked to the rise and fall of the Florentine Republic *(pp52–53)*, during which the religious leader Girolamo Savonarola was burned at the stake here.

Campanile

Salone dei Cinquecento
This vast council chamber, built in 1495, is decorated with Vasari's frescoes on the history of Florence.

Palazzo Vecchio

Grand Duke Cosimo I
Giambologna's equestrian statue (1595) celebrates the man who subjugated all Tuscany under his military rule (see pp54–5).

The Marzocco is a copy. The original of Donatello's heraldic lion is in the Bargello.

★ **Neptune Fountain**
Ammannati's Mannerist fountain (1575) of the Roman sea god surrounded by water nymphs commemorates Tuscan naval victories.

Pageantry
For centuries the piazza has been the city's venue for public rallies and festivities, as shown in this 18th-century engraving.

VISITORS' CHECKLIST

Map 4 D1 (6 D3). 🚌 A, B. Pedestrian area.

★ **Perseus**
Cellini's bronze statue (1554) of Perseus holding Medusa's head was meant to warn Cosimo I's enemies of their probable fate. The original of the base it rests on is in the Bargello.

The Uffizi café, on the roof of the Loggia dei Lanzi, offers fine views over the piazza.

★ **The Rape of the Sabine Women** *(1583)*
The writhing figures in Giambologna's famous statue were carved from a single block of flawed marble.

Hercules and Cacus (1533) by Bandinelli

The Loggia dei Lanzi (1382) is named after Cosimo I's bodyguards, the Lancers. Also known as Loggia di Orcagna, after the architect, it is lined with ancient Roman statues.

★ **David**
The original of Michelangelo's celebrated statue of David was moved from its initial location in the Piazza della Signoria into the Accademia in 1873 (see p94).

STAR FEATURES

★ David by Michelangelo

★ Neptune Fountain by Ammannati

★ The Rape of the Sabine Women by Giambologna

★ Perseus by Cellini

Palazzo Vecchio ⓱

The Palazzo Vecchio ("Old Palace") still fulfils its original role as Florence's town hall. It was completed in 1322 when a huge bell, used to call citizens to meetings or warn of fire, flood or enemy attack, was hauled to the top of the imposing belltower. The palazzo has retained its medieval appearance, but much of the interior was remodelled for Duke Cosimo I when he moved into the palace in 1540. Leonardo and Michelangelo were asked to redecorate the interior, but it was Vasari who finally undertook the work. His many frescoes (1563–5) glorify Cosimo and his creation of the Grand Duchy of Tuscany.

★ **Sala dei Gigli (Room of the Lilies)**
Gold fleurs-de-lis, emblems of Florence, cover the walls in between Ghirlandaio's frescoes (1485) of Roman statesmen.

PALACE GUIDE

A monumental staircase leads to the first-floor Salone dei Cinquecento, with its frescoed walls and marble statues. Above this is a suite of decorated rooms once used by the rulers of Florence. Parts of the Salone dei Cinquecinto, the Studiolo of Francesco I, the Treasury of Cosimo I and the staircase of the Duke of Athens are only accessible by tour. The tours follow the "secret routes" made for the rulers.

Heraldic Frieze
Shields on the façade symbolize episodes in Florentine history. The crossed keys represent Medici papal rule.

Loeser collection

Campanile

Cortile della Dogana

Museum entrance

★ **Cortile and Putto Fountain**
A copy of Verrocchio's Putto Fountain was placed in the courtyard by Vasari in 1565.

KEY TO FLOORPLAN

- ☐ Ground floor
- ☐ First floor
- ☐ Mezzanine floor
- ☐ Second floor
- ☐ Temporary exhibition space
- ☐ Non-exhibition space

Eleonora di Toledo's Rooms
Cosimo I's wife had a suite of rooms decorated with scenes of virtuous women. Penelope, wife of the Greek hero Odysseus, is shown waiting faithfully for her husband to return.

VISITORS' CHECKLIST

Piazza della Signoria. **Map** 4 D1 (6 D3). **Tel** 055 276 82 24. 🚌 A, B. **Open** 9am–7pm daily (to 2pm Thu). Last adm: 45 mins before closing. Some extended hours in summer. ♿
The Secret Routes
Open Mon–Fri.
Closed 1 Jan, Easter, 1 May, 15 Aug, 25 Dec. **Adm charge**.
📷 compulsory. 🚫 📷

The Map Room

The Quartiere degli Elementi contains Vasari's allegories of Earth, Fire, Air and Water.

Putto with Dolphin
Verrocchio's bronze fountain head (1470) is displayed in the Terrazzo di Giunone. The small room next door has fine views of San Miniato al Monte.

Pope Leo X's rooms

The Salone dei Cinquecento was a meeting place for the leaders of the Florentine Republic *(see pp52–3).*

Cappella di Eleonora
Egyptian soldiers in pursuit of Moses drown in the Red Sea, in the biblical frescoes (1540–45) by Bronzino in Eleonora di Toledo's chapel.

easury
imo I

★ Victory by Michelangelo
Michelangelo's nephew presented this statue (1533–4), intended for the tomb of Pope Julius II, to Cosimo I in 1565, following the Duke's military triumph over Siena.

STAR FEATURES

★ Cortile and Putto Fountain

★ Victory by Michelangelo

★ Sala dei Gigli

The Uffizi ⑱

The Uffizi was built in 1560–80 as a suite of offices *(uffici)* for Duke Cosimo I's new administration *(see p50)*. The architect, Vasari, used iron reinforcement to create an almost continuous wall of glass on the upper storey. From 1581 Cosimo's heirs used this well-lit space to display the Medici family art treasures, creating what is now the oldest gallery in the world. There are plans to double the entire exhibition space by 2007.

Main staircase

Entrance Hall

Entrance

The Loggia dei Lanzi terrace merits a visit for its unusual views of the Piazza della Signoria *(see pp76–7)*.

Bar

Corridor ceilings are frescoed in the "grotesque" style of the 1580s, inspired by Roman grottoes.

GALLERY GUIDE

Ancient Greek and Roman sculptures are in the corridor around the inner side of the horseshoe-shaped building. The paintings are hung in a series of rooms off the main corridor, in chronological order, to show the development of Florentine art from Gothic to Renaissance and beyond. Many well-known paintings are in rooms 7–18. Five new rooms opened on the ground floor in 2004. To avoid queues, book your ticket and visiting time in advance (see p296). Pick up a gallery guide for advice on layout changes.

The Ognissanti Madonna
Giotto's grasp of spatial depth in this altarpiece (1310) was a milestone in the mastery of perspective.

Buontalenti staircase

Entrance to the Vasari Corridor *(see pp106–7)*

STAR PAINTINGS

- ★ The Duke and Duchess of Urbino by Piero della Francesca

- ★ The Birth of Venus by Botticelli

- ★ The Holy Family by Michelangelo

- ★ The Venus of Urbino by Titian

★ The Venus of Urbino *(1538)*
Titian's sensuous nude was condemned for portraying the goddess in such an immodest pose.

★ **The Duke and Duchess of Urbino** *(1460)*
*Piero della Francesca's panels are among the first
true Renaissance portraits. He even recorded the
Duke's hooked nose – broken by a sword blow.*

The Tribune,
decorated in
red and gold,
contains the
works that
the Medici
valued most.

★ **The Birth of Venus** *(1485)*
*Botticelli's captivating image shows the Roman
goddess of love, born in a storm in the Aegean
sea. She is blown ashore by the
winds and greeted by nymphs,
ready to wrap her in a cloak.*

**Boy Removing a
Thorn from his Foot**
*This ancient Roman statue is,
like many of the collection's
antique sculptures, based
on a Greek original.*

**Vasari's Classical
Arno façade**

KEY

☐ East Corridor

☐ West Corridor

☐ Arno Corridor

☐ Gallery Rooms 1–45

☐ Non-exhibition space

★ **The Holy Family** *(1507)*
*Michelangelo's painting, the
first to break with the conven-
tion of showing Christ on the
Virgin's lap, inspired
Mannerist artists through its
expressive handling of colour
and posture* (see p27).

Exploring the Uffizi's Collection

The Uffizi offers an unrivalled opportunity to see some of the greatest works of the Renaissance. The collection was born from the immense wealth of the Medici family *(see pp50–51)*, who commissioned work from many great Florentine masters. Francesco I housed the family collection at the Uffizi in 1581. His descendants added to it until 1737, when Anna Maria Lodovica, last of the Medici, bequeathed it to the people of Florence.

GOTHIC ART

Following the collection of antiquities in room 1, the gallery's next six rooms are devoted to Tuscan Gothic art from the 12th to 14th centuries.

Giotto (1266–1337) introduced a degree of naturalism that was new in Tuscan art. The angels and saints in his *Ognissanti Madonna* (1310), in room 2, express a range of human emotions, from awe and reverence to puzzlement. The throne in this painting, and the temple in Lorenzetti's *Presentation in the Temple* (1342) in room 3, show a concern for three-dimensional depth quite at odds with the flatness of much Gothic art.

Giotto's naturalism extends throughout the works in room 4, devoted to the 14th-century Florentine School. One of the most obvious examples is the *Pietà* (1360–65), attributed to Giottino. Look at the difference

between the characters' expressions, their medieval, rather than Biblical, style of dress and the blood, still fresh on the cross.

EARLY RENAISSANCE

A better understanding of geometry and perspective allowed Renaissance artists to create an illusion of space and depth in their works. Paolo Uccello (1397–1475) was obsessed with perspective; witness his nightmarish *The Battle of San Romano* (1456) *(see p48)* in room 7.

Also in this room are two panels by Piero della Francesca (1410–92), depicting the Duke and Duchess of Urbino on one side and representations of their virtues on the other. Painted between 1465 and 1470, these are two of the first Renaissance portraits.

If these works seem coldly experimental, Fra Filippo

Lippi's *Madonna and Child with Angels* (1455–66), in room 8, is a masterpiece of warmth and humanity. Like so many Renaissance artists, Lippi uses a religious subject to celebrate earthly delights, such as feminine beauty and the Tuscan landscape.

Madonna and Child with Angels (1455–66) by Fra Filippo Lippi

BOTTICELLI

The Botticelli paintings in rooms 10–14 are the highlight of the Uffizi's collection. The brilliant colours and crisp draughtsmanship of, for instance, *The Birth of Venus* (about 1485) *(see p81)*, are a reminder that Renaissance artists often experimented with

Primavera (1480) by Botticelli

new pigments to achieve striking colour effects. The subject of this painting, the Roman goddess Venus, is also significant. By painting Venus instead of the Christian Virgin, Botticelli expressed the fascination with Classical mythology common to many Renaissance artists.

The same is true of his other famous work, *Primavera* (about 1480). It breaks with the tradition of Christian religious painting by illustrating a pagan rite of spring. Other works to see here include the *Adoration of the Magi* (about 1475), a thinly disguised Medici family portrait *(see p51)*.

LEONARDO DA VINCI

Detail from *The Annunciation* (1472–5) by Leonardo da Vinci

Room 15 contains works attributed to the young Leonardo. Still under the influence of his teachers, he was already developing his own masterly style, as in *The Annunciation* (1472–5) and the unfinished *Adoration of the Magi* (1481).

THE TRIBUNE

The octagonal tribune, with its mother-of-pearl ceiling, was designed in 1584 by Buontalenti so that Francesco I could display all his favourite works from the Medici collection in one room.

Notable paintings include Bronzino's portrait (1545) of Eleonora di Toledo with her son, Giovanni *(see p51)*, and the same artist's portrait of Bia, Cosimo I's illegitimate daughter. It was painted just before her

Portrait of *Bia* (1542) by Bronzino

early death in 1542. *The Medici Venus*, probably dating to the 1st century BC, is a Roman copy of the Greek original by Praxiteles. A small room off the Tribune contains a copy of the Hellenistic sculpture, *The Hermaphrodite*.

NON-FLORENTINE ART

The works in rooms 19 to 23 show how rapidly the artistic ideas and techniques of the Renaissance spread beyond Florence. Umbrian artists like Perugino (1446–1523) and Northern European painters such as Dürer (1471–1528) are well represented.

THE ARNO CORRIDOR

The corridor overlooking the Arno, which links the east and west wings of the Uffizi, offers fine views of the hills to the south of Florence.

The ancient Roman statues displayed here were mainly collected by the Medici during the 15th century. Their anatomical precision and faithful portraiture were much admired and copied by Renaissance artists, who saw themselves as giving rebirth to Classical perfection in art.

The Roman statues were equally popular during the 17th and 18th centuries with visitors on their way to Rome on the Grand Tour *(see p55)*. The Renaissance works, which attract visitors today, were largely ignored until John Ruskin, the art historian, wrote about them in the 1840s.

HIGH RENAISSANCE AND MANNERISM

Michelangelo's *The Holy Family* (1506–8), in room 25, is striking for its vibrant colours and the unusually twisted pose of the Virgin *(see p81)*. This painting proved to be enormously influential with the next generation of Tuscan artists, notably Bronzino (1503–72), Pontormo (1494–1556) and Parmigianino (1503–40). The latter's *Madonna of the Long Neck* (about 1534) in room 29, with its contorted anatomy and bright, unnatural colours, is a remarkable example of what came to be known as the Mannerist style.

Two other masterpieces of the High Renaissance are located nearby. Raphael's tender *Madonna of the Goldfinch* (1506), in room 26, still shows signs of earthquake damage dating to 1547. Titian's *The Venus of Urbino* (1538), said to be one of the most beautiful nudes ever painted, is in room 28.

Madonna of the Goldfinch (1506) by Raphael

LATER PAINTINGS

Works by Rubens (1577–1640) and Van Dyck (1599–1641) are in room 41 (sometimes closed), while Rembrandt (1606–69) can be found in room 44. New rooms on the ground floor hold paintings by Caravaggio (1573–1610) and his school, as well as by Guido Reni (1577–1642).

CITY CENTRE NORTH

This area of Florence is stamped with the character of Cosimo il Vecchio. The man who founded the great Medici dynasty maintained his position of power by astute management of the city's financial affairs, as opposed to resorting to threats and violence. Cosimo was a highly educated and sophisticated man with a passion for building, and he wanted the churches, palazzi and libraries that he built to last a thousand years, like the buildings of ancient Rome. To this end, he commissioned some of the greatest architects and artists of the time

Roundel on Spedale degli Innocenti

to build the churches of San Lorenzo and San Marco as well as the Medici's first home, the Palazzo Medici Riccardi. He is regarded as one of the great innovators of the Renaissance in Florence. Even after the Medici family had moved across the river Arno to the Palazzo Pitti in 1550, the Grand Dukes made their final journey back to the north of the city to be buried in the extravagant Cappelle Medicee in San Lorenzo. For the tombs in the New Sacristy, Michelangelo contributed his magnificent allegorical sculptures, *Day and Night*, and *Dawn and Dusk*.

SIGHTS AT A GLANCE

Churches and Synagogues
San Lorenzo pp90–91 ❷
San Marco pp96–7 ❼
Santa Maria Maddalena dei Pazzi ⓰
Santissima Annunziata ⓮
Tempio Israelitico ⓱

Historic Buildings
Palazzo Medici Riccardi ❺
Palazzo Pucci ❹
Spedale degli Innocenti ⓬

Museums and Galleries
Cenacolo di Sant'Apollonia ❻
Conservatorio ❿
Galleria dell'Accademia ❾
Museo Archeologico ⓯
Opificio delle Pietre Dure ⓫

Gardens
Giardino dei Semplici ❽

Streets, Piazzas and Markets
Mercato Centrale ❶
Piazza della Santissima Annunziata ⓭
Piazza di San Lorenzo ❸

KEY

▨	Street-by-Street map *See pp92–3*
▨	Street-by-Street map *See pp86–7*
🛈	Tourist information

0 metres 300
0 yards 300

◁ *Virgin and Child* by Fra Angelico (c.1440) in San Marco

Street-by-Street: Around San Lorenzo

Bust, Palazzo Medici Riccardi

This area is stamped with the character of Cosimo il Vecchio, founder of the Medici dynasty, who commissioned San Lorenzo and the Palazzo Medici Riccardi. Around San Lorenzo, a huge general market fills the streets, its colourful awnings almost obscuring the various monuments. The market is a reminder that Florence has always been a city of merchants. Many of the products on sale – leather goods and silk, wool and cashmere garments – are very good value especially if, like the Florentines, you are prepared to bargain.

Cheap cafés and cooked meat stalls abound in the vicinity of the market. They sell traditional Italian take-away foods, such as tripe and roast suckling pig, chicken and rabbit.

Mercato Centrale
Built in 1874, the central market is packed with fish, meat and cheese stalls downstairs, while fruit and vegetables are sold upstairs beneath the glass and cast-iron roof ❶

Palazzo Riccardi-Manelli, begun in 1557, stands on the site of the house where Giotto was born in 1266.

VIA DELL' ANTONINO
VIA SANT' ARIENTO
VIA FAENZA
VIA DELL' AMORINO
VIA DEL MELARANCIO
PIAZZA DI MADONNA DEGLI ALDOBRANDINI
VIA DEL GIGLIO
VIA DELL' ALLORO
VIA DE' CONTI
VIA F. ZANNETTI

Biblioteca Mediceo-Laurenziana

The Cappelle Medicee are situated in San Lorenzo, but are reached from a separate entrance in Piazza di Madonna degli Aldobrandini. Michelangelo designed the New Sacristy and two Medici tombs. Some of his pencil sketches survive on the walls inside.

STAR SIGHTS

★ San Lorenzo

★ Palazzo Medici Riccardi

The Biblioteca Riccardiana, founded in the 16th century, was opened to the public in 1715. It comprises a series of frescoed reading rooms which house a collection of precious manuscripts, including Dante's *Divine Comedy.*

LOCATOR MAP
See Florence Street Finder maps 5, 6

Via de' Ginori is lined with fine 16th-century palazzi.

San Giovannino degli Scolopi church was begun by Ammannati in 1579.

★ **Palazzo Medici Riccardi**
The palazzo, built between 1444–64, served as the Medici family home and the headquarters of their banking empire ❺

Palazzo Pucci
This is the home of designer Emilio Pucci ❹

★ **San Lorenzo**
The unfinished façade belies the noble interior, which was designed for the Medici by Brunelleschi in 1425–46 ❷

KEY

– – – Suggested route

0 metres	100
0 yards	100

Giovanni delle Bande Nere, Grand Duke Cosimo I's father (*see p51*), is depicted in battle dress in this statue by Baccio Bandinelli (1540).

Mercato Centrale

Mercato Centrale ❶

Via dell'Ariento 10–14. **Map** 1 C4 (5 C1). **Open** *7am–2pm Mon–Sat.* **Underground car park Open** *24 hours a day, seven days a week.*

Right in the heart of the San Lorenzo street market is Florence's busiest food market, the bustling Mercato Centrale. It is housed in a vast two-storey building made of cast-iron and glass, which was built in 1874 by Giuseppe Mengoni. During restoration in 1980, a mezzanine floor was constructed and a car park was added in the basement. For reduced rate parking, have a market vendor stamp your receipt. On the ground floor there are dozens of stalls selling meat, fish, cheese and typical Tuscan takeaway foods, such as *porchetta* (roast suckling pig). Fruit, vegetables and flowers are sold on the top floor.

San Lorenzo ❷

See pp90–91.

Piazza di San Lorenzo ❸

Map 1 C5 (6 D1). summer: *7am– 8pm; winter: 8am–8pm Tue–Sat.*

At the western end of the piazza, near the entrance to San Lorenzo church, there is a statue of Giovanni delle Bande Nere, mercenary and father of Cosimo I, first Medici Grand Duke *(see p49).* It was carved by Baccio Bandinelli in 1540, and is almost hidden from view among the market stalls stretching all the way up the side of San Lorenzo church and into the streets leading off the piazza. The stalls closest to the church cater mostly for tourists, selling leather goods, T-shirts and souvenirs. In the streets around the market, everything from lentils to bargain-priced clothes is sold. The neighbouring shops have become an integral part of the market, selling cheeses, hams, home-baked bread, pastries, fabrics and table linen.

Statue of Giovanni delle Bande Nere in Piazza di San Lorenzo

Palazzo Pucci ❹

Via de' Pucci 6. **Map** 2 D5 (6 E1). **Tel** *055 28 30 61.* **Closed** *to the public.*

The Palazzo Pucci is the ancestral home of clothes designer Emilio Pucci, Marchese di Barsento. The Pucci family, traditionally friends and allies of the Medici, feature prominently in Florence's history, and this large palace was built in the 16th century to designs by Bartolomeo Ammannati.

Emilio Pucci's boutique is at Via della Vigna Nuova 97–99r. *Haute couture* clients are fitted out in the palatial rooms which are above the showroom. Pucci is most famous for smart but casual clothes, and designed the stylish blue uniforms worn by Florentine traffic police, the *vigili urbani (see p276).*

San Lorenzo street market

Palazzo Medici Riccardi ❺

Via Cavour 1. **Map** 2 D5 (6 D1). *Tel 055 276 03 40.* **Cappella dei Magi Open** *9am–7pm Thu–Tue.* **Closed** *1 May, 25 Dec.* **Adm charge.** *Booking is advisable in busy periods.* 🚫 ♿

Home of the Medici for 100 years from 1444, the palazzo was later acquired by the Riccardi family and now houses government offices. It was built to an austere design by Michelozzo for Cosimo il Vecchio, who rejected Brunelleschi's original plans as being too flamboyant – Cosimo did not want to flaunt his wealth. The windows on either side of the entrance were added in 1517 and designed by Michelangelo.

Through the main door, the courtyard walls are covered in ancient Roman masonry fragments. The roundels above the arcade show scenes copied from antique intaglios now on display in the Museo degli Argenti *(see p123)*. Donatello's statue of David (now in the Bargello, *see pp68–9*) used to be here, but today the place of honour is given to Bandinelli's marble statue of *Orpheus*.

Only a few rooms in the palazzo are open to the public. In the Cappella dei Magi is a colourful fresco of *The Procession of the Magi* painted in 1459–60 by Benozzo Gozzoli. It depicts several members of the Medici dynasty *(see pp48–9)*. The Sala di Luca Giordano is named after the Neapolitan artist who painted its walls with *The*

Statuary in the garden of the Palazzo Medici Riccardi

The Last Supper (1445–50) by Andrea del Castagno in Sant'Apollonia

Apotheosis of the Medici in High Baroque style in 1683. A selection of marble sculptures from the Medici Riccardi collection is on display in a recently renovated wing. The palazzo often plays host to temporary art exhibitions, for which there is an additional admission charge.

Cenacolo di Sant'Apollonia ❻

Via XXVII Aprile 1. **Map** 2 D4. *Tel 055 238 86 07.* **Open** *8:15am–1:50pm daily.* **Closed** *1st & 3rd Sun, 2nd & 4th Mon of the month.* 📷 ♿

The cloister and refectory of what was originally a convent for the Camaldolite order of nuns are now used by the students of Florence University. On the main wall of the refectory is a fresco of *The Last Supper* painted in 1445–50, one of the few surviving works by Andrea del Castagno, pupil of Masaccio and among the first Renaissance artists to begin to experiment with perspective. Here Judas sits isolated in the foreground of the picture, disrupting its balance and breaking up the long white strip of tablecloth. He is shown in profile with the face of a satyr: a mythological creature, half-man, half-goat, often used in Renaissance paintings to represent evil.

San Marco ❼

See pp96–7.

Giardino dei Semplici ❽

Via Micheli 3. **Map** 2 E4. *Tel 055 275 74 02.* **Open** *9am–1pm Mon–Fri, Sun in spring; call for info.* **Closed** *1 Jan, 6 Jan, 25 Apr, Easter Sun & Mon, 1 May, 13–17 Aug, 1 Nov, 24–26 Dec, 31 Dec.* 📷 ♿

Giardino dei Semplici

The word "Semplici" refers to the raw ingredients, "simples", used by medieval apothecaries in preparing medicine – thus the Giardino dei Semplici was where medicinal herbs were grown and studied. It was set up in 1545 by Niccolò Tribolo for Cosimo I in the area between Via Micheli, Via Giorgio la Pira and Via Gino Capponi. The garden retains its original layout but now the collection includes tropical plants as well as flora native to Tuscany.

Around the garden are small specialist museums: a geology collection includes fossils; the mineralogy section shows the geological structure of Elba, whose ores attracted bronze traders in the 10th century BC. The botanical museum has specimens of rare plants.

San Lorenzo ❷

San Lorenzo was the parish church of the Medici family, and they lavished their wealth on its adornment. Brunelleschi rebuilt the church in Renaissance Classical style in 1419, although the façade was never completed. In 1520 Michelangelo began work on the Medici tombs and designed the Biblioteca Mediceo-Laurenziana in 1524

to house the manuscripts collected by the Medici. In both the New Sacristy and the Cappella dei Principi, extensive scaffolding has been erected (for an indefinite period) to protect visitors from falling marble.

The huge dome by Buontalenti echoes that of Brunelleschi's Duomo *(see pp64–5)*.

★ Cappella dei Principi
The marble decoration of the Medici mausoleum, begun in 1604 by Matteo Nigetti, was not completed until 1962.

The Old Sacristy was designed by Brunelleschi (1420–29) and painted by Donatello.

★ Michelangelo's Staircase
The Mannerist pietra serena sandstone staircase to the Biblioteca is one of Michelangelo's most innovative designs. It was built by Ammannati in 1559.

Michelangelo designed the desks and ceiling of the Biblioteca, which is entered from Manetti's graceful, tiered cloister, built in 1462.

The Martyrdom of St Lawrence
Bronzino's huge Mannerist fresco of 1659 is a masterly study of the human form in various contorted poses (see p27).

The formal cloister garden is planted with clipped box hedges, pomegranate and orange trees.

★ Medici Tombs
Michelangelo's monumental funerary figures, symbolizing Night, Day, Dawn and Dusk, are among his greatest works.

Six Grand Dukes are buried in the Cappella dei Principi.

VISITORS' CHECKLIST

Piazza di San Lorenzo (Basilica and Biblioteca), Piazza di Madonna degli Aldobrandini (Cappelle Medicee). **Map** 1 C5 (6 D1). 🚌 *many routes.* **Basilica** *Tel 055 21 66 34.* **Open** 10am–5pm Mon–Sat. 🕊 *8am, 9:30am, 6pm daily (also 11am Sun & relig hols).* 🛇 **Adm charge.** **Biblioteca** *Tel 055 21 44 43.* **Open** *9am–1pm Mon–Sat.* **Closed** *public hols.* **Cappelle Medicee** *Tel 055 238 86 02 (055 29 48 83 to book).* **Open** *8:30am–5pm daily (to 1:50pm public hols; last adm: 30 mins before closing).* **Closed** *1st, 3rd & 5th Mon, 2nd & 4th Sun of the month.* **Adm charge.** 📷

The campanile was built in 1740.

Donatello's Pulpits
Donatello was 74 when he began work on the bronze pulpits in the nave in 1460; they depict Christ's Passion and Resurrection.

A simple stone slab marks the unostentatious grave of Cosimo il Vecchio (1389–1464), founder of the Medici dynasty.

St Joseph and Christ in the Workshop
Pietro Annigoni (1910–88) is one of the few modern artists whose work is seen in Florence.

Michelangelo submitted several designs for the façade of San Lorenzo, but it remains unfinished.

Entrance to church

STAR FEATURES

★ Cappella dei Principi

★ Michelangelo's Staircase

★ Medici Tombs by Michelangelo

Street-by-Street: Around San Marco

The buildings in this part of Florence once stood on the fringes of the city, serving as stables and barracks. The Medici menagerie, including lions, elephants and giraffes, was housed here. Today it is the student quarter, and in term-time Piazza di San Marco is filled with young people waiting for lectures at the university or at the Accademia di Belle Arti. This is the world's oldest art school, set up in 1563, with Michelangelo as a founder *(see p94).*

The Palazzo Pandolfini was designed by Raphael in 1516.

Michelangelo taught himself to draw from the statues in the Medici gardens.

★ San Marco
This Dominican convent is now a museum housing Savonarola's cell and the spiritual paintings of Fra Angelico (1395–1455) **7**

Piazza di San Marco is a lively meeting-place for students.

VIA DEGLI ARAZZIERI

VIA SAN GALLO

VIA CAVOUR

PIAZZA DI SAN MARCO

VIA RICASOLI

Cenacolo di Sant'Apollonia
The refectory of this former convent features Andrea del Castagno's The Last Supper *(1450)* **6**

Conservatorio
Florence's academy of music has an excellent library **10**

★ Galleria dell' Accademia
This gallery, famous for Michelangelo's David, *also contains Bonaguida's* Tree of the Cross *(1330)* **9**

Opificio delle Pietre Dure
Precious mosaics are restored here **11**

STAR SIGHTS

- ★ Galleria dell'Accademia
- ★ San Marco
- ★ Spedale degli Innocenti

Santissima Annunziata
*The Medici funded the rebuilding of this
church, begun in 1444 by Michelozzo. The
atrium was frescoed by Andrea del Sarto* ⑭

LOCATOR MAP
*See Florence Street Finder
map 2*

Giardino dei Semplici
*Research into plant
remedies has been under-
taken here since 1543* ⑧

★ **Spedale degli Innocenti**
*The city orphanage (see
pp48–9) was Brunelleschi's
first completed Classical
design. Andrea della Robbia
added cameos of swaddled
infants in the 1480s, as an
inspiration to charity* ⑫

Museo Archeologico
*Etruscan vases and
bronzes form part of
this major collection* ⑮

Grand Duke Ferdinando I
was Giambologna's last
statue and was cast by Tacca
in 1608, using the bronze from
cannons captured as battle
trophies by the Tuscan navy.

KEY

– – – Suggested route

0 metres   50

0 yards   50

The central section of the 15th-century *Cassone Adimari* by Scheggia

Galleria dell'Accademia ❾

Via Ricasoli 60. **Map** 2 D4 (6 E1). *Tel 055 238 86 09 (information); 055 29 48 83 (reservations).* **Open** *8:15am– 6:50pm Tue–Sun (extended hours in summer).* **Closed** *1 Jan, 1 May, 25 Dec.* **Adm charge.** ⌀ 🚻 🏠

The Academy of Fine Arts in Florence was founded in 1563 and was the first school in Europe set up to teach the techniques of drawing, painting and sculpture. The art collection displayed in the gallery was formed in 1784 with the aim of providing the students of the academy with material to study and copy.

Since 1873, many of Michelangelo's most important works have been in the Accademia. Perhaps

Madonna del Mare (c.1470) by Sandro Botticelli

the most famous of all dominates the collection: Michelangelo's *David* (1504). This colossal Classical statue (5.2 m/17 ft) depicts the biblical hero who killed the giant Goliath. It was commissioned by the city of Florence and positioned in front of the Palazzo Vecchio. This established Michelangelo, then aged 29, as the foremost sculptor of his time. In 1873 it was moved to the Accademia, to protect it from the weather and pollution. One copy of *David* is now to be found in its original position in Piazza della Signoria *(see pp76–7)* and a second stands in the middle of Piazzale Michelangelo *(see p131)*.

Michelangelo's other masterpieces include a statue of St Matthew finished in 1508, and the *Quattro Prigioni* (the four prisoners) which were sculpted between 1521 and 1523 and intended to adorn the tomb of Pope Julius II. Presented to the Medici in 1564 by Michelangelo's cousin, the muscular figures struggling to free themselves from the stone are among the most dramatic of his works. The statues were moved to the

David by Michelangelo

Grotta Grande in the Boboli Gardens in 1585, where casts of the originals can now be seen *(see pp124–5)*.

The gallery contains an important collection of paintings by 15th- and 16th-century local artists: contemporaries of Michelangelo such as Fra Bartolomeo, Filippino Lippi, Bronzino and Ridolfo del Ghirlandaio. There are many major works including the *Madonna del Mare* (Madonna of the Sea), attributed to Botticelli (1445–1510), and *Venus and Cupid* by Jacopo Pontormo (1494–1556), based upon a preparatory drawing by Michelangelo. Also on display is an elaborately painted wooden chest, the *Cassone Adimari*, by Scheggia, Masaccio's step-brother. Dating from around 1440, it was originally used as part of a bride's trousseau, and is covered with details of Florentine daily life, clothing and architecture. The bridal party are pictured standing in front of the Baptistry.

Pacino di Bonaguida's *Tree of Life* (1310) is a prominent painting among the collections of Byzantine and late 13th- and 14th-century religious art much of which is stylized and heavily embossed with gold.

The Salone della Toscana (Tuscany Room) is full of 19th-century sculpture and paintings by members of the Accademia, and a series of original plaster models by the sculptor Lorenzo Bartolini. Born in 1777, he became professor at the Accademia in 1839, a post he held until his death in 1850. His work includes busts of major figures such as the poet Lord Byron and the composer Franz Liszt.

Detail from **14th-century** *Madonna and Saints* in the Accademia

Conservatorio Musicale Luigi Cherubini ⑩

Piazza delle Belle Arti 2. **Map** 2 D4 (6 E1). *Tel* 055 29 21 80. **Library** *closed* to the public.

Some of Italy's finest musicians trained at this musical academy, named after the Florentine composer Luigi Cherubini (1760–1842). The conservatory owns a range of ancient musical instruments, now on display in the Palazzo Vecchio *(see pp78–9)*. The collection was acquired by Ferdinando, the last of the Medici Grand Dukes, and includes violins, violas and cellos made by Stradivari, Amati and Ruggeri. There is also a harpsichord by Bartolomeo Cristofori, who invented the piano in the early 18th century. He was responsible for many of the most important acquisitions.

The conservatory has one of the best music libraries in Italy, holding many original manuscripts by composers like Monteverdi and Rossini.

Pietre dure table (1849) by Zocchi

Opificio delle Pietre Dure ⑪

Via degli Alfani 78. **Map** 2 D4 (6 F1). *Tel* 055 265 11. **Open** 8:15am– 1:45pm Mon–Sat (to 7pm Thu). **Closed** public hols. **Adm charge**. 🔲

Situated in the former monastery of San Niccolò, the *opificio* (factory) is a national institute specializing in teaching the Florentine craft of producing inlaid pictures using marble and semi-precious stones. This tradition has flourished since the end of the 16th century, when it was funded through the patronage of the Medici Grand Dukes, who decorated their mausoleum with *pietre dure*.

There is a museum in the same building displaying 19th-century workbenches, tools, vases and portraits showing *pietre dure* work. Several table tops decorated with *pietre dure* are on display: one inlaid with a harp and garlands by Zocchi, made in 1849, another with flowers and birds, designed by Niccolò Betti in 1855. A stockpile of exquisite marbles and other semi-precious stones dates back to Medici times.

Spedale degli Innocenti ⑫

Piazza della Santissima Annunziata 12. **Map** 2 D4 (6 F1). *Tel* 055 249 17 08. **Open** 8:30am–2pm Thu–Tue (last adm: 30 mins before closing). **Closed** 1 Jan, Easter, 25 Dec. **Adm charge**. 🔲

This "hospital" is named after Herod's biblical Massacre of the Innocents following the birth of Jesus. It opened in 1444 as the first orphanage in Europe, and part of the building is still used for this purpose. UNICEF, the United Nations Children's Fund, also has offices here. Brunelleschi's arcaded loggia *(see pp48–9)* is decorated with glazed terracotta roundels, added by Andrea della Robbia around 1498, showing babies wrapped in swaddling bands. At the left-hand end of the portico is the *rota*, a rotating stone cylinder on which mothers could place their unwanted children anonymously and ring the orphanage bell. The stone was then turned around and the child was taken in.

Within the building there are two elegant cloisters built to Brunelleschi's designs. The larger Chiostro degli Uomini (Men's Cloister), built between 1422 and 1445, is decorated with *sgraffito* designs of cherubs and roosters scratched into the wet plaster. The smaller Women's Cloister (1438) leads to a gallery which has several paintings donated by children from the orphanage who went on to be successful in later life. Outstanding among these is the *Adoration of the Magi* (1488) painted by Domenico del Ghirlandaio, showing the massacre in the background.

Andrea della Robbia's roundels (c.1490) on the Spedale degli Innocenti

San Marco ⊙

The convent of San Marco was founded in the 13th century and enlarged in 1437 when Dominican monks from nearby Fiesole moved here at the invitation of Cosimo il Vecchio. He paid a considerable sum to have the convent

Dominican friar in grey habit

rebuilt by his favourite architect, Michelozzo, whose simple cloisters and cells are the setting for a remarkable series of devotional frescoes (c.1438–45) by Fra Angelico.

Cells 38 and 39 were reserved for Cosimo il Vecchio when he retreated to the convent to find spiritual sustenance and peace.

The Mocking of Christ
Fra Angelico's beautiful allegorical fresco (c.1440) shows Jesus blindfolded and being struck by a Roman guard.

Cells 12 to 15 contain relics of the religious fanatic Savonarola, made prior of San Marco in 1491 *(see pp52–3).*

An ancient cedar stands in Michelozzo's Sant'Antonino cloister.

Entrance to the church (Chiesa di San Marco)

The Deposition *(1435–40)*
This poignant scene of the dead Christ, and other works by Fra Angelico and his School, are displayed in the former Pilgrims' Hospice.

Entrance to Museo di San Marco

KEY TO FLOORPLAN

- ☐ Ground floor
- ☐ First floor
- ☐ Non-exhibition space

Sant'Anton cloister

The dormitory cells contain scenes from *The Life of Christ*, intended to inspire prayer and contemplation.

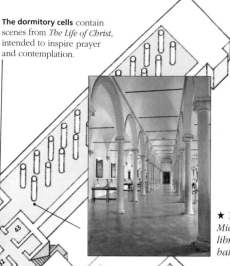

VISITORS' CHECKLIST

Piazza di San Marco. **Map** 2 D4.
🚌 *many routes*. **Church Tel** 055 28 76 28. **Open** 7am–noon, 4–8pm. 🕆 7:30am, 6:30pm Mon–Sat; 10:30am, 11:30am, 12:30pm, 6:30pm Sun & relig hols. 📷 👤 **Museum Tel** 055 238 86 08 (reservations: 055 29 48 83). **Open** 8:15am–1:50pm daily (to 6:50pm Sat, to 7pm Sun; last adm: 30 mins before closing). **Closed** 2nd & 4th Mon & 1st, 3rd & 5th Sun of month, 1 Jan, 1 May, 25 Dec. **Adm charge.** ⌀ 👤 🛍

★ **Library**
Michelozzo designed Europe's first public library, in a light and airy colonnaded hall, for Cosimo il Vecchio in 1441.

★ **The Annunciation** (*c.1440*)
Fra Angelico shows his mastery of perspective by placing Gabriel and the Virgin in an elaborate loggia, inspired by Michelozzo.

The Entombment
Fra Angelico's tender fresco (c.1442) in Cell 2 shows Mary Magdalene and St. John mourning Christ.

Staircase to first floor

★ **The Crucifixion** (*1441–42*)
Fra Angelico was moved to tears as he painted this image of the Crucifixion of Christ in the Chapter House.

STAR FEATURES

★ The Annunciation by Fra Angelico

★ The Crucifixion by Fra Angelico

★ Library by Michelozzo

Mannerist fountain by Pietro Tacca in Piazza della Santissima Annunziata

Piazza della Santissima Annunziata ⓭

Map 2 D4.

The delicate nine-bay arcade on the eastern side of this elegant square was designed by Brunelleschi in 1419 and forms the façade to the Spedale degli Innocenti (see p48). Brunelleschi's round arches gave rise to the Classical style widely copied by Renaissance architects. In the centre of the square is an equestrian statue of Duke Ferdinando I, started by Giambologna towards the end of his career. It was finished in 1608 by his assistant, Pietro Tacca, who also designed the two stylized Mannerist bronze fountains in the square.

A fair is held annually in the piazza on the feast of the Annunciation, 25 March, when homemade sweet biscuits called *brigidini* are sold from the stalls.

Santissima Annunziata ⓮

Piazza della Santissima Annunziata.
Map 2 E4. **Tel** 055 26 61 81.
Open 7:30am–12:30pm, 4–6:30pm daily. ⓟ

The Church of the Holy Annunciation was founded by the Servite order in 1250 and later rebuilt by Michelozzo between 1444 and 1481. There is a series of early 16th-century frescoes in the atrium by Mannerist artists Rosso Fiorentino, Andrea del Sarto and Jacopo Pontormo, but many of these frescoes have suffered from damp and are fading. The most celebrated are *The Journey of the Magi* (1511) and *The Birth of the Virgin* (1514) by del Sarto.

The interior is dark and heavily decorated, with a frescoed ceiling completed by Pietro Giambelli in 1669.

The church also boasts one of the most revered shrines in Florence, a painting of the Virgin Mary begun in 1252 by a monk. Devout Florentines believe it was finished by an angel, and many newly wed couples traditionally come here after their wedding ceremony to present a bouquet of flowers to the Virgin and pray for a long and fruitful marriage. Nine chapels radiate from the sanctuary. The central one was reconstructed by Giambologna to use as his tomb, and contains bronze reliefs and a crucifix sculpted by him.

Through the door in the north transept of the church is the Chiostro dei Morti (Cloister of the Dead), so called because it was originally used as a burial ground and is packed with memorial stones. The fresco above the entrance porch is by Andrea del Sarto. Painted in 1525, it shows the Holy Family resting on their flight to Egypt and is usually known as *La Madonna del Sacco*, since Joseph is depicted leaning on a sack.

The Cappella di San Luca off the cloister has been owned by the Accademia delle Arte del Disegno since 1565 and a special service dedicated to artists is held here every year on St Luke's day (which falls on 18 October). Benvenuto Cellini is among the artists buried in the vault below.

The Birth of the Virgin (1514) by Andrea del Sarto

The François Vase, covered in figures from Greek mythology

Museo Archeologico ⑮

Via della Colonna 38. **Map** 2 E4. *Tel* 055 23 57 50. *Open* 2–7pm Mon, 8:30am–7pm Tue, Thu, 8:30am–2pm Wed, Fri–Sun (phone to check). *Closed* 1 Jan, 1 May, 25 Dec. *Adm charge*. 📷 ♿

The Archaeological Museum is in a palazzo built by Giulio Parigi for the Princess Maria Maddalena de' Medici in 1620. It now exhibits outstanding collections of Etruscan, Greek, Roman and ancient Egyptian artifacts.

A section on the second floor is dedicated to Greek vases, with a room given over to the François Vase, found in an Etruscan tomb at Fonte Rotella near Chiusi *(see p228)*. Painted and signed in 570 BC, it is decorated with six rows of black and red figures depicting scenes from Greek mythology. The Etruscan collection was very badly damaged by the 1966 flood and only a fraction is now on display, although restoration work is being continued.

In addition to the splendid series of bronze Etruscan statues, on the first floor of the museum there are two famous bronzes. The *Chimera (see p42)*, sculpted in the 4th century BC, is a mythical lion with a goat's head imposed on its body and a serpent for a tail, shown here towering in terror. It was ploughed up

Bronze Etruscan warrior

in a field near Arezzo in 1553 and presented to Cosimo I de' Medici by Giorgio Vasari, the artist, author and critic. The *Arringatore* (Orator) was found c.1566 near Lake Trasimeno in central Italy and is inscribed with the name of an Etruscan aristocrat, Aulus Metullus. The sculpture dates from the 1st century BC, and the figure, splendidly dressed in a Roman toga, appears to be addressing his audience.

Part of the Egyptian collection was acquired during a joint French and Tuscan expedition in 1829. It is rich in wooden, cloth and bone artifacts, preserved in the dry atmosphere of the desert tombs in which they were found. They include a near-complete chariot of bone and wood found in a tomb near Thebes (dating to c.15th century BC), along with textiles, hats, ropes, furniture, purses and baskets.

Santa Maria Maddalena dei Pazzi ⑯

Borgo Pinti 58. **Map** 2 E5. *Tel* 055 247 84 20. **Church and chapter house** *Open* 9am–noon, 3–7pm daily. *Closed* for mass 5:30–6pm. 📷

This former convent has been restored following the floods of 1966. Originally run by the Cistercian order, it was taken over by Carmelites in 1628, and Augustinian monks have lived here since 1926. The chapterhouse, which is entered from the crypt, contains the famous *Crucifixion and Saints fresco* painted in 1493–6 by Perugino (his real name was Pietro Vannucci), who was one of the founders of the Umbrian School of artists. This beautiful and well-preserved fresco is regarded as a masterpiece, bearing all Perugino's trademarks, most notably the background, which is a detailed landscape of wooded hills and winding streams painted in soft blues

and greens. The main chapel, decorated with coloured marble by Ciro Ferri (1675), is one of the best examples of the High Baroque style in a Florentine church. In 1492 Giuliano da Sangallo designed the church's unusual and striking portico, with its square-topped, Ionic-style arcades.

Tempio Israelitico ⑰

Via Farini 4. **Map** 2 F5. *Tel* 055 24 52 52. **Synagogue and Museum** *Open* Oct–Mar: 10am–1pm, 2–4pm Sun–Thu, 10am–1pm Fri; Apr–Oct: 10am–1pm, 2–5pm Sun–Thu, 10am–1pm Fri. 📷 *Closed* Jewish hols.

Interior of the Tempio Israelitico

The green copper-covered dome of Florence's main synagogue stands out on the horizon as you look down on the city from the surrounding hills. As elsewhere in Europe, Jews in Florence were alternately welcomed and persecuted over the years. In the early 17th century they flocked to Livorno and then to Florence when it was freed from its strong political ties with Spain by Grand Duke Ferdinando I (1549–1609).

In the Inquisition, Grand Duke Cosimo III (1642–1723) passed laws forbidding Christians to work for Jewish families and businesses. In the 1860s the Jewish ghetto was cleared to make way for the Piazza della Repubblica *(see p112)*. The synagogue was built by Marco Treves in 1874–82 in Spanish-Moorish style. It has a museum of ritual objects dating to the 17th century.

CITY CENTRE WEST

A t one end of this part of Florence is the main railway station – a rare example of modern architecture in the city centre. At the other end, a magnet for visitors and Florentines alike, is the Ponte Vecchio, the city's oldest bridge. It is lined with jewellers' shops, here since 1593, and presents a scene little changed since.

Detail from Strozzi Chapel in Santa Maria Novella

Between these two focal points there is something to interest most people, from the frescoes of Santa Maria Novella and Santa Trinità to the awesome Palazzo Strozzi. Nearby is Piazza della Repubblica,

originally laid out as part of the grandiose plans to remodel Florence when it was briefly the nation's capital. Most locals may consider it an eyesore, but the cafés here have always been very popular. This is also the part of Florence in which to shop, from the leather goods, silks and woollens of the Mercato Nuovo to the elegant showrooms of the top couturiers in Via della Vigna Nuova and Via de' Tornabuoni. In the smaller streets off these, local artisans still continue Florence's proud tradition of craftsmanship, from stonecutting to restoration work.

SIGHTS AT A GLANCE

Museums and Galleries
Museo Marino Marini
  (San Pancrazio) ❶
Palazzo Davanzati ❿
Palazzo Rucellai ❷

Churches
Ognissanti ⓰
*Santa Maria Novella
  pp110–11* ⓱
Santa Trinità ❼
Santi Apostoli ❽

Bridges
Ponte Vecchio pp106–7 ❾

Markets
Mercato Nuovo ⓬

Historic Buildings
Palazzo Antinori ⓮
Palazzo di Parte Guelfa ⓫
Palazzo Strozzi ❺
Stazione di Santa
  Maria Novella ⓲

Historic Streets and Piazzas
Piazza della Repubblica ⓭
Piazza di Santa Trinità ❻
Via dei Fossi ⓯
Via de' Tornabuoni ❹
Via della Vigna Nuova ❸

KEY

▢	Street-by-Street map *See pp102–3*
ℹ	Tourist information
FS	Railway station

0 metres 400
0 yards 400

◁ **View from Ponte Santa Trinità towards Piazza di Santa Trinità**

Street-by-Street: Around Piazza della Repubblica

Underlying the street plan of modern Florence is the far older pattern of the ancient Roman city founded on the banks of the Arno. Nowhere is this more evident than in the rectilinear grid of narrow streets in the western half of the city centre. Here the streets lead north from the river Arno to the Piazza della Repubblica, once the site of the forum, the main square of the ancient Roman city. It later became the city's main food market *(see p54)* until the city authorities decided to tidy it up in the 1860s, building the triumphal arch that now stands in today's café-filled square.

Palazzo Strozzi
This monumental palazzo dominates the square **5**

Piazza di Santa Trinità
The square is marked by an ancient Roman column **6**

★ **Santa Trinità**
Ghirlandaio's frescoes, The Life of St Francis *(1483), depict scenes that took place in this area. Here, a child is restored to life, after falling from the Palazzo Spini-Ferroni* **7**

Palazzo Spini-Ferroni,
a medieval palazzo featured in Ghirlandaio's frescoes in Santa Trinità, now houses the fashion boutique of Salvatore Ferragamo *(see p108).*

The statues of the Four Seasons decorating the approaches to Ponte Santa Trinità were erected in 1608 to celebrate the wedding of Cosimo I.

KEY

– – – Suggested route

0 metres		200
0 yards		200

Santi Apostoli
A plaque claims Charlemagne as founder **8**

LOCATOR MAP
See Florence Street Finder
maps 5, 6

★ **Piazza della Repubblica**
*The Roman-style triumphal
arch celebrates Florence's
stint as Italy's capital
(1865–71)* ⓭

Mercato Nuovo
*Designed as a
covered general
market in 1547,
Mercato Nuovo is
full of expensive
souvenir stalls* ⓬

Palazzo Davanzati
*Frescoes with exotic birds
decorate the Sala dei
Papagalli, which was once
the dining room of this
14th-century palazzo* ⓾

★ **Ponte Vecchio**
*Giotto's pupil, Taddeo Gaddi, designed this
medieval bridge in 1345. It is the oldest –
and most popular – of Florence's bridges
and retains many of its original features* ⑨

**Palazzo di
Parte Guelfa**
*This was the head-
quarters of the Guelphs,
the dominant political
party of medieval
Florence* ⓫

STAR SIGHTS

★ Piazza d Repubblica
★ Ponte Vecchio
★ Santa Trinità

Museo Marino Marini (San Pancrazio) ❶

Piazza San Pancrazio. **Map** 1 B5 (5 B2). *Tel 055 21 94 32. Open 10am–5pm Mon, Wed–Sat. Closed Sat in June, July, Sept, 1 May, Aug, 25 Dec. Adm charge.*

The former church of San Pancrazio has been turned into a museum devoted to the work of Italy's best known abstract artist, Marino Marini (1901–80). Marini was born in Pistoia, where more of his work can be seen in the Palazzo del Comune and in the newly opened Centro Marino Marini (*see p186*). Marini studied art in Florence before moving on to teaching in Monza and at the prestigious Brera Academy in Milan. He is noted for rugged and elemental bronzes, many of them on the theme of horse and rider, which express a range of moods and experiences, from sombre weariness to joyous eroticism.

San Pancrazio itself is one of the oldest churches in Florence. It was founded in

Bronze statue, *Cavaliere* (1949), by Marini in the Museo Marino Marini

the 9th century, though its most attractive features are from the Renaissance period, including a graceful Classical façade and porch (1461–7) by Leon Battista Alberti.

San Pancrazio was the parish church of the wealthy merchant Giovanni Rucellai. Inside, in the Cappella di San Sepolcro, built by Alberti in 1467, is Rucellai's tomb, which is modelled on the Holy Sepulchre in Jerusalem (the tomb of Christ).

Palazzo Rucellai ❷

Via della Vigna Nuova 16. **Map** 1 C5 (5 B2). **Fratelli Alinari Museum of the History of Photography** *open 9am–6pm Mon–Sat.*

Built in 1446–57, this is one of the most ornate Renaissance palaces in the city. It was commissioned by Giovanni Rucellai, whose wealth derived from the family business, the import of a rare and costly red dye made from a lichen found only on Majorca. The dye was called *oricello*, from which the name Rucellai is derived.

Giovanni commissioned several buildings from the architect Leon Battista Alberti, who went on to write an influential architectural treatise called *De Re Aedificatoria* (Concerning Architecture) in 1452. Alberti designed this palace almost as a textbook illustration of the major Classical orders. In ascending order of complexity, the pilaster strips on the ground floor are Doric, those above are Ionic and those on the top floor are Corinthian.

Two symbols are carved into the entablature: the Rucellai's billowing sails of Fortune and the ring symbol of the Medici family. The ring is a reminder that Bernardo Rucellai formed an alliance with the Medici in the 1460s by marrying Lorenzo de' Medici's sister, Lucrezia. The Loggia del Rucellai, opposite the palace, was built to commemorate the marriage.

The palazzo used to house the Museo Alinari, but the collection has moved to Largo Fratelli Alinari 15. The Alinari brothers began taking pictures of Florence in the 1840s, soon after the invention of photography. The firm they set up in 1852 specialized in supplying top-quality prints, postcards and art books to foreigners who flocked to the city during the 1800s. Today, this archive of their photographs provides a fascinating insight into the social history of Florence over the last 150 years. The museum is due to open its new premises, in the former Leopoldine complex in Piazza Santa Maria Novella, by 2006.

19th-century view of Lungarno degli Acciaiuoli, from Palazzo Rucellai

Via della Vigna Nuova ❸

Map 3 B1 (5 B3).

Reflecting its associations with wealthy Renaissance Florentines, such as the Rucellai, Via della Vigna Nuova has a number of fashionable clothes shops. All the major Italian designers can be found here, as well as smaller shops selling quality silks, cashmeres and lingerie.

Among the top names doing business along Via della Vigna Nuova are Dolce & Gabbana (No. 25r), Valentino (No. 47r) and Versus-Versace (No. 38r).

Armani shop, Via della Vigna Nuova

Via de' Tornabuoni ❹

Map 1 C5 (5 C2). **Ferragamo Museum Tel** 055 336 04 56. **Open** 9am–1pm, 2–6pm Mon–Fri. **Closed** Aug. ☑ for groups of 10 or more.

Via de' Tornabuoni is the most elegant shopping street in Florence, lined with boutiques such as Salvatore Ferragamo (No. 14r), Enrico Coveri (No. 81r), Gucci (No. 73r), Prada for men (No. 67r), Prada for women (No. 53r), Armani (No. 48/50r), Bulgari (No. 61r) and Cartier (No. 40r). The Ferragamo Museum (No. 2) focuses on the firm's efforts in shoe-making. The medieval tower at the end of the street, now a hotel, used to be a private club for local aristocrats.

THE BIGGEST PALAZZO IN FLORENCE

The Strozzi family were exiled from Florence in 1434 for their opposition to the Medici, but in 1466 the banker Filippo Strozzi, having built up a fortune in Naples, returned to the city, determined to outdo his great rivals. He became a man obsessed. For years he bought up and demolished other palaces around his home. At last, he acquired enough land to achieve his ambition: to build the biggest palace ever seen in Florence. Having spent so much money to get this far, nothing was left to chance. Astrologers were brought in to choose the most favourable day on which to lay the foundation stone, and the walls of the monumental palace began to rise in 1489. Two years later Filippo Strozzi was dead, and, though his heirs struggled on with the building, the cost of pursuing Filippo's grandiose vision finally left them penniless and bankrupt.

Filippo Strozzi (1428–91)

Palazzo Strozzi ❺

Piazza degli Strozzi. **Map** 3 C1 (5 C3). **Piccolo Museo di Palazzo Strozzi closed** for restoration.

The Strozzi Palace is awesome because of its sheer size: 15 buildings were demolished to make way for it, and although it is only three storeys high, each floor is as tall as a normal palazzo. The palace was commissioned by the wealthy banker Filippo Strozzi, but he died in 1491, only two years after the foundation stone was laid.

The building was not completed until 1536, and three major architects had a hand in its design – Giuliano da Sangallo, Benedetto da Maiano and Simone del Pollaiuolo (also known as Cronaca). The exterior, built of huge rusticated masonry blocks, remains unspoiled. Look out for the original Renaissance torch-holders, lamps and rings for tethering horses, which adorn the corners and façades.

To the left of the courtyard entrance, the Piccolo Museo di Palazzo Strozzi explains the building's history through models and drawings. The elegance of the courtyard itself has been destroyed by a huge iron fire escape, constructed when the building was converted to a major exhibition venue. In recent years, it has hosted world-class exhibitions of art and antiquities.

The palace also houses various learned institutes and an excellent library, the Gabinetto Vieusseux, named after the 19th-century Swiss scholar Gian Pietro Vieusseux. He founded a scientific and literary association in 1818, which was attended by, among others, the French author Stendhal.

Exterior of Palazzo Strozzi, with masonry block rustication

Ponte Vecchio ❾

The Ponte Vecchio, or Old Bridge – indeed, the oldest bridge in Florence – was built in 1345. It was the only bridge in the city to escape being blown up during World War II. There have always been workshops on the bridge, but the butchers, tanners and blacksmiths who were here originally (and who used the river as a convenient rubbish tip) were evicted by Duke Ferdinando I in 1593 because of the noise and stench they created. The workshops were rebuilt and let to the more decorous goldsmiths, and the shops lining and over-hanging the bridge continue to specialize in new and antique jewellery to this day.

Private Corridor
The aerial corridor built by Vasari along the eastern side of the bridge is hung with the self-portraits of many great artists, including Rembrandt, Rubens and Hogarth.

Medieval Workshops
Some of the oldest work-shops have rear extensions overhanging the river, supported by timber brackets called sporti.

The three-arched medieval bridge rests on two stout piers with boat-shaped cutwaters.

VASARI'S CORRIDOR

The Corridoio Vasariano was built in 1565 by Giorgio Vasari and links the Palazzo Vecchio to the Palazzo Pitti, via the Uffizi. This private elevated walkway, also known as *Percorso del Principe* ("Prince's Route"), allowed members of the Medici family to move between their residences without having to step into the street below and mix with the crowds. The Corridor is occasionally open by guided tour only; tickets must be booked in advance.

Palazzo Vecchio

The Uffizi

Ponte Vecchio

Arno

Palazzo Pitti

Bust of Cellini
A bust of Benvenuto Cellini (1500 –71), the most famous of all Florentine goldsmiths, was placed in the middle of the bridge in 1900.

★ **Bridge at Sunset**
The Ponte Vecchio is especially attractive when viewed in the setting sun from Ponte Santa Trinità, or from one of the river embankments.

VISITORS' CHECKLIST

Map 3 C1 (5 C4). 🚌 *B, D.* **Vasari Corridor** *Tel 055 29 48 83.*

★ **Jewellers' Shops**
The shops sell everything from affordable modern earrings to precious antique rings.

Mannelli Tower
This medieval tower was built to defend the bridge. The Mannelli family stubbornly refused to demolish it to make way for the Vasari Corridor.

The Vasari Corridor, supported on brackets, circumvents the Mannelli tower.

Circular windows called *oculi* (eyes) light the corridor.

Viewpoint
There are few better places for enjoying the river views; buskers, portrait painters and street traders congregate on the bridge, adding to the colour and bustle.

STAR FEATURES

★ Jewellers' Shops

★ Bridge at Sunset

Piazza di Santa Trinità

Piazza di Santa Trinità ❻

Map 3 C1 (5 C3).

Noble Palazzi line this busy square. To the south is the Palazzo Spini-Ferroni, originally built in 1290 but much rebuilt in the 19th century; today the ground floor houses the famous boutique of Salvatore Ferragamo *(see p284)*, specializing in shoes and leather goods. To the north, on the corner with Via delle Terme, is the Palazzo Bartolini-Salimbeni. Built during 1520–29, it is one of the city's best examples of High Renaissance architecture. In between the two palazzi is a column of oriental granite originally from the Baths of Caracalla in Rome and given to Cosimo I by Pope Pius IV in 1560. The figure of Justice on top was made in 1581.

Just south of the square is the Ponte Santa Trinità, considered the most beautiful bridge in Florence. It affords fine views of the surrounding hills and especially of the Ponte Vecchio *(see pp106–7)*. It was originally built in wood in 1252, and then rebuilt by Ammannati in 1567 as a monument to Cosimo I's defeat of Siena. Michelangelo is credited with the elegant design, based on an intriguing elliptical curve echoing those on the famous Medici tombs *(see p91)*. The statues of the Four Seasons at each end were added in 1608 for Cosimo II's marriage to Maria of Austria. The bridge was restored after it was blown up by the Germans in 1944, and the statues were dredged up from the river bed.

Look west from here to the golden-yellow Palazzo Corsini (1648–56), with statues on the roof balustrade. It is one of the best examples of Baroque architecture in Florence.

Santa Trinità ❼

Piazza di Santa Trinità. **Map** 3 C1 (5 C3). **Tel** 055 21 69 12. **Open** 8am–noon, 4–6pm Mon–Sat, 4–6pm Sun. 📷 ♿

The nave of Santa Trinità

The original church, built in the second half of the 11th century by the Vallombrosan monastic order, was very plain – a reflection of the austerity of the order, which was founded in Florence in 1092 to restore the simplicity of monastic rule. Gradually, the building became more ornate, with a Baroque façade added in 1593. Inside, the east wall shows traces of its Romanesque predecessor.

Ghirlandaio's frescoes in the Sassetti Chapel (right of the High Altar) show what the church looked like in 1483–6. In one scene St Francis of Assisi performs a miracle in the Piazza di Santa Trinità, with the church and the Palazzo Spini-Ferroni in the background. The donors of the chapel, Francesco Sassetti and his wife Nera Corsi, are portrayed on either side of the altar. In another scene, St Francis is receiving the Rule of the Franciscan order from Pope

Ponte Santa Trinità

Honorius III in the Piazza della Signoria. Sassetti, who was general manager of the Medici bank, is shown with his son, Teodoro, and with Lorenzo de' Medici to his right, along with Antonio Pucci. Lorenzo's sons are climbing up steps with their tutors, led by the Humanist scholar Agnolo Poliziano, or Politian. The altar painting, *The Adoration of the Shepherds* (1485), is also by Ghirlandaio; he is the first, dark-haired shepherd. The black sarcophagi of Sassetti and his wife are by Giuliano da Sangallo.

Santi Apostoli ⑧

Piazza del Limbo. **Map** 3 C1 (5 C4). *Tel 055 29 06 42.* **Open** *10am–noon, 4–7pm daily.* 🚫

The little church of the Holy Apostles is, along with the Baptistry, among the oldest surviving churches in Florence. Florentines like to think that the church was founded in 800 AD by the first Holy Roman Emperor, Charlemagne, but it more likely dates to 1059–1100. The church has a simple Romanesque façade and the basilican plan typical of early Christian churches, but with 16th-century side aisles.

Santi Apostoli fronts Piazza del Limbo, so called because there was a cemetery here for infants who died before they were baptized. Hence, according to medieval theology, their souls dwelt in limbo – halfway between heaven and hell.

Della Robbia glazed terracotta tabernacle in Santi Apostoli

Ponte Vecchio ⑨

See pp106–7

Fresco in a bedroom in the Palazzo Davanzati

Palazzo Davanzati ⑩

Via Porta Rossa 13. **Map** 3 C1 (5 C3). *Tel 055 238 86 10.* **Open** *8:30am–1:50pm daily.* **Closed** *1 Jan, 1 May, 25 Dec, 1st, 3rd & 5th Mon and 2nd & 4th Sun of the month.*

Also known as the Museo dell'Antica Casa Fiorentina, the Palazzo Davanzati is preserved as a typical house of wealthy Florentines of the 14th century. Long closed for structural repairs, the museum is expected to re-open by 2006. In the meantime, a small exhibition, including photographs and a few items from the museum, has been organized in the entrance of the building. The entrance courtyard was designed to trap unwanted visitors; pelting holes in the vaulted ceiling were used for dropping missiles. In the more peaceful inner courtyard, a staircase links all the floors. In one corner is a well and a pulley system so buckets of water could be raised to each floor – this ingenious mechanism was quite a luxury since most households had to fetch all their water from a public fountain.

The main living room on the first floor looks plain,

but hooks beneath the ceiling show that the walls would have been hung with tapestries. Many rooms have bathrooms attached, and are decorated with frescoes of scenes from a French romance.

Palazzo di Parte Guelfa ⑪

Piazza di Parte Guelfa. **Map** 3 C1 (6 D3). **Closed** *to the public.*

This characterful building served as the headquarters of the Guelph party and the residence of its captains from around 1266, after the Guelphs began to emerge as the stronger of the two medieval factions struggling for control over Florence. In the complex politics of the period, the Guelphs supported the Pope and the Ghibellines took the side of the Holy Roman Emperor in the dispute over who should rule northern Italy *(see p46)*.

The lower part of the building dates to the 13th century, but the upper part was added by Brunelleschi in 1431. There are *stemmae* (coats-of-arms) under the crenellations. The elegant open staircase, added in 1589, is by Vasari.

Emblem of the Guelphs

Santa Maria Novella ⑰

The Gothic church of Santa Maria Novella
contains some of the most important works
of art in Florence. The church was built by
the Dominicans from 1279 to 1357. Beside
the church is a cemetery walled in with
avelli (grave niches), which continue along
the façade and the wall beyond. The
cloisters form a museum. Here, the frescoes
in the Spanish Chapel show the Dominicans
as whippets – *domini canes* or hounds of
God – rounding up the "stray sheep".

Green Cloister
*The name comes from the green
tinge to Uccello's Noah and the
Flood frescoes, unfortu-
nately damaged by
the 1966 floods.*

**Monastic
buildings**

★ **Spanish Chapel**
*The chapel used by the Spanish
courtiers of Eleonora of Toledo, the
wife of Cosimo I (see p51), has
dramatic frescoes on the theme
of salvation and damnation.*

★ **The Trinity**
*Masaccio's pioneering
work is a masterpiece
of perspective and
portraiture (see p26).*

Entrance to museum

Entrance

The billowing sail emblem of
the Rucellai *(see p104)* appears
on the façade because they
paid for its completion in 1470.

Alberti added the volutes
in 1458–70 to hide the roofs
over the side chapels.

Strozzi Chapel
The 14th-century frescoes by Nardo di Cione and his brother, Andrea Orcagna, were inspired by Dante's epic poem, The Divine Comedy. *Dante himself is portrayed in the* Paradise *fresco on the left, along with members of the Strozzi family.*

VISITORS' CHECKLIST

Piazza di Santa Maria Novella.
Map 1 B5 (5 B1).
A, 6, 11, 36, 37.
Church Tel 055 21 59 18.
Open 9:30am–5pm Mon–Thu;
1–5pm Fri–Sun. 7:30am,
8:30am, 6pm Mon–Sat;
8:30am, 10:30am, noon,
6pm Sun & religious hols.
Adm charge.
Museum Tel 055 28 21 87.
Open 9am–5pm Mon–Thur,
Sat; 9am–2pm Sun.
Adm charge.

The arcade arches are emphasized by grey and white banding.

★ Tornabuoni Chapel
Ghirlandaio's famous fresco cycle, The Life of John the Baptist *(1485), portrays Florentine aristocrats and contemporary costumes and furnishings. Opposite is his other masterpiece,* The Life of the Virgin.

★ Filippo Strozzi Chapel
Filippino Lippi's dramatic frescoes show St John raising Drusiana from the dead and St Philip slaying a dragon. Boccaccio set the beginning of The Decameron *in this chapel.*

The walls of the old cemetery are decorated with the emblems and badges of wealthy Florentines.

Interior
The nave piers are spaced closer at the east end to create the illusion of an exceptionally long church.

STAR FEATURES

★ The Trinity by Masaccio

★ Filippo Strozzi Chapel

★ Tornabuoni Chapel

★ Spanish Chapel

Mercato Nuovo ⓬

Map 3 C1 (6 D3). **Open** Apr–Oct:
9am–7pm daily; Nov–Mar:
9am–7pm Tue–Sat.

The Mercato Nuovo (New
Market) is sometimes called
the "Straw Market" because
goods woven out of straw,
such as hats and baskets,
were sold here from the end
of the 19th century until the
1960s. In fact, it was
originally built in 1547–51 as
a central market for silk and
other luxury goods. Today's
stallholders sell leather goods
and souvenirs, and on
summer evenings buskers
gather to entertain visitors.

To the south of the market
is a little fountain called Il
Porcellino. This is a 17th-
century copy in bronze of the
Roman marble statue of a
wild boar that can be seen in
the Uffizi. Its snout gleams
like gold, thanks to the
superstition that any visitor
who rubs it will return to
Florence some day. Coins
dropped in the water basin
below are collected and
distributed to
the city's
charities.

Bronze boar in Mercato Nuovo

Piazza della Repubblica ⓭

Map 1 C5 (6 D3).

Until 1890, when the present
square was laid out, this had
been the site of the Mercato
Vecchio (Old Market) and
before that of the ancient
Roman forum. A single
column from the old market
still stands on the square,
topped by an 18th-century
statue of Abundance.
Dominating the western side
of the square is a triumphal
arch built in 1895 to celebrate

**One of the many pavement cafés in
Piazza della Repubblica**

the fact that Florence was
then the capital of Italy. The
demolition of the Old Market
was intended as the first step
in a wholesale remodelling of
Florence, but leading members of the English community
led an international campaign
opposing this grand scheme,
which would have led to the
destruction of almost every
historic building in the city
centre. Fortunately, the
campaign was successful and
the demolition halted.

The square, popular with
both tourists and locals, is
lined with pavement cafés,
such as the very smart Gilli
(No. 39r) or the Giubbe Rosse
(No. 13–14r), so called
because of the red jackets of
the waiters. In the early part
of this century, the Giubbe
Rosse was the haunt of writers
and artists, including those of
Italy's avant-garde Futurist
movement. Rinascente, one of
Florence's department stores
(see p287), is on the eastern
side of the square.

Palazzo Antinori ⓮

Piazza Antinori 3. **Map** 1 C5 (5 C2).
Closed to the public. **Cantinetta
Antinori Tel** 055 29 22 34.
Open 12:30–2:30pm, 7–10:30pm
Mon–Fri. 🍴 🍷

The Palazzo Antinori,
originally the Palazzo Boni e
Martelli, was built in 1461–6
and with its elegant courtyard
is considered one of the
finest small Renaissance
palazzi of Florence. It was

acquired by the Antinori
family in 1506 and has
remained with them since.

The family owns large and
productive estates all over
Tuscany and in the neigh-
bouring region of Umbria,
producing a range of well-
regarded wines, olive oils and
liqueurs. You can sample
these in the frescoed wine bar
to the right of the courtyard,
the Cantinetta Antinori.

The wine bar also
specializes in typical Tuscan
cuisine, with dishes such
as *crostini alla toscana*,
together with traditional
cheeses and a range of
other produce from the
Antinori estates.

Via dei Fossi ⓯

Map 1 B5 (5 B3).

**Shop in Via dei Fossi selling
reproduction statuary**

Via dei Fossi and the nearby
streets contain some of
the most absorbing shops
in Florence, many of them
specializing in antiques and
works of art and statuary, and
in classic Florentine products.
Bottega Artigiana del Libro
(Lungarno Corsini 40r) stocks
handmade marbled papers,
albums, notebooks and
carnival masks. Fallani Best
(Borgo Ognissanti 15r) has
Art Nouveau and Art Deco
furnishings and sculpture,
and Antonio Frilli (Via dei
Fossi 26r) specializes in marble
sculpture – original Art
Nouveau works and copies of
famous Renaissance pieces.
Neri (Via dei Fossi 57r) also

sells top-quality antiques and G Lisio (Via dei Fossi 41r), makes handwoven tapestries and rich Renaissance-style fabrics. Attached to the convent of the same name, the frescoed Farmacia di Santa Maria Novella (Via della Scala 16r) dates to the 16th century and sells toiletries and liqueurs made by Dominican monks.

Ognissanti ⓰

Borgo Ognissanti 42. **Map** 1 B5 (5 A2). *Tel* 055 239 87 00. *Open* 8:30am–12:30pm, 3:30–5:30pm Mon–Fri; 9:30–10:30am, 3:30–5pm Sat; 9:30–10:30am, 3:30–6pm Sun. *Closed* first and last Mon of month. ♿ 🚻 **Cenacolo del Ghirlandaio** *Open* 9am–noon Mon, Tue & Sat (348 645 03 90).

The church of All Saints, or Ognissanti, was the parish church of the merchant family of the Vespucci, one of whose members, the 15th-century navigator Amerigo, gave his name to the New World. Amerigo is depicted in Ghirlandaio's fresco of the *Madonna della Misericordia* (1472) in the second chapel on the right.

Amerigo Vespucci was the first to realize that the land discovered by Columbus was a new continent, not the eastern shore of the Indies. He made two voyages following

The cloister of Ognissanti with 17th-century frescoes

Columbus's route and, because his letters enabled cartographers to draw the first maps *(see p75)* of the new land, it was given his name.

Ognissanti is also the burial place of Sandro Botticelli. His fresco of *St Augustine* (1480) can be seen on the south wall. It is complemented by Ghirlandaio's *St Jerome* (1480) on the opposite wall.

Alongside the church is a cloister and refectory, containing Ghirlandaio's fresco *The Last Supper* (1480), with its background of birds and trees.

Santa Maria Novella ⓱

See pp110–11.

Stazione di Santa Maria Novella ⓲

Map 1 B4 (5 B1). *Closed* 1:30–4:15am daily. **Train information** *open* 7am–9pm daily. **Ticket office** *open* 5:45am–11pm daily. **Bag deposit** *open* 6am–midnight daily. **Assistance** *open* 7am–9pm daily. *Tel* 055 235 61 20. **Disabled passengers assistance** *open* 7am–9pm daily. *Tel* 055 235 22 75. ℹ️ *Open* 8:30am–5:30pm Mon–Sat. **Chemist** *open* 24 hrs. 🍴

A fine example of modern architecture in Italy, the central railway station was designed in 1935 by a group of Tuscan "Functionalist" artists, including Piero Berardi and Giovanni Michelucci. They believed that a building's form should reflect its purpose.

Ghirlandaio's *Madonna della Misericordia* (1472) in Ognissanti, with the boy Amerigo Vespucci

OLTRARNO

Oltrarno means "across the Arno", and living on the south bank of the river was once considered inferior. Here lived people who did not have sufficient wealth to build a palazzo within the city centre. That stigma did not change until the household of the Medici Grand Dukes moved to Oltrarno in 1550.

MEDICI POWER BASE

The Palazzo Pitti became the base from which Tuscany was ruled for the next 300 years. Eleonora di Toledo, the Spanish wife of Cosimo I, purchased the Palazzo Pitti in 1549. Suffering from a wasting disease, perhaps malaria or tuberculosis, Eleonora persuaded Cosimo that her health might well improve if they lived in the relatively rural setting of Oltrarno. Over the years the Palazzo Pitti

Statue, Museo Bardini

increased almost threefold in size in comparison with the original plans, and the Boboli Gardens were laid out on the land around it. A few Florentine aristocrats followed the Medici lead and moved across the river to make their homes here. In the late 16th and 17th centuries, many palazzi were built in the area surrounding Via Maggio and Piazza di Santo Spirito. Today, this is primarily a quiet area full of artisan workshops and antique shops, contrasting with the elegant palazzi and the unfinished austere façade of Santo Spirito. The local merchants' association organizes guided tours, events and fairs to expose visitors to the artisan treasures on the south bank. It is a fascinating area to wander around and discover the true character of Florence.

SIGHTS AT A GLANCE

Churches
Brancacci Chapel pp126–7 **⑩**
Santa Felicità **⑤**
San Frediano in Cestello **⑪**
Santo Spirito **①**

Museums and Galleries
Cenacolo di Santo Spirito **②**
Museo Bardini **⑧**
Museo "La Specola" **⑨**
Palazzo Pitti pp120–21 **⑥**

Gardens
Boboli Gardens pp124–5 **⑦**

Streets and Piazzas
Piazza di Santo Spirito **③**
Via Maggio **④**

KEY

Street-by-Street map
See pp116–17

| 0 metres | 500 |
| 0 yards | 500 |

◁ **Rooftops of the Oltrarno and the spire and dome of Santo Spirito**

Street-by-Street: Oltrarno

Medici coat of arms

For the most part, the Oltrarno area consists of relatively small houses and shops selling antiques, bric-à-brac and foodstuffs. The Via Maggio breaks this pattern, with its numerous imposing 16th-century palazzi close to the Medici's Palazzo Pitti. As it is one of the main routes into the city, the road is busy and there is constant traffic noise. Step into the side streets, however, and you escape the noise and bustle to discover traditional Florence; restaurants are authentic and reasonably priced, and the area is full of workshops restoring antique furniture.

Cenacolo di Santo Spirito
The old refectory is used to display medieval and Renaissance sculpture ❷

Santo Spirito
Simplicity is the keynote of Brunelleschi's last church. It was completed after his death in 1446 ❶

Palazzo Guadagni (1500) was the first in the city to be built with a rooftop loggia, setting a trend among the aristocracy.

Palazzo di Bianca Cappello
(1579) is covered in ornate *sgraffito* work and was the home of the mistress of Grand Duke Francesco I *(see pp50–51).*

STAR SIGHTS

★ Palazzo Pitti

★ Boboli Gardens

KEY

– – – Suggested route

0 metres   100

0 yards   100

Casa Guidi was the home of the poets Robert Browning and Elizabeth Barrett Browning from 1846–61, after their secret wedding.

The fountain and gargoyle in Piazza de' Frescobaldi were designed by Buontalenti in the 16th century.

Ponte Santa Trinità

PIAZZA DE' FRESCOBALDI

LOCATOR MAP
See Florence Street Finder map 5

CITY CENTRE NORTH
CITY CENTRE WEST
CITY CENTRE EAST
Arno
OLTRARNO

Ponte Vecchio

BORGO SAN JACOPO

VIA TOSCANELLA
VIA DELLO SPRONE
V.D.RAMAGLIANTI
VIA DE VELLUTINI
VIA DE VELLUTI
VIA TOSCANELLA
VIA DE' GUICCIARDINI
ZA DE' PITTI

Palazzo Guicciardini

★ **Palazzo Pitti**
This massive 16th-century palazzo contains several important museums ❻

Masks and murals are made by hand at Frieze of Papier Mâché, one of the unusual shops in Piazza de' Pitti.

★ **Boboli Gardens**
Florence's largest public park was built as the private garden to the Palazzo Pitti. It contains Classical sculptures such as Stoldo Lorenzi's Neptune (1588) spearing fish ❼

Santo Spirito ❶

Piazza di Santo Spirito. **Map** 3 B2
(5 A4). ▦ D. **Tel** 055 21 00 30.
Open 10am–noon, 4–5:30pm
Mon–Fri (only am on Wed),
4–5:30pm Sat & Sun. ⚲

The Augustinian foundation of
this church dates from 1250.
The present building has an
unfinished 18th-century façade,
which dominates the northern
end of Piazza di Santo Spirito.
Brunelleschi designed the
church in 1435, but it was not
completed until the late 1400s,
well after his death.

Inside, the harmony of the
proportions has been somewhat spoiled by the elaborate
Baroque baldacchino and the
High Altar, which was finished
in 1607 by Giovanni Caccini.
The church has 38 side altars,
decorated with 15th- and 16th-
century Renaissance paintings
and sculpture, among them
works by Cosimo Rosselli,
Domenico Ghirlandaio and
Filippino Lippi. The latter
painted a *Madonna and Child*
(1466) for the Nerli Chapel in
the south transept.

In the north aisle, a door
beneath the organ leads to
a vestibule with an ornate
coffered ceiling. It was
designed by Simone del
Pollaiuolo, more commonly
known as Cronaca, in 1491.
The sacristy adjoining the
vestibule was designed by
Giuliano da Sangallo in 1489.

Cenacolo di Santo Spirito ❷

Piazza di Santo Spirito 29. **Map** 3 B1
(5 B4). **Tel** 055 28 70 43. **Open** Apr-
Nov: 9am–2pm Tue–Sun; Dec–Mar:
10:30am–1:30pm Tue–Sun. **Closed** 1
Jan, Easter Sun, 1 May, 15 Aug, 25
Dec. **Adm charge**. ⚲ 📷

All that survives of the
monastery that stood next to
Santo Spirito is the refectory
(*cenacolo*), now a small
museum. Inside is a fresco,
The Crucifixion (1360–65),
attributed to the followers of
Andrea Orcagna and his
brother Nardo di Cione. In a
city that has a wealth of
Renaissance art, this is a rare
and beautiful example of
High Gothic religious work.

The Fondazione Salvatore
Romano, a collection of
11th-century Romanesque
sculpture, is displayed in
the refectory.

The façade of Palazzo Guadagni

Piazza di Santo Spirito ❸

Map 3 B2 (5 A4). ▦ D. ⛵ 2nd
(Antiques) & 3rd (Organic) Sun of
month.

This part of Florence is best
appreciated by wandering
around the square and its
market, looking at the many
furniture restorers' workshops
and medieval palazzi. The
biggest house in the square is
the Palazzo Guadagni at No.
10, on the corner with Via
Mazzetta. It was built around
1505, probably to the designs
of Cronaca. The windows have
distinctive stone surrounds
with tear-drop shaped key-
stones. The top floor forms an
open loggia, the first of its kind
to be built in the city. The
loggia set a fashion among
16th-century Florentine aristocrats, who incorporated the
design into their own palazzi.

Via Maggio ❹

Map 3 B2 (5 B5).

Opened in the mid-13th
century, this road became a
fashionable residential area
after the Medici Grand Dukes
moved to the Palazzo Pitti in
1550 (see pp120–21). It is lined
with 15th- and 16th-century
palazzi, such as the Palazzo
Ricasoli at No. 7, and antique
shops. Via Maggio runs into
Piazza di San Felice, where a
plaque marks the Casa Guidi.
The English poets Elizabeth
and Robert Browning rented
an apartment here after
eloping in 1847. Inspired by
Tuscan art and landscape, this
is where they wrote much of
their best poetry.

Colonnaded aisle in Santo Spirito

The Virgin from *The Annunciation* (1528) by Pontormo

Santa Felicità ❺

Piazza di Santa Felicità. **Map** 3 C2 (5 C5). **Tel** 055 21 30 18. **Open** 9am–noon, 3–6pm Mon–Sat, 1:30–6pm Sun.

A church has stood on this site since the 4th century AD, but the current building dates from the 11th century. It was extensively remodelled by Ferdinando Ruggieri in 1736–9, but some original Gothic features and the porch added by Vasari in 1564 were retained.

The Capponi family chapel to the right of the entrance houses two masterpieces by Mannerist artist Jacopo da Pontormo: *The Annunciation* and *The Deposition*. Painted in 1525–8, the frescoes make use of vivid colours such as light green, salmon pink, apricot and gold. The roundels around the base of the ceiling vault depict the Four Evangelists, also painted by Pontormo, with help from his pupil Agnolo Bronzino.

Palazzo Pitti ❻

See pp120–23.

Boboli Gardens ❼

See pp124–5.

Museo Bardini ❽

Piazza de' Mozzi 1. **Map** 4 D2 (6 E5). **Tel** 055 234 24 27. **Closed** for restoration until further notice. Call for more information. **Adm charge**.

Stefano Bardini was a 19th-century antiquarian and avid collector of architectural materials – mostly salvaged from the churches and palazzi demolished when the Piazza della Repubblica was built in the 1860s (see p112). In 1883 he built his palazzo in Piazza de' Mozzi almost entirely from recycled medieval and Renaissance masonry, including carved doorways, chimney pieces and staircases as well as painted and coffered ceilings. The rooms are full of sculpture, statues, paintings, armour, musical instruments, ceramics and antique furnishings. In 1922 this collection of antiquities was bequeathed to the people of Florence.

Museo Bardini, Piazza de' Mozzi

Museo "La Specola" ❾

Via Romana 17. **Map** 3 D2 (5 B5). **Tel** 055 22 88 251. **Open** 9am–1pm Mon, Tue, Thur–Sat. **Closed** public hols. in English, on request. **Adm charge**.

This unusual museum is in the Palazzo Rottigiani, built in 1775 and now used by the natural science faculty of Florence University. The name "la Specola" refers to the observatory built on the roof of the building by Grand Duke Pietro Leopoldo in the late 18th century. It now contains the museum, which has a zoological section exhibiting vast numbers of preserved animals, insects and fish, and an anatomical section with some extremely realistic 18th-century wax models showing various grotesque aspects of human physiology and disease.

Brancacci Chapel ❿

See pp126–7.

San Frediano in Cestello ⓫

Piazza di Cestello. **Map** 3 B1 (5 A3). D, 6. **Tel** 055 21 58 16. **Open** 9–11:30am, 4:30–6pm Mon–Sat, 5–6:30pm Sun.

The San Frediano area, with its small, low houses, has long been associated with the wool and leather industries. The parish church of San Frediano in Cestello stands beside the Arno looking across the river. It has a bare stone exterior with a large dome that is a local landmark. It was rebuilt on the site of an older church in 1680–89 by Antonio Maria Ferri: the fresco and stuccowork inside are typical of the late 17th and early 18th centuries. Nearby is a well-preserved stretch of the 14th-century city walls. The Porta San Frediano, built in 1324, has a tower overlooking the road to Pisa. Its wooden doors have retained their original 14th-century locks and detailed ironwork.

The dome and plain façade of San Frediano in Cestello

Palazzo Pitti ❻

The Palazzo Pitti, begun in 1457, was originally built for the banker Luca Pitti. Its huge scale was developed into its actual shape by the Medici, who one century later bought the palazzo when building costs bankrupted Pitti's heirs. In 1550 it became the main Medici residence and subsequently all Florentine rulers lived here. Today the richly decorated rooms exhibit treasures from the Medici collections *(see pp122–3)* and the Habsburg-Lorraine court.

Inner Courtyard
Ammannati designed the courtyard in 1560–70. The Artichoke Fountain by Francesco Susini (1641) was topped by a bronze artichoke, since lost.

The Boboli Gardens were laid out where stone had been quarried to build the Palazzo Pitti *(see pp124–5).*

★ Palatine Gallery
The gallery contains many masterpieces, among which is the highest concentration of Raphael's paintings.

The side wings were added in 1828 by the Dukes of Lorraine, who ruled the city after the Medici.

Frescoes by Pietro da Cortona (1641–5) cover the ceilings in the Palatine Gallery.

Brunelleschi is thought to have designed the façade of the palazzo, which was later extended to three times its original length.

★ Museo degli Argenti
As well as silverware, the museum displays gold, stone and glassware. This view of Piazza della Signoria (see pp76–7) is made of precious stones.

STAR SIGHTS

★ Palatine Gallery

★ Museo degli Argenti

Galleria d'Arte Moderna
The gallery, on the second floor of the palazzo, spans the years from 1784 to 1924. The Tuscan Maremma (c.1850), by Giovanni Fattori, is a highlight of the collection.

The Carriage Museum offers another glimpse of the sumptuous, opulent life of the dukes.

Galleria del Costume
The clothes reflect changing fashion at the court of the Grand Dukes during the 18th and 19th centuries.

VISITORS' CHECKLIST

Piazza Pitti. **Map** 3 C2 (5 B5). D, 11, 36, 37. **Palatine Gallery & Royal Apartments** *Tel 055 238 86 14.* **Open** *8:15am–6:50pm Tue–Sun.* **Closed** *1 Jan, 1 May, 25 Dec.* **Galleria d'Arte Moderna** *Tel 055 238 86 01.* **Galleria del Costume** *Tel 055 238 87 13.* **Both open** *8:15am–1:50pm daily.* **Closed** *2nd & 4th Sun and 1st, 3rd & 5th Mon of the month.* **Museo degli Argenti** *Tel 055 238 87 09.* **Open** *same as Boboli Gardens (see p125).* **Museo delle Porcellane** (enter via Boboli Gardens, *see p125*). *Tel 055 238 86 05.* **Open** *same as Boboli Gardens (see p125).* **All museums closed** *public hols. Ticket offices close 45 mins before the museums.* **Adm charge** *for each museum.* **Palatine Gallery** *ticket admits to* **Royal Apartments**. **Galleria d'Arte Moderna** *ticket admits to* **Galleria del Costume**.

Entrance to museums and galleries

Massive Windows
The windows of the Palazzo Pitti were built to be larger than the main door of the Palazzo Medici Riccardi.

Royal Apartments
The south wing was used for ceremonial occasions and receiving ambassadors.

Exploring the Palazzo Pitti

The Palatine gallery was realized by the Medici family and the Habsburg-Lorraine duchies in the 1600s and 1700s. The frescoed halls were hung with works from their private collection and the gallery was opened to the public in 1833. Other attractions include the royal apartments, the Medici collection of jewellery and treasures, the gallery of modern art and an exhibition of Italian clothing from the 18th, 19th and 20th centuries.

THE PALATINE GALLERY

The gallery contains a superb collection of works dating from the Renaissance and Baroque. They are hung as the 17th- and 18th-century Grand Dukes wished, placed purely for their effect, regardless of subject or chronology. The decoration of the rooms in the gallery reflects the tastes and preoccupations of the time. Rooms 4 to 8 are painted with Baroque ceiling frescoes begun by Pietro da Cortona between 1641–7, and finished by his pupil Ciro Ferri in 1666. They allegorize the education of a prince by the gods. In Room 1, the prince is torn from the love of Venus by Minerva (knowledge) and in the following rooms he is taught science from Apollo, war from Mars and leadership from Jupiter. Finally Saturn welcomes him to Mount Olympus, home of the gods in Roman mythology.

The other rooms in the gallery were private apartments and range from the opulence of the formal drawing rooms to the severity of Napoleon's bathroom (Room 27) *(see p55)*, in a suite of rooms designed by Giuseppe Cacialli for the emperor in 1813 following his conquest of northern Italy.

Mary Magdalene by Titian (c.1535)

Although some of the Medici collection has been transferred to the Uffizi over the years, the Palatine Gallery is still packed with masterpieces by artists such as Botticelli, Perugino, Titian, Andrea del Sarto, Pontormo, Tintoretto, Veronese, Caravaggio, Rubens and Van Dyck, among others. There are approximately 1,000 paintings here, providing a vast survey of 16th- and 17th-century European painting.

The Sala di Venere (Venus) is dominated by the statue of *Venus Italica* by Antonio Canova, commissioned by Napoleon in 1810 as a replacement for *The Medici Venus* in the Uffizi Gallery, which was to be taken to Paris. Napoleon was not normally so generous, as his agents were renowned for stealing a large number of fine works of art from Italy during the Napoleonic Wars.

Several of Titian's works in the following rooms were commissioned by the Duke of Urbino. *La Bella* (1536) is a portrait of a lovely but unknown woman, whom he also used as a model in other paintings. His portrait, *Mary Magdalene*, in the Sala di Apollo, was painted between 1530–35 in an overtly sensual manner, bathed in soft light.

Some of Raphael's best High Renaissance work is in the Palatine, including *Portrait of a Woman* (c.1516) and

THE PALATINE GALLERY
The gallery is on the first floor of the Palazzo Pitti.

Madonna of the Chair by Raphael (c.1516)

Stairs to ground floor

Sala di Venere

Sala di Apollo

Sala di Marte

Sala di Giove

Sala di Saturno

East stairs

Venus Italica by Antonio Canova (1810)

Madonna of the Chair (c.1510) in the *tondo* (roundel) form which became very popular during the Renaissance.

The Consequences of War by Peter Paul Rubens (1638) is an allegorical painting of the Thirty Years' War (1618–48), showing Venus preventing Mars from unleashing his fury on the cowering, beleaguered figure of Europe, completely robed in black mourning.

ROYAL APARTMENTS

The Throne Room

The Royal Apartments on the first floor of the south wing of the palazzo were built in the 17th century. They were decorated with frescoes by various Florentine artists and a series of portraits of the Medici by the Flemish painter Justus Sustermans, who worked at the court between 1619–81. In the late 18th and early 19th centuries, the apartments were completely revamped in Neo-Classical style by the Dukes of Lorraine when they succeeded the Medici dynasty as the rulers of Florence *(see pp54–5)*.

The apartments are lavishly appointed with ornate gold and white stuccowork ceilings and rich decoration, as on the walls of the Parrot Room, which are covered with an opulent crimson fabric detailed with a bird design. The apartments' varied ownership is revealed in their design, which embraces three distinct artistic periods.

MUSEO DEGLI ARGENTI

This museum is on the ground and mezzanine floors, below the Palatine Gallery, in the rooms used by the Medici as their summer apartments. It displays the massive private wealth of the Medici dynasty: the collection encompasses rare and beautiful examples of ancient Roman glassware, ivory, carpets, crystal and amber and fine works by Florentine and

14th-century gold and jasper vase

German goldsmiths. The pride of the collection are 16 *pietre dure* vases displayed in the Sala Buia. These belonged to Lorenzo the Magnificent and are from the ancient Roman and Byzantine periods.

The family's lavish tastes are reflected in the museum's polished ebony furniture inlaid with semi-precious marbles and stones. Portraits of the Medici hang throughout the rooms, including a series of the Grand Duchesses, and Cosimo I and his family carved in an onyx cameo.

GALLERIA D'ARTE MODERNA

Here the paintings span the period from 1784 to 1924; many of them were collected by the Dukes of Lorraine to decorate the Palazzo Pitti.

The present museum has combined this collection with pictures donated by the state and various private collectors. The museum contains Neo-Classical, Romantic and religious works, but probably the most important collection is of the group of late 19th-century artists known as the *Macchiaioli* (spotmakers), similar to French Impressionists. The *Macchiaioli* used bright splashes of colour to represent the sun-dappled Tuscan landscape. This collection was given to the city of Florence in 1897 by the art critic Diego Martelli, and includes paintings by Giovanni Fattori *(see p121)* and Giovanni Boldini. Two works by Camille Pissarro hang in the same room.

GALLERIA DEL COSTUME

Opened in 1983, the gallery is on the ground floor of the Palazzo Meridiana. This was designed in 1776 by Gaspare Maria Paoletti for the Royal Family; they lived until the abolition of the monarchy *(see p52)*. The exhibits reflect the changing tastes in the courtly fashion of the late 18th century up to the 1920s. Some of the rooms have been restored to correspond to a 1911 inventory. The gallery has recently been renovated.

The Italian Camp after the Battle of Magenta (c.1855) by Giovanni Fattori

Boboli Gardens 🟣

The Boboli Gardens were laid out for the Medici in 1550, one year after they bought the Palazzo Pitti. A perfect example of stylized Renaissance gardening, they were opened to the public in 1766. The more formal parts of the garden, nearest the palazzo, consist of box hedges clipped into symmetrical geometric patterns. These lead to wild groves of ilex and cypress trees, planted to create a contrast between artifice and nature. Statues of varying styles and periods are dotted around, and the vistas were planned to give views over Florence.

★ Amphitheatre
Stone for the Palazzo Pitti was quarried here and the hollow was turned into a stage for the first-ever opera performances.

Kaffeehaus
The Rococo-style pavilion, built in 1774, now houses a coffee house. It is open during the summer and offers beautiful views over the city.

Forte di Belvedere

Ganymede Fountain

Entrance to palazzo and gardens

Galleria del Costume

The Neptune Fountain was built between 1565–8 by Stoldo Lorenzi.

★ La Grotta Grande
The casts of Michelangelo's Quattro Prigioni (see p94) are built into the walls of this Mannerist folly (1583–93), which also houses Vincenzo de' Rossi's Paris with Helen of Troy (1560) and Venus Bathing (1565) by Giambologna.

Bacchus Fountain *(1560)*
A copy of the original by Valerio Cioli, the statue shows Pietro Barbino, Cosimo I's court dwarf, as Bacchus, the Roman god of wine, astride a turtle.

Lunette of Boboli Gardens
The Flemish artist Giusto Utens painted this picture of the Palazzo Pitti and Boboli Gardens in 1599.

The Porcelain Museum is accessed via the Rose Garden.

Viottolone
The avenue of cypress trees, planted in 1612, is lined with Classical statues.

★ **L'Isolotto (Little Island)**
The centrepiece of the moated garden is Giambologna's Oceanus Fountain (1576). The original statue of Oceanus has been moved to the Bargello
(see pp68–9).

Hemicycle (semicircular lawn)

Entrance

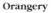

Orangery
Zanobi del Rosso's Orangery (1777–8) was built to protect rare, tender plants from frost.

STAR FEATURES

★ Amphitheatre

★ La Grotta Grande

★ L'Isolotto
   (Little Island)

Brancacci Chapel ⑩

The church of Santa Maria del Carmine is famous for *The Life of St Peter* frescoes in the Brancacci Chapel, commissioned by the Florentine merchant Felice Brancacci around 1424. Masolino began the work in 1425 but many of the scenes are by his pupil, Masaccio, who died before completing the cycle. Filippino Lippi finished the work 50 years later, in 1480. Masaccio's use of perspective in *The Tribute Money* and the tragic realism of his figures in *The Expulsion of Adam and Eve* placed him at the vanguard of Renaissance painting. Many great artists, including Leonardo and Michelangelo, later visited the chapel to study his pioneering work.

In every scene, St Peter is distinguished from the crowds as the figure in the orange cloak.

St Peter Heals the Sick
Masaccio's realistic portrayal of cripples and beggars was revolutionary in his time.

The grouping of stylized figures in Masaccio's frescoes reflects his interest in the sculpture of his contemporary Donatello *(see p69)*.

Masaccio's simple style allows us to focus on the figures central to the frescoes without distracting detail.

Expulsion of Adam and Eve
Masaccio's ability to express emotion is well illustrated by his harrowing portrait of Adam and Eve being driven out of the Garden of Eden, their faces wracked by misery, shame and the burden of self-knowledge.

KEY TO THE FRESCOES: ARTISTS AND SUBJECTS

☐ Masolino

☐ Masaccio

☐ Lippi

1 Expulsion of Adam and Eve
2 The Tribute Money
3 St Peter Preaching
4 St Peter Visited by St Paul
5 Raising the Emperor's Son;
 St Peter Enthroned
6 St Peter Healing the Sick

7 St Peter Baptizing the Converts
8 St Peter Healing the Cripple;
 Raising Tabitha
9 Temptation of Adam and Eve
10 St Peter and St John Giving Alms
11 Crucifixion; Before the Proconsul
12 The Release of St Peter

VISITORS' CHECKLIST

Piazza del Carmine. **Map** 3 A1
(5 A4). **Tel** 055 238 21 95. 🚌
D. **Open** 10am–5pm Mon,
Wed–Sat; 1–5pm Sun (arrive
early). **Closed** Tue, public hols.
Adm charge. 📷

Masolino's *Temptation of
Adam and Eve* is gentle
and decorous,
in contrast with the
emotional force of
Masaccio's painting
on the opposite wall.

Woman in a Turban
*The freshness of Masaccio's
original colours is seen in
this rediscovered roundel,
hidden behind the altar
for 500 years.*

St Peter is depicted
against a background
of Florentine
buildings.

Two Figures
*Masolino's work is painstakingly
decorative in contrast with
Masaccio's simpler style.*

Before the Proconsul
*Filippino Lippi was called in to complete the unfinished
cycle of frescoes in 1480. He added this emotional scene
showing the Proconsul sentencing St Peter to death.*

FOUR GUIDED WALKS

In Florence the countryside is never very far away, and you can be walking down quiet, rural lanes within just a few minutes of leaving the Ponte Vecchio *(see pp106–7)*, in the bustling heart of the city. The first walk is popular with the Florentines, who like to stroll on a Sunday beneath the city walls and take in the panoramic views that can be enjoyed from San Miniato al Monte and the Piazzale Michelangelo. Fiesole, the setting for the second walk, is 8 km (5 miles) north of Florence. It was once a powerful Etruscan city, but was later eclipsed by the rise of Florence, so that it is now merely a village. There are archaeological remains to provide a hint of its previous glory. The third walk shows Renaissance Florence at its best, taking in Brunnelleschi's cupola and many of the grand palazzi. The last walk ends in the serene Piazza Santa Spirito after exploring the Florentine backstreets.

Bust, Museo Faesulanum

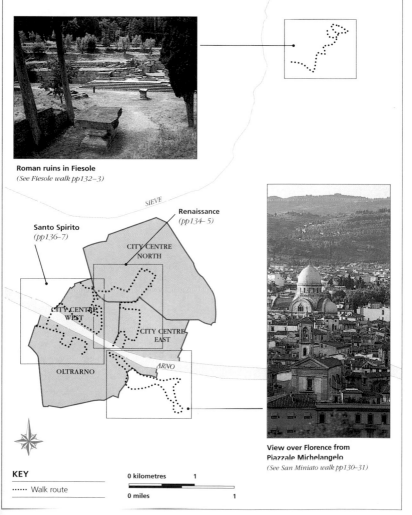

Roman ruins in Fiesole
(See Fiesole walk pp132–3)

SIEVE

Renaissance
(pp134–5)

Santo Spirito
(pp136–7)

CITY CENTRE NORTH

CITY CENTRE WEST

CITY CENTRE EAST

ARNO

OLTRARNO

View over Florence from Piazzale Michelangelo
(See San Miniato walk pp130–31)

KEY

...... Walk route

| 0 kilometres | 1 |
| 0 miles | 1 |

◁ **Looking up the steps to the church of San Miniato al Monte**

A Two-Hour Walk to San Miniato al Monte

This walk takes you from the centre of Florence to the exquisitely decorated church of San Miniato al Monte high on a hill in the south of the city. The route follows quiet lanes along the city walls, and then takes in the bustling Piazzale Michelangelo, packed with souvenir stalls, before returning to the town centre.

No. 19 Costa di San Giorgio ③

From the Ponte Vecchio ① walk south down Via de' Guicciardini and take the second turning left into the square fronting Santa Felicità ②. On the left of the church, take the steep road to the right, Costa di San Giorgio. No. 19 ③ was once the home of Galileo. The Porta San Giorgio (St George's Gate) ④ is straight ahead at the end of the lane.

Built in 1260, this is the oldest city gate to survive in Florence. The weathered fresco within the arch is *The Virgin with St George and St Leonard* by Bicci di Lorenzo (1460). On the outer face of the arch is a carving of St George fighting the dragon, a copy of the original 1284 work, which has been removed and is currently being restored.

The Forte di Belvedere ⑤ is to the right through the gate, and was designed by Bernardo Buontalenti in 1590. Originally the fortress was built to guard the city against attack from its political rivals, but it soon became a private refuge for the Medici Grand Dukes. From here there are extensive views over the Boboli Gardens ⑥ below, and across to the olive groves and cypress trees in the countryside south of the city. Head downhill along Via di Belvedere, which runs along

a stretch of city walls (to the left) dating from 1258. Porta San Miniato ⑦, a small arch in the wall, is situated at the bottom of the hill.

San Miniato al Monte

Turn right into Via del Monte alle Croci and walk uphill for 500 m (550 yds) to the Viale Galileo Galilei. Bear right and cross the road to the vast stone steps leading to the terrace in front of San Miniato al Monte ⑧. Catch your breath and admire the view of the Forte di Belvedere.

San Miniato al Monte is one of the most unspoiled of all the Romanesque churches in Tuscany. It was built in 1018 over the shrine of the early Christian martyr, San Miniato (St Minias). He was a rich Armenian merchant beheaded for his beliefs by Emperor Decius in the 3rd century. The façade was begun around 1090 and has geometric patterning in green-grey and white marble, typical of the Romanesque style. The statue on the gable shows an eagle carrying a bale of cloth, the symbol of the powerful Arte di Calimala (guild of wool

The façade of San Miniato al Monte ⑧

View across to San Miniato al Monte from Forte di Belvedere ⑤

importers) who financed the church in the Middle Ages. The restored 13th-century mosaic below the gable shows Christ, the Virgin and St Minias. Inside the church, the High Altar is raised above the nave and there is a Byzantine-style mosaic in the apse, again of St Minias with Christ and the Virgin. Below this is the crypt, built using columns salvaged from ancient Roman buildings. The floor of the nave is covered with seven marble mosaic panels of lions, doves and the signs of the Zodiac (1207); similar intarsia work panels can be seen on the raised marble choir and

13th-century mosaic on San Miniato façade

pulpit. In the north wall is the funeral chapel of the 25-year-old Cardinal of Portugal, Iacopo di Lusitania, who died in Florence in 1439. Antonio Rossellino carved the figure of the cardinal guarded by angels on the elaborate marble tomb (1466). The terracotta roundels on the ceiling, showing the Holy Spirit and Virtues, were painted by Luca della Robbia (1461). Outside, the massive belltower was begun in 1523 by Baccio

d'Agnolo, but was never finished. Cannons were installed here to shoot at the Medici troops during the Siege of Florence (see pp52–3). The cemetery ⑨ surrounding the church opened in 1854 and this contains tombs the size of miniature houses, built to show off family wealth.

Leave San Miniato by an arch in the buildings to the west and follow the path that

San Salvatore al Monte ⑩

threads down to the church of San Salvatore al Monte ⑩. Here steps lead down to the Viale Galileo Galilei; take a right turn to reach Piazzale Michelangelo ⑪. The piazzale was laid out in the 1860s by Giuseppe Poggi, and is dotted with copies of Michelangelo's famous statues. It is lined with souvenir stalls and has far-reaching views over the rooftops of central Florence.

Either take the No. 13 bus back to the city centre, or the stone steps on the west side of the piazza down to Porta San Niccolò ⑫, a 14th-century gateway in the city wall. Go left along Via di San Niccolò and Via de' Bardi, lined with medieval buildings. This includes the 13th-century Palazzo de' Mozzi ⑬ on Via de' Bardi; the Museo Bardini ⑭ (see p119) is opposite. From here you can return along the Arno to the Ponte Vecchio ①.

TIPS FOR WALKERS

Starting point: Ponte Vecchio.
Length: 3 km (2 miles).
San Miniato al Monte: Open Apr–Sep 8am–noon, 2–7pm daily; Oct– Mar 8am–noon, 2:30–6pm daily.
Stopping-off points: There are several cafés along the route.

KEY

····· Walk route

🌣 Viewing point

metres 500
yards 500

David in Piazzale Michelangelo ⑪

A Two-Hour Walk through Fiesole

The village of Fiesole stands in the foothills of the Mugello region, 8 km (5 miles) north of Florence, and has substantial Roman and Etruscan remains. The area has been a popular summer retreat since the 15th century, thanks to its fresh breezes and hilltop position.

The belltower of the Duomo ②

Piazza Mino da Fiesole

The No. 7 bus arrives at its last stop, in Fiesole's main square ①, after a 30-minute journey from Florence through countryside dotted with villas. Settled in the 7th century BC, Fiesole was a powerful force in central Italy by the 5th century BC. It began to decline after the Romans founded Florence in the 1st century BC, but kept its independence until 1125, when Florentine troops razed most of the city. The Duomo of San Romolo ② in the piazza was begun in 1028 and has a massive belltower. The bare Romanesque interior has columns which are topped with reused Roman capitals.

TIPS FOR WALKERS

Starting point: Piazza Mino da Fiesole.
Length: 1.5 km (1 mile). Allow 2–3 hours for the walk to include time to visit the various museums. Note that Via di San Francesco is steep.
Badia Fiesolana: Open Sunday morning for services.
Getting there: No. 7 bus from Santa Maria Novella bus station, or Piazza di San Marco in Florence.
Stopping-off points: There are several cafés around Piazza Mino da Fiesole. The tiny ice-cream parlour Il Tucano (Via Gramsci 8) is also worth a stop.

From here, walk up the square to the front of the 14th-century Palazzo Comunale ③. Here there is a bronze statue of King Vittorio Emanuele II and Garibaldi, called *Incontro di Teano* (Meeting at Teano) ④. Returning to the church, take the first turning right, down Via Dupre, to the Roman theatre ⑤ and into the archaeological park.

The bronze statue
Incontro di Teano ④

After its defeat by Florence in 1125, Fiesole went into a decline, and many Etruscan and Roman remains went

undisturbed until excavation in the 1870s. The Teatro, built in the 1st century BC, is used for the annual Estate Fiesolana festival *(see pp38–9)*. Its tiers of stone seats can hold 3,000 spectators. Next to the theatre is the Museo Faesulanum ⑥, built in 1912–14. Inside are finds from the Bronze Age onwards: coins, jewellery and ceramics, bronzes and marble sculpture. The building is a copy of the 1st-century Roman temple whose remains are in the northern part of the complex. It is built on Etruscan foundations, and part of the Roman frieze dating from the 1st century BC is still intact. There are some partly restored Roman baths close by ⑦, and, at

Roman theatre complex ⑤

Badia Fiesolana

⑯

VIA DELLA BADIA DEI ROCCETTINI

⑮

KEY

•••• Walk route

⚜ Viewpoint

0 metres	250
0 yards	250

the northern edge of the park, 4th-century BC Etruscan walls ⑧. From the theatre turn into Via Dupre to Museo Bandini ⑨ to the right, with a collection of medieval religious paintings built up by local aristocrat Angelo Bandini in the 19th century.

Back in Piazza Mino da Fiesole, turn right down Via di San Francesco to the left of the Palazzo Vescovile ⑩. There are views over Florence and back to Fiesole ⑪ on the road up to Sant'Alessandro church ⑫, which has a Neo-Classical façade combined with a 9th-century

Fiesole from Via di San Francesco

Façade of Badia Fiesolana ⑯

Romanesque interior. Original Roman columns used in the nave are made out of *cipollino* (onion ring) marble. From here carry on up to San Francesco ⑬, a Franciscan friary founded in 1399 and restored in 1907. It has a pretty cloister and a museum of artifacts collected by the monks.

From Fiesole to San Domenico

Retrace your steps or walk through the park back to the town centre. Continue down Via Vecchia Fiesolana. On the left is the Villa Medici ⑭, built in 1461 by Michelozzo for Cosimo de' Medici. Walk down Via Bandini and Via Vecchia Fiesolana to San Domenico. In this little hamlet is the 15th century

The 15th-century church of San Francesco ⑬

church of San Domenico ⑮, with two good works by Fra Angelico, Dominican prior of the monastery here until 1437. The *Madonna with Angels* and *The Crucifixion* are in the chapter house and were both painted around 1430.

Opposite, Via della Badia dei Roccettini leads to the Badia Fiesolana ⑯, a pretty church with a Romanesque façade of inlaid marble. The interior is decorated with local grey sandstone, *pietra serena*. The No. 7 bus back to Florence can be caught from the village square in San Domenico.

A 90-Minute Walk Around Renaissance Florence

This walk takes in the Renaissance heart of the city and passes some of its greatest landmarks. Ideally, it should be done early on in your visit to get a real feel for the place, and if you incorporate a climb up Giotto's Campanile, you will get a bird's eye view of the narrow streets, the characteristic red-tiled rooftops and the many towers that are not so easy to see from ground level.

View of Ponte Vecchio and Vasari corridor ①

rooftops, is the Badia Fiorentina ⑥, one of the city's oldest churches. Across the street is the forbidding ex-prison building that now houses the Bargello museum ⑦ *(see pp68–9)* and its superb collection of sculpture. Continue north up Via Proconsolo. At no. 10 stands Palazzo Pazzi-Quaratesi, once the home of the Pazzi family of bankers, protagonists in the famous Pazzi conspiracy against the Medici of 1478. At no. 12 is

Ponte Vecchio to Piazza di San Firenze

The walk begins in the centre of the Ponte Vecchio ① *(see pp106–7)*, where butcher's and grocery shops were first built in the 13th century, then replaced by goldsmiths at the end of the 16th century. The bust here is of Benvenuto Cellini, the most famous gold-smith of them all. Note the Vasari Corridor with its round windows running over the shops on the eastern side of the bridge. Walk north up Via Por Santa Maria. A short way along on the right is Vicolo Santo Stefano and the ancient, deconsecrated church of Santo Stefano al Ponte ②, which was badly damaged in 1993 when a car bomb exploded in nearby Via Lambertesca. Further up Por Santa Maria is the Mercato Nuovo ③ *(see p112)*, a site on which there has been a market for centuries. The famous bronze *"porcellino"* (wild boar) is on the southern side; he is a copy of a copy of a sculpture by Tacca. It is said that if you rub his snout you will return to Florence one day. Turn right into Piazza della Signoria, past the open air sculpture gallery of the Loggia dei Lanzi ④ and turn right to walk the length of the Uffizi gallery portico *(see pp80–81)*

and back along the opposite side. Turn right and take Via della Ninna out of the square; turn left at the end into Piazza di San Firenze ⑤. On the corner of Via dei Gondi stands Sangallo's late 15th-century Palazzo Gondi whose graceful courtyard is now occupied by a flower shop. The huge Baroque building opposite (1772–5) houses the law courts; to its left is the 17th-century church of San Filippo Neri, which has a painted ceiling.

Via del Proconsolo to Via dei Servi

At the north end of the square on the left, its tall, slim tower rising above the surrounding

Flower shop in the courtyard of Palazzo Gondi

Buontalenti's Palazzo Nonfinito *(see p70)* begun in 1593 and "unfinished", which today houses the Anthropological Museum and its wonderfully old-fashioned collection of curios. Via Proconsolo emerges at the east end of the Duomo ⑧ *(see pp64–5)*. Skirt around the south side of this massive building, past the stone plaque known as *"Il Sasso di Dante"* ⑨, where the poet would sit and contemplate the construction of the cathedral; it's on the left just before Via dello Studio.

Enter Piazza di San Giovanni with its extraordinary religious buildings, crowds of visitors, and postcard sellers. Just south of the Baptistery at the top of Via de' Calzaiuoli is the 14th-century Loggia del

Bigallo ⑩. Piazza di San Giovanni is the heart of religious Florence and if you have the time and energy to climb the 400-odd steps of the Giotto's Campanile, you will be rewarded by a close-up of the great dome by Brunelleschi *(see pp64–5)*, and a view of the city below.

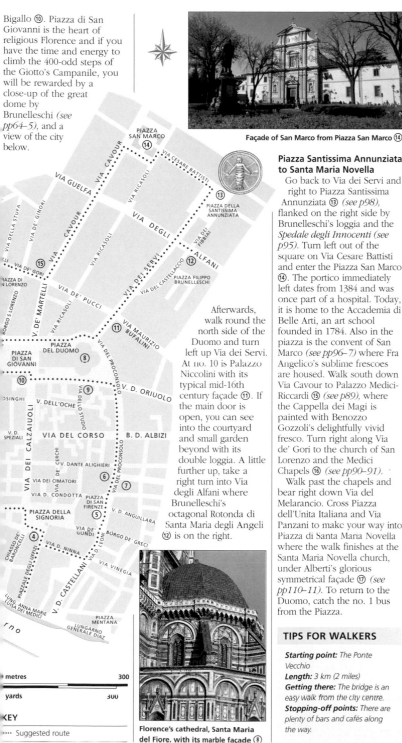

Façade of San Marco from Piazza San Marco ⑭

Piazza Santissima Annunziata to Santa Maria Novella

Go back to Via dei Servi and right to Piazza Santissima Annunziata ⑬ *(see p98)*, flanked on the right side by Brunelleschi's loggia and the *Spedale degli Innocenti (see p95)*. Turn left out of the square on Via Cesare Battisti and enter the Piazza San Marco ⑭. The portico immediately left dates from 1384 and was once part of a hospital. Today, it is home to the Accademia di Belle Arti, an art school founded in 1784. Also in the piazza is the convent of San Marco *(see pp96–7)* where Fra Angelico's sublime frescoes are housed. Walk south down Via Cavour to Palazzo Medici-Riccardi ⑮ *(see p89)*, where the Cappella dei Magi is painted with Benozzo Gozzoli's delightfully vivid fresco. Turn right along Via de' Gori to the church of San Lorenzo and the Medici Chapels ⑯ *(see pp90–91)*.

Afterwards, walk round the north side of the Duomo and turn left up Via dei Servi. At no. 10 is Palazzo Niccolini with its typical mid-16th century façade ⑪. If the main door is open, you can see into the courtyard and small garden beyond with its double loggia. A little further up, take a right turn into Via degli Alfani where Brunelleschi's octagonal Rotonda di Santa Maria degli Angeli ⑫ is on the right.

Walk past the chapels and bear right down Via del Melarancio. Cross Piazza dell'Unità Italiana and Via Panzani to make your way into Piazza di Santa Maria Novella where the walk finishes at the Santa Maria Novella church, under Alberti's glorious symmetrical façade ⑰ *(see pp110–11)*. To return to the Duomo, catch the no. 1 bus from the Piazza.

TIPS FOR WALKERS

Starting point: The Ponte Vecchio
Length: 3 km (2 miles)
Getting there: The bridge is an easy walk from the city centre.
Stopping-off points: There are plenty of bars and cafés along the way.

Florence's cathedral, Santa Maria del Fiore, with its marble façade ⑧

metres 300
yards 300

KEY

···· Suggested route

A 90-Minute Walk to Piazza Santo Spirito

This walk begins under the clock at the Santa Maria Novella train station, which is one of the city's few significant modern buildings. It takes you to one of Florence's greatest churches, leads along one of the city's most fashionable shopping streets, and visits Piazza Santa Trinità, with its elegant medieval palaces. You cross the Arno river into the western limits of the Oltrarno area with its fascinating artisan workshops, taking in Piazza del Carmine and finishing in the heart of the Bohemian district at Piazza Santo Spirito.

View across the Piazza Santa Maria Novella to the parish church ③

Stazione di Santa Maria Novella

Begin under the digital clock on the south side of Florence's main train station ① *(see p113)*. Designed in 1935, this is one of the few important "modern" buildings in a city dominated by Medieval and Renaissance architecture. The Italians invented the digital clock and the one here is an early version. Cross over Piazza della Stazione and bear left towards the back of the great parish church of Santa Maria Novella *(see pp110–11)* ②. Follow the arched recesses along one side of the church, which were once the family vaults of Florentine nobles, and you will emerge in the Piazza Santa Maria Novella ③, a rather scruffy square that is undergoing radical

renovation. At the southern end is the Loggia di San Paolo, a copy of Brunelleschi's famous Loggia degli Innocenti dating from 1489. In the 17th century the piazza was used for carriage races and the two obelisks sitting on turtles marked the turning points. Exit the square on the south side along Via dei Fossi and turn left into Via della Spada, a busy local shopping street. On the right is the former church of San Pancrazio ④, one of the oldest in Florence and, today, home to the Museo Marino Marini *(see p104)*. Turning left into Via delle Belle Donne, right into Via del Trebbio and right again will bring you out in Via de' Tornabuoni with its impressive mansions and designer shops *(see p105)*. On the corner is Palazzo Antinori ⑤ *(see p112)*, built by Giuliano da Maiano from 1461–69; you can walk into the splendid courtyard. Note the 17th-century church of San Gaetano across the road with its a fine Baroque façade.

A designer shop in chic Via de' Tornabuoni

Piazza Santa Trinità

Walk past Palazzo Strozzi *(see p105)* and down to Piazza Santa Trinità ⑥ *(see p108)*, which marks the meeting of three ancient Roman roads and is lined with noble palaces. Walk towards the river and turn right along Lungarno Corsini. At no. 2 is Palazzo Masetti ⑦, today occupied by the British Consulate but once the home of Bonnie Prince Charlie's widow, the Countess of Albany, who later married the dramatist Vittorio Alfieri.

The huge building a little further down on the right is Palazzo Corsini ⑧; it houses the Corsini family's private art collection (entrance on

Via del Parione), which includes works by artists such as Botticelli.

At Piazza Carlo Goldoni (named after the playwright whose statue is on the far side), continue west along Borgo Ognissanti which opens onto the Arno at Piazza Ognissanti ⑨. Palazzo Lenzi, on the right, was built in the mid-15th century and has a

| 0 metres | | 30 |
| 0 yards | | 300 |

KEY

····· Suggested route

🚊 Train station

façade decorated with sgraffiti; today it is home to the French Consulate. Overlooking the square is the church of Ognissanti *(see p113)*, which contains Botticelli's tomb and frescoes by Ghirlandaio. The latter's

One of the artisan workshops in the Oltrano area

del Cestello ⑪, where the entrance to the church of San Frediano in Cestello *(see p119)* faces the river. Return to Borgo San Frediano turning right into Piazza del Carmine ⑫. The church of Santa Maria del Carmine is famous for its Brancacci Chapel *(see pp126–7)*, which is decorated with frescoes begun by Masolino and Masaccio, and finished by Filippino Lippi.

Leave the square at the southernmost corner along Via Santa Monica and turn left into Via dei Serragli where there is a pretty tabernacle. Walk towards the river and turn right into Via di Santo Spirito. Note the Medici Crest at no. 58r, the 13th–14th-century Torre de' Lanfredini stands at no. 40r and Palazzo Frescobaldi (home of the wine-growing Frescobaldi family) is at nos. 5-13. Turn into Via de' Coverelli and walk to Piazza Santo Spirito ⑬, the heart of this Bohemian district and the walk's end. To return to the city centre, catch bus no. 11 to the Duomo.

famous *The Last Supper*, is housed in the convent refectory next door, reached through a frescoed cloister.

Across the River Arno

Cross the Ponte Amerigo Vespucci and walk on to Borgo San Frediano, a delightful area that's filled with artisan workshops and characteristic houses set on narrow streets. To the right is Porta San Frediano ⑩, built in 1324, whose massive wooden doors are still intact. The adjoining stretch of city wall is particularly well preserved.

Double back along Borgo San Frediano and turn left down Via Cestello into Piazza

TIPS FOR WALKERS

Starting point: Santa Maria Novella Train Station.
Length: 3.5 km (2 miles)
Getting there: You can walk to the station from the city centre.
Stopping-off points: There are plenty of bars and cafés along the way.

A pavement café in the Piazza di Santo Spirito ⑬

FLORENCE STREET FINDER

Map references given for sights, restaurants, hotels and shops in Florence refer to the maps in the *Florence Street Finder* (*see* How the Map References Work *opposite*).

Where two map references are provided, the second (in brackets) relates to the large-scale maps, 5 and 6.

A complete index of street names is on pages 146–7. The key map below shows the area of Florence covered by each of the six maps in the *Florence Street Finder*. The maps encompass the four city-centre areas (colour-coded pink), which include all the sights. (*See also* Florence City Centre, *pp16–17.*)

0 metres 750
0 yards 750

HOW THE MAP REFERENCES WORK

The first figure tells you which Street Finder map to turn to.

Ognissanti ⑯

Borgo Ognissanti 42. **Map** 1 B5
(5 A2) **Tel** 055 239 87 00.
Open 8am–noon, 4–7pm.

The letter and number are a grid reference. You will find the letters at the top and bottom of the map and the numbers at the sides.

The second reference refers to the large-scale maps of Florence (5 & 6). It is read in exactly the same way as the first.

The map continues on map 3 of the Street Finder.

The key to the abbreviations used in the Street Finder is on page 146.

KEY TO STREET FINDER

▪	Major sight
▪	Places of interest
▪	Railway station
🚌	Bus terminus
🚍	Coach terminus
P	Parking
🛈	Tourist information office
✚	Hospital with casualty unit
🚓	Police station
✝	Church
✡	Synagogue
⊠	Post office
=	Railway line
	Pedestrianized street
—	City wall

SCALE OF MAPS 1–2 & 3–4

| 0 metres | 200 | |
| 0 yards | 200 | 1:11,000 |

SCALE OF MAPS 5–6

| 0 metres | 125 | |
| 0 yards | 125 | 1:6,000 |

Street Finder Index

KEY TO ABBREVIATIONS USED IN THE STREET FINDER

d.	di, del, dell',	**Lung.**	Lungarno	**P.te**	Ponte
	dello, della, dei,	**P.**	Piazza	**S.**	San, Sant', Santa, Santo
	de', delle, degli	**P.ta**	Porta	**SS.**	Santi, Santissima
				V.	Via
				Vic.	Vicolo
				V.le	Viale

A

XX Settembre, V.   1 C2
XXVII Aprile, V.   1 C4
Acciaiuoli, Lungarno
  degli   3 C1 (5 C4)
Acqua, V. dell'   6 E3
Adua, P.   1 B4
Agli, V. degli   1 C5 (5 C2)
Agnolo, V. dell'   4 E1
Alamanni, V. Luigi   1 B4
Albero, V. dell'   1 B5 (5 A1)
Albizi, Borgo d.   2 D5 (6 E3)
Alfani, V. degli   2 D4 (6 E1)
Alfieri, V. Vittorio   2 F4
Alighieri, V.   4 D1 (6 E3)
Alinari,
  Largo Fratelli   1 C4 (5 B1)
Allegri, Borgo   4 E1
Alloro, V. dell'   1 C5 (5 C1)
Altoviti, Chiasso degli   5 C3
Amendola, V.le   4 F1
Amorino, V. dell'   5 C1
Angiolieri, Piazzetta d.   5 C4
Anguillara, V. d.   4 D1 (6 E3)
Anselmi, V. d.   3 C1 (5 C3)
Antinori, P. degli   5 C2
Arazzieri, V. degli   2 D4
Archibusieri, Lungarno
  degli   3 C1 (6 D4)
Arcovata, V. dell'   1 A1
Ardiglione, V. dell'   3 B2 (5 A4)
Ariento, V. dell'   1 C4 (5 C1)
Ariosto, V.le Ludovico   3 A1
Armati, Chiasso degli   5 C1
Arte della Lana, V. dell'   6 D3
Artisti, V. degli   2 F4
Avelli, V. degli   1 C5 (5 B1)

B

Badesse, V. delle   6 F3
Baldinucci, P. Filippo   1 B2
Baluardo, V. del   3 B3
Banchi, V. dei   1 C5 (5 C2)
Bandini, V. Angelo Maria   1 B1
Bandini, V. Sallustio   1 B1
Barbadori, V. de'   5 C4
Barbano, V. di   1 C3
Barbera, V. Gaspero   1 B1
Barbi, Vic. del   2 E2
Bardi, V. de'   3 C2 (6 D5)
Bargellini, Largo Piero   4 E1
Baroncelli, Chiasso de'   6 D4
Bartolini, V. Lorenzo   3 A1
Bastioni, Rampa dei   4 F3
Bastioni, V. dei   4 E2
Battisti, V. Cesare   2 D4
Beccaria, P. Cesare   4 F1
Belfiore, V.le   1 A4
Belle Donne, V. d.   1 C5 (5 C2)
Bellini, V. Lorenzo   3 A5
Belvedere, V. di   4 D3
Benci, V. de'   4 D2 (6 E4)
Benedetta, V.   1 B5 (5 A2)
Beneventi, V. Girolamo   2 E3
Bentaccordi, V. de'   6 E4
Berchet, V. Giovanni   2 E2
Bersaglio, V. del   2 F2
Bezzecca, V.   2 D1
Bianchi, V. Celestino   1 C1
Biffi, V. de'   2 D5 (6 D1)
Bobolino, V. del   3 B3
Boccaccio, V. Giovanni   2 F2
Bolognese, V.   2 F1
Bombarde, V. delle   5 C3
Bonaini, V. Francesco   1 B2
Boni, V. de'   5 C2
Bonizzi, V. dei   6 E2
Bonsi, P. de'   6 D5
Borghini, V. Vincenzo   2 F1
Botticelli, V. Sandro   2 F3
Brache, V. delle   6 E4
Brunelleschi, P.   2 D5 (6 F1)
Brunelleschi,
  V. de'   1 C5 (6 D2)
Bruni, V. de'   2 E1
Bruni, Viuzzo de'   2 E1
Bufalini, V. Maurizio   6 E2

Buonarroti, V.
  Michelangelo   4 E1
Burella, V. delle   4 D1 (6 E3)

C

Cadorna, V.le dei   1 C2
Caduti nei Lager, P.le   1 B3
Calamandrei, Piazzetta   6F3
Caldaie, V. delle   3 B2 (5 A5)
Calimala   3 C1 (6 D3)
Calimaruzza   6 D3
Calza, P. della   3 A3
Calzaiuoli, V. dei   6 D3
Camaldoli, V. di   3 A1
Campanile, V. del   6 D2
Campidoglio, V. del   5 C2
Campora, V. delle   3 A3
Camporeggi, V. di   2 D3
Campuccio, V. d.   3 A2 (5 A5)
Canacci, V. de'   1 B5 (5 A1)
Canneto, V. del   6 D5
Canneto, Vic. del   6 D5
Canonica, V. della   6 D2
Cantagalli, V.   3 A4
Canto de' Nelli, V. del   6 D1
Canto Rivolto, V. del   6 E4
Cantù, Largo Cesare   2 D1
Capaccio, V. di   6 D3
Capitolo, P. del   6 E2
Capponi, V. Gino   2 E3
Capponi, V. Pier   2 E3
Carafa, V. Ettore   2 F1
Cardatori, V. dei   3 A1
Carducci, V. Giosue   2 F5
Carmine, P. del   3 A1 (5 A4)
Carraia, P.te alla   3 B1 (5 B3)
Casine, V. delle   4 E1
Casone, V. del   3 A2
Cassia, V.   1 A3
Castellaccio, V. d.   2 D5 (6 E1)
Castellani, V. de'   4 D1 (6 E4)
Castelli, V. Benedetto   3 A5
Castello d'Altafronte,
  V. del   6 E4
Catalani, V. Alfredo   1 A2
Cava, Vic. della   3 C2 (6 D5)
Cavalleggeri, P. dei   4 E2
Cavour, V.   2 D4 (6 D1)
Cellini, Lung. Benvenuto   4 F2
Cenacolo di Santo
  Spirito   3 B1 (5 B4)
Cennini, V. Bernardo   1 B4
Cerchi, V. de'   6 D3
Cerchi, Vic. de'   6 D3
Cernaia, V. della   1 C2
Cerretani, V. de'   5 C2
Cestello, P. di   3 B1 (5 A3)
Cestello, V. di   3 A1
Cherubini, V.   2 E4
Chiara, V.   1 C4
Chiesa, V. della   3 A2 (5 A5)
Ciechi, Volta dei   6 F2
Cimarosa, V. Domenico   1 A3
Cimatori, P. dei   6 D3
Cimatori, V. dei   4 D1 (6 D3)
Cinque Giornate, V. d.   1 B2
Ciompi, P. dei   4 E1
Circondaria, V.   1 A1
Cirillo, V. Domenico   2 F1
Cironi, V. Piero   1 A1
Cittadella, V.   1 A3
Colonna, V. della   2 E4 (6 F1)
Conce, V. delle   4 E1
Conciatori, V. dei   4 E1
Condotta, V. d.   4 D1 (6 D3)
Conti, P. Augusto   2 F4
Conti, V. de'   5 C1
Cornino, Chiasso   5 C3
Corno, V. del   6 E4
Corridoni, V. Filippo   1 A1
Corsi, V. de'   5 C2
Corsica, V.le   1 A1
Corsini, Lung.   3 B1 (5 B3)
Corso, V. del   2 D5 (6 D3)
Corti, Viuzzo delle   4 F3
Cosseria, V.   1 B2
Coste, Rampa delle   6 D5

Costituzione, P. della   1 C2
Coverelli, V. de'   3 B1 (5 B4)
Crimea, V.   1 B2
Crispi, V. Francesco   1 C2
Cristofori, V.   1 A3
Crocifisso, P. del   1 A4
Crocifisso, V. del   6 F3
Cure, P. delle   2 F2
Curtatone, V.   1 A5

D

Da Castiglione, V. Dante   3 A4
Da Diacceto, V. Iacopo   1 A4
Da Foiano, V. Benedetto   3 B4
Da Palestrina, V.   1 A3
Da Verrazzano, V.   4 E1 (6 F4)
Da Vinci, V. Leonardo   2 E2
Davanzati, P. de'   3 C1 (5 C3)
D'Azeglio, P. Massimo   2 F5
De Lauger, V. Cesare   2 F2
De' Medici, Lungarno
  Anna Maria Luisa   6 D4
De' Ricci, V. Scipione   1 B1
Degli Uberti, V. Farinata   3 A4
Del Lungo, P. Isidoro   2 E3
Del Verrocchio, V.   4 F1
Della Bella, V. Giano   3 A2
Della Robbia, V. dei   2 F3
Demidoff, P.   4 D2 (6 F5)
Di Lando, V. Michele   3 B4
Di Savoia, V. Mafalda   2 E2
Diaz, Lung. Gen.   4 D2 (6 E4)
Dionisi, V. Fausto   1 C3
Dogana, V. della   2 D4
Dolfi, V. Giuseppe   1 C3
Donatello, P.le   2 F4
Drago d'Oro, V.   3 A1
Duca degli Abruzzi, V.le   4 F1
Duca d'Aosta, V.   2 D3
Duomo, P. del   2 D5 (6 D2)

E

Erta, Passo all'   4 E4
Erta Canina   4 E3

F

Fabbri, V. Egisto   1 B2
Fabroni, V. Giovanni   1 B1
Faentina, V.   2 E2
Faenza, V.   1 C4 (5 C1)
Farini, V. Luigi Carlo   2 E5
Fattori, V. Giovanni   2 F3
Federighi, V. de'   5 B3
Ferrucci, P. Francesco   4 F2
Fibbiai, V. dei   2 D4 (6 F1)
Ficino, V. Marsilio   2 E2
Fico, V. del   4 E1 (6 F3)
Fiesolana, V.   2 E5
Finiguerra, V.   1 B5 (5 A2)
Fiordaliso, V. del   5 C3
Firenzuola, V. Agnolo   2 F2
Fiume, V.   1 C4
Fornace, V. della   4 F2
Forte di San Giorgio,
  V. del   3 C2
Fortezza, V. della   1 C3
Foscolo, V. Ugo   3 A3
Fossi, V. dei   1 B5 (5 B3)
Fra' Bartolommeo, V.   2 E3
Fra' Domenico
  Buonvicini, V.   2 F3
Fra' Girolamo
  Savonarola, P.   2 F3
Fra' Iacopo
  Passavanti, V.   2 F2
Fra' Silvestro Maruffi, V.   2 E2
Frescobaldi, P. d.   3 B1 (5 B4)

G

Galdi, V. Matteo   2 F1
Galileo, P.le   3 C4
Galileo Galilei, V.le   3 C5
Galluzzi, V. Riguccio   1 B1
Gamberaia, Viuzzo di   4 E4
Garibaldi, V. Giuseppe   1 A5
Gattaia, Viuzzo di   4 F4
Gelsomino, V. del   3 A5

Genovesi, V. Antonio   2 F1
Georgofili, V. de'   6 D4
Geppi, V. de'   5 B4
Ghiacciaie, V. delle   1 A2
Ghibellina, V.   4 D1 (6 E3)
Ghiberti, P. Lorenzo   4 F1
Giacomini, V. de'   5 C2
Giacomini, V. Antonio   2 E2
Giambologna, V.   2 F4
Gianni, V. Francesco   1 B1
Giardino, V. del   4 E2
Giglio, P. del   6 D2
Giglio, V. del   1 C5 (5 C2)
Giglio, Vic. del   6 D2
Ginori, V. de'   2 D4 (6 D1)
Giordani, V. Pietro   2 F4
Giordano, V. Luca   2 F4
Giovine Italia, V.le   4 F1
Giraldi, V. de'   4 D1 (6 E3)
Giramonte, V.   4 E4
Giramontino, V.   4 D4
Girolami, V. de'   6 D4
Giudici, P. de'   4 D1 (6 E4)
Giusti, V. Giuseppe   2 E4
Goldoni, P. Carlo   3 B1 (5 B3)
Gomitolo dell'Oro, V.   6 D2
Gondi, V. de'   6 E3
Gordigiani, V. Luigi   1 A1
Gori, V. de'   6 D1
Gramsci, V.le Antonio   2 F4
Grazie, Lung. d.   4 D2 (6 F5)
Grazie, P.te alle   4 D2 (6 E5)
Greci, Borgo de'   4 D1 (6 E4)
Guasti, V. Cesare   1 B1
Guelfa, V.   1 C4
Guerrazzi, V.   2 F4
Guicciardini,
  Lungarno   3 B1 (5 B4)
Guicciardini, V. d.   3 C2 (5 C5)

I

Il Magnifico, V. Lorenzo   1 C1
Indipendenza, P. dell'   1 C3
Inferno, V. dell'   3 C1 (5 C3)
Isola delle Stinche, V.   6 F1
Italia, Corso   1 A5

J

Jahier, V. Piero   2 F1

L

La Croce, Borgo   4 F1
La Farina, V. Giuseppe   2 F1
La Marmora, V. Alfonso   2 E3
La Noce, Borgo   6 D1
La Pira, V. Giorgio   2 D4
Lambertesca, V.   6 D4
Lamberti, V. de'   6 D3
Lambruschini, V.   1 C1
Lami, V.le Giovanni   1 C1
Landini, V. Francesco   1 A1
Landino, V. Cristoforo   2 D1
Lane, Viuzzo delle   2 F1
Lastri, V. Marco   1 A1
Laura, V.   2 E4
Lavagnini, V.le Spartaco   1 C3
Lavatoi, V. dei   6 F4
Leone, V. del   3 A4
Leone X, V.   1 C1
Leoni, V. dei   4 D1 (6 E4)
Leopardi, V. Giacomo   2 F4
Levi, V. Alessandro   2 E1
Libertà, P. della   2 E3
Limbo, P. del   5 C4
Locatelli, V. Antonio   1 A2
Lorenzoni, V. Giovanni   1 B1
Lungo il Mugnone, V.   2 F1
Lungo le Mura di Santa
  Rosa, V.   3 A2
Lupi, V. Bonifacio   2 D3
Lupo, V.   4 E4

M

Macci, V. de'   4 E1
Machiavelli, V.le Niccolò   3 A4
Madonna degli Aldobrandini,
  P. di   1 C5 (5 C1)

Madonna della Pace,
V. della 3 B3
Madonna della Tosse,
V. della 2 E2
Maffia, V. 3 B2 (5 A5)
Magalotti, V. de' 6 E4
Magalotti, V.le Lorenzo 3 A5
Magazzini, V. dei 6 E3
Magenta, V. 1 A5
Maggio, V. 3 B2 (5 B5)
Magnoli, Costa d. 3 C2 (6 D5)
Malcontenti, V. dei 4 E1
Malenchini, V. Vincenzo 6 E4
Manetto, Chiasso di 6 D4
Mantellate, V. delle 2 D3
Manzoni, V. Alessandro 2 F5
Maragliano, V. 1 A2
Marcello, V. Benedetto 1 A3
Marsili, V. de' 5 B5
Martelli, V. de' 2 D5 (6 D2)
Martiri del Popolo, V. d. 4 E1
Marucelli, V. Francesco 1 C1
Masaccio, V. 2 F2
Mascagni, V. Paolo 3 A4
Mascherino, V. del 3 B3
Matteotti, V.le Giacomo 2 E3
Mattonaia, V. della 2 F5
Mayer, V. Enrico 1 B1
Mazzetta, V. 3 B2 (5 B5)
Medici, V. de' 6 D3
Melarancio, V. del 5 C1
Melegnano, V. 1 A5
Mentana, P. 4 D1 (6 E4)
Mercato Centrale, P. del 1 C4
Metastasio, V. Pietro 3 A3
Mezzo, V. di 2 E5
Michelangelo, P.le 4 F3
Michelangelo, V.le 4 F3
Micheli, V. Pier Antonio 2 D3
Michelozzi, V. de' 5 B5
Milanesi, V. Gaetano 1 B2
Mille, V.le dei 2 F2
Milton, V.le Giovanni 1 C2
Minima, V. 3 A2
Minzoni, V.le 2 E2
Modena, V. Gustavo 2 E3
Monachi, V. Ser Ventura 4 F2
Monaco, V. Guido 1 A3
Monalda, V. 5 C2
Montanara, V. 2 F3
Montanelli, V. Giuseppe 1 C1
Monte alle Croci, V. del 4 E3
Montebello, V. 1 A5 (5 A2)
Montelungo, P.le 1 B3
Monti, V. Vincenzo 3 A3
Mori, V. de' 3 A2
Moro, V. del 5 B2
Mosca, V. della 6 E4
Mozzi, P. de' 4 D2 (6 E5)
Muratori, P. 1 B2

N
Nardi, V. Iacopo 2 F4
Nazionale, V. 1C4
Neri, V. de' 4 D1 (6 E4)
Neri, V. Pompeo 1 B1
Nerli, P. de' 3 A1
Niccolini, V. 2 F5
Nievo, V. Ippolito 1 C2
Ninna, V. della 4 D1 (6 D4)
Nove Febbraio, V. 2 D2
Nuova de' Caccini, V. 2 E5

O
Oche, V. dell' 2 D5 (6 D2)
Ognissanti, Borgo 1 A5 (5 A2)
Ognissanti, P. d' 1 B5 (5 A2)
Olio, P. dell' 6 D2
Oriani, V. Alfredo 1 C1
Oriuolo, V. dell' 2 D5 (6 E2)
Orti Oricellari,
V. degli 1 A5 (5 A1)
Orto, V. dell' 3 A1
Ortone, V. dell' 4 F1
Osteria del Guanto, V. 6 E4
Ottaviani, P. degli 1 B5 (5 B2)

P
Pagano, V. Mario 2 F1
Paganini, V. 1 C1
Palazzuolo, V. 1 A5 (5 A1)
Palchetti, V. dei 5 B2
Palestro, V. 1 A5
Pallone, V. del 2 F2
Palmieri, V. 4 E1 (6 F3)
Pandolfini, V. de' 4 D1 (6 E3)
Panicale, V. 1 C4
Panzani, V. 1 C5 (5 C1)

Paoletti, V. Ferdinando 1 C1
Paolieri, V. Ferdinando 4 F1
Parioncino, V. 5 B3
Parione, V. 3 B1 (5 B3)
Parlascio, V. del 6 E4
Pascoli, V. Giovanni 2 E2
Pazzi, P. de' 6 E3
Pecori, V. de' 1 C5 (5 C2)
Pecori Giraldi, Lung. 4 F2
Pellegrino, V. del 2 D3
Pellicceria 6 D3
Pellico, V. Silvio 2 F5
Pepe, V. Guglielmo 2 F2
Pepi, V. de' 2 E5 (6 E4)
Pergola, V. della 2 E5 (6 F2)
Pergola, Vic. della 2 E5 (6 F2)
Peri, V. Iacopo 1 B3
Peruzzi, P. de' 4 D1 (6 E4)
Pesce, V. del 3 C1 (6 D4)
Pescioni, V. de' 1 C5 (5 C2)
Petrarca, V.le Francesco 3 A2
Piaggione, V. del 3 A1
Pian dei Giullari, V. del 3 C5
Piattellina, P. 3 A1
Piave, P. 4 F2
Pico della Mirandola, V. 2 F3
Pietrapiana, V. 4 E1
Pietro Leopoldo, P. 1 B1
Pilastri, V. de' 2 E5
Pindemonte, V. Ippolito 3 A3
Pinti, Borgo 2 E5 (6 F2)
Pinzochere, V. delle 4 E1
Pitti, P. de' 3 B2 (5 B5)
Pitti, Sdrucciolo d. 3 B2 (5 B5)
Poerio, V. Fratelli 2 F1
Poggi, P. Giuseppe 4 E2
Poggi, V. Enrico 1 C3
Poggi, V.le Giuseppe 4 E2
Poggio Imperiale, V.le d. 3 A4
Poliziano, V. Agnolo 2 D2
Ponte alla Carraia 3 B1 (5 B3)
Ponte all'Asse, V. del 1 A2
Ponte alle Grazie 4 D2 (6 E5)
Ponte alle Mosse, V. del 1 A4
Ponte alle Riffe, V. del 2 F1
Ponte Amerigo Vespucci 1 A5
Ponte Rosso, V. del 2 E2
Ponte San Niccolò 4 F2
Ponte Santa Trinità 3 C1 (5C4)
Ponte Vecchio 3 C1 (5 C4)
Por Santa Maria, V. 6 D4
Porcellana, V. del 1 B5 (5 A2)
Porta al Prato, P.le della 1 A4
Porta Romana, P.le della 3 A3
Porta Rossa, V. 3 C1 (5 C3)
Porte Nuove, V. delle 1 A3
Portinari, V. Folco 6 E2
Pratello, V. del 1 C4
Presto, V. del 6 E3
Presto di San Martino,
V. del 3 B2 (5 B4)
Preti, V. dei 3 B2 (5 A5)
Proconsolo, V. d. 2 D5 (6 E2)
Pucci, V. de' 2 D5 (6 D1)
Puccinotti, V. Francesco 1 C2
Purgatorio, V. del 3 C1 (5 B3)

R
Ramaglianti, V. de' 5 C4
Redi, V.le Francesco 1 A2
Renai, V. dei 4 D2 (6 E5)
Repubblica, P. d. 1 C5 (6 D3)
Ricasoli, Chiasso 5 C3
Ricasoli, V. 2 D5 (6 E1)
Richa, V. Giuseppe 1 B2
Ridolfi, V. Cosimo 1 C3
Righini, V. Guglielmo 3 C5
Risorgimento, V. del 2 D2
Roma, V. 1 C5 (6 D2)
Romana, V. 3 A3
Romitino, V. del 2 D1
Romito, V. del 1 B2
Ronco, V. del 3 B3
Rondinelli, V. de' 5 C2
Rosa, V. della 6 F3
Rosina, V. 1 C4
Rosselli, V.le Fratelli 1 A4
Rossi, P. de' 5 C5
Rossini, V. Gioacchino 2 D2
Rucellai, P. de' 5 B3
Rucellai, V. Bernardo 1 A4
Ruffini, V. Fratelli 2 D2
Ruote, V. delle 2 D3
Rustici, V. de' 6 E4

S
Sacchetti, V. Franco 2 F2
Saltarelli, P. de' 6 D4
Salvagnoli, V. Vincenzo 1 C3

Salvemini, P. 2 E5 (4 E1)
Salvestrina, V. 2 D3
Salvini, V. Anton Maria 2 F1
Sant'Agostino, V. 3 B1 (5 A4)
Sant'Ambrogio, P. di 2 E5
Sant'Anna, V. 2 D3
Santissima Annunziata,
P. della 2 D4
Sant'Antonino, V. 1 C5 (5 C1)
Santi Apostoli, Borgo 5 C3
Santa Caterina
d'Alessandria, P. di 2 D3
Santa Caterina
d'Alessandria, V. di 2 D3
Santa Caterina da Siena,
V. di 1B5 (5 A1)
Santa Cecilia, P.etta di 6 D3
San Cristofano, V. 4 E1
Santa Croce,
Borgo 4 D1 (6 F4)
Santa Croce, P. di 4 E1 (6 F4)
Sant'Egidio, V. 6 F2
Sant'Elisabetta, V. 6 D2
San Felice, P. di 3 B2 (5 B5)
Santa Felicità, P.d 3 C1 (5 C4)
Santa Firenze, P. di 4 D1 (6 E3)
San Francesco di
Paola, V. di 3 A2
San Frediano,
Borgo 3 A1 (5 A3)
San Gallo, V. 2D4
San Giorgio,
Costa di 3 C2 (6 D5)
San Giovanni,
P. di 1 C5 (6 D2)
San Giovanni, V. 3 A1
San Giuseppe, V. di 4 E1
Sant'Ilario a Colombaia,
V. di 3 A4
San Jacopino, P. di 1 A2
San Jacopino, V. 1 A2
San Jacopo,
Borgo 3 C1 (5 C4)
San Leonardo, V. di 3 C5
San Lorenzo, Borgo 6 D2
San Lorenzo, P. d. 1 C5 (6 D1)
Santa Lucia, V. 1 A5
San Marco, P. di 2 D4
Santa Margherita, V. (6 E3)
Santa Maria, V. 3 B2 (5 A5)
Santa Maria Maggiore,
P. di 5 C2
Santa Maria Novella,
P. di 1 B5 (5 B2)
Santa Maria Nuova,
Ospedale di 2 D5 (6 F2)
Santa Maria Nuova, P. di 6 F2
Santa Maria Soprarno,
P. di 3 C2 (6 D4)
San Michele Visdomini,
P. di 6 E1
San Miniato al Monte,
V. di 4 F3
Santa Monaca, V. 3 B1 (5 A4)
San Niccolò, Pescaia di 4 F2
San Niccolò, P.te 4 F2
San Niccolò, V. di 4 D2
Sant'Onofrio, V. 3 A1
San Paolino, P. di 1 B5 (5 B2)
San Paolino, V. di 5 B2
San Pier Maggiore, V. di 6 F3
San Remigio, P. d. 4 D1 (6 E4)
Santa Reparata, V. 2 D4
Santa Rosa, Lungarno di 1 A5
Santa Rosa,
Pescaia di 1 B5 (5 A3)
San Salvatore al Monte,
V. di 4 F3
Santo Spirito, P. di 3 B2 (5 A5)
Santo Spirito, V. di 3 B1 (5 A4)
Santa Trinità, P. d. 3 C1 (5 C3)
Santa Trinità,
P.te 3 C1 (5 C4)
San Zanobi, V. 1 C4
Sapiti, V. de' 5 C4
Saponaio, V. del 6 E4
Sassetti, V. de' 5 C3
Sauro, P. Nazario 3 B1 (5 A3)
Scala, V. della 1 A4 (5 A1)
Scarlatti, V. Alessandro 1 A3
Scarpuccia, Costa 4 D2 (6 D5)
Seggiole, V. delle 4 D1 (6 F3)
Senese, V. 3 A5
Sercambi, V. Giovanni 2 F1
Serragli, V. de' 3 A3 (5 A5)
Serristori, Lung. 4 E2 (6 E5)
Serumido, V. 3 A4
Servi, V. dei 2 D5 (6 E2)
Settembrini, V. Luigi 2 F1

Sguazza, V. 5 B5
Sighele, V. Scipio 1 A1
Signoria, P. della 4 D1 (6 D3)
Slataper, V. Scipio 1 A1
Soderini, Lung. 1 A5 (5 A3)
Sole, V. del 1 C5 (5 B2)
Solferino, V. 1 A4
Spada, V. della 5 B2
Spadolini, V. Guido 1 B3
Spano, V. Pippo 2 E2
Spaventa, V. Silvio 2 E2
Speziali, V. degli 6 D3
Spontini, V. 1 A2
Sprone, V. dello 3 C1 (5 B4)
Statuto, V. dello 1 C2
Stazione, P. della 1 B5 (5 B1)
Stella, Borgo d. 3 B1 (5 A4)
Strozzi, P. degli 3 C1 (5 C3)
Strozzi, V. degli 1 C5 (5 C3)
Strozzi, V.le Filippo 1 B3
Studio, V. dello 6 E2
Stufa, V. della 1 C5 (6 D1)
Susini, V. Antonio 4 E5

T
Tacca, V. Pietro 4 F5
Taddea, V. 1 C4
Targioni Tozzetti, V. 1 A2
Tasso, P. Torquato 3 A1
Tavolini, V. dei 4 D1 (6 D3)
Teatina, V. 1 C5 (5 C2)
Tegolaio, Borgo 3 B2 (5 A5)
Terme, V. delle 3 C1 (5 C3)
Tessitori, V. dei 3 A1
Thouar, V. Pietro 4 F1
Tintori, Corso d. 4 D2 (6 F4)
Tintori, Volta dei 6 F5
Tiratoio, P. del 3 A1
Tiratoio, V. del 3 A1
Tornabuoni, V. d 1 C5 (5 C2)
Torre del Gallo, V. della 4 D5
Torricelli, V.le
Evangelistica 3 B5
Torrigiani, Lung. 4 D2 (6 D5)
Torta, V. 4 D1 (6 F3)
Toscanella, V. 3 C2 (5 C4)
Toscanelli, V. Paolo 2 E2
Tosinghi, V. de' 6 D2
Trebbio, V. del 5 C2
Trento, V. 2 D1
Trieste, V. 2 D1
Tripoli, V. 4 E2

U
Uffizi, P.le degli 6 D4
Ulivo, V. dell' 4 E1
Unganelli, P. degli 4 D4
Unità Italiana,
P. dell' 1 C5 (5 C1)

V
Vagellai, V. dei 4 D1 (6 E4)
Valfonda, V. 1 B4
Valori, V. Francesco 2 E3
Vanini, V. Giulio Cesare 2 D2
Vannucci, V. Atto 1 B1
Varchi, V. Benedetto 2 F5
Vasari, P. Giorgio 2 F3
Vecchietti, V. de' 1 C5 (5 C2)
Vecchio, P.te 3 C1 (5 C4)
Velluti, V. de' 3 B2 (5 B4)
Vellutini, V. de' 5 B4
Venezia, V. 2 E3
Ventiquattro Maggio, V. 1 B2
Verdi, V. 4 E1 (6 F3)
Verzaia, P. di 3 A1
Vespucci, Lung.
Amerigo 1 A5 (5 A2)
Vespucci, P.te Amerigo 1 A5
Vieusseux, P. Giampietro 1 B1
Vigna Nuova, V.
della 3 B1 (5 B3)
Vigna Vecchia,
V. della 4 D1 (6 E3)
Villani, V. 3 A2
Vinegia, V. 6 E4
Vittoria, P. della 2 D2
Vittorio Emanuele II, V. 1 C1
Viviani, V. Vincenzo 3 C5
Volsanminiato, V. 4 D5
Volta, V.le Alessandro 2 F2

XZ
Ximenes, V. Leonardo 3 A5
Zannetti, V. Ferdinando 6 D1
Zara, V. 2 D3
Zecca Vecchia, Lung. d. 4 E2
Zobi, V. Antonio 1 B1
Zoli, Largo Adone 2 E2

Map references in parentheses refer to the larger scale map.

TUSCANY AREA BY AREA

TUSCANY AT A GLANCE 150–151
WESTERN TUSCANY 152–167
NORTHERN TUSCANY 168–189
EASTERN TUSCANY 190–205
CENTRAL TUSCANY 206–229
SOUTHERN TUSCANY 230–241

Tuscany at a Glance

Tuscany is rich in culture and landscape. Out of Florence, most visitors' first port of call is Pisa, in Western Tuscany, with its Leaning Tower. Northern Tuscany has mountains and beaches, and Eastern Tuscany the lush forests of the Mugello. Siena and San Gimignano in Central Tuscany draw their own visitors, while Southern Tuscany with its sparse vegetation and unspoiled beaches is more off the beaten track.

Sights in Tuscany are grouped within their own sections in this book, corresponding with the colour-coded map below.

NORTHERN TUSCANY

Lu

Pisa

NORTHERN TUSCANY
Pages 168–189

WESTERN TUSCANY
Pages 152–167

SOUTHERN TUSCANY
Pages 230–241

| 0 kilometres | 20 |
| 0 miles | 20 |

EASTERN TUSCANY
Pages 190–205

FLORENCE

EASTERN TUSCANY

Chianti

San Gimignano

CENTRAL TUSCANY

Arezzo

Siena

Montepulciano

SOUTHERN TUSCANY

The Maremma

CENTRAL TUSCANY
Pages 206–229

WESTERN TUSCANY

uscany's hard-working economic engine, this area is characterized by its factories and ports, particularly Livorno. There are also some extraordinary sights, most famously the Leaning Tower of Pisa. To the south, the windswept ancient Etruscan town of Volterra, standing high on a barren plateau, has some of the finest museums and medieval architecture in Italy.

From the 11th to the 13th centuries, when at the height of its powers, Pisa dominated the Western Mediterranean. Its strong navy opened up extensive trading links with North Africa, and brought to Italy the benefits of Arabic scientific and artistic achievement.

These new ideas had a profound effect on 12th- and 13th-century architects working in western Tuscany. Many of the era's splendid buildings, for instance Pisa's Duomo, Baptistry and Campanile, are decorated with complex geometric patterns made from beautiful inlaid marble, alternating with bizarre arabesques.

During the 16th century the Arno estuary began to silt up, ending Pisan supremacy. In 1571, work began to establish Livorno as the region's main port. This proved so successful that it remains Italy's second busiest port. Pisa, meanwhile, has become the gateway to Tuscany following the extensive development of Galileo Galilei airport. The Arno valley is mainly an industrial area, with huge factories producing glass, furniture, motorcycles, leather and textiles. Even so, there are some rewarding sights lurking within the urban sprawl, like the Romanesque church of San Piero a Grado or the entertaining museum in Vinci, which contains models of many of Leonardo da Vinci's brilliant inventions.

South of the Arno valley, the landscape is pleasant but unremarkable, consisting of rolling hills and expanses of agricultural land. But the imposing ancient town of Volterra, with its unmatched collection of Etruscan artifacts, demands a visit.

Landscape of rolling hills near Volterra

◁ **The Leaning Tower, rising above the terracotta roofs of Pisa**

Exploring Western Tuscany

Pisa, with its world-famous leaning tower, and Volterra, with a wealth of ancient Etruscan remains, are the highlights of the region. There is, however, much more to see, especially in the gentle hilly countryside that rises on either side of the Arno valley. It was here that Renaissance architects pioneered new styles of villa building; their work can be admired at Poggio a Caiano and Artimino. San Miniato is gloriously sited on a hilltop commanding extensive views; the museum in Vinci, on the other side of the valley, celebrates the inventive genius of Leonardo da Vinci.

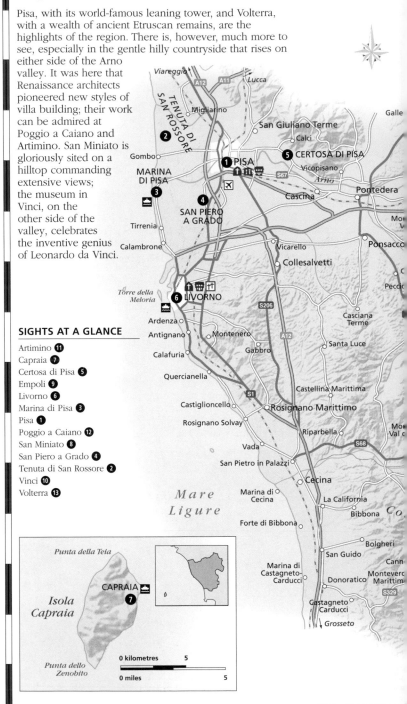

SIGHTS AT A GLANCE

Artimino **⑪**
Capraia **⑦**
Certosa di Pisa **⑤**
Empoli **⑨**
Livorno **⑥**
Marina di Pisa **③**
Pisa **①**
Poggio a Caiano **⑫**
San Miniato **⑧**
San Piero a Grado **④**
Tenuta di San Rossore **②**
Vinci **⑩**
Volterra **⑬**

0 kilometres   5
0 miles   5

Venezia Nuova in Livorno, with its canals and waterways

GETTING AROUND

Western Tuscany has a number of busy roads. A new express route, the Fi-Pi-Li, links Pisa with Florence, but travellers may find the old S67 more convenient for reaching the sights lining the Arno valley towards Florence. The S1 coastal road skirts Livorno on its way to Rome.

The region is well served by buses and trains. A regular rail service runs between Florence and Pisa, stopping at the major Arno valley towns.

It can be difficult to reach Volterra, as there is no train service, but several buses depart each day from Florence, Pisa and Livorno.

KEY

▬▬	Motorway
▬▬	Major road
▬	Secondary road
═	Minor road
▬▪▬	Main railway
—	Minor railway
△	Summit

The S68 highway to Volterra

Pisa ●

Inlaid marble, Duomo façade

From the 11th to the 13th centuries, Pisa's powerful navy ensured the city's dominance in the Western Mediterranean. Trading links with Spain and North Africa led to a scientific and cultural revolution *(see p46)* reflected in the splendid buildings of the era: the Duomo, Baptistry and Campanile. Pisa's decline was assured when the Arno began to silt up. Salt marsh, partly a nature reserve, now divides the city from the sea.

Campo dei Miracoli

🏛 Campo dei Miracoli
See pp158–9.

🏛 Museo delle Sinopie
Piazza del Duomo. **Open** Apr–Sep: 8am–7:30pm daily; Mar & Oct: 9am–5:30pm daily; Nov–Feb: 9am–4:30pm daily. **Adm charge**.

This fascinating museum displays sketches from the fresco cycle that once covered the walls of Campo Santo cemetery *(see pp158–9)*. The frescoes disintegrated when the cemetery was bombed in 1944, but the underlying sketches survived. They were removed from the walls for conservation before being rehoused in the museum. There are also displays showing how fresco artists went about their work.

🏛 Museo dell'Opera del Duomo
Piazza Duomo. **Tel** 050 56 05 47. **Open** Apr–Sep: 8am–7:20pm daily; Mar & Oct: 9am–5:20pm daily; Nov–Feb: 9am–4:20pm daily.

Adm charge. 🚻

Housed in the cathedral's 13th-century former Chapter House, the museum was opened in 1986. All the exhibits were formerly in the Duomo and Baptistry. Modern display methods ensure that they are excellently

presented. Exhibits such as the intricately inlaid marble arabesque panels and fine Corinthian capitals reveal the twin influences of Rome and Islam on Pisan architects in the 12th and 13th centuries. Be sure to see the imposing 10th-century hippogriff (half horse, half gryphon); this statue, cast in bronze by Islamic craftsmen, was looted by Pisan adventurers during the wars against the Saracens.

The museum also contains 13th-century statues and sculptures by Nicola and Giovanni Pisano, including Giovanni's ivory *Virgin and Child* (1300) carved for the Duomo's High Altar. There are paintings from the 15th to 18th centuries, a fine Roman and Etruscan archaeological collection, and ecclesiastical treasures and vestments dating from the 12th century.

The museum cloister offers a wonderful view of the Leaning Tower *(see p160)*.

🏛 Piazza dei Cavalieri
The Piazza dei Cavalieri stands at the heart of Pisa's student quarter. The huge building on the north side of the square, covered in exuberant black and white *sgraffito* decoration (designs scratched into wet plaster), is the Palazzo dei Cavalieri and houses one of Pisa University's most prestigious colleges: the Scuola Normale Superiore. The site was originally occupied by Pisa's medieval town hall, but Cosimo I ordered its destruction when the city fell under Florentine rule. The council chamber, however, was spared and is now a lecture hall. The present flamboyant building was designed in 1562 by Vasari, as the headquarters of the Cavalieri di San Stefano, an order of knights created by Cosimo in 1561. An equestrian statue of Cosimo by Pietro Francavilla (1596) stands outside. Santo Stefano dei Cavalieri

10th-century bronze hippogriff

Virgin and Child **polyptych (1321) by Simone Martini**

(1565–9), the knights' church, stands next to the Palazzo dei Cavalieri. Also designed by Vasari, it has a splendid gilded and coffered ceiling. The walls are hung with figureheads and battle standards. There is also a splendid organ (look out for notices of recitals).

On the other side of the Palazzo dei Cavalieri is the Palazzo dell'Orologio, incorporating the medieval town jail. The building, which is now housing a library, was the scene of a most shameful and gruesome historical episode. In 1288 Count Ugolino, mayor of Pisa, was accused of treachery and walled up with his sons and grandsons. The entire male side of the Ugolino family was wiped out.

🏛 Museo Nazionale di San Matteo
Piazzetta San Matteo in Soarta.
Tel 050 54 18 65. **Open**
8:30am–7pm daily (to
1pm Sun). **Closed**
1 Jan, 1 May, 15 Aug,
25 Dec. **Adm charge**.
The medieval convent of San Matteo, with its elegant Gothic façade, is located alongside the Arno. Many exhibits in the museum inside are poorly labelled and the rooms leading off the cloister are unnumbered. Nevertheless, the museum presents a unique opportunity to examine the complete sweep of Pisan and

Grand Duke Cosimo I

Florentine art from the 12th to the 17th centuries.

Most of the earliest works portray the Virgin and Child. These include Simone Martini's fine polyptych (1321) and a 14th-century statue, the *Madonna del Latte*, attributed to Nino Pisano, another member of the talented family of sculptors. The half-length statue, in gilded marble, shows Christ feeding at his mother's breast. A number of early Renaissance pieces deserve to be sought out, particularly Masaccio's *St Paul* (1426), Gentile da Fabriano's radiant 15th-century *Madonna and Child*, and Donatello's reliquary bust of *San Rossore* (1424–7).

PISA TOWN CENTRE

Campo dei Miracoli ①
Museo Nazionale di San Matteo ⑤
Museo dell'Opera del Duomo ③
Museo delle Sinopie ②
Piazza dei Cavalieri ④
Santa Maria della Spina ⑥
San Paolo a Ripa d'Arno ⑦

0 metres 500
0 yards 500

Key to symbols see back flap

Campo dei Miracoli

Cemetery memorial

Pisa's world famous Leaning Tower is just one of the splendid religious buildings that rise from the emerald-green lawns of the "Field of Miracles". Lying to the northwest of the city centre, it is partnered by the Duomo, begun in 1063, the Baptistry of 1152–1284 and the Campo Santo cemetery begun in 1278. These buildings combine definite Moorish elements, such as inlaid marble in geometric patterns (arabesques), with delicate Romanesque colonnading and spiky Gothic niches and pinnacles.

Campo Santo
The cemetery contains earth from the Holy Land and carved Roman sarcophagi.

The domed Cappella de Pozzo wa added in

The Triumph of Death
These late 14th-century frescoes depict various allegorical scenes such as this of a knight and lady overwhelmed by the stench of an open grave.

★ **Baptistry Pulpit**
Nicola Pisano's great marble pulpit, completed in 1260, is carved with lively scenes from The Life of Christ.

Upper gallery

VISITORS' CHECKLIST

Piazza dei Miracoli. *Tel 050 56 05 47.* 🚌 *3, 11.* **Duomo open** daily; Mar–Oct: 10am–7:30pm (from 1pm Sun; to 5:30pm Mar & Oct); Nov–Feb: 10am–12:45pm, 3–4:45pm. ✝ 8am, 9:30am daily; also 11am, 12:10pm, 6pm Sun (5pm in winter). **Adm charge.** 📷 **Baptistry & Campo Santo open** daily; Nov–Feb: 10am–4:30pm; Mar & Oct: 9am–5:30pm; Apr–Sep: 8am–7:30pm. **Adm charge** (cumulative tickets available). 📷 **Tower open** daily; book admission time in advance. **www**.opapisa.it

★ **Portale di San Ranieri**
Bonanno Pisano's bronze panels for the south transept doors depict The Life of Christ. *Palm trees and Moorish buildings show Arabic influence.*

Frescoes were added to the dome's interior after a fire in 1595.

The Leaning Tower *(see p160)* was completed in 1350, when its seven bells were hung.

Fragments of the 11th-century marble floor survive beneath the dome.

A frieze shows that work began in 1173.

Gleaming white Carrara marble decorates the walls.

Cathedral Pulpit
The carved supports for Giovanni Pisano's pulpit (1302–11) symbolize the Arts and Virtues.

This 12th-century wall tomb is for Buschetto, the Duomo's original architect.

★ **Duomo Façade**
Coloured sandstone, glass and majolica plates decorate the lombard style 12th-century façade. Its patterned surface includes knots, flowers and animals in inlaid marble.

STAR FEATURES

★ Portale di San Ranieri

★ Baptistry Pulpit by Nicola Pisano

★ Duomo Façade

The Leaning Tower of Pisa

All the buildings of the Campo dei Miracoli lean because of their shallow foundations and sandy silt subsoil, but none tilts so famously as the Torre Pendente – the Leaning Tower. Begun in 1173, the tower began to tip sideways before the third storey was completed. Even so, construction continued until its completion in 1350. Recent engineering interventions have corrected the tilt by 38 cm (14 in), and the tower was reopened in December 2001.

Belfry
The bell chamber at the top of the tower is smaller in diameter than the other seven storeys. Its addition in 1350 brought the total height to 54.5 m (179 ft).

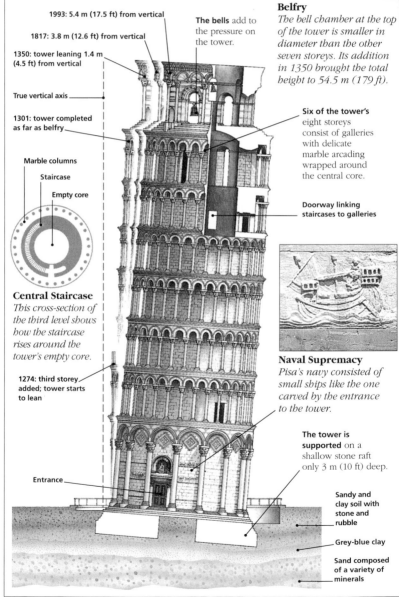

1993: 5.4 m (17.5 ft) from vertical

1817: 3.8 m (12.6 ft) from vertical

1350: tower leaning 1.4 m (4.5 ft) from vertical

The bells add to the pressure on the tower.

True vertical axis

1301: tower completed as far as belfry

Marble columns

Staircase

Empty core

Six of the tower's eight storeys consist of galleries with delicate marble arcading wrapped around the central core.

Doorway linking staircases to galleries

Central Staircase
This cross-section of the third level shows how the staircase rises around the tower's empty core.

1274: third storey added; tower starts to lean

Naval Supremacy
Pisa's navy consisted of small ships like the one carved by the entrance to the tower.

The tower is supported on a shallow stone raft only 3 m (10 ft) deep.

Entrance

Sandy and clay soil with stone and rubble

Grey-blue clay

Sand composed of a variety of minerals

Santa Maria della Spina by the river Arno in Pisa

🔒 Santa Maria della Spina

Lungarno Gambacorti. **Tel** 055 321 54 46. **Open** Oct–Mar: 10am–2pm Tue–Sun; Apr, May & Sep: 10am–1.30pm, 2:30– 5pm Tue–Sun (to 7pm Sat & Sun); Jun–Aug: 11am–1.30pm, 2:30–6pm Tue–Fri, 11am–8pm Sat & Sun.

The roofline of Santa Maria della Spina bristles with spiky Gothic pinnacles, miniature spires and niches sheltering statues of apostles and saints. The church was built to house an unusual relic: a thorn from the Crown of Thorns forced on to Christ's head during the cruel mock coronation that preceded His crucifixion.

🔒 San Paolo a Ripa d'Arno

Piazza San Paolo a Ripa d'Arno. **Tel** 050 415 15. **Open** by appt.

Worth visiting for its impressive 12th-century façade, this church was built in the same Pisan-Romanesque style as the Duomo (see pp158–9).

The Romanesque chapel (see p44) at the east end is dedicated to St Agatha. It is built entirely from brick, with a cone-shaped roof; Islamic influence is said to account for its unusual octagonal shape.

Tenuta di San Rossore ②

Road map B2. Pisa. **Tel** 050 52 55 00 (050 53 01 01 for tours). **Open** 8am–5:30pm Sat, Sun & public hols (Apr–Sep: to 7:30); guided tours: 8am–2pm Mon–Fri. English (by appt).

North of the Arno, this area is part of the Parco Naturale di San Rossore, a nature reserve stretching to the north of Tuscany. Wild boar and deer roam among the pine forests and salt marsh. Gombo, to the west, is where the drowned body of the poet Shelley was found in 1822.

Marina di Pisa ③

Road map B2. 3,000. Sun in summer, Tue in winter.

Moorings at Marina di Pisa, at the mouth of the river Arno

Much of the salt marsh to the west of Pisa has now been drained and reclaimed, and a large US Air Force base (Camp Darby) now occupies the area south of the Arno. There are extensive sandy beaches on the Arno estuary, and here lies Marina di Pisa, a seaside resort with some pretty Art Nouveau houses, backed by pine woods.

On the drive there you may catch sight of grazing camels – these are the descendants of a large herd established under Duke Ferdinand II in the mid-17th century. The village of Tirrenia, with its sandy beaches, lies 5 km (3 miles) south of Marina di Pisa.

San Piero a Grado ④

Road map B2. **Tel** 050 96 00 65. **Open** 8am–7pm daily.

San Piero is a handsome 11th-century church built on the spot where St Peter is believed to have first set foot on Italian soil in AD 42. According to the New Testament Book of Acts, he arrived at a set of landing steps by the Arno. Archaeologists have discovered the foundations of Roman port buildings underneath the present church, which stands at the point where the Arno once flowed into the sea. Silt deposits mean that the church now stands some 6 km (3.5 miles) from the shore.

An unusual feature of the church is the lack of any façade. Instead, it has semicircular apses at both the east and west ends. The exterior is decorated with blind arcading and with Moorish-style ceramic plates set into the masonry around the eaves – an unusual feature that it shares with the Duomo in San Miniato (see p163).

The present church was built during the reign of Pope John XVIII (1004–9) and the varied capitals of the nave come from ancient Roman buildings. High up on the nave walls there are frescoes by Deodato Orlandi, painted around 1300, on The Life of St Peter. These are interspersed with portraits of all the popes from St Peter to John XVII.

Interior of San Piero a Grado, with frescoes by Deodati Orlandi

The 18th-century Certosa di Pisa

Certosa di Pisa ❺

Road map C2 (località Calci). ⬛ *from Pisa.* **Tel** *050 93 84 30.* **Open** *8:30am– 6:30pm Tue–Sat, 9am–noon Sun (adm half past the hour; last adm: 1 hour before closing).* **Adm charge**.

This Carthusian monastery was founded in 1366 and rebuilt during the 18th century. The splendid church is lavishly decorated, and some buildings form the University of Pisa's **Museo di Storia Naturale.** Exhibits include 16th-century anatomical wax models.

Nearby is the **Pieve di Calci,** a fine 11th-century Roman-esque church. The unfinished campanile is alongside.

🏛 Museo di Storia Naturale

Certosa di Pisa. **Tel** *050 221 29 70.* **Open** *mid-Sep–mid-Jun: 9am–6pm Tue–Sat, 10am–7pm Sun; mid-Jun–mid-Sep: 10am–7pm Tue–Fri, 4pm–midnight Sat, Sun. Closed public hols, 1–10 Jun.* **Adm charge.** ♿ *partial.*

🔓 Pieve di Calci

Piazza della Propositura, Calci. **Open** *daily.* ♿

Livorno ❻

Road map B3. 🏛 *168,370.* 🚊 ⬛ ⛴ ℹ *Piazza Cavour 6. (0586 20 46 11).* ⛴

The fact that Livorno is now a bustling city, Italy's second busiest container port, is thanks to Cosimo I. In 1571 he chose Livorno, then a tiny fishing village, as the site for Tuscany's new port after Pisa's harbour silted up. From 1607–21 the English marine engineer Sir Robert Dudley built the great sea wall that protects the harbour.

In 1608 Livorno was declared a free port, open to all traders, regardless of religion or race. Jews, Protestants, Arabs, Turks and others who came here, fleeing wars or religious persecution, contributed greatly to the city's success.

🏛 Piazza Grande

When the architect Buon-talenti planned the new city of Livorno in 1576, he envisaged the huge Piazza Grande at the heart of a network of wide avenues.

The square's original appear-ance has, however, been lost. This is partly due to contro-versial post-war rebuilding, which cut the square into two halves: the present Piazza Grande, to the south, and the Largo Municipio, to the north.

🔓 Duomo

Piazza Grande. **Open** *daily.*
A prominent victim of Livorno's wartime bombing was the late 16th-century cathedral by Pieroni and Cantagallina. It was rebuilt in 1959, retaining the original entrance portico, with its Doric arcades.

The original building was designed by Inigo Jones, who served his apprenticeship under the architect Buontalenti. Jones later used an almost identical design for the arcades of his Covent Garden piazza in London.

🏛 Piazza Micheli

The piazza, with its views of the 16th-century Fortezza Vecchia, contains Livorno's best-known monument: the *Monumento dei Quattro Mori.*

Bandini's bronze figure of Duke Ferdinand I dates to 1595; but Pietro Tacca's four Moorish slaves, also cast in bronze, were not added until 1626. Naked and manacled, the dejected slaves are a stark reminder that Livorno once had a thriving slave market.

Venezia Nuova canals

🏛 Venezia Nuova

Originally laid out in the middle of the 17th century, this area, which includes the 18th-century octagonal church of Santa Caterina, is spread between a handful of canals, reminiscent of Venetian waterways. Although it only covers a few blocks, Venezia Nuova is one of the city's most scenic areas.

Monumento dei Quattro Mori **by Bandini and Tacca in Piazza Micheli**

Fortezza Vecchia, Livorno harbour

The Fortezza Nuova, surrounded by a moat, dates to 1590. Its interior has been converted to a public park.

🏛 Piazza XX Settembre

Lying south of the Fortezza Nuova, the piazza is renowned for its bustling "American Market". The market's name derives from the large amounts of American army surplus sold here after World War II.

A US army base, Camp Darby, still operates to the north of Livorno.

🏛 English Cemetery

Via Giuseppe Verdi 63. **Tel** 0586 89 73 24. **Open** by appt. 🚻
The 19th-century memorials to British and American emigrés, long untended, are considerably overgrown. Among them is the grave of Tobias Smollett (1721–71), the misanthropic Scottish novelist. He claimed to live in Italy for health reasons, and, predictably, constantly complained about the place.

🏛 Museo Civico

Via San Jacopo Acquaviva. **Tel** 0586 80 80 01. **Open** 10am–1pm, 4–/pm Tue–Sun. **Closed** Easter, 1 May. **Adm charge**.
The Museo Civico houses temporary exhibitions and several paintings by Giovanni Fattori (1825–1908), an artist of the *Macchiaioli* School *(see p123)*, whose work was similar to that of the French Impressionists.

Capraia ❼

🚢 from Livorno. 🏃 300. 🛈 Pro Loco, The Port (0586 90 51 38).

This tiny mountainous island appeals mainly to keen bird watchers and divers who go to explore the rocky coastline.

Nearby Gorgona, a penal colony, can also be visited by booking in advance. Contact the tourist information office in Livorno.

San Miniato ❽

Road map C2. 🏃 3,852. 🚌
🛈 Piazza del Popolo 3 (0571 427 45). 🛒 Tue, 1st & 2nd Sun of each month.

San Miniato suffers from its proximity to the vast industrial conurbation of the Arno valley. Straddling the crest of one of the region's highest hills, it manages, however, to remain somewhat aloof. There are a number of fine historic buildings, including the 13th-century Rocca (castle) built for Frederick II (1194–1250), the German Holy Roman Emperor.

The town played a major part in Frederick's Italian military campaigns. He dreamed of rebuilding the ancient Roman empire that lay divided between papal and Imperial authority. To this end he conquered large areas of Italy. His battles fuelled fierce local struggles between the imperial Ghibellines and the papal Guelphs *(see p46)*.

Local people still refer to the town as San Miniato *al Tedesco* (of the German).

Façade of Duomo in San Miniato

🛈 Duomo

Piazza del Duomo. **Open** daily.
Only the red-brick façade survives from the original 12th-century building. The majolica plates set within it show evidence of trade with Spain or North Africa. They seem to represent the North Star and the constellations of Ursus Major and Minor: key reference points for early navigators.

The campanile, the Torre di Matilda, is named in honour of the great Countess Matilda *(see p45)*, who was born in Livorno in 1046.

🏛 Piazza della Repubblica

The Piazza della Repubblica (also known as the Piazza del Seminario) occupies a long, narrow space dominated by the decorated façade of the 17th-century seminary. The frescoes and *sgraffito* (scenes scratched out of plaster) on the façade show allegories of the Virtues painted below quotations from key religious texts, for instance the writings of Pope Gregory (540–604).

To the right of the seminary are several well-restored 15th-century shops. Buildings like these can be seen in many medieval frescoes, such as Lorenzetti's 14th-century *Good Government (see p46)*.

Piazza Farinata degli Uberti in Empoli

Empoli ⑨

Road map C2. 🏛 *43,500.* 🚆
🚌 ℹ *Via Giuseppe del Papa 98 (0571 76 115).* 🔄 *Thu.*

An industrial town, specializing in textiles and glass manufacturing, Empoli is worth visiting for the excellent Museo della Collegiata.

🏛 Piazza Farinata degli Uberti

Empoli's arcaded main square is surrounded by a number of 12th-century buildings, notably the church of Sant'Andrea, with its black and white marble façade. The large fountain dating to 1827, with water nymphs and lions, is by Luigi Pampaloni.

🏛 Museo della Collegiata di Sant'Andrea

Piazza della Propositura 3. **Tel** *0571 762 84.* **Open** *9am–noon, 4–7pm Tue–Sun.* **Closed** *public & relig hols.* **Adm charge.**
The museum contains a collection of Renaissance paintings and sculpture. Of particular interest are Masolino's *Pietà* fresco (1425) and a marble font by Rossellino, dating to 1447.

⛪ Santo Stefano

Via dei Neri. **Open** *for concerts & exhibitions.*
Visitors to Santo Stefano can see fresco fragments by Masolino, dating to 1424, and two 15th-century Annunciation statues by Rossellino. Bicci di Lorenzo's painting, *St Nicholas*

Façade of the seminary in Piazza della Repubblica

🏛 Museo Diocesano d'Arte Sacra

Piazza Duomo. **Tel** *0571 41 82 71.* **Open** *10am–1pm, 3–7pm Tue–Sun (Nov–Mar: to 6pm).* **Adm charge.**
Located next to the Duomo, the Museo Diocesano d'Arte Sacra contains a number of important 15th-century works gathered from local churches. These include a *Crucifixion* by Filippo Lippi and a terracotta bust of Christ attributed to Verrocchio.

🏰 Rocca

Open *10am–7pm Tue–Sun.*
A staircase behind the Museo Diocesano leads towards Frederick II's ruined 13th-century Rocca (castle). While the remains are run down, the site offers extraordinary views along the entire Arno valley, from Fiesole to Pisa.

Pietà by Masolino in Museo della Collegiata

of Tolentino (1445), in the second chapel on the north side, shows Empoli as it was in the mid-15th century.

Vinci ⑩

Road map C2. 🏛 *2,000.*
🚌 🔄 *Wed.*

This hilltop town is the birthplace of Leonardo da Vinci (1452–1519). To celebrate his extraordinary genius, the 13th-century castle in the centre of the town was restored in 1952 to create the **Museo Leonardiano**. Among the displays are wooden models of Leonardo's machines and inventions, based on the drawings from his notebooks shown alongside. These range from his conception of a car, to an armoured tank and even a machine-gun. A pair of skis, designed for walking on water, show that he could occasionally miss the mark. The museum is best avoided on Sundays, when it can be extremely crowded.

Close to the museum is Santo Stefano church and the font in which Leonardo was baptized. His actual birthplace the **Casa di Leonardo**, is 2 km (1.25 miles) from the town centre at Anchiano. This simple farmhouse is worth visiting if you feel like a pleasant, undemanding walk through superb poppy fields; but don't expect

For hotels and restaurants in this region see pp256–57 and pp273–74

to be overawed by the exhibits. These mostly consist of a few reproduction drawings.

⚏ Museo Leonardiano
Castello dei Conti Guidi. *Tel 0571 560 55.* **Open** *Mar–Oct: 9:30am–7pm daily; Nov–Feb: 9:30am–6pm daily.* **Adm charge**.

⚏ Casa di Leonardo
Anchiano. *Tel 0571 560 55.* **Open** *Mar–Oct: 9:30am–7pm daily; Nov–Feb: 9:30am–6pm daily.*

Model bicycle based on drawings by Leonardo, Museo Leonardiano

Artimino ⓫

Road map C2.

Artimino is a fine example of a *borgo*, a small fortified hamlet. Despite its proximity to the industrial conglomerations of Florence and Prato, the views from this hilltop site are of wooded green hills, with not a factory in sight. The hamlet itself is only remarkable for the unspoiled Romanesque church of San Leonardo. Outside the walls, however, higher up the hill, lies the **Villa di Artimino**, designed by Buontalenti in 1594 for Grand Duke Ferdinando I. It is often referred to as the

"Villa of a Hundred Chimneys", because of the numerous and highly ornate chimney pots crowding the roofline. The building is now used as a conference centre, but the Museo Archeologico Etrusco in the basement, which exhibits Etruscan and Roman artifacts, is open to the public.

Lovers of the work of Pontormo (1494–1557) should set aside time to visit the church of **San Michele** in Carmignano, only 5 km (3 miles) north of Artimino. It contains his great masterpiece, *The Visitation* (1530).

⚏ Museo Leonardiano
Castello dei Conti Guidi. *Tel 0571 560 55.* **Open** *Mar–Oct: 9:30am–7pm daily; Nov–Feb: 9:30am–6pm daily.* **Adm charge**.

⚏ Casa di Leonardo
Anchiano. *Tel 0571 560 55.* **Open** *Mar–Oct: 9:30am–7pm daily; Nov–Feb: 9:30am–6pm daily.*

Poggio a Caiano ⓬

Road map C2. *Tel 055 87 70 12.* **Open** *daily (except 2nd and 3rd Mon of each month).* **Adm charge**.

The Villa di Poggio a Caiano, built by Giuliano da Sangallo for Lorenzo de' Medici (*see p50*) in 1480, was the first Italian villa to be designed in the Renaissance style. Its original severity is

Villa di Artimino

now softened by the graceful, curved staircase (added in 1802–7) leading up to the villa terrace, with its views of the gardens and parkland beyond.

The villa's principal room is the barrel-vaulted *salone*, with its 16th-century frescoes by Andrea del Sarto and Franciabigio. They were commissioned by the future Leo X, the Medici pope, to portray his family as great statesmen in the manner of ancient Roman figures.

The *salone* also contains Pontormo's colourful *Conette* fresco (1521). Surrounding the circular window of the end wall, it portrays the Roman garden deities, Vertumnus and Pomona – a perfect evocation of a Tuscan summer afternoon.

Among the other rooms is the bedchamber of Bianca Cappello, mistress and later wife of Grand Duke Francesco I. The couple died here within a few hours of each other, apparently poisoned. They may, however, simply have succumbed to a lethal viral infection.

Villa di Poggio a Caiano from the set of lunettes by Giusto Utens (*see p71*)

Volterra ⑬

Situated, like many Etruscan cities, on a high plateau, Volterra offers uninterrupted views over the surrounding hills. In many places the ancient Etruscan walls still stand. Volterra's famous Museo Guarnacci contains one of the best collections of Etruscan artifacts in Italy. Many of the exhibits were gathered from the numerous local tombs.

Stucco figure in the Duomo

After its museums and medieval buildings, the city is famous for its craftsmen who carve beautiful white statues from locally mined alabaster.

🏛 Museo Etrusco Guarnacci

Via Don Minzoni 15. *Tel* 0588 863 47. **Open** 9am–7pm daily (2 Nov–15 Mar: to 1:30pm). **Closed** 1 Jan, 25 Dec. **Adm charge** (also allows entry at the Pinacoteca e Museo Civico and the Museo d'Arte Sacra). ♿

The pride of the Guarnacci Museum is its collection of 600 Etruscan funerary urns. Adorned with detailed carving, they offer a unique insight into Etruscan customs and beliefs (see pp42–3).

The museum's two main exhibits are on the first floor. Room 20 contains the terracotta "Married Couple" urn. The elderly couple on the lid are portrayed realistically, with haggard, careworn faces.

Room 22 contains an even more unusual exhibit, the elongated bronze known as the *Ombra della Sera* (Shadow of the Evening). This name was bestowed by the poet Gabriele d'Annunzio, who said the bronze reminded him of the shadow thrown by a human figure in the dying light of the evening sun. It is probably a votive figure dating to the 3rd century BC, but it is difficult to speak of it with any certainty; unusually, it was cast with no clothes or jewellery to indicate rank, status or date. It is only by chance that this remarkable figure survived. Ploughed up by a farmer in 1879, it was used as a fire poker until someone recognized it as a masterpiece of Etruscan art.

Ombra della Sera

Detail from *The Deposition* (1521) by Rosso Fiorentino

🏛 Pinacoteca e Museo Civico

Via dei Sarti 1. *Tel* 0588 875 80. **Open** mid-Mar–Oct: 9am–7pm daily; Nov–mid-Mar: 9am–1:30pm daily. **Closed** 1 Jan, 25 Dec. **Adm charge** (also allows entry at the Museo Etrusco Guarnacci and the Museo d'Arte Sacra).

Volterra's excellent art gallery is situated in the 15th-century Palazzo Minucci-Solaini. The best works are by Florentine artists. In Ghirlandaio's *Christ in Majesty* (1492), Christ hovers above an idealized Tuscan landscape. It was meant for the San Giusto monastery, which was abandoned after a landslip like the one shown in the middle distance and beyond. Luca Signorelli's *Madonna and Child with Saints* (1491) shows his debt to Roman art through the reliefs on the base of the Virgin's throne. His *Annunciation* (1491) is another beautiful composition.

The museum's main exhibit is Rosso Fiorentino's Mannerist work (see p27), *The Deposition* (1521). Attention is focused on the grief-stricken figures in the foreground and the pallid, empty shell of Christ's body, its dead weight symbolizing that His spirit is elsewhere.

🔒 Duomo

Piazza San Giovanni. **Open** daily.

Work on Volterra's cathedral began in the 1200s and continued intermittently over the next two centuries.

To the right of the High Altar stands a Romanesque wood-carving of *The Deposition* (1228). The Altar itself is flanked by graceful marble angels carved by Mino da Fiesole in 1471; they face the same artist's elegant tabernacle, carved with figures of Faith, Hope and Charity.

The nave, remodelled in 1581, has an unusual coffered ceiling with stucco figures of bishops and saints painted in rich blue and gold. The pulpit in the middle of the nave, dates to 1584, but was created using sculptural reliefs from the late 12th and early 13th centuries. The *Last Supper* panel, facing into the nave and thought to be the work of the

View from Volterra over the surrounding landscape

Detail from one of the panels decorating the Duomo pulpit

Pisan artist Guglielmo Pisano, has a number of humorous details including a monster snapping at the heels of Judas. Nearby, in the north aisle, Fra Bartolomeo's *The Annunciation* (1497) hangs above one of the side chapel altars.

More sculptures are housed in the oratory off the north aisle, near the main entrance. The best is a tableau of the Epiphany, preserved behind glass. The remarkably humane painted terracotta figures of the Virgin and Child in the foreground are believed to be by Zaccaria da Volterra (1473–1544), a local sculptor.

🏛 Museo d'Arte Sacra

Via Roma 13. **Tel** *0588 862 90*. **Open** *9am–1pm, 3–6pm daily (Nov–Mar: 9am–1pm only)*. **Closed** *1 Jan, 1 May, 25 Dec*. **Adm charge** *(also allows entry at the Museo Etrusco Guarnacci and the Pinacoteca e Museo Civico)*.

This museum, in the Palazzo Arcivescovile, contains sculpture and architectural fragments from the Duomo and a few local churches. The main exhibit is a 15th-century della Robbia terracotta of St Linus, Volterra's patron saint.

The collection also has a range of church bells, from the 11th to 15th centuries, some church silver and several illuminated manuscripts.

🎭 Teatro Romano

Viale Ferrucci. **Open** *Apr–Oct: 10am–1pm, 2–5pm daily, except when raining*. **Adm charge.**

Situated just outside the city walls, the ancient Roman theatre, dating to the first century BC, is one of the best-preserved in Italy. Enough of the original structure has survived to enable an almost complete reconstruction.

VISITORS' CHECKLIST

Road map *C3.* 🏠 *12,200.* 🚌 *Via Giusto Turazza 2 (0588 861 50).* 🛒 *Sat.* 🎪 *Astiludio (1st Sun in Sep).* **www**.provolterra.it

🏛 Piazza dei Priori

This fine square is dominated by the Palazzo dei Priori, dating to 1208. A sober building, it is said to have been the model for the Palazzo Vecchio in Florence (*see pp78–9*).

The 13th-century Porcellino tower, on the other side of the square, is named after the small pig, now almost worn away, carved at its base.

🏛 Arco Etrusco

One of Volterra's more unusual sights, the Etruscan arch is in fact part Roman. Only the columns and the severely weathered basalt heads, representing Etruscan gods, date to the 6th-century BC original. The features of each head are now barely visible.

Plaque outside the Palazzo dei Priori

VOLTERRA

Arco Etrusco ⑥
Duomo ④
Museo d'Arte Sacra ③
Museo Guarnacci ⑦
Piazza dei Priori ⑤
Pinacoteca e Museo Civico ②
Teatro Romano ①

0 metres 250
0 yards 250

Key to symbols *see back flap*

NORTHERN TUSCANY

O*f all the regions of Tuscany, this one offers something for everyone. The historic towns are rich in art, architecture and music festivals, while many sporting activities can be enjoyed along the coast or in the mountains. The landscape, too, is marked by a vast range of features, from marble quarries to market gardens, and from mountain ranges and nature reserves to beaches.*

The heavily populated Lucchese plain between Florence and Lucca is dominated by industry: the textile factories of Prato produce three out of every four woollen garments exported from Italy.

But in spite of their large suburbs, cities such as Prato, Pistoia and, above all, Lucca have rewarding churches, museums and galleries within their historic city centres.

The land between the cities is fertile and is therefore intensively cultivated. Asparagus and cut flowers are two of the most important crops, and the wholesale flower market at Pescia is one of the biggest in Italy. East of Lucca towards Pescia are garden centres and nurseries where huge quantities of young trees and shrubs are grown in long, neat rows.

North of the Lucchese plain the scenery is very different again. A series of foothills is covered in olive groves which produce some of the finest oil in Italy. Then, the land rises to the wild and mountainous areas of the Garfagnana, the Alpi Apuane (Apuan Alps) and the Lunigiana, with its fortified towns and castles built by the Dukes of Malaspina. Here you will find some of Tuscany's highest peaks, rising to 2,000 m (6,550 ft) or more. Vast areas of the mountains are designated as nature parks and the wild scenery attracts ramblers, trekkers and riders as well as hang-gliding enthusiasts.

Finally, the coastal area, known as the Versilia, includes some of Italy's most elegant and popular beach resorts. It stretches from the famous marble-quarrying town of Carrara in the north down to the area's main town, Viareggio, and to Torre del Lago Puccini, the lakeside home of Giacomo Puccini, where he wrote nearly all his operas.

Lucca's Piazza del Mercato, echoing the shape of the original Roman amphitheatre

◁ The village of Vagli di Sotto on Lago di Vagli in the Parco Naturale delle Alpi Apuane

Exploring Northern Tuscany

The beautiful town of Lucca is a favourite base for
exploring. Northwards, industrial suburbs give way to
the olive groves, chestnut woods and bare mountains of the
Alpi Apuane and the Garfagnana region, a popular area for
outdoor sports, from trekking and canoeing to skiing. Castles
dot the rugged Lunigiana,
while beaches line the
Versilia. Due east are
large towns with
historic centres:
Pistoia and Prato.

Orrido di Botri near Bagni di

KEY

══	Motorway
───	Secondary road
⋯⋯	Minor road
───	Scenic route
───	Main railway
───	Minor railway
══	Regional border
△	Summit

Parma

Passo della Cisa

Montelungo

Pontremoli

Zeri

Mulazzo

Villafranca in Lunigiana

Bagnone

Tavernelle

Passo del Cerreto

Fivizzano

Sillano

Orecchie

Genoa

Aulla

Piazza al Serchio

Equi Terme

Castiglione di Garfagnana

Fosdinovo

Monte Pisanino 1945m

Lago di Vagli

PARCO NATURALE DELLE ALPI APUANE

Sarzana

La Spezia

CARRARA

CASTELNUO DI GARFAGNA

Massa-Carrara

Galli

Bocca di Magra

Massa

Marina di Carrara

Stazzema

Fo

Marina di Massa

Seravezza

Forte dei Marmi

Pietrasanta

Cinquale

Camaiore

Marina di Pietrasanta

Lido di Camaiore

Massarosa

VIAREGGIO

TORRE DEL LAGO PUCCINI

Lago di Massaci

Migliarino

Pisa

Lago di Massaciuccoli at Torre del Lago Puccini

For additional map symbols see back flap

GETTING AROUND

Lucca, Montecatini Terme, Prato and Pistoia are all on the A11 autostrada and are easy to reach by car from Pisa, Florence and other major cities outside Tuscany, such as Bologna. There are several trains a day between Pisa and Florence via Lucca, Montecatini Terme, Prato and Pistoia, and along the coast between Pisa and Carrara. From Lucca you can also travel by train up the Serchio valley to Castel-nuovo di Garfagnana. But, since this is a mountainous region, much of it is only accessible by car.

SIGHTS AT A GLANCE

Bagni di Lucca **8**
Barga **6**
Carrara **2**
Castelnuovo di Garfagnana **5**
Collodi **12**
The Garfagnana **7**
Lucca **11**
The Lunigiana **1**
Montecatini Terme **14**
Parco Naturale
   delle Alpi Apuane **4**
Pescia **13**
Pistoia **15**
Prato **16**
Torre del Lago Puccini **10**
The Versilia **3**
Viareggio **9**

The hamlet of Montefegatesi in the Alpi Apuane

Sun, sand and sea – essential components of a holiday at a beach resort of the Versilia

The Lunigiana ❶

Road map A1. **FS** 🚍 *Aulla.*
ℹ️ *Aulla (0187 42 14 39).*

The Lunigiana (Land of the Moon) area is named after the port of Luni – so called because of the moon-like luminescence of the marble shipped from here in Roman times. From the 16th century onwards, the Dukes of Malaspina fortified villages against banditry and built castles at Massa, Fosdinovo, Aulla, Fivizzano and Verrucola.

At Pontremoli, the 14th-century Castello del Piagnaro houses the **Museo delle Statue-Stele Lunigianesi**, which shows prehistoric carved stone figures from the region.

🏛️ **Museo delle Statue-Stele Lunigianesi**
Castello del Piagnaro, Pontremoli.
Tel *0187 83 14 39.* **Open** *Apr–Sep:
9am– noon, 3–6pm Tue–Sun;
Oct–Mar: 9am– noon, 2–5pm
Tue–Sun.* **Adm charge.**

Carrara ❷

Road map B1. 🏚️ *70,000.* **FS**
🚍 ℹ️ *Viale XX Settembre 46
(0585 84 44 03).* 🛍️ *Mon.*

Carrara is world famous for its white marble. The 300 or so quarries near the town date to Roman times, making this the oldest industrial site in continuous use in the

world. In Carrara itself there are numerous showrooms and workshops where the marble is sawn into sheets or sculpted into statues and ornaments. Many of the workshops welcome visitors. You can also discover more about the techniques of crafting marble at the **Museo Civico del Marmo**.

Carrara's **Duomo** uses the local marble to good effect in its Pisan-Romanesque façade featuring a rose window. In the same square is the house where Michelangelo used to stay on his visits to buy marble for his sculptures. The façade is marked by a plaque and by carvings of the sculptor's tools.

Tour buses from Carrara regularly visit the quarries at Colonnata and at Fantiscritti, where a museum displays various marble quarrying

techniques. You can also drive there, following the numerous signs that say "Cave di Marmo"

🏛️ **Museo Civico del Marmo**
Viale XX Settembre. **Tel** *0585 84 57
46.* **Open** *Oct–Apr: 9am–5pm
Mon–Sat; May–Sep: 10am–6pm
Mon–Sat (Jul & Aug: to 8pm).*

🏛️ **Duomo**
Piazza del Duomo. **Open** *daily.*

The Versilia ❸

Road map B2. **FS** 🚍 *Viareggio.*
ℹ️ *Viale Carducci 10, Viareggio
(0584 96 22 33).* **www**.versilia.
turismo.toscana.it

The Versilia, sometimes called the Tuscan Riviera because of the many beach resorts that line this 30-km (18-mile) strip, stretches from Marina di Carrara in the north

A quarry in the marble-bearing hills around Carrara

down to Marina di Torre del Lago Puccini. In the 1820s, towns such as Massa, Pietra Santa and Camaiore developed marinas and lidos along the part of the coast they controlled. These inland towns are linked by roads to their coastal twins. Here villas and hotels with fine walled gardens line the streets, with the mountains of the Alpi Apuane as a backdrop.

The beaches are divided into numerous bathing establishments run by hotels or private operators, who charge for use of the beach and its facilities. Forte dei Marmi is perhaps the most beautiful of these resorts, much favoured by wealthy Florentines and Milanese.

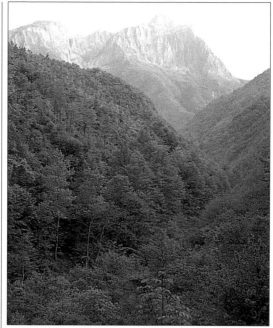

The Turrite Secca valley in the Parco Naturale delle Alpi Apuane

Poster for the Versilia

Parco Naturale delle Alpi Apuane ➍

Road map B1. **FS** 🚌 *Castelnuovo di Garfagnana.* 🚶 *Castelnuovo di Garfagnana (0583 64 43 54).*

The Parco Naturale delle Alpi Apuane, northwest of Castelnuovo di Garfagnana, was designated a nature reserve in 1985. Monte Pisanino is the highest peak in the area at 1,945 m (6,320 ft). It towers above Lago di Vagli, an artificial lake covering the drowned village of Fabbrica. Nearby are Vagli di Sotto (*see p168*) and Vagli di Sopra, ancient villages with rugged stone houses.

To the south, in the valley of the Turrite Secca, a spectacular mountain road leads to Seravezza, passing through a white-walled tunnel called the

Galleria del Cipollaio. Northwest, at Arni, are the Marmitte dei Giganti (Giants' Cooking Pots), great hollows left by the glaciers of the Ice Age.

Southeast at Calomini is a 12th-century rock-cut hermitage, home to a Capuchin monk. Further on is the Grotta del Vento (Cave of the Wind), at Fornovolasco. To the east, past Barga, at Coreglia Antelminelli, is the **Museo della Figurina di Gesso**, devoted to the history of locally made

The 13th-century Rocca at Castelnuovo di Garfagnana

plaster figurines, once sold by traders all over Europe.

🏛 **Museo della Figurina di Gesso**
Via del Mangano 17, Coreglia Antelminelli. **Tel** *0583 780 82.* **Open** *9am–1pm Mon–Fri, 10am–1pm Sat–Sun, 3pm–5pm daily.* **Adm charge.**

Castelnuovo di Garfagnana ➎

Road map B1. 🏘 *6,300.* **FS** 🚌 🚶 *Via Cavalieri di Vittorio Veneto (0583 64 43 54).* 🛒 *Thu.*

Visitors to the Garfagnana use the town as a base for sporting activities. For details, head to the information office or the **Cooperativa Garfagnana Vacanze**. The 13th-century Rocca (castle) houses the town hall. Ludovico Ariosto, author of the epic poem *Orlando Furioso* (1516), was town governor in 1522–25.

🎿 **Cooperativa Garfagnana Vacanze**
Piazza delle Erbe 1. **Tel** *0583 651 69.* **Open** *Jun–Sep: 9am–1pm, 3–7pm daily; Oct–May: 9am–1pm, 3:30–5:30pm daily.*

Barga ❻

Road map C1. 🏛 *11,000*. **FS** ▣
🚌 *Sat.*

Barga is the most attractive of the towns that line the Serchio valley leading northwards from Lucca, and it makes an excellent base for touring the Garfagnana area. The little walled town with its steep streets paved with stone is the setting for a highly regarded opera festival held in July and August in the 18th-century Teatro dell'Accademia dei Differenti. The festival is always well attended.

View over Barga rooftops

🏛 Duomo

Propositura. **Open** *daily.*
Barga's Duomo stands on a grassy terrace at the highest point in the town. There are glorious views from here of the gleaming white marble and limestone peaks of the Alpi Apuane.

The 11th-century Duomo is dedicated to San Cristoforo (St Christopher). The exterior is decorated with interesting Romanesque carvings of interlaced knots, wild beasts and knights in armour. Over the north portal, a frieze thought to be a scene from a folk tale depicts a banquet.

Inside, a huge wooden statue of St Christopher dates to the 12th century, and there is a gilded tabernacle guarded by two charming terracotta angels by Luca della Robbia.

Most impressive of all is the massive marble pulpit, standing fully 5 m (16.5 ft) tall, supported by pillars which in turn rest on the back of man-eating lions. The pulpit is the work of Guido Bigarelli of Como and dates to the early 13th century. The lively sculptures on the upper part

depict the Evangelists, the Three Magi, the Annunciation, the Nativity and the Baptism of Christ.

The Garfagnana ❼

Road map C1. **FS** ▣ *Castelnuovo di Garfagnana.* 🚹 *Via Cavalieri di Vittorio Veneto, Castelnuovo di Garfagnana (0583 64 43 54).*

This mountainous region can be explored from Barga, Seravezza, or Castelnuovo di Garfagnana (*see p173*). Here too is the Parco Naturale delle Alpi Apuane (*see p173*). From Castelnuovo a scenic drive takes you to the Alpe Tre Potenze. You can return via San Pellegrino in Alpe with its **Museo Etnografico**, and also visit the nature park **Parco dell' Orecchiella** and the **Orto Botanico Pánia di Corfino** with its collection of local Alpine plants.

Romanesque sculpture in Pieve di Brancoli

🏛 Museo Etnografico
Via del Voltone 15, San Pellegrino in Alpe. **Tel** *0583 64 90 72.* **Open** *Tue–Sun (phone for times).* **Adm charge**.

🌿 Parco dell'Orecchiella
Centro Visitatori, Orecchiella. **Open** *Jun & Sep: Sat & Sun; Jul–15 Sep: daily; Apr–Nov: Sun.* 🖝

🌿 Orto Botanico Pánia di Corfino
Parco dell'Orecchiella. **Open** *Jul–Aug daily; May–Jun & Sep: Sun.*

Bagni di Lucca ❽

Road map C2. 🏛 *7,402*. ▣
🚹 *Via Umberto I 3 (0583 88 88 81).*
🚌 *Wed & Sat.*

Visitors come to Bagni di Lucca for its lime sulphate springs. In the 19th century it was one of Europe's most fashionable spa towns (*see p185*): the Casino, built in 1837, was the first to be licensed in Europe. Also from that time are the Neo-Gothic **English Church**, the elegant **Palazzo del Circolo dei Forestieri** restaurant and the **Cimitero Anglicano** (Protestant Cemetery). Bagni di Lucca makes a good base for exploring the surrounding hills cloaked in chestnut woods. You can walk to Montefegatesi, a hamlet surrounded by the peaks of the Alpi Apuane, and then continue to Orrido d Botri, a dramatic gorge. To the south of Bagni is San Giorgio or **Pieve di Brancoli**, one of many Romanesque churches in the area founded during the reign of Countess Matilda (1046–1115) (*see p45*).

The Ponte della Maddalena is a hump-backed bridge across the River Serchio just north of the village of Borgo a Mozzano. It is called Ponte del Diavolo (Devil's Bridge) because, according to local legend, the Devil offered to build the bridge in return for possession of the first soul to

Ponte della Maddalena or "Devil's Bridge" near Bagni di Lucca

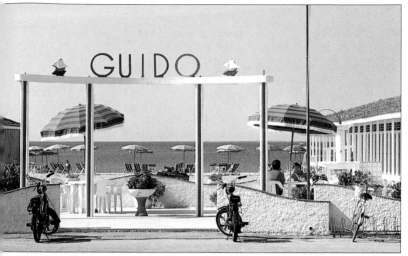

A seaside café in the popular beach resort of Viareggio

cross it; the canny villagers agreed and, when it was finished, sent a dog across.

🏛 English Church
Via Crawford. **Tel** *0583 80 99 11.*
Open *by appt.*

🏛 Palazzo del Circolo dei Forestieri
Piazza Varraud 10. **Tel** *0583 860 38.* **Open** *Tue–Sun.* &

🏛 Cimitero Anglicano
Via Letizia. **Tel** *0583 80 99 11.*
Open *by appt.*

🏛 Pieve di Brancoli
Vinchiana. **Tel** *0583 96 52 81.*
Open *by appt.*

Viareggio ❾

Road map B2. 🏠 *60,000.*
🚆 🚌 🛈 *Viale Carducci 10 (0584 96 22 33).* 🛒 *Thu.*

Viareggio is famous for its elegant "Liberty" style (Art Nouveau) villas and hotels, built in the 1920s after the original boardwalk and timber chalets of the resort went up in flames in 1917. One example is the Gran Caffè Margherita, designed by Galileo Chini *(see p194).* The harbour has an interesting mix of boatyards, luxury yachts and fishing boats, and offers fine views of the Versilia coastline. Viareggio's carnival, held on Sundays from February to Lent and on Shrove Tuesday, is famous throughout Italy *(see p38).*

Torre del Lago Puccini ❿

Road map B2. 🏠 *11,500.* 🚆 🚌
🛈 *Viale Kennedy 2 (0584 35 98 93).*
🛒 *Fri (Jul & Aug): also Sun).* **Teatro Opera Puccini Tel** *0584 35 93 22.*

The composer Giacomo Puccini (1858–1924) *(see p179)* lived here, beside Lago di Massaciuccoli, to indulge his passion for shooting waterfowl. He and his wife are buried in the **Museo Villa Puccini,** in the mausoleum between the piano room and the gun room where he kept his rifle ("my second favourite instrument"). The operas are performed in the open-air theatre in summer *(see p35).* The reed-fringed lake is now a nature reserve for rare migrant birds.

🏛 Museo Villa Puccini
Piazzale Belvedere Puccini 266.
Tel *0584 34 14 45.* **Open** *Apr–Sep: 10am–12:30pm, 3–6pm daily; Oct–Mar: 9am–noon, 3–5pm Tue–Sun.* **Adm charge.** &

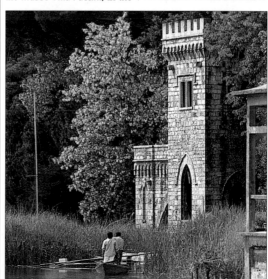

Near Puccini's lakeside home at Torre del Lago Puccini

Street-by-Street: Lucca ⓫

Lucca became a colony of ancient Rome in 180 BC, and the town's Roman legacy is still evident in the regular grid pattern of its streets. The remarkable elliptical shape of the Piazza del Mercato (see p169) is a survival of the amphitheatre. The name of the church of San Michele in Foro indicates that it stands beside the Roman forum, laid out as the city's main square in ancient times and still serving that function to this day. San Michele is just one of Lucca's many churches built in the 12th and 13th centuries in the elaborate Pisan-Romanesque style.

Most of the Renaissance palazzi of Piazza San Michele are now offices.

Casa di Puccini
This plaque marks the birthplace of Giacomo Puccini (1858–1924), composer of some of the world's most popular operas.

★ San Michele in Foro
The Madonna on the south-west corner of the church is a copy of the original inside, carved by Matteo Civitali (1436–1501).

The Palazzo Ducale, once home to Lucca's rulers, has a Mannerist colonnade by Ammannati (1578).

San Giovanni (1187)

Piazza Napoleone
The square is named after Napoleon, whose sister, Elisa Baciocchi, was ruler of Lucca (1805–15). The statue is of her successor, Marie Louise de Bourbon.

STAR SIGHTS

* ★ San Martino
* ★ San Michele in Foro

Via Fillungo
Several shop fronts in Lucca's main shopping street are decorated with Art Nouveau details.

To San Frediano

To Anfiteatro Romano

VIA SANT' ANDREA

VIA DEL CARMINE

VIA SAN GREGORIO

V. D CHIAVI D'ORO

VISITORS' CHECKLIST

Road map C2. 🏘 100,000.
🚉 Piazza Ricasoli. 🚌 Piazzale Verdi. ℹ Piazza Santa Maria 35 (0583 91 99 31). 🛒 Wed, Sat. Antiques: 2nd Sat & 3rd Sun of month. 🎭 Palio della Balestra (12 Jul); Estate Musicale (Jul–Sep); Luminara di Santa Croce (13 Sep). **www**.luccaturismo.it

SANTA CROCE

PIAZZA BERNADINI

VIA SANT' ANASTASIO

VIA GUINIGI

VIA SANTA CROCE

PIAZZA DEI SERVI

VIA A. VALLISNERI

Torre dei Guinigi
This medieval tower with holm-oak trees growing at the top is a familiar landmark of Lucca.

To Villa Bottoni and Museo Nazionale di Palazzo Mansi

Museo dell'Opera della Cattedrale
This recently opened museum features the treasures of San Martino.

VIA DELL' ARCIVESCOVADO

To Giardino Botanico

★ **San Martino**
Lucca's cathedral dates from the 11th century. Its marble façade is asymmetrical to accommodate the adjoining belfry. With its columns, arcades and rich decoration, the façade is an outstanding example of the exuberant Pisan-Romanesque style.

KEY

- - - Suggested route

0 metres 300

0 yards 300

Exploring Lucca

Mosaic in San Frediano

Lucca is enclosed by massive red brick walls which help to give the city its special character by shutting out traffic and the modern world. Built in 1504–1645, the walls are among the best-preserved Renaissance defences in Europe. Within these walls, Lucca is a peaceful city of narrow lanes, preserving intact its original ancient Roman street plan. Unlike several of Tuscany's hilltop cities, Lucca is flat: many locals use bicycles, which lends the city added charm.

Lucca viewed from the top of the Guinigi Tower

🏰 San Martino
See pp180–81.

🏛 Anfiteatro Romano
Piazza del Mercato.

Almost none of the ancient Roman amphitheatre survives: the stone was gradually stolen for use elsewhere, leaving the atmospheric arena-shaped Piazza del Mercato of today *(see p169)*. The piazza is enclosed by medieval houses that were built up against the walls of the amphitheatre. Its shape, perfectly preserved, is a striking reminder that Lucca was founded by the Romans around 180 BC. Low archways at north, south, east and west

mark the gates through which beasts and gladiators would once have entered the arena.

🏛 Palazzo dei Guinigi
Via Sant'Andrea 41. **Tel** *0583 31 68 46.* **Tower Open** *Mar–Sep: 9am–8pm daily (Nov–Feb: to 5:30pm); Oct: 10am–6pm daily.* **Closed** *25 Dec.* **Adm charge.**

This house was once owned by the powerful Guinigi family, rulers of the city in the 15th century. They kept Florence at bay, so Lucca was never conquered by the Medici, remaining independent until

the late 1700s. The red brick palazzo, built in the late 14th century, has late-Gothic windows. The striking 41-m (133-ft) defensive tower alongside, the Torre del Guinigi, has a small roof garden, hence the ilex (holm-oak) trees sprouting incongruously at the top.

🌸 Giardino Botanico
Via dell'Orto Botanico 14. **Tel** *0583 44 21 60.* **Open** *9am–1pm Tue–Sat, 9am–1pm, 3:30–6:30pm Sun.* **Closed** *Sun (Nov–Mar).* **Adm charge.** ♿

Lucca's delightful botanical garden, tucked into an angle of the city walls, was laid out in 1820. It displays a wide range of Tuscan plants.

🏛 Museo della Cattedrale
Piazza Antelminelli 5. **Tel** *0583 49 05 30.* **Open** *10am–5pm daily (to 6pm Sat & Sun and Apr–Oct).* **Closed** *1 Jan, 25 Dec.* **Adm charge.** ♿

Housed in the 14th-century former Archbishop's Palace, the museum displays the treasures of the Duomo, San Martino. These include the 11th-century carved stone head of a king from the original façade. There is also a rare 12th-century Limoges enamel casket, which possibly held a relic of St Thomas à Becket. The Croce di Pisani made by Vincenzo di Michele in 1411 is a masterpiece showing Christ hanging from the Tree of Redemption, surrounded by angels, the Virgin, St John and the other Evangelists.

🏛 Museo Nazionale Villa Guinigi
Via della Quarquonia. **Tel** *0583 49 60 33.* **Open** *9am–7pm Tue–Sun (to 1pm Sun).* **Closed** *1 Jan, 1 May, 25 Dec.* **Adm charge** *(a cumulative ticket also allows entry at the Museo Nazionale di Palazzo Mansi).*

This Renaissance villa was built for Paolo Guinigi, who ruled Lucca from 1400 until 1430. The ground floor holds sculpture from Lucca and surrounds, including fine Romanesque reliefs from Lucca's churches. The gallery on the floor above displays paintings, furnishings, and

Romanesque lion at Museo Nazionale Guinigi

The beautiful galleried staircase at Palazzo Pfanner

choir stalls from Lucca's cathedral, inlaid with marquetry views of the city in 1529.

🏛 Palazzo Pfanner

Tel 340 923 30 85. *Closed* to the public. *Gardens* **Open** Mar–Oct: 10am–6pm daily. **Adm charge**.

The imposing Palazzo Pfanner, built in 1667, has a delightful formal garden to the rear, which can also be viewed from the ramparts. Laid out in the 18th century, the garden's central avenue is lined with Baroque statues of ancient Roman gods and goddesses, alternating with lemon trees in huge terracotta pots.

Unfortunately, the house, with its rich collection of 18th- and 19th-century court costumes, is closed to the public.

🏟 Piazza Napoleone and Piazza del Giglio

Piazza Napoleone was laid out in 1806 when Lucca was under the imposed rule of Elisa Baciocchi, Napoleon's sister. The statue in the square is of her successor, Marie Louise de Bourbon. She faces the massive Palazzo Ducale, with its elegant colonnade built by Ammannati in 1578. Behind her is the Piazza del Giglio, with the Teatro del Giglio (1817) on the south side of the square. The theatre is famous for its productions of operas by Puccini, who was born in Lucca.

🏛 Casa di Puccini

Corte San Lorenzo 8 (Via di Poggio). *Tel* 0583 584 02 87. **Open** Mar–May & Oct–Dec: 10am–1pm, 3–6pm Tue–Sun; Jun–Sep: 10am–6pm daily. **Adm charge**.

The 15th-century house in which Giacomo Puccini (1858–1924) was born contains portraits of the great composer, costume designs for his operas and the piano he used when composing his last opera, *Turandot*. Left unfinished at his death, it was completed by Franco Alfano and first performed two years later at La Scala, Milan.

The composer Giacomo Puccini

🏛 Museo Nazionale di Palazzo Mansi

Via Galli Tassi 43. *Tel* 0583 555 70. **Open** 9am–7pm Tue–Sat. **Adm charge** (a cumulative ticket also allows entry at the Museo Nazionale Guinigi). 📷

Lucca's picture gallery is in the impressive 17th-century Palazzo Mansi, with paintings and furnishings of the same period, typical of the time when Mannerism was being superseded by Baroque and Rococo art. There are also works by Bronzino, Pontormo, Sodoma, Andrea del Sarto, Tintoretto and Salvatore Rosa.

🏟 Ramparts

Complete circuit: 4.2 km (2.5 miles).

A promenade runs along the top of the city walls, built in 1504–1645. Marie Louise de Bourbon made the ramparts into a public park in the early 19th century, with a double avenue of trees. It makes a delightful walk with fine views of Lucca. There are occasional guided tours of the chambers and passages inside one of the bastions. For more information on the tours, contact Compagnia Balestrieri Lucca on 338 237 1277.

The Porta San Donato along the tree-lined ramparts walk

San Martino

Lucca's extraordinary cathedral, with its façade abutting incongruously on to the campanile, is dedicated to St Martin. He is the Roman soldier depicted on the façade dividing his cloak with a sword to share with a needy beggar. This and other scenes from the life of the saint form part of the complex decorations covering the 13th-century façade. There are also reliefs depicting *The Labours of the Months* and intricate panels of inlaid pink, green and white marble showing hunting scenes, peacocks and flowers.

Threshing, the Labour of September

The altar painting in the Sacristy, *The Madonna and Saints* (1449–94), is by Ghirlandaio.

Domed chapels encircling the apse

Romanesque blank arcades and carved capitals

Matteo Civitali's marble Tempietto (1484)

★ **Tomb of Ilaria del Carretto**
The Sacristy houses Jacopo della Quercia's beautiful portrait in marble (1405–6) of Paolo Guinigi's bride.

★ **Volto Santo**
This revered 13th-century wooden effigy was believed by medieval pilgrims to have been carved by Christ's follower, Nicodemus, at the time of the Crucifixion.

STAR FEATURES

★ Façade
★ Volto Santo
★ Tomb of Ilaria del Carretto

★ Façade
*The gabled façade has three tiers
of ornate colonnading (1204).
Every one of the carved columns
is different, and there are lively
hunting scenes above them.*

Circular clerestory
windows, in the nave and
above the aisle roof, light
the unusually tall nave of
the cross-shaped
church.

The campanile was
built in 1060 as a
defensive tower. The
upper two tiers were
added in 1261 when
the tower was joined
to the cathedral.

VISITORS' CHECKLIST

*Tel 0583 95 70 68. **Open** 7am–
6:30pm daily (to 5pm Oct–Mar).*
✝ *8am, 10:30am, noon Sun &
relig hols, 9am, 6pm Mon–Sat.*
*Sacristy & Museum **Open** daily;
hours vary. **Adm charge**.* 📷 ♿

St Martin
*This sculpture of the saint
dividing his cloak to share it
is a copy. The 13th-century
original is now just inside
the cathedral entrance.*

Inlaid Marble
*Scenes from daily life, myths
and poems cover the façade.
Look out for the maze pattern
on the right pier of the porch.*

Nicola Pisano (1200–78)
carved *The Journey of the
Magi* and *The Deposition*
round the left doorway.

Doorway Sculptures
*This 13th-century
relief depicts the
beheading of St
Regulus.* The Labours
of the Months *round
the central door show
the tasks appropriate
to each season.*

Apostles from the mosaic on the façade of San Frediano in Lucca

🔒 San Frediano

Piazza San Frediano. **Open** daily.

The striking façade of Lucca's San Frediano church features a colourful 13th-century mosaic, *The Ascension,* by the School of Berlinghieri. Inside, to the right, is a splendid Romanesque font which could easily be mistaken for a fountain, because it is so big and impressive. The sides are carved with scenes from *The Life of Christ* and the story of Moses. One dramatic scene shows Moses and his followers dressed in 12th-century armour, looking like Crusaders, as they pass through the divided Red Sea with an entourage of camels.

Amico Aspertini's frescoes (1508–9) in the second chapel in the north aisle tell the story of Lucca's precious relic, the Volto Santo *(see p180),* and give a good idea of what the city looked like in the early 16th century.

Also in the church is a coloured wooden statue of the Virgin, carved by Matteo Civitali, and an altarpiece carved from a single block of marble by Jacopo della Quercia in the Cappella Trenta. It is carved in the shape of a polyptych with five Gothic-spired niches.

🔒 San Michele in Foro

Piazza San Michele. **Open** daily.

As its name suggests, this church stands on the site of the ancient Roman forum. It has a wonderfully rich Pisan-Romanesque façade that competes in splendour with that of San Martino *(see pp180–81).* John Ruskin, the English artist and art historian whose work did so much to revive interest in Italian art during the 19th century *(see p55),* spent many hours sketching the rich mixture of twisted marble columns and Cosmati work (inlaid marble). The façade is almost barbaric in its exuberance, and the inlaid marble scenes depict wild beasts and

Detail from façade of San Michele in Foro

huntsmen on horseback rather than Christian subjects. Only the huge winged figure of St Michael, standing on the pediment and flanked by two angels, marks this out as a church. The splendour of the façade, built over a long period from the 11th to the 14th centuries, is matched by the arcading of the belltower.

The interior has little of interest except for Filippino Lippi's recently restored *Saints Helena, Jerome, Sebastian and Roch,* among the most beautiful of his paintings.

The square outside is circled by 15th- and 16th-century palazzi, which are now mostly occupied by banks, while the portico of the Palazzo Pretorio to the south shelters a 19th-century statue of Lucca's greatest artist and architect, Matteo Civitali (1436–1501).

🏛 Via Fillungo

Lucca's principal shopping street winds its way through the heart of the city towards the Anfiteatro Romano *(see p178).* It is a good place to stroll in the cool of the early evening. The upper end, towards San Frediano church, has several shops with Art Nouveau ironwork, while San Cristoforo, the 13th-century church halfway down the street, holds exhibitions of work by local artists.

🏛 Villa Bottini

Via Elisa. **Tel** 0583 49 14 49.
Garden open 9am–1pm Mon–Sat.

The pretty walled garden of this late 16th-century building is open to the public. It is also used occasionally in summer for outdoor concerts.

Villa Bottini and garden

A Day Out around Lucca

This motoring tour takes you by a scenic route to the best of the villas around Lucca. After leaving Lucca the first stop is the Romanesque church of San Giorgio at Pieve di Brancoli; then comes the ancient hump-backed Ponte della Maddalena, also known as Devil's Bridge *(see p174)*. In the spa town of Bagni di Lucca the pretty suspension bridge across the Lima dates from 1840. On reaching Collodi, explore the village on foot, as the streets are too steep and narrow for cars. The Villa Garzoni, with its splendid gardens, lies below the town, and the Pinocchio Park is on the other side of the road. Continue to the Villa Torrigiani, which is set in a fine park and contains 13th–18th- century porcelain and furnishings. The tour ends at the 17th-century Villa Mansi, with its Baroque façade and a garden enlivened by statues of Diana and other pagan deities.

Bagni di Lucca ③
Drive on along the S12 for 5 km (3 miles) to the spa town. Then continue along the same road through the town.

Villa Garzoni ④
Turn left at the T-junction on the S12 for Abetone, then right for Collodi and the Villa Garzoni with its terraced gardens.

Ponte della Maddalena ②
Continue for 8 km (5 miles) on the S12 to the bridge.

S12

②
Borgo a Mozzano

S12

Boveglio

① *Pieve di Brancoli*

Villa Basilica

Pinocchio Park ⑤
This children's theme park in Collodi is based on the famous puppet's adventures.

Collodi

④⑤

San Giorgio ①
Leave Lucca on the S12 to Abetone, staying on the right bank of the Serchio. After 10 km (6 miles) turn right for Pieve di Brancoli and San Giorgio.

Villa Reale
Marlia

⑦⑥
Segromigno in Monte

Camigliano

S435

LUCCA

Villa Mansi ⑦
Heading for Segromino in Monte, turn right at the first junction into Via Piaggiori; then follow signs to Villa Mansi.

Villa Torrigiani ⑥
South of Collodi turn right on the S435 for Lucca. After Borgonuovo, turn right for Camigliano Santa Gemma and left after 1.5 km (1 mile) for the villa.

KEY

▬▬ Tour route

〜 Other roads

0 kilometres   5

0 miles   2

Terme Tettuccio, Montecatini's oldest and most famous spa, rebuilt in 1925–8

Collodi ⓬

Road map C2. 🏃 *3,000.* ℹ *Via B Pasquinelli 54 (0583 97 82 05).*

There are two main sights in this town: the **Villa Garzoni** with its theatrical terraced gardens tumbling down the hillside and, for children, the **Pinocchio Park** *(see p183).*

The author of *The Adventures of Pinocchio* (1881), Carlo Lorenzini, was born in Florence but his uncle was custodian of the Villa Garzoni and Lorenzini frequently stayed here as a child. Fond memories led him to use Collodi as his pen name and in 1956 the town decided to repay the compliment by setting up the theme park.

The park consists of gardens featuring mosaics and sculptural tableaux based on the adventures of the puppet, plus a maze, playground, exhibition centre and children's restaurant.

🏯 **Villa Garzoni**
Tel 0572 42 95 90. **Villa** *closed* for restoration. **Garden** *open daily.* **Adm charge**.

🌳 **Pinocchio Park**
Tel 0572 42 93 42. **Open** *8:30am–sunset daily.* **Adm charge**. ♿ partial. **www**.pinocchio.it

Pescia ⓭

Road map C2. 🏃 *18,000.* 🚌 ℹ *Via B Pasquinelli 54, Collodi (0583 97 82 05).* 🛒 *Sat.*

Pescia's wholesale flower market is one of Italy's biggest, and there are some interesting sights to visit.

In the church of **San Francesco** are frescoes on *The Life of St Francis* (1235) by Bonaventura Berlinghieri (1215–74). The artist knew St Francis *(see p47)* and it is claimed that the frescoes are an accurate portrait of the saint. The **Duomo**, remodelled in Baroque style by Antonio

Ferri in 1693, has a massive campanile that was originally built as a tower within the city walls. It was given its onion-dome "cap" in 1771.

There is a small collection of religious paintings and illuminated manuscripts in the **Museo Civico**, and the **Museo Archeologico della Valdinievole** displays material excavated from nearby Valdinievole, the pretty "Vale of Mist".

⛪ **San Francesco**
Piazza San Francesco. **Open** *daily.*

⛪ **Duomo**
Piazza del Duomo. **Open** *daily.*

🏛 **Museo Civico**
Palazzo Galeotti, Piazza Santo Stefano 1. **Tel** *0572 47 79 44.* **Open** *1–7pm Mon, Wed, Fri, 8am–1pm Tue, Thu, Sat.*

🏛 **Museo Archeologico della Valdinievole**
Piazza Leonardoda Vinci 1. **Tel** *0572 47 75 33.* **Open** *9am–1pm Mon–Sat, 3–5pm Tue & Thu.*

Montecatini Terme ⓮

Road map C2. 🏃 *22,500.* 🚌 ℹ *Viale Verdi 66 (0572 77 22 44).* 🛒 *Thu.*

Of all Tuscany's many spa towns, Montecatini Terme is the most interesting. It has beautiful formal gardens and the architecture of its spas is particularly distinguished.

Terme Leopoldine (1926), built in the style of a Classical temple, is named after Grand Duke Leopoldo I, who first

The Pescia river, running through a fertile, cultivated landscape

Theatre building in Montecatini Alto's main square

encouraged the development of Montecatini Terme in the 18th century.

The most splendid is the Neo-Classical Terme Tettuccio (1925–8) with its circular, marble-lined pools, fountains and Art Nouveau tiles depicting languorous nymphs.

Terme Torretta, named after its mock medieval tower, is noted for its tea-time concerts, while Terme Tamerici has beautifully tended gardens.

Visitors can obtain day tickets to the spas to drink the waters and relax in the reading, writing and music rooms. More information is available from the Direzione delle Terme at Viale Verdi 41.

A popular excursion from Montecatini Terme is to take the funicular railway up to the ancient fortified village of Montecatini Alto. In the quiet main piazza, there are antique shops and well-regarded restaurants with outdoor tables. From the Rocca (castle) you can take in sweeping views over the mountainous countryside.

Nearby at Ponte Buggianese, in **San Michele** church, you can see modern frescoes by the Florentine artist Pietro Annigoni (1910–88) on the theme of Christ's Passion.

At Monsummano Terme, another of Tuscany's well known spa towns, the **Grotta Giusti** spa prescribes the inhalation of vapours from hot sulphurous springs found in the nearby caves.

Above Monsummano Terme is the fortified hilltop village of Monsummano Alto, with its ruined castle. Today, few people live in the sleepy village, with its pretty 12th-century church and crumbling houses, but there are some fine views from here.

🔒 **San Michele**
Ponte Buggianese.
Open by appointment.

🚰 **Grotta Giusti**
Monsummano Terme.
Tel 0572 907 71. Open 9am–7pm daily. Adm charge.
www.grottagiustispa.com

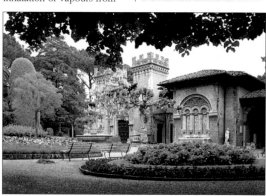

The Terme Tamerici, built in Neo-Gothic style in the early 20th century

---

TAKING THE WATERS IN TUSCANY

The therapeutic value of bathing was first recognized by the ancient Romans. They were also the first to exploit the hot springs of volcanic origin that they found all over Tuscany. Here they built bath complexes where the army veterans who settled in towns such as Florence and Siena could relax. Some of these spas, as at Saturnia *(see p238)*, are still called by their original Roman names.

Other spas came into prominence during the Middle Ages and Renaissance: St Catherine of Siena (1347–80) *(see p219)*, who suffered from scrofula, a form of tuberculosis, and Lorenzo de' Medici (1449–92), who was arthritic, both bathed in the sulphurous hot springs at Bagno Vignoni *(see p226)* to relieve their ailments. Tuscan spas really came into their own in the early 19th

1920s spa poster

century when Bagni di Lucca was one of the most fashionable spa centres in Europe, frequented by emperors, kings and aristocrats *(see p174)*. However, spa culture in the 19th century had more to do with social life: flirtation and gambling took precedence over health cures.

Today treatments such as inhaling sulphur-laden steam, drinking the mineral-rich waters, hydro massage, bathing and application of mud packs are prescribed for disorders ranging from liver complaints to skin conditions and asthma. Many visitors still continue the tradition of coming to fashionable spas such as Montecatini Terme or Monsummano Terme, not just for the benefits of therapeutic treatment but also for relaxation and in search of companionship.

Pistoia 🟫

The Cappella del Tau symbol

The citizens of Pistoia acquired a reputation for viciousness and intrigue in the 13th century and the taint has never quite disappeared. The cause was a feud between two of the city's rival factions, the Neri and Bianchi (Blacks and Whites), that spread to involve other cities. Assassination in Pistoia's narrow alleyways was commonplace. The favoured weapon was a tiny but deadly dagger called the *pistole* made by the city's ironworkers, who also specialized in surgical instruments. The city still thrives on metalworking: everything from buses to mattress springs is made here. Its historic centre has several fine buildings.

Baptistry opposite the Cattedrale

🏛 Cattedrale di San Zeno
Piazza del Duomo. **Tel** *0573 250 95.*
Open *8:30am–12:30pm, 3:30–7pm daily.* **Adm charge.** ♿ *side entrance.*
Cappella di San Jacobo Open *daily.*
Piazza del Duomo, the city's main square, is dominated by the Cattedrale di San Zeno and its bulky campanile, which was originally built in the 12th century as a defensive watchtower in the city walls.

The interior is rich in funerary monuments, including the tomb of poet Cino da Pistoia, in the south aisle. He is depicted in a relief (1337) lecturing to a class of young boys.

Nearby is the Cappella di San Jacobo, with its extraordinary silver altar decorated with over 600 statues and reliefs. The earliest of these date from 1287 and the altar was not completed until 1456. During that time, nearly every silversmith of note in Tuscany contributed to the extraordinarily rich design. Among them was Brunelleschi, who began his career working in metal before switching to architecture. Also in Piazza del Duomo, facing the Cattedrale, is the octagonal Baptistry, which was finished in 1359.

🏛 Museo di San Zeno
Palazzo dei Vescovi, Piazza del Duomo. **Tel** *0573 36 92 72.*
Open *10am–1pm, 3–5pm Tue, Thu & Fri.* **Adm charge.**
📷 ♿ *partial.*
In the beautifully restored Palazzo dei Vescovi (Bishop's Palace) is the Museo

della Cattedrale. In the basement, you can see the excavated remains of Roman buildings, and upstairs there are some fine reliquaries, crucifixes and chalices made by local goldsmiths during the 13th–15th centuries.

🏛 Museo Civico
Palazzo del Comune, Piazza del Duomo. **Tel** *0573 37 12 96.* **Open** *10am–6pm Tue–Sat (to 5pm in winter), 9:30am–12:30pm Sun.* **Adm charge.** ♿
On the opposite side of the square is the Palazzo del Comune (Town Hall), which has the Museo Civico upstairs. Exhibits here range from medieval altar paintings to the work of 20th-century Pistoian artists, architects and sculptors.

🏛 Centro Marino Marini
Palazzo del Tau, Corso Silvano Fedi 30. **Tel** *0573 302 85.*
Open *10am–6pm Mon–Sat.*
Adm charge. ♿
The work of Marino Marini (1901–80), Pistoia's most famous 20th-century artist, is housed in a museum dedicated to him in the Palazzo del Tau. On display are drawings and casts, which trace the development of his style. Marini specialized in sculpting primitive forms in bronze or clay. His subjects included a horse and rider (*see p104*), and Pomona, the ancient Roman goddess of fertility.

Pomona by Marino Marini

🏛 Cappella del Tau
Corso Silvano Fedi 70. **Tel** *0573 322 04.* **Open** *8am–2pm Mon–Sat.*
This chapel owes its name to the letter T (*tau* in Greek) which appeared on the cloaks of the monks who built it and which symbolized a crutch.

Inside the chapel there are frescoes on *The Creation* and the life of St Anthony Abbot, who founded the order, which is dedicated to tending the sick and crippled.

The Fall, in the Cappella del Tau

🏛 San Giovanni Fuorcivitas
Via Cavour. **Open** *daily.*
Just north of the Cappella del Tau is the 12th-century church of San Giovanni Fuorcivitas ("St John outside the city", since the church once stood beyond the city walls). Its north flank is strikingly clad in banded marble and there is a Romanesque relief of *The Last Supper* over the portal. Inside is Giovanni Pisano's holy water basin, carved in marble with figures of the Virtues, and an equally masterly pulpit by Guglielmo

Detail of frieze (1514–25) by Giovanni della Robbia, Ospedale del Ceppo

da Pisa, carved in 1270 with New Testament scenes. Both works are among the finest of this period, when artists were reviving the art of carving.

🏠 Sant'Andrea

Via Sant'Andrea 21. **Tel** 0573 219 12. **Open** 8am–12:30pm, 3:30–6pm daily (to 7pm in the summer).
This church is reached by walking through Piazza della Sala, the site of Pistoia's lively open-air market. There is a good Romanesque relief of *The Journey of the Magi* over the portal, and inside is Giovanni Pisano's pulpit (completed in 1301). This is considered by some to be his masterpiece, even more accomplished than the pulpit he later made for Pisa cathedral *(see p159)*. It is decorated with reliefs depicting scenes from the life of Christ.

🏠 San Bartolomeo in Pantano

Piazza San Bartolomeo 6. **Open** daily.
The beautiful Romanesque church of San Bartolomeo in Pantano, dating from 760, houses another celebrated pulpit, carved in 1250 by Guido da Como.

🏥 Ospedale del Ceppo

Piazza Giovanni XXIII.
This hospital and orphanage, founded in 1277, was named after the *ceppo*, or hollowed-out tree trunk, that was used in medieval times to collect donations for its work. The striking façade of the main building features coloured terracotta panels (1514–25) by Giovanni della Robbia illustrating the Seven Works of Corporeal Mercy. The portico is by Michelozzo.

VISITORS' CHECKLIST

Road map C2.
🏠 93,000.
🚉 Piazza Dante Alighieri.
🚌 Piazza San Francesco.
ℹ️ Palazzo dei Vescovi, Piazza del Duomo 4 (0573 216 22).
📅 Wed & Sat.
🎪 Giostra dell'Orso (25 Jul).

🐾 Zoo

Via Pieve a Celle 160a. **Tel** 0573 91 12 19. **Open** 9am–5pm daily (to 7pm in summer). **Adm charge**. ♿
There is a small, well-kept zoo just 4 km (2.5 miles) northwest of Pistoia at La Verginina.

Façade of San Bartolomeo

PISTOIA CITY CENTRE

Cappella del Tau ⑧
Cattedrale and Baptistry ⑥
Centro Marino Marini ⑨
Museo della Cattedrale ⑤
Museo Civico ④
Ospedale del Ceppo ②
Sant'Andrea ①
San Bartolomeo in Pantano ③
San Giovanni Fuorcivitas ⑦

Prato ⑯

Prato has been one of Italy's most important textile-manufacturing cities since the 13th century. One of its most famous citizens was the immensely wealthy Francesco di Marco Datini (1330–1410), who has been immortalized by Iris Origo in *The Merchant of Prato* (1957). Datini left all his money to charity, and the city contains several reminders of him, particularly in his own Palazzo Datini. Prato also attracts pilgrims from all over Italy who come to see the Virgin's Girdle, a prized relic kept in the Duomo and on view five times a year.

Duomo façade and pulpit

🛉 Duomo

Piazza del Duomo. *Tel 0574 26 234.* **Open** *7am–12:30pm, 3:30–7pm Mon–Sat, 7am–1pm, 3:30–8pm Sun.*
The Duomo stands on the main square, with the Pulpit of the Holy Girdle to the right of its façade, its frieze of dancing cherubs designed by Donatello (1438). Inside, the first chapel on the left holds the Virgin's Girdle, which is displayed from the pulpit on religious holidays. Frescoes by Agnolo Gaddi (1392–5) relate how the girdle reached Prato. In 1141 a local merchant married a Palestinian woman who brought it with her after inheriting it from the Apostle Thomas, who had been given it by the Virgin herself. Also in the Duomo is Fra Filippo Lippi's masterpiece, *The Life of John the Baptist* (1452–66).

🏛 Museo dell'Opera del Duomo

Piazza del Duomo 49. *Tel 0574 293 39.* **Open** *9:30am–12:30pm, 3–6:30pm Mon & Wed–Sat; 9:30am–12:30pm Sun.* **Adm charge** *(a cumulative ticket allows entry at the Museo Civico and the Castello dell'Imperatore, see p189).*
Donatello's original panels for the Holy Girdle pulpit are currently being restored, but

the museum also houses the reliquary (1446) made for the Girdle by Maso di Bartolomeo, and *St Lucy* by Filippino Lippi, the son of Fra Filippo Lippi.

🚏 Piazza del Comune

The streets around the Duomo contain several important buildings. The city's main street, Via Mazzoni, leads west to the Piazza del Comune with its Bacchus fountain. The original, made in 1659, is in the nearby Palazzo Comunale.

🏛 Museo Civico

Palazzo Pretorio, Piazza del Comune 19. *Tel 0574 61 63 02.* **Closed** *for restoration.* **Adm charge** *(see Museo dell'Opera del Duomo).* ♿ *partial.*
The Museo Civico houses the altar painting *The Story of the Holy Girdle* by Bernardo Daddi (1312–48) and Fra Filippo

Madonna del Ceppo by Fra Filippo Lippi in the Museo Civico

Lippi's *Madonna del Ceppo*, featuring a portrait of Francesco Datini, a patron of the Ceppo charity *(see p187)*. During restoration work, many paintings are on display at the Museo di Pittura Murale (Piazza S Domenico 8, 0574 440 501).

🏛 Palazzo Datini

Via Ser Lapo Mazzei 43. *Tel 0574 213 91.* **Open** *9:30am–noon, 4–7pm Mon–Sat.* ♿
This house where Francesco Datini lived is now a museum. Its archive contains 140,000 business letters and Datini's account books, on which Iris Origo based her biography.

The Story of the Holy Girdle by Bernardo Daddi in the Museo Civico

🔒 Santa Maria delle Carceri

Piazza delle Carceri. **Open** 7am–noon, 4–7pm daily.

Prato's most important church stands on the site of a prison (*carceri*) on whose wall an image of the Virgin miraculously appeared in 1484. With its harmoniously proportioned interior, the domed church (1485–1506) is a fine work by Renaissance architect Giuliano da Sangallo. Andrea della Robbia created the blue and white glazed terracotta roundels of the Evangelists (1490).

♣ Castello dell'Imperatore

Piazza delle Carceri. **Open** Wed–Sat, Sun morning & Mon. **Adm charge** (see Museo dell'Opera del Duomo). This castle (1237) was built by the German Holy Roman Emperor Frederick II during his campaign to conquer Italy.

🏛 Museo del Tessuto

Piazza del Comune. **Tel** 0574 611 503. **Open** 10:30am–6:30pm Mon, Wed–Sat (to 2:30pm Sat), 4–7pm Sun. 🚹 The history of Prato's textile industry, the basis of its wealth, is charted in this textile museum.

Located on the city's southern outskirts, it houses historic looms and examples of various types of cloth, such as lush Renaissance embroidery, velvets, lace and damask.

🏛 Centro per l'Arte Contemporanea Luigi Pecci

Viale della Repubblica 277. **Tel** 0574 53 17. **Open** 10am–4pm Wed–Mon (phone to check). **Adm charge**. 🚹 www.centropecci.it Near the Prato Est Autostrada exit, this cultural centre is an interesting modern building in its own right. It is used for changing displays of contemporary art, concerts and films. The permanent collection may be viewed by appointment.

The imposing Castello dell'Imperatore (1237), built by Frederick II

PRATO CITY CENTRE

Castello dell'Imperatore ⑦
Duomo ①
Museo Civico ④
Museo dell'Opera del Duomo ②
Palazzo Datini ⑤
Piazza del Comune ③
Santa Maria delle Carceri ⑥

Key to Symbols see back flap

0 metres 500
0 yards 500

EASTERN TUSCANY

From the forests of the Mugello and the Casentino to the heights of La Verna, this is an area of outstanding natural beauty.Hermits and mystics have long favoured its more remote reaches, where ancient monastic orders continue to flourish. Only this part of Tuscany could have produced an enigmatic artist like Piero della Francesca, whose celebrated frescoes decorate San Francesco in Arezzo.

Eastern Tuscany's main transport route, the A1 Autostrada, channels speeding traffic southwards along the Arno valley towards Arezzo and Rome. Away from this busy artery, Eastern Tuscany is a little-visited region of steep hills cloaked in beech, oak and sweet chestnut trees. It is particularly attractive in autumn, when the huge forests of the Mugello and the Casentino take on fiery shades of red and gold. This is also the season when mushrooms and truffles abound. Driving through the region at this time of year, you'll see them for sale at roadside stalls.

The tiny mountain pastures to the east of the region are grazed both by sheep, whose milk is made into cheese, and by beautiful white cattle, which were once highly prized by the Romans as sacrificial beasts.

This is also a land of saints, hermits and monasteries. The mountain-top sanctuary of La Verna is reputed to be the place where St Francis received the stigmata – marks resembling Christ's wounds. The 11th-century hermitage at Camaldoli was intended as the site for a Benedictine order who wished to live in complete isolation, but proved so popular with religious day-trippers that a visitors' centre soon had to be built nearby. The monastery at Vallombrosa has such glorious woodlands that John Milton was moved to describe them in his epic poem, *Paradise Lost* (1667).

For art-lovers, eastern Tuscany is the region of Piero della Francesca. His frescoes in Arezzo, largely ignored until the late 19th century, form one of the world's greatest fresco cycles.

Pieve di Santi Ippolito e Donato in Pratovecchio, between Poppi and Stia

◁ Fertile countryside surrounding Monterchi

Exploring Eastern Tuscany

The ancient city of Arezzo and the hilltop town of Cortona, with its steep streets, narrow, ladder-like alleys and ancient houses, will amply satisfy visitors in search of culture, art and architecture. The region will also appeal to those who love nature. The woodlands, meadows and streams are ideal for exploring on foot. There are plenty of well-marked paths and picnic areas to encourage you, especially within the beautiful ancient forests surrounding the monasteries at Vallombrosa and Camaldoli.

KEY

▬▬	Motorway
▬▬	Major road
▬▬	Secondary road
▭▭	Minor road
▬▪▬	Main railway
▬▬	Regional border
△	Summit
)(	Pass

```
0 kilometres        10
0 miles             10
```

Cortona, with its steep streets and medieval towers

GETTING AROUND

The region's main highways, the A1 Autostrada and the S71, linking Bibbiena, Poppi and the Casentino, offer swift access to most of the region. The remaining roads are delightfully rural, particularly the S70, with its fine views near Vallombrosa, but be prepared for steep gradients and hairpin bends. Some roads in the Casentino are very narrow. There are passing places, but a speed limit of 40 km/h (25 mph) means you should leave plenty of time for your journey.

Bus and rail transport is very limited. An intercity train service links Florence to Arezzo, from where there are irregular bus services to other major towns in the region.

SIGHTS AT A GLANCE

Anghiari **12**
Arezzo **14**
Bibbiena **7**
Borgo San Lorenzo **2**
Camaldoli **5**
Caprese Michelangelo **10**
The Casentino **9**
Cortona **17**
La Verna **8**
Lucignano **16**
Monte San Savino **15**
Monterchi **13**
The Mugello **1**
Poppi **6**
Sansepolcro **11**
Stia **4**
Vallombrosa **3**

Ancient forest in the Casentino: a rich
ecological enclave

Medieval street in Monte San
Savino

The Mugello ❶

Road map D2. 🚉 🚌 *Borgo San Lorenzo.* ℹ️ *Via Palmiro Togliatti 45, Borgo San Lorenzo (055 84 52 71). (Mon, Wed, Fri am).*

The Mugello is the area to the north and east of Florence.

The scenic S65 passes the **Parco Demidoff** at Pratolino, to the south of the region. Here you can see a giant statue of the mountain god, Appennino, carved by Giambologna in 1580. Just to the north, the **Convento di Montesenario** offers excellent views. Further east lies the wine town of Rufina, with its **Museo della Vita e del Vino della Val di Sieve**.

🌿 **Parco Demidoff**
Via Fiorentina 6, Pratolino. **Tel** 055 40 94 27. **Open** Apr–Sep: Thu–Sun; Mar & Oct: Sun. **Adm charge.** 🅰️

⛪ **Convento di Montesenario**
Via Montesenario 1, Bivigliano. **Tel** 055 40 64 41. **Church Open** daily. **Convent Open** by request.

🏛️ **Museo della Vita e del Vino della val di Sieve**
Villa di Poggio Reale, Rufina. **Tel** 055 839 79 32.

Borgo San Lorenzo ❷

Road map D2. 🏛️ 15,500. 🚉 🚌 ℹ️ *Villa Pecori Giraldi, Via Togliatti 69 (055 845 62 30). (Tue am, Fri–Sun pm).* 🍴 Tue.

Substantially rebuilt after an earthquake in 1919, this is the largest town of the Mugello. The parish church,

Tabernacle of St Francis in Borgo San Lorenzo

the **Pieve di San Lorenzo**, has an odd Romanesque campanile, circular in its lower stages and hexagonal above. In the apse, the wall paintings (1906) are by the Art Nouveau artist Galileo Chini. He also worked on the Tabernacle of St Francis (1926), a shrine outside the church, and the Santuario del Santissimo Crocifisso, a church on the edge of town.

To the west are the **Castello del Trebbio**, with its gardens, and the **Villa di Cafaggiolo**, with its bulging clock tower. Among the first Medici villas, both were built for Cosimo il Vecchio by Michelozzo di Bartolommeo (1396–1472).

⛪ **Pieve di San Lorenzo**
Via Cocchi 4. **Open** Mon–Sat, Sun pm.

♣ **Castello del Trebbio**
San Piero a Sieve. **Tel** 055 845 87 93 (Mon, Wed, pm Fri). **Open** Easter– Oct: Tue–Fri by appt. **Adm charge.** 🅰️

🏚️ **Villa di Cafaggiolo**
Cafaggiolo, Barberino di Mugello. **Open** daily by appt (groups only). **Tel** 055 849 81 03 (Mon, Wed, Fri am). **Adm charge.** 🅰️

Woodland landscape at Vallombrosa

Vallombrosa ❸

Road map D2. 🚌 *from Florence.* **T** 055 86 20 03. **Church open** from 3:30pm daily. **Abbey open** by appt.

Like the monasteries of the Casentino *(see p196)*, the abbey buildings at Vallombrosa are surrounded by woodland. The routes to this sight are all very scenic.

The Vallombrosan order was founded by Saint Giovan Gualberto Visdomini in 1038. He aimed to persuade like-minded aristocrats to join him in relinquishing their wealth and adopting a life of great austerity. Contrary to these worthy ideals, the order grew wealthy and powerful during the 16th and 17th centuries. was then that today's fortress-like abbey was built. Today the order comprises some 20 monks.

In 1638 the English poet John Milton (1608–74) visited the abbey. The beautiful scenery of this area inspired passage in his epic poem, *Paradise Lost*.

Façade of Santa Maria Assunta in Stia

Stia ❹

Road map D2. 🏘 *3,017.* 🚆 🚌
ℹ️ *Piazza Ianucci 65 (0575 50 41 06) (summer only).* 🍴 *Tue.*

Stia is a bustling, attractive village on the Arno. In the main piazza is the Romanesque church of **Santa Maria Assunta**, with a rather plain façade. Inside is a 16th-century terracotta *Madonna and Child* by Andrea della Robbia.

There are two medieval Guidi family castles close by: **Castello di Palagio**, with an attractive garden, and the **Castello di Porciano**, which houses an agricultural museum.

🏛 **Santa Maria Assunta**
Piazza Tanucci. **Open** *daily.* ♿

♟ **Castello di Palagio**
Via Vittorio Veneto. **Tel** *0575 58 33 88.* **Open** *Jul–Sep: Sat–Sun, Tue.* **Adm charge**.

♟ **Castello di Porciano**
Porciano. **Tel** *055 40 05 17.* **Open** *mid May – mid Oct: Sun.* ♿

Camaldoli ❺

Road map E2. 🚌 *from Bibbiena.* **Tel** *0575 55 60 12.* **Monastery open** *9am–12:30pm, 2:30–6:30pm daily.* **Hermitage Tel** *0575 55 60 21.* **Open** *8:30–11:15am, 3–6pm daily.* **Museo Ornitologico Forestale Tel** *0575 55 61 30.* **Adm charge**. ♿

The monastery was founded in 1046 and today houses 40 Carthusian monks. Visitors to Camaldoli will want to see not only the monastery

but the original *eremo* (hermitage), 2.5 km (1.5 miles) away. A narrow, winding road leads up from the monastic complex to the hermitage through thick forest. This ancient woodland, which is some of the most ecologically rich in Europe, was declared a National Park in 1991.

The hermitage dates back to 1012 when San Romualdo (St Rumbold) came here with a small group of followers, to cut themselves off completely from the outside world.

Today's monks lead a more gregarious life, running a small café in the monastery below. As you descend to the monastery complex you will also pass numerous picnic spots and some of the many local footpaths.

The monks still tend the magnificent beech and chestnut woodland that surrounds the ancient monastery, as their predecessors have for nearly 1,000 years. A pharmacy, dating to 1543, now sells soaps, toiletries and liqueurs made by the monks.

There is a small, privately owned ornithological museum across the road from the monastery, opposite the car park, which illustrates the area's rich bird life.

Poppi ❻

Road map E2. 🏘 *6,700.* 🚆 🚌
ℹ️ *Via Nazionale 14, Badia Prataglia (Mar–Dec Tue–Sun) (0575 55 90 54).* 🍴 *Tue.*

The older part of Poppi is located high above the town's bus and train termini. Its splendid castle, the imposing **Castello di Poppi**, can be seen from as far away as Bibbiena *(see p196)*. Just to the south of the town is the **Zoo Fauna Europa**, which specializes in the conservation of endangered European species like the Apennine wolf and the lynx.

Visible from Poppi, a short drive to the northwest up the Arno valley, is the 11th-century **Castello di Romena** where Dante stayed as a guest of the local rulers in the early 14th century. Romena's *pieve*, dating to 1152, is a typical example of a Romanesque village church.

♟ **Castello di Poppi**
Tel *0575 52 99 64.* **Open** *Apr–Oct: daily; Nov– Mar: Thu–Sun.* **Adm charge**. ♿ *partial.*

🦊 **Zoo Fauna Europa**
Poppi. **Tel** *0575 52 90 79.* **Open** *daily.* **Adm charge**. ♿

♟ **Castello di Romena**
Pratovecchio. **Tel** *0575 58 13 53.* **Closed** *for restoration.*

Castello di Poppi, which towers over Poppi and overlooks the entire Casentino

Casentino landscape

Bibbiena **7**

Road map E2. 🏛 *11,000*. 🚉 💠
i *Bibbiena train station (0575 59 30 98)*. 🍴 *Thu.*

One of the oldest towns in the region, Bibbiena was the subject of intense territorial feuding between Arezzo and Florence in medieval times. It is now the commercial centre of the Casentino region, surrounded by sprawling factories and industrial buildings.

The town's main attraction is the **Pieve di Santi Ippolito e Donato**. Dating from the 12th century, this church contains some fine Siena School paintings and an altarpiece by Bicci di Lorenzo (1373–1452).

Bibbiena's main square, the Piazza Tarlati, offers excellent views of Poppi *(see p195)*.

🏛 **Pieve di Santi Ippolito e Donato**
Piazza Tarlati. **Open** *8am–noon, 3–6pm daily.* 💠

La Verna **8**

Road map E2. 💠 *from Bibbiena*.
Tel *0575 53 41*. **Open** *6:30am–7:30pm daily.* 💠 *partial*.

The rocky outcrop on which La Verna monastery stands, called La Senna, was split, according to legend, by an earthquake when Christ died on the Cross. The site was given to St Francis by the local ruler, Count Orlando Cattani, in 1213, and it was here, in 1224, that the saint was miraculously marked with the stigmata – the wounds of Christ.

Today, the monastery is both a popular tourist sight and a charismatic religious centre. Its modern buildings are not particularly attractive, but they contain numerous sculptures by the della Robbia workshops. There are several waymarked paths through the surrounding woodland, leading to some excellent viewpoints.

The Casentino **9**

Road map E2. **FS** 💠 *from Bibbiena*. **i** *Bibbiena*.

The vast Casentino region, an area of tiny villages dotted among hills covered with ancient woodland, lies to the north of Arezzo. The river Arno has its source here, on the slopes of Monte Falterona.

Countless streams run down the region's valleys to join it, creating stunning waterfalls.

A favourite destination for walkers, the area is renowned for its abundant autumn mushroom crop *(see p202)*.

Caprese Michelangelo **10**

Road map E2. 🏛 *1,671*. 💠 *from Arezzo*. **i** *Via Capoluogo 1 (0575 79 37 76)*.

Michelangelo Buonarroti was born in Caprese on 6 March 1475, while his father served as the town's *podestà* – a combination of magistrate, mayor and chief of police. His birthplace is now a museum, the **Comune Casa Natale Michelangelo**, housing photos and copies of the artist's work. The town walls feature modern sculptures and have fine views over the alpine landscape. Michelangelo attributed his keen mind to the mountain air he breathed here as a child.

Michelangelo Buonarroti (1475–1564)

🏛 **Comune Casa Natale Michelangelo**
Casa del Podestà, Via Capoluogo 1.
Tel *0575 79 37 76*. **Open** *mid-Jun–Aug: 9:30am–6:30pm daily (to 7:30pm Sun & Aug); Sep–mid-Jun: 10am–5pm daily (to 6pm Sun).*

Sansepolcro **11**

Road map E3. 🏛 *15,700*. 💠
i *Via Matteotti 8 (0575 74 05 36)*.
🍴 *Tue, Sat.*

Sansepolcro is a busy industrial town, famous as the birthplace of the artist Piero della Francesca (1410–92). The **Museo Civico**, housed in the 14th-century Palazzo Comunale, contains a collection of his work. The most famous exhibit is Piero's fresco *The Resurrection* (1463), in which a curiously impassive Christ strides out of his tomb. The sleeping soldiers at his feet, in their Renaissance armour, seem trapped in time, while the Son of God takes

The monastery at La Verna, founded by St Francis in 1213

possession of a primitive, eternal landscape. Other works by Piero are displayed in the same room, notably the *Madonna della Misericordia* (1462).

Sansepolcro is home to a number of other major works. Chief among these are Luca Signorelli's 15th-century *Crucifixion* (also in the Museo Civico) and Rosso Fiorentino's Mannerist *Deposition* in **San Lorenzo** church.

🏛 Museo Civico
Via Aggiunti 65. **Tel** 0575 73 22 18.
Open Oct–May: 9:30am–1pm, 2:30–6pm daily; June–Sep: 9am–1:30pm, 2:30–7:30pm daily.
Adm charge.

⛪ San Lorenzo
Via Santa Croce. **Tel** 0575 74 05 36.
Open 10am–1pm, 3–6pm daily. ♿

Anghiari ⑫

Road map E3. 👥 5,874. 🚌
ℹ Via Matteotti 103 (0575 74 92 79). 🛒 Wed.

The Battle of Anghiari, between Florence and Milan in 1440, was to have been the subject of a fresco by Leonardo in Florence's Palazzo Vecchio. It was never painted – one of the greatest "lost" works of

Anghiari, a typical medieval walled town

the Renaissance. Today, this historic little town sits peacefully amid fields of tobacco, a traditional crop of the upper valley of the river Tevere (Tiber), which rises nearby on the slopes of Monte Fumaiolo.

🏛 Museo dell'Alta Valle del Tevere
Piazza Mameli 16. **Tel** 0575 78 80 01.
Open 8:30am–7pm Tue–Sat, 9am–1pm Sun. **Closed** 1 Jan, 1 May, 25 Dec.
Several major works, such as Jacopo della Quercia's fine wooden *Madonna* (1420), can be seen here. There are also displays of locally made furniture and toys.

⛪ Santa Maria delle Grazie
Propositura. **Open** daily. ♿
The town's main church, dating to the 18th century, contains a High Altar and tabernacle from the della Robbia workshops. There is also a 15th-century *Madonna and Child* painted by Matteo di Giovanni.

🏛 Museo della Misericordia
Via Francesco Nenci 13. **Tel** 0575 78 95 77. **Open** by appt.
The Misericordia, a charitable organization, was founded in the 13th century to look after ailing pilgrims on their way to Rome. Today it operates Tuscany's efficient ambulance service *(see p301)*. This small museum records their work.

Monterchi ⑬

Road map E3. 👥 1,910. 🚌
ℹ Arezzo. 🛒 Sun.

The cemetery chapel at Monterchi was the site chosen in 1460 by Piero della Francesca for his *Madonna del Parto* (Pregnant Madonna) *(see p28)*, possibly because his mother may be buried here. The recently restored fresco is now in the **Museo Madonna del Parto**. A work of haunting ambiguity, it simultaneously captures the Virgin's pride in the impending birth, the weariness of pregnancy and the sorrow borne of knowing that her child will be no ordinary man.

🏛 Museo Madonna del Parto
Via Reglia 1. **Tel** 0575 707 13.
Open 9am–1pm, 2–7pm Tue–Sun (until 6pm Nov–Mar). **Adm charge.**

The Resurrection (1463) by Piero della Francesca in Sansepolcro

Arezzo ⑭

One of the wealthiest cities in Tuscany, Arezzo produces gold jewellery for shops all over Europe. It is famous for Piero della Francesca's frescoes and for its antiques market. Following World War II, there was much rebuilding – broad avenues have replaced many of the medieval alleys. The Chimera fountain near the station is a reminder of the city's past. It is a copy of an Etruscan bronze *(see p42)* cast here in 380 BC.

Duomo façade, completed as recently as 1914

Chimera fountain

🏠 San Francesco
See pp200–201.

🏠 Pieve di Santa Maria
Corso Italia 7. **Tel** *0575 226 29.*
Open *8am–1pm, 3–6:30pm daily.*
Arezzo's main shopping street, Corso Italia, leads uphill to the Pieve di Santa Maria, which has a beautifully ornate Romanesque façade. Sadly, the complex filigree of interlaced arches has weathered badly.

The splendid campanile, the "tower of a hundred holes", dates to 1330. Its name derives from the many arches running through it.

🏯 Piazza Grande
The square is famous for its regular antiques market *(see p286)*. On the west side, the façade of the Palazzo della Fraternità dei Laici is decorated with a relief of the Virgin (1434) by Bernardo Rossellino. The lower half of the building dates from 1377. The belfry and clock tower date from 1552.

The north side of the square is occupied by a handsome arcade designed by Vasari in 1573.

⚓ Fortezza Medicea e Parco il Prato
Tel *0575 37 76 66.* **Open** *summer: 8am–8pm; winter: 8am–5pm.* ♿
Antonio da Sangallo the Younger's imposing fortress was built for Cosimo I during the 16th century. It was partly demolished in the 18th century, leaving only the ramparts intact. With its excellent views across the Arno valley, it remains an excellent spot for a picnic.

The same can be said of the city's large public park, the Parco il Prato, with its extensive lawns. It contains a huge statue (1928) of the great poet Petrarch. The house where he was born stands at the entrance to the park.

🏠 Duomo
Piazza del Duomo. **Open** *daily.*
Begun in 1278, the Duomo remained incomplete until 1510; its façade dates to 1914. A huge building, its Gothic interior is lit through windows containing beautiful 16th-century stained glass by Guillaume de Marcillat, a French artist who settled in Arezzo.

High on the wall to the left of the 15th-century High Altar can be seen the tomb of Guido Tarlati, bishop and ruler of Arezzo from 1312 until his death in 1327. Carved reliefs depict scenes from his unconventional life. Next to the tomb is a small fresco of Mary Magdalene by Piero della Francesca (1410–92).

The Lady Chapel, fronted by an intricate wrought-iron screen (1796), contains a terracotta *Assumption* by Andrea della Robbia (1435–1525).

🏛 Museo del Duomo
Piazzetta behind the Duomo 13.
Tel *0575 239 91.* **Open** *10am–12:30pm Thu–Sat. Ask the sacristan to let you in.* **Adm charge.**
Among the artifacts removed from the cathedral are three wooden crucifixes, dating from the 12th and 13th centuries. The oldest of these was painted by Margaritone di Arezzo in 1264.

Also of interest are Bernardo Rossellino's terracotta bas-relief of *The Annunciation* (1434), a number of frescoes by Vasari (1512–74) and an *Annunciation* by Spinello Aretino (1373–1410).

Apse of Pieve di Santa Maria and Palazzo della Fraternità dei Laici in Piazza Grande

Casa del Vasari

Via XX Settembre 55. **Tel** 0575 40 90 40.
Open 8:30am–7pm Mon, Wed–Sat,
9am–1pm Sun & public hols.
Vasari (1512–74) built
this house for himself
in 1540 and decorated
the ceilings and walls
with portraits of fellow
artists, friends and
mentors. He
also painted
himself looking
out of one of
the windows.

Detail of fresco from Casa del Vasari

A prolific painter
and architect, Vasari
is most famous for his book,
*Lives of the Most Excellent
Painters, Sculptors and
Architects* (1550). An account
of many great Renaissance
artists, it has, in spite of an
often cavalier attitude to the
truth, led to Vasari being described as the first art historian.

Museo Statale d'Arte Medioevale e Moderna

Via di San Lorentino 8. **Tel** 0575
40 90 50. **Open** 9am–7pm daily.
Adm charge.
The museum is housed in the
graceful 15th-century Palazzo
Bruni. Its courtyard contains

architectural fragments and
sculptures dating from the
10th to the 17th centuries.
The collection includes
one of the best displays
of majolica pottery in
Italy. There are also
several terracottas by
Andrea della Robbia
and his followers;
frescoes by Vasari
and Signorelli;
and paintings by
19th- and 20th-
century artists,
including members
of the Italian
Macchiaioli School *(see p123)*.

Anfiteatro Romano e Museo Archeologico

Via Margaritone 10. **Tel** 0575 208
82. **Open** 8:30am–7pm daily. **Closed**
1 Jan, 1 May, 25 Dec. **Adm charge**
for Museo Archeo-
logico.
A ruined Roman
amphitheatre
stands near the
Museo Archeologico,
to the south of Arezzo.
Famous for its extensive
collection of Roman
Aretine ware, the mu-
seum has a display

1st-century BC Aretine ware

showing how this high-quality
red-glazed pottery was produced during the 1st century
BC and exported throughout
the Roman Empire.

Santa Maria delle Grazie

Via di Santa Maria. **Open** daily.
Completed in 1449 and set in
its own walled garden, this
church, fronted by Benedetto
da Maiano's pretty loggia
(1482), stands on the south-
eastern outskirts of the
town. The High
Altar, by Andrea
della Robbia
(1435–1525),
encloses Parri di
Spinello's fresco of the
Virgin (1430). A damaged
fresco by Lorentino
d'Arezzo (1430–1505) is
on the right of the altar.

AREZZO

Anfiteatro Romano e
   Museo Archeologico ⑨
Casa del Vasari ①
Duomo ④
Fortezza Medicea e Parco il
   Prato ⑧
Museo del Duomo ③
Museo Statale d'Arte
   Medioevale e Moderna ②
Piazza Grande ⑦
Pieve di Santa Maria ⑥
San Francesco ⑤

0 metres   500
0 yards   500

Key to Symbols *see back flap*

San Francesco

The 13th-century church of San Francesco contains Piero della Francesca's *Legend of the True Cross* (1452–66), one of Italy's greatest fresco cycles. The frescoes, now visible again after a long restoration, show how the Cross was found near Jerusalem by the Empress Helena. Her son, the Emperor Constantine, adopted it as his battle emblem. In reality, Constantine granted the Christian faith official recognition through the Edict of Milan, signed in 313. He is said to have bequeathed the Empire to the Church in 337, although this was still hotly disputed when Piero painted the frescoes. Visitors have a limited time in the chapel and advance booking is mandatory.

Exaggerated Hats
Piero often depicted historical figures in Renaissance garb.

Judas reveal
where the C
is hidden.

The Cross
returns to
Jerusalem.

Painted Crucifix
The 13th-century Crucifix forms the focal point of the fresco cycle. The figure at the foot of the Cross represents St Francis.

The Empress Helena watches the Cross being dug up. The town shown in the background, symbolizing Jerusalem, is an accurate representation of 15th-century Arezzo.

The Annunciation, wit
its stately figures and a
of serenity, is typical o
Piero's enigmatic style.

The Defeat of Chosroes
The battle scene shows the chaos of Renaissance warfare. Piero was influenced by ancient Roman carving, especially the battle scenes that often decorated sarcophagi.

The Death of Adam
This vivid portrayal of Adam and Eve in old age illustrates Piero's masterly treatment of anatomy. He was one of the first Renaissance artists to paint nude figures.

The prophets appear to play no part in the narrative cycle; their presence may be for purely decorative reasons.

The buildings in the fresco reflect the newly fashionable Renaissance style in architecture (*see p25*).

The wood of the Cross is buried in a pit.

Constantine dreams of the Cross on the eve of battle.

Constantine adopts the Cross as his battle emblem.

The Queen of Sheba recognizes the wood of the Cross.

Solomon's Handshake
The Queen's handshake with Solomon, King of Israel, symbolizes 15th-century hopes for a union between the Orthodox and Western churches.

Mushrooms in Tuscany

Champignon
(*Marasmius oreades*)

The people of Tuscany consider mushrooms a great delicacy. Collecting fungi can be dangerous, unless you are an expert, but you can sample the best varieties in the region's restaurants. The smaller edible varieties are sometimes chopped and combined with mashed garlic to make a pasta sauce. As starters, many menus include *funghi trifolati* (sautéed mushrooms with garlic and parsley), or the region's most popular mushrooms, porcini, served *in gratella* (grilled). The prized truffle is often simply grated over home-made pasta; it has a pronounced flavour and should be used sparingly.

Gathering chanterelles *(right)* and saddle fungus *(left)*

Cauliflower fungus
(*Sparassis crispa*)

Field blewit
(*Lepista personata*)

Chanterelle
(*Cantharellus cibarius*)

Parasol
(*Lepiota procera*)

Cep
(*Boletus edulis*)

Oyster
(*Pleurotus ostreatus*)

Morel
(*Morchella esculanta*)

Champignon
(*Marasmius oreades*)

THE BEST TUSCAN MUSHROOMS

Prized species have a rich flavour and a firm texture. They are sold from mid-September to late November at shops and markets throughout the region.

Porcini

This popular mushroom, known in England as the cep, is one of the few wild species available all year, either fresh or dried.

Monte San Savino ⑮

Road map E3. 🏛 7,794. 🚊 🚌
ℹ Piazza Gamurrini 3 (0575
84 30 98). 🛒 Wed.

The town stands on the western edge of the Valdichiana, once a marshy and malaria-ridden plain that was drained by Cosimo I in the 16th century. It is now an area of rich farmland used to rear cattle whose meat is used for *Bistecca alla Fiorentina*, the famous beefsteaks served in Florentine restaurants *(p267)*.

Agriculture has made the town prosperous, and its streets are lined with handsome buildings and churches. Some of these are by the High Renaissance sculptor and architect Andrea Contucci, known as Sansovino (1460–1529), who was born in the town; a number are by Antonio da Sangallo the Elder (1455–1537), his contemporary.

The town's main street, Corso Sangallo, starts at the Porta Fiorentina town gate, built in 1550 to Giorgio Vasari's design. The street leads past the 14th-century Cassero, or Citadel, whose exterior walls are now almost entirely hidden by 17th-century houses. There are good views from the interior, which contains the tourist office and the small

Lucignano, with its circular street plan

Museo del Cassero with its extensive collection of local work. Further up the street is the handsome Classical Loggia dei Mercanti (1518–20), designed by Sansovino, and the Palazzo Comunale, originally built as the Palazzo di Monte by Sangallo for Cardinal Antonio di Monte in 1515. Sansovino's house can be seen in the Piazza di Monte. He laid out the square, built the fine double loggia with Ionic columns that fronts **Sant'Agostino** church and went on to design the cloister standing alongside it. Inside the church is a series of 15th-century frescoes illustrating scenes from *The Life of Christ*, and Vasari's *Assumption* altarpiece (1539). Sansovino's worn tomb slab lies beneath the pulpit.

Locally made vase, Museo di Ceramica

🏛 **Museo del Cassero**
Piazza Gamurrini. **Tel** 0575 84 30 98. Open by appt. **Adm charge**

🏠 **Sant'Agostino**
Piazza di Monte. **Open** daily. ♿

Lucignano ⑯

Road map E3. 🏛 3,349. 🚌
ℹ Piazza del Tribunale 1 (0575
838 01). 🛒 Thu.

An attractive medieval town, Lucignano contains many well-preserved 14th-century houses. The street plan is extremely unusual, consisting of a series of four concentric rings encircling the

hill upon which the town sits, sheltered by its ancient walls. There are four small piazzas at the centre.

The **Collegiata** is fronted by some attractive steps whose circular shape reflects the town's street plan. Completed by Orazio Porta in 1594, the church contains some fine gilded wooden angels added in 1706.

The 14th-century Palazzo Comunale houses the **Museo Comunale**. Its highlight is a massive gold reliquary, 2.5 m (8 ft) high, to which numerous artists contributed over the period 1350–1471. Because of its shape, it is known as the *Tree of Lucignano*.

Also of note are two 14th-century paintings by Luca Signorelli: a lunette showing St Francis of Assisi miraculously receiving the wounds of Christ to his hands and feet, and a *Madonna and Child*. There are several fine 13th- to 15th-century Siena School paintings and a small painting of the Madonna by Lippo Vanni (1341–75).

The vaulted ceiling of the main chamber, the Sala del Tribunale, has frescoes of famous biblical figures and characters from Classical mythology painted from 1438–65 by various Siena School artists.

🏠 **Collegiata**
Costa San Michele.
Tel 0575 83 61 22.

🏛 **Museo Comunale**
Piazza del Tribunale 22.
Tel 0575 83 80 01.
Open Tue, Thu–Sun.
Adm charge. ♿

Corso Sangallo in Monte San Savino

For hotels and restaurants in this region see pp259 and pp276–78

Cortona ⑰

Cortona is one of the oldest cities in Tuscany. It was founded by the Etruscans (see p42), whose work can still be seen in the foundations of the town's massive stone walls. The city was a major seat of power during the medieval period, able to hold its own against larger towns like Siena and Arezzo; its decline followed defeat by Naples in 1409, after which it was sold to Florence and lost its autonomy. The main street, Via Nazionale, is remarkably flat in comparison with the rest of Cortona. The numerous ladder-like alleys leading off it, for instance the Vicolo del Precipizio (Precipice Alley), are far more typical.

Medieval houses in Via Janelli

Palazzo Comunale

🏛 Palazzo Comunale

Closed to the public.
Dating from the 13th century, the building was enlarged at the beginning of the 16th century, to incorporate the distinctive tower. Its ancient steps are the ideal place to linger in the early evening.

🏛 Museo dell'Accademia Etrusca

Palazzo Casali, Piazza Signorelli 9. **Tel** 0575 63 04 15. **Open** Apr–Oct: 10am–7pm daily; Nov–Mar: 10am–5pm Tue–Sun. **Closed** 1 Jan, 25 Dec. **Adm charge**. 🅰 partial.
This is one of the region's most rewarding museums. It contains a number of major Etruscan artifacts, including a unique bronze chandelier (see p43) dating from the 4th century BC. There are also a number of Egyptian objects. These include a wooden model funerary boat dating to the second millennium BC.
On the west wall of the main hall is a beautiful fresco of Polymnia, the muse of song. It was once believed to be Roman and date from the

1st- or 2nd-century AD, but it is now known to be a brilliant 18th-century fake.

🔒 Duomo

Piazza del Duomo. **Open** daily. 🅰
The present Duomo was designed by Giuliano da Sangallo in the 16th century. Remains of an earlier Romanesque building were incorporated into the west façade. The entrance is through an attractive doorway (1550) by Cristofanello.

🏛 Museo Diocesano

Piazza del Duomo 1. **Tel** 0575 628 30. **Open** Apr–Oct: 10am–7pm daily; Nov–Mar: 10am–5pm Tue–Sun. **Adm charge**. 🅰
Housed in the 16th-century church of Gesù, the museum contains several masterpieces. Chief among these are Fra Angelico's *Annunciation* (1428–30), a *Crucifixion* by Pietro Lorenzetti (c.1280–

1348) and a *Deposition* by Luca Signorelli (1441–1523). There is also a Roman sarcophagus, featuring Lapiths and Centaurs, which was much admired by Donatello and Brunelleschi.

🏛 Via Janelli

The medieval houses in this short street are some of the oldest to survive in Italy. A striking feature is their overhanging upper floors, built out on massive timbers.

🔒 San Francesco

Via Maffei. **Closed** to the public.
The church was built in 1245 by Brother Elias, a native of Cortona, who succeeded St Francis as leader of the Franciscan order. He and Luca Signorelli (1441–1523), also born locally, are buried here.

The Annunciation (1428–30) by Fra Angelico in the Museo Diocesano

🏛 Piazza Garibaldi

Located on the eastern edge of town, this square is a favourite haunt of American students who come to Cortona each summer. It offers superb views of the handsome Renaissance church of Santa Maria delle Grazie al Calcinaio.

🏛 Via Crucis and Santa Margherita

The Via Crucis, a long uphill lane with gardens on either side, leading to the 19th-century church of Santa Margherita, was laid out as a war memorial in 1947. It is decorated with Futurist mosaics depicting episodes in Christ's Passion by Gino Severini (1883–1966).

The church, rebuilt from 1856–97 in the Romanesque-Gothic style, has excellent views over the surrounding country-side. Inside, to the right of the altar, lie a number of Turkish battle standards and lanterns captured during 18th-century naval battles. A single rose window remains from the original church.

Santa Maria delle Grazie

🏛 Santa Maria delle Grazie

Calcinaio. **Open** daily.
A 15-minute stroll from the centre of town, this remarkable Renaissance church (1485) is one of the few surviving works by Francesco di Giorgio Martini (1439–1502). The building is opened on request – ask at the caretaker's house, beyond a garden to the right of the main entrance.

The attractive High Altar (1519), built by Bernardino Covatti, contains a 15th-century image of the Madonna del Calcinaio. The stained glass is by Guillaume de Marcillat *(see p198)*.

VISITORS' CHECKLIST

Road map E3. 🚶 22,620.
🚈 Camucia, 5 km (3 miles) SE.
🚌 Piazza Garibaldi. **i** Via Nazionale 42 (0575 63 03 52). 🗓 Sat. 🎪 Sagra della Bistecca (14–15 Aug). **Shops closed** Mon am.

🏛 Tanella di Pitagora

Maestà del Sasso, on the road to Sodo. **Tel** 0575 63 04 15. **Open** daily. Book one day in advance at the Museo dell'Accademia Etrusca (see p200).
"Pythagoras's tomb" draws its name from a mix-up between Cortona and Pythagoras's birthplace, Crotone. Two Etruscan tombs nearby are called "melons" because of the grassy mounds around them.

Tanella di Pitagora, a Hellenic-style tomb on the plain below Cortona

CORTONA

Duomo ③
Museo dell'Accademia Etrusca ④
Museo Diocesano ②
Palazzo Comunale ⑤
Piazza Garibaldi ⑦

San Francesco ⑥
Santa Margherita ⑧
Via Janelli ①

Porta Montanina
Fortezza Medicea
⑧ Santa Margherita
VIA SANTA MARGHERITA
PIAZZALE MAZZINI
San Cristoforo
Porta Colonia
Sant'Antonio
VIA DEL SALVATORE
VICOLO M PERAZZI
VICOLO RADI
San Nicolò
VIA DELL'ORTO DELLA CERA
PIAZZA PESCAIA
VIA DELLE SANTUCCE
③ Duomo
Teatro Signorelli
VIA G. MAFFEI
VIA BERRETTINI
VIA SAN MARCO
VIA S. NICOLO
VIA SANTA MARGHERITA
Museo Diocesano ②
PIAZZA DEL DUOMO
Palazzo Fierli
VIA CASALI
VIA MONETTI
⑥ San Francesco
San Marco
Porta Berada
VIA JANELLI ①
Museo dell'Accademia Etrusca ④
Palazzo del Popolo
VIA G. MAFFEI
San Domenico
Giardino Pubblico
Porta a Maria
VIA ROMA
⑤ Palazzo Comunale
PIAZZA DELLA REPUBBLICA
Palazzo Ferretti
VIALE GIARDINI PUBBLICI
San Benedetto
VIA NAZIONALE
⑦ P
VIA GINO SEVERINI
VIA GUELFA
VIA COPPI
PIAZZA GARIBALDI
VIA DELLE MURA DEL MERCATO
VIA DEL MERCATO
Piazza del Mercato
Sant'Agostino
VIA S. SEBASTIANO
VIALE CESARE BATTISTI
STRADA UMBRO CORTONESE
Porta Sant'Agostino
Spirito Santo
Camucia-Cortona 5 km (3 miles)
🚈 Santa Maria delle Grazie al Calcinaio
AREZZO

Key to Symbols see back flap

| 0 metres | | 250 |
| 0 yards | | 250 |

CENTRAL TUSCANY

*W*ith Siena at its heart, this is an agricultural area of great scenic beauty, noted for its historic walled towns such as San Gimignano and Pienza. To the north of Siena is the Chianti Classico region, where some of Italy's best wines are produced; to the south is the Crete, with landscapes characterized by round clay hillocks, eroded of topsoil by heavy rain over the centuries.

The vine-clad hills to the north of Siena are dotted with farmhouses, villas and baronial castles. Many are now turned into luxury hotels or rental apartments, offering various leisure facilities such as tennis courts, swimming pools and riding stables: this is now one of the most popular areas for family holidays in the Tuscan countryside.

To the south of Siena, in the Crete, shepherds tend sheep whose milk is used to produce the *pecorino* cheese popular throughout Tuscany. Cypress trees, planted to provide windbreaks along roads and around isolated farms, are an important sculptural feature in this empty and primeval landscape.

Linking the two regions is the S2 highway, an ancient road along which pilgrims made their way in the Middle Ages, followed by travellers on the Grand Tour *(see p55)* in the 18th and 19th centuries. Romanesque churches line the roads, and the valleys and passes are defended by castles and garrison towns, most of which have hardly changed over the years.

CONSTANT CONFLICT

The history of the region is of a long feud between the two city states of Florence and Siena. Siena's finest hour was its victory in the Battle of Montaperti in 1260, but when Siena finally succumbed to the Black Death, and subsequently to a crushing defeat by Florence in the siege of 1554–5, the city went into decline.

As several other Central Tuscan cities experienced the same fate, this lovely region became a forgotten backwater, frozen in time. But after centuries of neglect, the graceful late-medieval buildings in many of the towns are now being well restored, making this the most architecturally rewarding part of Tuscany to explore.

The beautifully preserved fortified town of Monteriggioni

◁ **A house in San Quirico d'Orcia, bathed in the morning light**

Exploring Central Tuscany

The beautiful city of Siena, with its narrow streets and medieval buildings of rose-coloured brick, is the natural starting place for exploring the heart of Tuscany. From here it is only a short drive to the castle-dotted landscapes of Chianti to the north, or to historic towns such as San Gimignano and Montepulciano. Although these towns are full of visitors during the day, at night they revert to their timeless Tuscan character and many have first-class restaurants serving local fare. The landscape is of cypresses, olive groves, vineyards, simple churches and stone farmhouses.

Wicker-covered *damigiane* (demijohns) transporting local Chianti wine

GETTING AROUND

The S2 is the main road south through Siena. The S222 links Florence with Siena and is known as the *Chiantigiana* (Chianti Way) as it passes through the Chianti wine-growing area. Both routes are well served by bus services, and tour operators in both cities offer tours of the main sites. Train services are limited to one line between Florence and Siena. A car is a great advantage, especially for visiting the Chianti wine estates.

KEY

▬▬	Motorway
▬▬	Major road
▬▬	Secondary road
▬▬	Minor road
▬▬	Scenic route
▬▬	Main railway
▬▬	Minor railway
▬▬	Regional border
△	Summit

0 kilometres   10

0 miles   10

View over Siena from the surrounding hills

Landscape with cypresses typical of the Crete area

SIGHTS AT A GLANCE

Asciano ⑤
Bagno Vignoni ⑩
Chiusi ⑬
Colle di Val d'Elsa ②
Montalcino ⑧
Monte Oliveto Maggiore ⑥
Montepulciano ⑫
Monteriggioni ③
Pienza ⑪
Sant'Antimo ⑭
San Galgano ⑦
San Gimignano ①
San Quirico d'Orcia ⑨
Siena ④

Palazzo Campana, the gateway to Colle Alta

San Gimignano **1**

See pp212–15.

Colle di Val d'Elsa **2**

Road map C3. 🏛 *17,200.* **FS** 🚌
ℹ *Via Campana 43 (0577 92 27 91).* 🛒 *Fri.*

Colle di val d'Elsa has a lower and an upper town. Colle Alta, the upper town, is of great medieval architectural interest. Arnolfo di Cambio, who built the Palazzo Vecchio in Florence *(see pp78–9)*, was born here in 1232. In the modern lower town shops sell locally made crystal glass.

🏛 Palazzo Campana
Closed to the public.
This Mannerist palazzo was built on a viaduct in 1539 by Baccio d'Agnolo, forming a gateway to Colle Alta.

🔒 Duomo
Piazza del Duomo. **Open** *4–5pm Mon–Fri, Sun morning (for Mass only).* **Tel** *0577 92 01 80.*
The Duomo has a marble Renaissance pulpit carved with bas-reliefs of the Madonna (1465), attributed to Giuliano da Maiano. The façade was rebuilt in 1603.

🏛 Museo Archeologico
Palazzo Pretorio, Piazza del Duomo. **Tel** *0577 92 04 90.* **Open** *Oct–Apr: 3:30–5:30pm Tue–Fri, 10am–noon, 3–6pm Sat & Sun; May–Sep: 10am–noon, 5–7pm Tue–Sun (from 4pm Sat & Sun).* **Adm charge.**
The museum houses many Etruscan funerary urns. The building was once a jail: Communist slogans written on the walls survive from the 1920s.

🏛 Museo d'Arte Sacra
Via del Castello 31. **Tel** *0577 92 38 88.* **Open** *see Museo Civico.*
This museum features 14th-century frescoes by Bartolo di Fredi, Sienese paintings and a Etruscan pottery. In 2005 it will move to Palazzo San Pietro, in Via Gracco del Secco.

Sgraffito cherub, Museo Civico

🏛 Museo Civico
Via del Castello 31. **Tel** *0577 92 38 88.* **Open** *Apr–Oct: 10am–noon, 4–7pm Tue–Sun; Nov–Mar: 10am–noon, 3:30–6:30pm Sat & Sun.* **Adm charge.**
The museum is in the Palazzo dei Priori, whose façade is decorated with *sgraffito* work scratched in the plaster, incorporating cherubs and Medici coats of arms. There is a small collection of Siena School paintings and Etruscan pottery. The chapel next to the main room has a portico decorated with frescoes by Simone Ferri in 1581. In 2005 the museum will move to Palazzo San Pietro, in Via Gracco del Secco.

🔒 Santa Maria in Canonica
Via del Castello. **Open** *sporadically.*
The Romanesque church has a simple belltower and a stone façade decorated with brickwork. The interior was altered in the 17th century, and now contains a tabernacle by Pier Francesco Fiorentino, showing scenes from the lives of the Madonna and Child.

⚓ Porta Nova
Via Gracco del Secco. **Open** *daily.*
This large Renaissance fortress was designed by Giuliano da Sangallo in the 15th century to guard against attack from the Volterra road. Two heavily fortified cylindrical towers are on the outside of the building.

Monteriggioni **3**

Road map D3. 🏛 *720.* 🚌 ℹ
Piazza Roma 21 (0577 30 48 10).

Monteriggioni is a gem of a medieval hilltop town. It was built in 1203 and ten years later became a garrison town. It is totally encircled by high walls with 14 heavily fortified towers, built to guard the northern borders of Siena's territory against invasion by Florentine armies
Dante used the town as a simile for the abyss at the

Craft shop in the main piazza of Monteriggioni

heart of his *Inferno*, which compares Monteriggioni's ring-shaped citadel . . . "crowned with towers" to giants standing in a moat.

The walls, which are still perfectly preserved, are best viewed from the direction of the Colle di Val d'Elsa road. Within the walls, the sleepy village consists of a large piazza, a pretty Romanesque church, a few houses, a couple of craft shops, restaurants, and shops selling many of the excellent local Castello di Monteriggioni wines.

Siena ➍

See pp216–23.

Asciano ➎

Road map D3. 🚶 6,250. 🚂 🚌 ℹ *Corso Matteotti 18 (0577 71 95 10).* 🛍 *Sat.*

The road from Siena to Asciano passes through the strange Crete landscape of clay hillocks, almost bare of vegetation and looking like massive anthills. Asciano itself is medieval, and retains much of its fortified wall, built in 1351. The main street, Corso Matteotti, is lined with smart shops and Classical *palazzi*. At the top of the street, in Piazza della Basilica, there is a large fountain built in 1472. Facing it is the late 13th-century Romanesque **Basilica di Sant'Agata**.

The Romanesque Basilica di Sant'Agata in Asciano

Temptation of St Benedict (1508) by Sodoma in Monte Oliveto Maggiore

Alongside the church is the **Museo d'Arte Sacra**, which houses a collection of late Siena School masterpieces, including Duccio's *Madonna and Child* and Ambrogio Lorenzetti's unusual *St Michael the Archangel*. The **Museo Archeologico** is in the old San Bernardino church, and displays local Etruscan finds from the **Necropoli di Poggio Pinci**, 5 km (3 miles) east of the village. The artifacts come from tombs built between the 7th and 4th centuries BC. On Via Mameli, the **Museo Amos Cassioli** has a display of portraits by Cassioli, who lived here from 1832–91, and other modern works by local artists.

🛐 **Basilica di Sant'Agata**
Piazza della Basilica. **Open** daily.

🏛 **Museo d'Arte Sacra**
Piazza della Basilica.
Tel 0577 71 82 07. **Open** by appt.

🏛 **Museo Archeologico**
Corso Matteotti 46.
Open Tue–Sun. **Adm charge**.

⛏ **Necropoli di Poggio Pinci**
Poggio Pinci. *Tel 0577 71 95 10.*
Closed temporarily due to structural hazards. Due to re-open in 2006.

🏛 **Museo Amos Cassioli**
Via Mameli. *Call tourist information for opening times. Adm charge.* ♿

Monte Oliveto Maggiore ➏

Road map D3. *Tel 0577 70 76 11.*
Open 9:15am–noon, 3:15–5pm daily (to 6pm in the summer).

The approach to this abbey is through thick cypresses, with stunning views of eroded cliffs and sheer drops to the valley floor. It was founded in 1313 by the Olivetan order, who were dedicated to restoring the simplicity of Benedictine monastic rule. The 15th-century rose-pink abbey church is a Baroque building with outstanding choir stalls of inlaid wood.

Alongside is the Great Cloister (1427–74), whose walls are covered by a cycle of frescoes on the life of St Benedict, begun by Luca Signorelli, a pupil of Piero della Francesca, in 1495. He completed nine panels; the remaining 27 were finished by Sodoma in 1508. The cycle, which begins on the east wall with Benedict's early life, is considered a masterpiece of fresco painting for its combination of architectural and naturalistic detail.

Street-by-Street: San Gimignano ❶

The distinctive skyline of San Gimignano must have been a welcome sight to the faithful in medieval times, for the town lay on the main pilgrim route from northern Europe to Rome. This gave rise to its great prosperity at that time, when its population was twice what it is today. The plague of 1348, and later the diversion of the pilgrim route, led to its economic decline. However, since World War II it has been recovering rapidly thanks to tourism and local wine production. For a small town, San Gimignano is rich in works of art, and good shops and restaurants.

Sant'Agostino
Here Bartolo di Fredi painted Christ, Man of Sorrows.

To Sant'Agostino

Via San Matteo, in contrast with the more commercial Via San Giovanni, caters mainly for the local residents, selling food and wine, clothes and other typical Tuscan products.

Rocca (1353)

La Buca, Via San Giovanni, selling local wine and wild boar ham

Museo Ornitologico

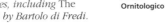

★ **Collegiata**
This 11th-century church is covered in delightful frescoes, including The Creation *(1367) by Bartolo di Fredi.*

Museo d'Arte Sacra
The museum contains religious paintings, sculpture and liturgical objects from the Collegiata.

STAR SIGHTS

★ Collegiata
★ Piazza del Duomo
★ Palazzo del Popolo

KEY

– – – Suggested route

0 metres	250
0 yards	250

For hotels and restaurants in this region see pp260–62 and pp278–80

★ Piazza del Duomo
Among the historic buildings located here is the Palazzo Vecchio del Podestà (1239), whose tower is probably the town's oldest.

There are spectacular views from the top of the Torre Grossa.

VISITORS' CHECKLIST

Road map C3. 🏠 7,041. 🚌 *Porta San Giovanni.* ℹ️ *Piazza del Duomo 1 (0577 94 00 08).* 🛒 *Thu.* **Shops closed** *Mon am (summer); souvenir shops stay open.* 🎉 *Patron Saints' Festivals: 31 Jan, 12 Mar; Ferie delle Messi: 3rd weekend of June; Fiera di Santa Fina: 1st wk of Aug; Fiera di Sant' Agostino: 29 Aug; Festa della Madonna di Pancole: 8 Sep.* **www**.comune.sangimignano.si.it

★ Palazzo del Popolo
The impressive town hall (1288–1323) has a huge Maestà by Lippo Memmi in the council chamber.

Piazza della Cisterna is named after the well at its centre.

Museo Civico
This gallery, found on the upper floors of the Palazzo del Popolo, houses The Madonna with Saints Gregory and Benedict (1511), which was one of the last works to be painted by Pinturicchio.

'ia San Giovanni is ned with shops elling local goods.

Exploring San Gimignano

Fresco in Sant'Agostino

The "city of beautiful towers" is one of the best-preserved medieval towns in Tuscany. Its stunning skyline bristles with tall towers dating from the 13th century: 14 of the original 76 have survived. These windowless towers were built to serve both as private fortresses and symbols of their owners' wealth. In the Piazza della Cisterna, ringed by a jumble of unspoilt 13th- and 14th-century *palazzi*, is a wellhead built in 1237. Shops, galleries and jewellers line the two main streets, Via San Matteo and Via San Giovanni, which still retain their medieval feel.

San Gimignano's skyline, almost unchanged since the Middle Ages

♖ Palazzo Vecchio del Podestà
Piazza del Duomo.
Closed to the public; visitors can observe only from the outside.
The Palazzo Vecchio del Podestà (the old mayor's palace) is in a group of public buildings clustered around the central Piazza del Duomo. It has a vaulted loggia and the 51-m (166-ft) Torre della Rognosa, one of the oldest towers in San Gimignano. A law was passed in 1255 forbidding any citizen to build a higher tower, but the rule was often broken by rival families.

⛫ Museo Civico
Palazzo del Popolo, Piazza del Duomo. **Tel** *0577 99 03 12.*
Museum & Tower open
Mar–Oct: 9:30am–7pm daily; Nov–Feb: 10am–5pm daily.
Adm charge.
The Museo is on the south side of the Piazza del Duomo, in the Palazzo del Popolo (town hall). Its tower,

finished in 1311, is the tallest in the city, at 54 m (175 ft). This is open to the public and the views from the top are quite stunning. Worn frescoes in the courtyard feature the coats of arms of city mayors and magistrates, as well as a 14th-century *Virgin and Child* by Taddeo di Bartolo. The first public room is the Sala di Dante, where an inscription records the poet's plea to the

12th-century well and medieval *palazzi* in the triangular Piazza della Cisterna

city council in 1300 to support the Guelph (pro-pope) alliance led by Florence. The walls are covered with hunting scenes and a huge *Virgin Enthroned* by Lippo Memmi (1317).

The floor above has a small art collection, which includes Pinturicchio's *Madonna with Saints Gregory and Benedict* (1511) painted against a landscape of blues and greens. The painting of *San Gimignano and his Miracles* by Taddeo di Bartolo shows the saint holding the town – recognizably the same city we see today. The *Wedding Scene* frescoes by Memmo di Filippucci (early 14th-century) show a couple sharing a bath and going to bed – an unusual record of life in a wealthy household in 14th-century Tuscany.

⛫ Museo d'Arte Sacra
Piazza Pecori. **Tel** *0577 94 22 26.*
Open *Apr–Oct: 9:30am–7:30pm daily; Nov–Jan & Mar: 9:30am–5pm daily.* **Closed** Feb. **Adm charge**.
The museum is entered from Piazza Pecori, where buskers play in summer. A chapel on the ground floor contains elaborate tomb slabs. The first floor houses paintings, sculpture and liturgical objects from the Collegiata. A marble bust (1493), by Benedetto da Maiano, commemorates the scholar Onofrio di Pietro.

♜ Collegiata
Piazza del Duomo. **Tel** *0577 94 03 16.*
Open *Nov–Jan: 9:30am–5pm daily (from 1pm Sun); Mar: 9:30am–5pm daily; Apr–Oct: 9:30am–7:30pm daily (to 5pm Sat).* **Adm charge**.
The plain façade of this 12th century Romanesque church belies its exotic interior it is one of the most frescoed churches in Italy. The arches bordering the central aisle are painted in striking blue and white stripes, and the deep blue paint of the vaulted roof is speckled with gold stars. The aisle walls are extensively covered with dramatic fresco cycles of scenes from the Bible. In the north aisle the frescoes are on three levels and comprise 26 episodes

The ceiling of the Collegiata, painted with gold stars

from the Old Testament, including *The Creation of Adam and Eve, Noah and his Ark, Moses Crossing the Red Sea* and *The Afflictions of Job*, finished by Bartolo di Fredi in 1367. On the opposite walls are scenes from the life of Christ, dated 1333–41, now attributed to Lippo Memmi, a pupil of Simone Martini. At the back of the church, on the nave walls, are scenes from *The Last Judgment*, painted by Taddeo di Bartolo (1393–6). They depict the souls of the damned being tortured in hell by devils relishing their task.

The tiny Santa Fina chapel, off the south aisle, is covered with a cycle of frescoes by Ghirlandaio (1475) telling the life story of St Fina; legend has it that she spent most of her short life in prayer. The towers of San Gimignano feature in the background of the funeral scene.

Under an arch to the left of the Collegiata is a courtyard containing the loggia to the Baptistry, frescoed with an *Annunciation* painted in 1482 by Ghirlandaio.

⋔ Rocca

Piazza Propositura. **Open** *daily.*
The Rocca, or fortress, was built in 1353. It now has only one surviving tower following its dismantling by Cosimo I de' Medici in the 16th century. It encloses a public garden filled with fig and olive trees, and commands superb views over the vineyards where wine has been produced for hundreds of years.

⛪ Sant'Agostino

Piazza Sant'Agostino. **Tel** *0577 90 70 12.* **Open** *7am–noon, 3–7pm daily.*
This church was consecrated in 1298 and has a simple façade, contrasting markedly with the heavily decorated Rococo interior (c.1740) by Vanvitelli, architect to the kings of Naples. Above the main altar is the *Coronation of the Virgin* by Piero del Pollaiuolo, dated 1483, and the choir is entirely covered in a cycle of frescoes of *The Life of St Augustine* (1465), by the Florentine artist Benozzo Gozzoli and his assistants.

In the Cappella di San Bartolo, on the right of the main entrance, is an elaborate marble altar completed by Benedetto da Maiano in 1495. The bas-relief carvings show the miracles performed by St Bartholomew, all topped by flying angels and a roundel of the Madonna and Child.

Detail from *The Life of St Augustine*

🏛 Museo Ornitologico

Via Quercecchio. **Tel** *0577 94 13 88.* **Open** *Apr–Sep: 11am–6pm daily.* **Adm charge**.
The museum is in an elaborate 18th-century Baroque church. This is in total contrast to the sturdy cases of stuffed birds that form the collection, put together by a local dignitary.

Fresco from the early 14th-century *Wedding Scene* cycle by Memmo di Filippucci in the Museo Civico

Street-by-Street: Siena ●

Unicorn *contrada* symbol

The principal sights of Siena are found in the network of narrow streets and alleys around the fan-shaped Piazza del Campo. Scarcely any street is level, as Siena, like Rome, is built on seven hills. This adds to the pleasure of exploring: one minute the city is laid out to view before you and the next you are in a warren of medieval houses. Packed into Siena are the 17 *contrade* (parishes) whose animal symbols are everywhere on carvings, plaques and car stickers.

Aerial bridges and corridors linking buildings on opposite sides of the street are characteristic of Siena.

Via della Galluzza leads up to the house where St Catherine was born in 1347.

★ Duomo
Statues of prophets carved by Giovanni Pisano in the 1290s fill the Gothic niches of the marble façade (see pp220–21).

Each tier of the Duomo's belltower has one window fewer than the floor above.

Antique shops line the streets near the Duomo square.

Museo dell'Opera Metropolitana
Statue of Remus. Legend tells that his son Senius founded Siena.

KEY
- - - Suggested route

0 metres 300
0 yards 300

Loggia della Mercanzia
Built in 1417, the arcade is where Siena's merchants and money dealers carried out their business.

Fonte Gaia

VIA BANCHI DI SOTTO

VIA RINALDINA

VIA DI PANTANETO

VIA DEL PORRIONE

PIAZZA DEL CAMPO

Torre del Mangia

VIA DI SALICOTTO

PIAZZA DEL MERCATO

VIA DUPRE

Steps linking the steep streets

VISITORS' CHECKLIST

Road map D3. 🏠 56,900.
FS Piazza Stazione.
🚌 Piazza San Domenico.
ℹ️ Piazza del Campo 56
(0577 28 05 51). **Open**
9am–7pm daily. 🛒 Wed. 🎺
Palio: 2 Jul, 16 Aug; Settimana
Musicale Chigiana: Jul.
www.terresiena.it

The Logge del Papa, or Pope's colonnade, was built in honour of Pius II in 1462.

Palazzo Piccolomini
Rossellino, the architect who built Pienza (see p226), designed this palazzo for Pius II's family.

★ **Piazza del Campo**
The Campo (field) is divided into nine marked sectors, symbolizing the Council of Nine, which was responsible for the government of the medieval city.

★ **Palazzo Pubblico**
The graceful Gothic town hall was completed in 1342. At 102 m (330 ft), the belltower is the second highest medieval tower to be built in Italy.

STAR SIGHTS

★ Duomo

★ Piazza del Campo

★ Palazzo Pubblico

Exploring Siena

Siena is a city of steep medieval alleys surrounding the Piazza del Campo. The buildings around the square symbolize the golden age of the city between 1260 and 1348, when wealthy citizens contributed to a major pro- gramme of civic building. Siena's decline began in 1348 when the Black Death hit the city, killing a third of the population; 200 years later many more died in an 18- month siege ending in defeat by the Florentines. The victors repressed all further development and building in Siena, which remained frozen in time, crammed with medieval buildings which have recently been renovated.

Muccio and Francesco di Rinaldo between 1338–48, it is named after the first bell ringer, who was nicknamed *Mangiaguadagni* (literally "eat the profits") because of his great idleness. (It was the bell ringer's responsibility to warn the citizens of impending danger.) There are 505 steps to the top of the tower, which has views across Tuscany.

Aerial view of Siena's Piazza del Campo and surrounding palazzi

☗ Piazza del Campo

The shell-shaped 12th-century Piazza del Campo is bordered by elegant *palazzi*. It has an elaborate fountain as its focal point, the Fonte Gaia, a rectangular marble basin decorated by statues. The fountain now seen in the square is a 19th-century copy of the original, which was carved by Jacopo della Quercia in 1409–19. This was removed to preserve it from the ravages of the weather.

The reliefs on the fountain depict Adam and Eve, the Madonna and Child, and the Virtues. Water is fed into it by a 25-km (15-mile) aqueduct, which has brought fresh water into the city from the hills since the 14th century.

☗ Torre del Mangia

Piazza del Campo. **Tel** *0577 29 22 63*. **Open** *10am–4pm (mid-Mar–Oct: to 7pm; extended hours in summer).* **Closed** *25 Dec.* **Adm charge**.
The belltower to the left of the Palazzo Pubblico is the second- highest in Italy, at 102 m (330 ft). Built by the brothers

☗ Palazzo Pubblico

Piazza del Campo 1. **Tel** *0577 29 22 63.* **Museo Civico Open** *mid-Mar–Oct: 10am–7pm daily; Nov–mid-Mar: 10am–5:30pm daily (extended hours in summer).* **Closed** *25 Dec.* **Adm charge**.
The Palazzo Pubblico serves as the town hall, but the state rooms are open to the public. The main council chamber is called the Sala del Mappa- mondo, after a map of the world painted by Ambrogio Lorenzetti in the early 1300s. One wall is covered by Simone Martini's *Maestà* (Virgin in Majesty). Painted in 1315, it depicts the Virgin Mary as the Queen of Heaven, attended by the Apostles, saints and angels. Opposite is Martini's fresco of the mercenary Gui- doriccio da Fogliano (1330).

The walls of the adjacent chapel are covered with frescoes of the *Life of the Virgin* (1407) by Taddeo di Bartolo, and the choir stalls (1428) feature wooden panels inlaid with biblical scenes.

The Sala della Pace contains the famous *Allegory of Good and Bad Government*, a pair of frescoes by Ambrogio Lorenzetti, finished in 1338. In *The Good Government (see pp46–7)* civic life flourishes, while *The Bad Government* reveals ruins and rubbish- strewn streets.

Fonte Gaia in Piazza del Campo

Guidoriccio da Fogliano by Simone Martini (1330) in the Palazzo Pubblico

The Sala del Risorgimento is covered with late 19th-century frescoes illustrating the events leading up to the unification of Italy under King Vittorio Emanuele II *(see pp54–5)*.

🏛 Palazzo Piccolomini

Via Banchi di Sotto 52. *Tel 0577 24 71 45.* **Open** 9am–1pm Mon–Sat. **Closed** 1st two weeks in Aug.
This imposing private palazzo was built in the 1460s by Rossellino for the very wealthy Piccolomini family. It houses the *Tavolette di Biccherna*, municipal ledgers from the 13th century, with covers by Sano di Pietro, Ambrogio Lorenzetti, Domenico Beccafumi and others.

🏛 Pinacoteca Nazionale

Via San Pietro 29. *Tel 0577 28 11 61.* **Open** 8am 1:30pm Sun, Mon, 8am–7pm Tue–Sat. **Closed** 1 Jan, 1 May, 25 Dec. **Adm charge**. ♿
Housed in the 14th-century Palazzo Buonsignori, this gallery contains important works by the Siena School. Lorenzetti's *Two Views*, painted in the 14th century, are early examples of landscape painting, and Pietro da Domenico's *Adoration of the Shepherds* (1510) shows how the art of the Siena School remained stylized long after Renaissance naturalism had

influenced the rest of Europe. There is also a striking *Deposition* (1502) by Sodoma.

🔒 Duomo
See pp220–21.

🏛 Museo dell'Opera Metropolitana

Piazza del Duomo 8. *Tel 0577 28 30 48.* **Open** mid-Mar–Oct: 9am–7:30pm daily (to 6pm in Oct); Nov–mid-Mar: 9am– 1:30pm. **Closed** 1 Jan, 25 Dec. **Adm charge**.
This museum is built into the unfinished side aisle of the Duomo *(see pp220–21)*. Part of it houses the sculpture from the exterior of the Duomo, which had become eroded outside. Duccio's double-sided *Maestà*, one of the best Siena School works, has a room to itself. Painted between 1308–11, it depicts the Madonna and Child on one side and scenes from *The Life of Christ* on the other. A loggia on the top floor offers views of the town and countryside.

Pisano's Simone (c.1300) in the Museo dell'Opera del Duomo

🏛 Santa Maria della Scala

Piazza del Duomo. *Tel 0577 22 48 11.* **Open** 10am–6pm daily. **Adm charge**. ♿ 🏛
This former hospital is now a museum housing a collection of paintings and sculpture. In the Sala del Pellegrino,

frescoes by Domenico di Bartolo depict hospital scenes from the 1440s, including monks attending to the sick.

Cloister of Casa di Santa Caterina

🏛 Santuario e Casa di Santa Caterina

Costa di Sant'Antonio. *Tel 0577 247 393.* **Open** 9am–12:30pm, 3–6pm daily (3:30–6pm in winter).
Siena's patron saint, Catherine Benincasa (1347–80), was the daughter of a tradesman. She took the veil aged eight, and experienced many visions of God, from whom she also received the stigmata. Her eloquence persuaded Gregory XI to return the seat of the papacy to Rome in 1376, after 67 years of exile in Avignon. She died in Rome and was canonized in 1461. Today, her house is surrounded by chapels and cloisters. It is decorated with paintings of events from her life by artists such as Pietro Sorri and Francesco Vanni, both her contemporaries.

Siena Duomo

Siena's Duomo (1136–1382) is one of the most spectacular in Italy, and one of the few to have been built south of the Alps in full Gothic style. Many ordinary citizens helped to cart the black and white stone used in its construction from quarries on the outskirts of the city. In 1339, the Sienese decided to build a new nave to the south with the aim of making it the biggest church in Christendom. This plan came to nothing when plague hit the city soon afterwards, killing off much of the population. The uncompleted nave now contains a museum of Gothic sculpture.

★ **Pulpit Panels**
Carved by Nicola Pisano in 1265–8, the panels on the octagonal pulpit depict scenes from The Life of Christ.

★ **Inlaid Marble Floor**
The Massacre of the Innocents is one of a series of scenes in the inlaid marble floor. The marble is usually uncovered each year, in September and October.

Nave
Black and white marble pillars support the vault.

Chapel of St John the Baptist

STAR FEATURES

★ Inlaid Marble Floor
★ Piccolomini Library
★ Pulpit Panels by Pisano

★ **Piccolomini Library**
Pinturicchio's frescoes (1509) portray the life of Pope Pius (see p226). Here he presides at the betrothal of Frederick III to Eleonora of Portugal.

Unfinished Nave
If completed, the nave would have measured 50 m (162 ft) in length and 30 m (97 ft) in breadth.

VISITORS' CHECKLIST

Piazza del Duomo. *Tel* 0577 28 30 48. Pollicino. **Duomo open** 10:30am–7:30pm Mon–Sat (to 6:30 Nov–mid-Mar), 1:30–6:30pm Sun (to 5:30 Nov–mid-Mar). 8, 9 & 11am Mon–Sat, 8 & 11am, 12:15 & 6:30pm (Sep–Mar: 5:30) Sun. **Fee** to see marble floor. **Library open** daily; mid-Mar–Oct: 9am–7:30pm (from 2 Sun); Nov–mid-Mar: 10am–1pm, 2–5pm (only pm Sun).

Archway leading to the Baptistry

The side aisle of the unfinished nave was roofed over and turned into the Museo dell'Opera del Duomo.

Column base in unfinished nave

The façade was built in two parts: the doors in 1284–97, the rest in 1382–90.

Façade Statues
Many statues on the façade have been replaced by copies; the originals are in the Museo dell'Opera del Duomo.

Entrance to Duomo

Sun Symbol
Hoping to end bloodshed and rivalry, St Bernardino of Siena (1380–1444) wanted the feuding Sienese to give up all loyalty to their contrada *emblems and unite under this symbol of the risen Christ.*

The Sienese Palio

One of the contrada symbols

The Palio is Tuscany's most celebrated festival and takes place on 2 July and 16 August each year in the Campo *(see p218)*. It is a bareback horse race and was first recorded in 1283, but may have had its origins in Roman military training. The jockeys represent the 17 *contrade* or districts; the horses are chosen by the drawing of straws and are then blessed at the local *contrada* churches. The races are preceded by heavy betting and pageantry, but only last about 90 seconds each. The winner is awarded a *palio* (banner).

Ringside View
Huge sums are paid for a view of the races.

Flag-Throwing
The Sienese display their flag-throwing skills in the procession and pageantry before the race.

Medieval Knight
The traditional outfits worn in the processions are all hand-made.

Racing Crowds
Thousands of people cram into the piazza to watch the race, and rivalry is intense between competitors.

Galloping towards the finish

Traditional drummer taking part in pre-race pageant

View across the Campo during a race

The façade of San Domenico

🔒 San Domenico

Piazza San Domenico. *Open daily.*
This barn-like Gothic church
was begun in 1226 and its
belltower was added in 1340.
Inside is an exquisite chapel
dedicated to St Catherine
(see p219). It was built in
1460 to store her preserved
head, which is now kept in a
gilded marble tabernacle on
the altar. This is surrounded
by frescoes showing
Catherine

in a state of religious fervour,
painted by Sodoma in 1526.
The marble pavement is
attributed to Giovanni di
Stefano.

Catherine experienced
many of her visions and
received her stigmata in the
Cappella delle Volte at the
west end of the church. Here
there is an authenticated
portrait of her by
contemporary Andrea Vanni,
dated around 1380.

🏰 Fortezza Medicea

Viale Maccari. **Fortezza** *Open daily.*
Enoteca ☎ *0577 28 84 97.* **Open**
noon–1am Tue–Sat, noon–8pm Mon.
Theatre *Open Nov–Apr:
performances only.* **Closed** *May–Oct.*
This huge red-brick fortress
was built for Cosimo I by
Baldassarre Lanci in 1560,
following Siena's defeat by the
Florentines in the 1554–5 war.
More than 8,000 Sienese died
either from battle wounds or
through starvation and disease
in the 18-month siege,
reducing the town's
population to a mere 6,000.
The town was repressed by its
Florentine masters, its banking
and wool industries were
suppressed and all building
work ended.

The fortress now houses an
open-air theatre, and from the
entrance bastions there are
glorious views of the countryside. The Enoteca Italiana, a
wine shop, is in one of the
bastions on the Lizza, the garden fronting the fort. It offers
visitors the chance to taste and
buy from a comprehensive list
of quality Italian wines.

Casa di Santa
 Caterina ③
Duomo ⑤
Fortezza Medicea ①
Museo dell'Opera
 Metropolitana ④
Palazzo Piccolomini ⑦
Palazzo Pubblico ⑨
Piazza del Campo ⑥
Pinacoteca Nazionale ⑩
San Domenico ②
Santa Maria della Scala ⑪
Torre del Mangia ⑧

SIENA CITY CENTRE

0 metres 200
0 yards 200

Key to Symbols *see back flap*

KEY
See p216–17

The ruined abbey at San Galgano, surrounded by dense woodland

San Galgano 🟡

Road map D4 (località Chiusdino).
🚌 *from Siena.* **Abbey and oratory**
open daily.

The ruined Cistercian abbey
is in dense woodland in a
superb setting. It is very
remote but well worth the
effort of getting there for the
beauty of the surroundings
and the majesty of the ruined,
roofless building. Begun in
1218, the abbey is Gothic in
style; unusual in Tuscany, this
reflects the French origins of
the Cistercian monks who
designed and built it.

The monks avoided contact
with civilization and divided
their lives between prayer
and labour, clearing the hills
of vegetation to graze their
sheep. Despite the Cistercian
emphasis on poverty, the
monks became wealthy from
the sale of wool; by the middle
of the 14th century, the abbey
was corruptly administered
and gradually fell into decline.

In the late 14th century, the
English mercenary Sir John
Hawkwood sacked the abbey
and by 1397 the abbot was
the sole occupant. Numbers
recovered for a time but the
abbey was eventually dissolved
in 1652. Empty for many years,
the cloister and other monastic
buildings alongside the church
are now being restored for
the Olivetan order of nuns.

On a hill above the abbey is
the beehive-shaped chapel of
Montesiepi, built on the site
of St Galgano's hermitage
around 1185, a few years
after his death in 1181.

St Galgano's sword stands
embedded in a stone just
inside the door of the circular
oratory. The 14th-century
stone walls of the side chapel
are covered with frescoes
showing scenes from
Galgano's life by Ambrogio
Lorenzetti (1344); some are
now in a poor state of repair.

The shop alongside the
chapel sells locally-made
herbs, wines, olive oils and
toiletries along with books
on the history of the region.

Montalcino 🟡

Road map D4. 🏘 *5,100.* 🚌
ℹ️ *Costa del Municipio 8 (0577
84 93 31).* **Closed** *Mon.* 🅿️ *Fri.*

Montalcino's foremost
activity is wine-producing,
as is evident from the
number of shops where you
can both sample and buy
the excellent local Brunello
wines *(see p268).*

The town, situated on the
top of a hill, is of timeless
character and the streets are
narrow, winding and steep.
The highest point is the
14th-century **Fortezza** and
its impressive ramparts,
built by Cosimo I in 1571.

THE LEGEND OF ST GALGANO

Galgano was born in 1148, the
son of noble parents, and grew
into a brave but dissolute young
knight. He saw his life as futile
and turned to God, renouncing
the material world. When he
tried to break his sword
against a rock as a symbol of
his rejection of war, it was
swallowed by the stone. This
he interpreted as a sign of
God's approval. He built a
hut on the site of today's
chapel at Montesiepi, and
died a hermit in 1181. In 1185
Pope Urban III declared him
a saint and an example to all
Christian knights.

Montalcino's 14th-century Fortezza

Spectacular views over the surrounding countryside are available from the walkway on the ramparts.

There is an Enoteca (wine shop) in the grounds of the Fortezza, where the Brunello red wines are on sale.

Inside the fortress there is an ancient Sienese battle standard, a reminder that the town gave refuge to a band of rebels after Florence conquered Siena in 1555. In remembrance of this, flag-bearers from the village of Montalcino are given the honour of leading the parade before the Palio in Siena every year (*see p222*).

As you walk down into the town from the Fortezza, the monastery of Sant'Agostino and its 14th-century church, with an attractive rose window, are on the right. Just beyond is the **Palazzo Vescovile**, formerly the bishop's palace. The **Palazzo Comunale** stands on the Piazza del Popolo. Constructed in the 13th and 14th centuries, its tall, slim tower rises above the town.

The Duomo, San Salvatore, was designed in 1818–32 by Agostino Fantastici, and replaced the original Romanesque church building.

⚜ **Fortezza**
Piazzale della Fortezza. **Tel** 0577 84 92 11. **Enoteca open** Nov–Mar: 9am–6pm daily; Apr–Oct: 9am–8pm daily. **Adm charge** for ramparts.

🏛 **Palazzo Vescovile**
Via Spagni 4. **Tel** 0577 84 81 68. **Closed** to the public.

🏛 **Palazzo Comunale**
Costa del Municipio 1. **Tel** 0577 84 93 31. **Closed** to the public.

San Quirico d'Orcia ❾

Road map E4. 🏠 *2,390.*
🚌 ℹ *Via Dante Alighieri 33 (0577 89 72 11).* 🛒 *2nd & 4th Tue of month.*

Collegiata in San Quirico

Standing just inside the city walls, San Quirico d'Orcia's pride is the **Collegiata**, featuring three ornately carved Romanesque portals built onto an 8th-century structure. Begun in 1080, the capitals and lintels of the portals are carved with details of dragons, mermaids and other mythical beasts.

The church commemorates the 3rd-century martyr St Quiricus, who was killed at the age of five by the Romans for the simple act of declaring himself a Christian. Quiricus is depicted in the elaborate altar piece by Sano di Pietro, along with the Virgin and Child and other saints.

Next to the church is the 17th-century **Palazzo Chigi**, whose frescoed interior has recently been restored. The **Horti Leonini** nearby is a 16th-century garden of box hedges nestling within the town walls. It was intended as a refuge for pilgrims, and is now used as a public sculpture garden during the summer months.

⛪ **Collegiata**
Via Dante Alighieri. **Tel** 0577 89 72 36. **Open** 8am–5pm daily.

🏛 **Palazzo Chigi**
Piazza Chigi. **Open** 10am–1pm, 4–7pm (Oct–Mar: 3:30–6:30pm) Tue–Sun.

🌿 **Horti Leonini**
Piazza Libertà. **Tel** 0577 89 72 11. **Open** sunrise–sunset daily. ♿ partial.

Flower-covered house in the pretty town of Montalcino

The Terme di Bagno Vignoni

Bagno Vignoni ⑩

Road map D4. 👥 *32.* 🚌 *from Siena.* ℹ️ *0577 88 73 65.*

This is a tiny medieval spa village which consists of a handful of houses built round a huge piazza containing an arcaded, stone-lined pool. Constructed by the Medici, it is full of hot sulphurous water which bubbles up to the surface from the volcanic rocks deep underground. The healing quality of the water has been known since Roman times and, according to legend, famous people who have sought a cure in Bagno Vignoni include St Catherine of Siena *(see p215)* and Lorenzo the Magnificent (to relieve his arthritis). The pool is no longer open for bathing but is still well worth a visit to admire the architecture. Sulphur pools in the grounds of the Posta Marcucci hotel are open for swimming.

Coat of arms of Pope Pius II

Pienza ⑪

Road map E4. 👥 *1,300.* 🚌 ℹ️ *Corso il Rossellino 59 (0578 74 90 71).* 🛒 *Fri.*

The centre of Pienza was completely redesigned in Renaissance times by Pope Pius II *(see p47)*. Born here in 1405, when it was called Corsignano, Aeneas Sylvius Piccolomini became known as a leading Humanist scholar and philosopher. He was elected pope in 1458 and in the following year decided to

commission a new centre in Corsignano and rename it Pienza in his own honour. He planned to transform his birthplace into a model Renaissance town, but the grand scheme never progressed beyond the handful of buildings around the Piazza Pio II. The architect Bernardo Rossellino was commissioned to build a Duomo, papal palace and town hall, which were completed in three years. Subsequently Rossellino was caught embezzling papal funds, but Pius II forgave him because he was so delighted with his new buildings.

Away from the grandeur of the main square, Pienza is a quiet agricultural town with shops selling local produce like *pecorino*, cheese made from sheep's milk *(see p255)*.

🏛 Duomo

Piazza Pio II. **Open** *daily.*
The Duomo was built by the architect Rossellino in 1459, and is now suffering from serious subsidence at its eastern end. There are cracks in the walls and floor of the nave, but this does not detract at all from the splendid Classical proportions of this Renaissance church. It is flooded with light from the vast stained-glass windows requested by Pius II; he wanted a *domus vitrea* (literally "a house of glass") which would symbolize the spirit of intellectual enlightenment of the Humanist age.

🏛 Palazzo Piccolomini

Piazza Pio II. **Tel** *0578 74 85 03.*
Open *10am–12:30pm, 3–6pm Tue–Sun (guided tours only).* **Closed** *mid-Nov–mid-Dec.* **Adm charge.**
The palazzo is next door to the Duomo and was home to Pius II's descendants until 1968. Rossellino's design for the building was influenced by Leon Battista Alberti's Palazzo Rucellai in Florence *(see p104).* The apartments open to the public include Pius II's bedroom and library, which are full of his belongings. At the rear of the palazzo there is an arcaded courtyard and a triple-tiered loggia. The spectacular view looks across the garden and takes in the wooded slopes of Monte Amiata.

Courtyard in Palazzo Piccolomini

🏛 Pieve di Corsignano

Via delle Fonti. **Tel** *0578 74 82 03.*
Open *by appt or through tourist office.*
Pope Pius II was baptized in this 11th-century Romanesque parish church on the outskirts of Pienza. It has an unusual round tower and a doorway decorated with flower motifs.

Pienza's piazza and the town hall, viewed from the steps of the Duomo

The church of Madonna di San Biagio on the outskirts of Montepulciano

Montepulciano ⑫

Road map E4. 🏘 *14,000.* 🚌
ℹ *Via Gracciano nel Corso 59
(0578 75 73 41).* 🛒 *Thu.*

Montepulciano is built
along a narrow limestone
ridge and, at 605 m (1,950 ft)
above sea level, is one of the
highest of Tuscany's hilltop
towns. The town is encircled
by walls and fortifications
designed by Antonio da
Sangallo the Elder in 1511
for Cosimo I. Inside the walls
the streets are crammed with
Renaissance-style palazzi and
churches, but the town is
chiefly known for its good
local Vino Nobile wines *(see
p256)*. A long winding street
called the Corso climbs up
into the main square, which
crowns the summit of the hill.

On the Corso is the Art Deco
Caffè Poliziano, which has an
art gallery in the basement.
In July the café hosts a jazz
festival and the town fills with
musicians who perform at the
Cantiere Internazionale d'Arte
(see p33), an arts festival
directed by the German composer Hans Werner Henze.

In August there are two
festivals: the Bruscello takes
place on the 14th, 15th and
16th, when hordes of actors
re-enact scenes from the
town's turbulent history. For
the Bravio delle Botti, on the
last Sunday in August, there is
a parade through the streets
followed by a barrel race and
a banquet to end the day.

🏛 Madonna di San Biagio
Via di San Biagio 14. *Open daily.* ♿
This beautiful church on the
outskirts of Montepulciano is
perched on a platform below
the city walls. Built of honey-
and cream-coloured travertine,
it is Sangallo's masterpiece, a
Renaissance gem begun in
1518. The project occupied
him until his death in 1534.
The façade is being restored.

🏛 Palazzo Bucelli
Via di Gracciano del Corso 73. *Closed.*
The lower façade of the
palazzo (1648) is studded
with ancient Etruscan reliefs
and funerary urns collected
by its 18th-century antiquarian
owner, Pietro Bucelli.

🏛 Sant'Agostino
Piazza Michelozzo. *Open daily.*
Michelozzo built the church
in 1427, with an elaborate
carved portal featuring the
Virgin and Child flanked by
St John and St Augustine.

🏛 Palazzo Comunale
Piazza Grande 1. *Tel 0578 75 70 34.*
In the 15th century,
Michelozzo added a tower
and façade on to the original
Gothic town hall. The
building is now a smaller
version of the Palazzo
Vecchio *(see pp72–9)*.
The tower is open only
during the summer months.

🏛 Palazzo Tarugi
Piazza Grande. *Closed.*
This imposing 16th-century
palazzo is located next to the
town hall.

🏛 Duomo
Piazza Grande. *Open daily.*
The Duomo was designed
between 1592 and 1630 by
Ippolito Scalza. The façade
is unfinished and plain, but
the interior is Classical in
proportions. It is the setting
for an earlier masterpiece
from the Siena School, the
Assumption of the Virgin
triptych painted by Taddeo
di Bartolo in 1401. Placed
over the High Altar, it is rich
in bright, jewel-like colours
and heavily embossed with
gold leaf.

Taddeo di Bartolo's triptych (1401)

🏛 Santa Maria dei Servi
Via del Poliziano. *Open by appt.* ♿
The Corso continues from the
Piazza up to the Gothic church
of Santa Maria dei Servi. The
wine bar alongside sells Vino
Nobile from medieval storage
cellars cut out of the limestone cliffs below the town.

Etruscan frieze in the Museo Nazionale Etrusco in Chiusi

Chiusi ⑬

Road map E4. 🏘 *10,000.* FS 🚌
ℹ️ *Piazza Duomo 1 (0578 22 76
67).* 🚐 *Mon, Tue.*

Chiusi was one of the
most powerful cities in the
Etruscan league, reaching the
height of its influence in the
7th and 6th centuries BC *(see
pp42–3).* There is a large
number of Etruscan tombs in
the surrounding countryside.

🏛 Museo Archeologico
Nazionale
Via Porsenna 93. **Tel** *0578 201 77.*
Open *9am–2pm daily (to 1pm Sun
& hols).* **Adm charge.** ♿
The museum, founded in 1871,
is packed with cremation urns,
vases decorated with black
figures and Bucchero ware,
burnished to resemble bronze.
Most of these were excavated
from local tombs, which can
be visited by arrangement
with the museum.

🔓 Duomo
Piazza del Duomo. **Open** *daily.*
The Romanesque cathedral is
built from recycled Roman
pillars and capitals. The decorations on the nave walls seem
to be mosaics, but in fact were
painted by Arturo Viligiardi
in 1887. There is a Roman
mosaic under the High Altar.

🏛 Museo della Cattedrale
Piazza del Duomo. **Tel** *0578 22 64 90.*
Open *Jun–mid-Oct: 9:30am–12:45pm
4–7pm daily; mid-Oct–May 9:30am–
12:45pm Mon–Sat, 3:30–6:30pm
Sun.* **Adm charge.** ♿ *partial.*
The museum has a display of
Roman, Lombardic and medi-
eval sculpture. Visits can be
arranged here to the under-

ground galleries beneath the
city, dug by the Etruscans and
used as Christian catacombs
in the 3rd–5th centuries.

Sant'Antimo ⑭

Road map D4. **Custodian** *0577 83
56 59.* **Open** *10:30am–12:30pm,
3–6:30pm Mon–Sat, 9:15–10:45am,
3–6pm Sun.* ♿

This beautiful abbey church
(see pp44–5) has inspired
many poets and painters and
enchants everyone who

comes here. The creamy travertine church is set against a
background of tree-clad hills
in the Starcia valley. The very
earliest surviving church on
the site dates back to the 9th
century, but locals prefer to
think the church was founded
by the Holy Roman Emperor
Charlemagne in 781. The
main part of the church was
built in 1118 in the French
Romanesque style, and the
exterior is decorated with
interlaced blank arcades
carved with the symbols
of the Four Evangelists.

The soft, honey-coloured
alabaster interior has an odd
luminous quality which is
seen to change according to
time of day and season. The
capitals in the nave are carved
with geometric designs, leaf
motifs and biblical scenes.
Recorded plainsong echoes
around the walls, adding to
the eerie atmosphere.

The Augustinian monks
who tend the church sing
Gregorian chant at mass
every Sunday and there are
organ concerts in the church
during July and August.

The beautiful abbey church of Sant'Antimo

A Day Out in Chianti

This tour takes in the main villages of the Chianti Classico wine region. Castles and wine estates line the route, and vineyards offer tastings and sell direct to the public. Look for signs along the way saying "vendita diretta".

The first stop on leaving Siena is the Castello di Brolio, which has been owned by the Ricasoli family since 1167. From Brolio, drive to Gaiole, diverting to see the 13th-century castle at Meleto. Gaiole is a very quiet agricultural town with a stream running down the main street; wine can be sampled here at the local cooperative. In Badia a Coltibuono there is a restaurant *(see p292)* and a Romanesque church, and Radda in Chianti offers extensive views over the Parco Naturale della Viriglia. At Castellina in Chianti, there is a 15th-century underground passage built for defence purposes, and the Enoteca Vini Gallo Nero (Via della Rocca 13), which is a showcase for the region's wines *(see pp268–9)*.

Badia a Coltibuono ④
At the crossroads in Gaiole, follow the signs to Montevarchi and divert to the left off the main road before heading right towards the village of Badia.

Radda in Chianti ⑤
Return to the main road from Badia and drive on to Radda.

S429

Castellina in Chianti ⑥
From Radda drive straight on to Castellina, and from there follow the signs back to Siena.

Gaiole in Chianti ③
The main road from Meleto leads to Gaiole.

Meleto ②
Follow the signs to Gaiole from Brolio. After 9 km (5.5 miles) turn right to see the castle at Meleto.

Lecchi

S222

Vagliagli

S408

The Gallo Nero (black cockerel) is the symbol of the Chianti Classico Consortium.

CONSORZIO DEL GALLO NERO · CHIANTI CLASSICO

Pieve Asciata

Castello di Brolio ①
Leave Siena on the S408 to Gaiole in Chianti. After 15 km (9 miles) turn right to Brolio, leading to the Castello di Brolio.

SIENA

S408

KEY

- Tour route
- Other roads

0 km 2
0 miles 2

SOUTHERN TUSCANY

*T*he southernmost part of Tuscany has a very different feel to any other Tuscan region. Thanks to the hotter, drier and sunnier climate, the hills are cloaked in aromatic Mediterranean scrub, known as macchia. Palm trees grow in the towns and along the edge of the sandy beaches, and great strands of prickly pear cactus are traditionally used to mark field boundaries in the countryside.

The coastline, lined with fishing villages and beaches, is very popular in the summer, with numerous holiday villages and caravan sites. Resorts such as Monte Argentario have a much more exclusive image, and are favoured by the wealthy, yacht-owning Italians from Rome and Milan. Inland, the region's wild and unspoiled hills are popular with sportsmen, who come to hunt for wild boar and deer.

The transformation of the marshy coastal strip, known as the Maremma, into a holiday playground is a recent development. The ancient Etruscans, followed by the Romans *(see p42)*, drained its swamps to create richly fertile farming land. After the collapse of the Roman Empire, the drainage channels became choked, turning the Maremma into an inhospitable wilderness of marshland and stagnant pools plagued by malaria-carrying mosquitoes. Re-draining of the land began again in the late 18th century and, with the help of insecticides, the malaria-mosquito was finally eliminated in the 1950s.

LITTLE DEVELOPMENT

The region slumbered from Roman times and for long periods was virtually uninhabited except for farmers and fishermen. Consequently there are few cities or major architectural and artistic monuments. On the other hand, archaeological remains have survived because there were few people here to salvage the stone for new buildings. The relative lack of intensive farming means the region is still rich in wildlife, from butterflies and orchids to tortoises and porcupines.

Detail of Romanesque *tympanum* on the Duomo at Massa Marittima

◁ The Strada Panoramica at Monte Argentario

Exploring Southern Tuscany

Away from the coastal resorts, this region remains
relatively undiscovered; quiet roads and a lack of
tourists only add to the pleasure of exploring rock-
cut tombs in Sovana, bathing in hot
sulphurous springs at Saturnia or
wandering through the Maremma
spotting the wildlife. For a busier
atmosphere, visit the resorts of
Orbetello and Monte Argentario,
which have plenty of choice for
shopping, restaurants and nightlife.

Statue above gateway, Orbetello

KEY

=== Major road

— Secondary road

=== Minor road

— Scenic route

=== Main railway

— Minor railway

=== Regional border

△ Summit

Marina di
Castagneto-
Carducci

Donoratico

Monteverdi
Marittimo

Castagneto
Carducci

Colline Metalli

Sassetta

San Vincenzo

*Monte Calvo
648m*

Suvereto

Riva degli Etruschi

Campiglia Marittima

MASSA MA

*Golfo di
Baratti*

Venturina

Valpi

Populonia

Marina di Salivoli

PIOMBINO **2**

Prato Ranieri

Gavo

Follonica

Scarl

Canale di Piombino

*Golfo di
Follonica*

Capo Vita

Cavo

*Isola
Palmaiola*

Punta Ala

*Poggio Bal
630m*

PORTOFERRAIO **3**

5 RIO MARINA

Marciana
Marina

Riva del Sole

4

Procchio

San Martino

MARCIANA

Castiglione
della Pescaia

Pomonte

Lacona

Porto Azzurro

Marina
di Campo

Capoliveri

Isola d' Elba

*Punta di
Fetovàia*

Punta dei Ripalti

GETTING AROUND

The S1 coastal route cannot
cope with the traffic in
summer and is best avoided.
A busy railway line runs
alongside; most trains stop
at Grosseto and Orbetello,
and buses from Grosseto
serve most towns in the area.
Vehicle and passenger ferries
depart from Piombino to
Elba every 30 minutes during
the day in summer. Bus
services from Portoferraio
cover all parts of the island.

View across the rooftops of Massa Marittima to the hills beyond

Sandy beaches at Procchio on the north coast of Elba

SIGHTS AT A GLANCE

Ansedonia ⓮
Capalbio ⓮
Grosseto ❻
Marciana ❹
The Maremma ❼
Massa Marittima ❶
Monte Argentario ⓬
Orbetello ⓫
Piombino ❷
Pitigliano ❿
Portoferraio ❸
Rio Marina ❺
Saturnia ❽
Sovana ❾

Massa Marittima ●

Road map C4. 🏠 *9,469.* 🚌
🏢 *Amatur, Via Todini 3–5 (0566 90 27 56).* 🛒 *Wed.*

Set in the Colline Metallifere (metal-bearing hills), from which lead, copper and silver ores were mined, Massa Marittima is far from being a grimy industrial town. Its history is closely associated with mining and there are some excellent examples of Romanesque architecture.

🏛 Duomo
The Romanesque cathedral is dedicated to St Cerbone, a 6th-century saint whose story is told in stone above the door.

🏛 Museo Archeologico & Pinacoteca
Palazzo del Podestà, Piazza Garibaldi. **Tel** *0566 90 22 89.* **Open** *Tue–Sun.* **Adm charge.**
This 13th-century building has an archaeological museum with material from Paleolithic to Roman times.

🏛 Museo della Miniera
Via Corridoni. **Tel** *0566 90 22 89.* **Open** *Mar–Jan: Tue–Sun (guided tours only).* **Adm charge.**
Parts of this museum of mining are located within a worked-out mine shaft. The exhibits explain mining techniques and locally found minerals.

Piombino ●

Road map C4. 🏠 *36,774.* 🚊 🚌
🚢 🏢 *Via Ferruccio 4 (0565 22 56 39).* 🛒 *Wed.*

Piombino is a busy town dominated by iron and steel works. It is at the end of the Massoncello peninsula and was originally an island.

The skyline of Massa Marittima

A Day Out on Elba

Elba's most famous resident was Napoleon, who spent nine months here after the fall of Paris in 1814. Today the island is mainly populated by holidaymakers, who come by ferry from Piombino, 10 km (6 miles) away on the mainland. The main town is Portoferraio, with an old port and a modern seafront with smart hotels. The landscape of the island is varied: on the west coast there are sandy beaches, suitable for all water sports; inland, olive groves and vineyards line hillsides, and vegetation covers the mountains. The east coast is more rugged, with high cliffs and stony beaches.

Marciana Marina ③
Return to the main road and follow the coast round, past Procchio with its long sandy bays. From here it is 7.5 km (4.5 miles) to the marina.

Marciana Alta ④
From the marina take the main road into the hills to the old medieval town. After 8 km (5 miles) turn left on to a minor road leading to the cable car up to the top of Monte Capanne.

KEY

▬▬	Tour route
═══	Other roads

0 km   2
0 miles   2

Marina di Campo ⑤ Stay on the coast road, round the west end of the island, until Marina di Campo.

It is the main port for ferries to Elba, which run every half hour in summer and also at fairly frequent intervals in winter. Nearby are the extensive ruins of Etruscan Populonia and the **Museo Etrusco Gasparri**, which contains a collection of bronze and terracotta works found in the surrounding necropolises.

🏛 **Museo Etrusco Gasparri**
Populonia. *Tel 0565 293 39.* **Open** *9am–sunset daily.* **Adm charge.** ♿

Portoferraio ❸

Road map B4. 🚶 *11,500.* 🚌 ⛴ ℹ *Calata Italia 43 (0565 91 46 71).* 🛒 *Fri.*

The ferry from mainland Piombino arrives here. The town has a pretty harbour but the main sights are Napoleon's two houses. In the centre of Portoferraio is the **Palazzina Napoleonica** (also known as the Villetta dei Mulini), a modest house built around two windmills. **Villa**

San Martino, his country residence, had a Classical façade imposed on it by the Russian emigré, Prince Demidoff, in 1851. Egyptian-style frescoes in the house, painted in 1814, are a reminder of Napoleon's Nile campaigns of 1798–9.

🏛 **Palazzina Napoleonica**
Villa Napoleonica dei Mulini.
Tel 0565 91 58 46. **Open** *9am–7pm Mon, Wed–Sun (to 1pm Sun).* **Closed** *Tue.* **Adm charge.** ♿

🏛 **Villa San Martino**
San Martino. *Tel 0565 91 46 88.* **Open** *9am–7pm Tue–Sun (to 1pm Sun).* **Closed** *Mon.* **Adm charge.**

Marciana ❹

Road map B4. 🚶 *3,000.* 🚌
ℹ *Municipio, Marciana Alta (0565 90 12 15).*

On Elba's Northwest coast is Marciana Marina, and further inland the well-preserved medieval town of Marciana Alta. The **Museo**

Shady beaches and inlets at Marciana Marina on Elba

Civico Archeologico houses exhibits from Etruscan ships wrecked off Elba. From here, take the cable car up Monte Capanne, Elba's highest peak at 1,018 m (3,300 ft).

🏛 **Museo Civico Archeologico**
Via del Pretorio, Marciana Alta.
Tel 0565 90 12 15. **Open** *Apr–Sep: daily.* **Adm charge.**

Villa San Martino ② Divert right off the main road to San Martino, and on to Napoleon's country residence.

Portoferraio ① Take the main coast road towards Marciana Marina.

Cavo ⑨ Drive for 7.5 km (4.5 miles) to Cavo, along the east coast, to see the scenic northern tip of Elba.

Rio Marina ⑧ This mining town, 12 km (7.5 miles) to the north, has an excellent museum of mineralogy.

Porto Azzurro ⑦ Return to the main road and carry on for 2 km (1.25 miles) to Elba's second largest port, a fashionable resort overlooking a lovely bay dominated by a 17th-century fortress.

Capoliveri ⑥ Follow the road round the south of the island and divert to the right just before Porto Azzurro to visit this charming old mining village.

The Maremma ❼

Maremma butterfly

The ancient Romans were the first to cultivate the marshes of the Maremma, but after the collapse of their empire the area went virtually uninhabited until the 18th century. The land has since been reclaimed, the irrigation canals unblocked and farming developed on the fertile soil. The Parco Naturale dell'Uccellina was set up in 1975 to protect the abundant local flora and fauna and prevent more development taking place.

Wildlife
The undergrowth and marshes are home to wild boar and other wildlife.

This salt marsh, cut by irrigation canals, is home to herons, storks and other wading birds.

Entry permits are sold at Alberese.

SPERGOLAIA

Fiume Ombrone

PRATINI

Torre di Castelmarino

Canoes can be hired to explore the irrigation canals.

A7

P

MARINA DI ALBERESE

Torre di Collelungo

There are picnic tables on the beach in the shade of pine trees.

Sea lilies and hollies grow along the sandy shoreline, backed by groves of parasol pines, mastic trees and juniper.

Beaches
The shoreline south of Marina di Alberese has wide, sandy beaches sheltered by steep cliffs.

Torre di Castelmarino
The cliffs are crowned by 16th-century watchtowers, part of a defence system built by the Medici to protect the coastal region from attack.

For hotels and restaurants in this region see p263 and pp280–81

★ Abbazia di San Rabano

The ruined Cistercian abbey, built in the 12th century, stands close to the park's highest peak, Poggio Lecci. The tower and fortifications date back to the 14th century, the time of the fierce battles between Pisa and Siena.

The hills running parallel to the coast are cloaked in scrub called *macchia*, consisting of rosemary, broom, rock rose, sea lavender and rowan trees.

★ Waymarked Paths

Footpaths give access to areas where you can see butterflies, lizards and poisonous snakes, including vipers.

Birds of prey hunt in remote parts of the parkland.

ALBERESE SCALO

Il Uccellina

bano

FONTEBLANDA

Rocca di Talamone

Talamone is a fishing village.

TALAMONE

Long-horned Cattle
The docile white Maremma cattle are raised by cowboys (butteri) who also stage rodeos.

VISITORS' CHECKLIST

Centro Visite di Alberese. **Road map** D5. **Tel** 0564 40 70 98. **www**. parcomaremma.it **Marginal areas Open** 9am–1 hr before sunset daily (mid-Jun–Sep: 7:30–10am, 4–6pm daily). **Entrances** Alberese, Marina di Alberese, Talamone. **Itineraries: A/5, A/6**: nature trails 5 km (3 miles), 2 hrs; **A/7**: Ombrone estuary, 4 km (2.5 miles), 2 hrs; **T/1, T/2**: short trails (Oct–mid-Jun only). 📷 🎫 adv booking (only in spring). **Inner park areas Open** 9am–1 hr before sunset Wed, Sat, Sun and public hols; **Closed** 1 May, 25 Dec. **Entrance** Alberese. Tour transport departs from Pratini, 9 km (5.5 miles). **Itineraries: A/1**: Abbazia di San Rabano, 6 km (3.75 miles), 5 hrs; **A/2**: Le Torri, 5 km (3 miles), 3 hrs; **A/3**: Le Grotte, 8 km (5 miles), 4 hrs; **A/4**: Cala di Forno, 12 km (7.5 miles), 6 hrs. **Note:** A/3 and A/4 are closed mid-June–Sep. **Adm charge.** 📷 🎫 mid-Jun–Sep: compulsory for **A/1** (7am) and **A/2** (4pm). **Park regulations:** Dress adequately and bring drinking water. Some walks are strenuous.

KEY

═══ Roads

▬▬▬ Paths

════ Canals and rivers

– – Itineraries

0 km   1

0 miles   1

STAR FEATURES

★ Waymarked Paths

★ Abbazia di San Rabano

Rio Marina ❺

Road map B4. 🏚 *2,038.* 🚌
ℹ *Lungomare G Marconi 2,
Gli Spiazzi (0565 96 20 04).* 🚢 *Mon.*

Around Rio Marina there are
still open-cast mines which
extract the ores that attracted
the Etruscans to Elba. The
Museo dei Minerali explains
the geology of the island.
Shops in the town centre sell
jewellery made of local semi-
precious stones.

🏛 Museo dei Minerali
Palazzo Comunale. *Tel 0565 96
27 47.* **Open** *Apr–mid-Oct: daily;
mid-Oct–Mar: by appt.* **Adm charge.**

Grosseto ❻

Road map D4. 🏚 *71,472.*
FS 🚌 ℹ *Via Monterosa 206
(0564 46 26 11).* 🚢 *Thu.*

Grosseto is the largest town
in southern Tuscany. World
War II destroyed many
buildings, but the 16th-century
walls still stand and several of
the bastions are now parks.

🏛 Museo Civico
Archeologico e d'Arte
della Maremma
Piazza Baccarini 3. **Open** *Oct–Feb:
9am–1pm Tue–Sun (also 4–6pm Sat);
Mar–Apr: 9am–1pm, 4–6pm Tue–Sun;
May–Sep: 10am–1pm, 5–8pm Tue–
Sun.* **Closed** *1 Jan, 1 May, 25 Dec.*
The museum has Etruscan and
Roman artifacts from Roselle
and Vetulonia. There is also a
collection of coins, intaglios
(carved stones) and pottery.

Grosseto, a busy town full of
narrow streets and shops

Cascate del Gorello, free for all to enjoy in Saturnia

The Maremma ❼

See pp236–7.

Saturnia ❽

Road map D5. 🏚 *550.* 🚌 ℹ *Piazza
Vittorio Veneto 10 (0564 60 12 80).*

Holidaymakers come to
Saturnia to enjoy the good
Maremma food or seek a
health cure in the modern spa
of Terme di Saturnia. Others
prefer to bathe for free in the
hot sulphurated waters of the
waterfall at Cascate del
Gorello on the Montemerano
road. This is a pretty spot,
with its pools and rocks
stained coppery green.

Sovana ❾

Road map E5. 🏚 *100.*

Sovana sits on a ridge high
above the Lente valley. Its
main street is lined with cafés,
restaurants and shops. The
13th-century Romanesque
Rocca Aldobrandesca,

named after the Teutonic fam
that ruled in the area until 16
is now in ruins.
   The frescoes of the late 15th
century Siena School in the
medieval church of **Santa Ma**
were discovered under the
whitewashed walls. The main
altar is sheltered by a 9th-
century canopy that was
originally in the Romanesque
Duomo. This 12th-century
building incorporates sculptu
from earlier churches built on
the same site.
   The Etruscans dug tombs
nearby in the soft limestone
cliffs bordering the river Lent
The most complete set of
Necropoli Etrusca can be
found in a valley just to the
west of Sovana.

⚜ Rocca Aldobrandesca
Via del Pretorio. **Closed.**

⛪ Santa Maria
Piazza del Pretorio. **Open** *daily.*

⛪ Duomo
Piazza del Pretorio. **Open** *daily in
summer; Sat, Sun only in winter.*

⛪ Necropoli Etrusca
Poggio di Sopra Ripa. **Tel** *0564 61
40 74.* **Open** *Mar–Nov: 9am–7pm
daily; Dec–Feb: 9am–5pm Sat & Sun.*

Cafés and shops in Sovana's medieval piazza

Pitigliano ⑩

Road map E5. 🏘 4,361. 🚌
🛈 Piazza Garibaldi 51 (0564
51 71 11). 🗓 Wed.

Pitigliano looks spectacular perched on a plateau, high above cliffs carved out by the river Lente. The houses seem to grow out of the cliffs, which are riddled with caves cut out of soft limestone. The caves have been used for many years to store wines and olive oils.

A maze of tiny medieval streets passes through the Jewish ghetto, formed when Jews fleeing from Catholic persecution took refuge here in the 17th century. The Palazzo Orsini in the town centre has its water supply brought in by an aqueduct, built in 1545, that overhangs Via Cavour. The **Museo Palazzo Orsini** in the palazzo has a

small exhibition of work by the artist Francesco Zuccarelli (1702–88). He also painted two of the altarpieces in the medieval **Duomo**, whose huge belltower supports a bell which weighs 3 tonnes.

The **Museo Etrusco** contains finds from ancient local settlements.

🏛 **Museo Palazzo Orsini**
Piazza della Fortezza Orsini. **Tel** 0564 61 60 74. **Open** 10am–1pm, 3–7pm (to 5pm in winter) Tue–Sun. **Closed** Mon. **Adm charge**.

🛈 **Duomo**
Piazza San Gregorio. **Open** daily. ♿

🏛 **Museo Etrusco**
Piazza della Fortezza Orsini 59. **Tel** 0564 61 40 67. **Open** summer: 10am–1pm, 3–7pm Thu–Tue; winter: 3–4pm Thu–Tue.

Orbetello ⑪

Road map D5. 🏘 15,455. 🚉 🚌
🛈 Piazza della Repubblica 1 (0564 86 04 47). 🗓 Sat.

Orbetello is a crowded resort bordered by two tidal lagoons. Part of the northernmost lagoon is managed by the Worldwide Fund for Nature as a wildlife park.

The town was the capital of a tiny Spanish state, called the Presidio, from 1557 until 1808, when it was absorbed into the Grand Duchy of Tuscany. The Porta del Soccorso bears the coat of arms of the king of Spain. Inside the gates is the **Polveriera Guzman**, which was originally used as an arsenal. The Duomo, **Santa Maria Assunta**, also has Spanish-style decoration, but the altar in the Cappella di San Biagio is typically Romanesque in design.

The Fontone di Talamone, in Piazza della Repubblica, is a terracotta plinth from the Roman Etruscan era.

Coat of arms on the Porta del Soccorso

🏛 **Polveriera Guzman**
Viale Mura di Levante. **Open** Call Tourist Information for details.

🛈 **Santa Maria Assunta**
Piazza del Duomo. **Open** daily.

View over Pitigliano showing soft limestone cliffs and caves bordering the river Lente

Porto Ercole, near Monte Argentario

Monte Argentario ⑫

Road map D5. 🏘 *14,000.* 🚌
ℹ *Piazzale Sant'Andrea, Porto Santo Stéfano (0564 81 42 08).* 🚌 *Tue.*

Monte Argentario was an island until the early 18th century, when the shallow waters separating it from the mainland began to silt up, creating two sandy spits of land, known as *tomboli*, that enclose the Orbetello lagoon. Orbetello itself was linked to the island in 1842, when a dyke was constructed linking the mainland to Terrarossa.

The two harbour towns of Porto Ercole and Porto Santo Stéfano are both favoured by wealthy yacht owners. There are good fish restaurants in both towns *(see p263)*, and from the Strada Panoramica there are views over rocky coves, cliffs and bays. Ferries from Porto Santo Stéfano go to the island of Giglio, popular with Italian tourists for its sandy beaches and rich wildlife.

In the summer the Porto Santo Stéfano ferry also calls at Giannutri, a privately owned island where visitors are not allowed to stay overnight.

Ansedonia ⑬

Road map D5. 🏘 *300.*

Ansedonia is a prosperous village of luxurious villas and gardens, high on a hill above the coast. The ruins of the city of Cosa, founded by the Romans in 173 BC, are on the summit of the hill looking over Ansedonia. The **Museo di Cosa**, containing relics from the ancient settlement, is close by. East of Ansedonia is a long stretch of sandy beach and the remains of the Etruscan Canal. The date and purpose of the canal

An Etruscan Tour

The Etruscans gained much of their wealth from Tuscany's vast mineral resources, and their monied classes were cultured and worldly. Both their elaborate burial sites and the artifacts found in their tombs give us an insight into their lives *(see pp42–3)*. Etruscan burial sites were carved into soft rock or built of huge stone slabs with rock-cut roads leading down to the tombs.

Grosseto ① The Museo Civico Archeologico has a collection of Etruscan artifacts found in local tombs.

ALSO WORTH SEEING

Museo Archeologico, Florence *(see p99).*

Museo Etrusco, Volterra *(see p166).*

Vulci and **Tarquinia** These excavated sites, just over the Tuscany border in Lazio, have impressive Etruscan ruins, painted tombs and art collections.

This Etruscan bone brooch, called a *fibula*, was found near Grosseto and is now in the Museo Archeologico in Florence.

Talamone ⑦ Follow the S74 to the S1. Turn right and after 8 km (5 miles) fork off to the left, into the Maremma, for the Etruscan temple, Roman villa and baths.

0 kilometres   5

0 miles   5

For hotels and restaurants in this region see p263 and pp280–81

The Etruscan Canal at Ansedonia

are debatable, but it may have been dug in Roman times to keep the harbour free of silt. Alternatively, it may have been part of a canal leading to the Lago di Burano, 5 km (3 miles) down the coast. This lagoon is 4 km (2.5 miles) long and has been turned into a wild-life refuge (*rifugio faunistico*) by the Worldwide Fund for Nature. It is a very important habitat for wading birds.

🏛 Museo di Cosa
Via delle Ginestre 35, Ansedonia. **Tel** 0564 88 14 21. **Open** 9am–7pm daily. **Closed** 1 Jan, 25 Dec. **Adm charge.**

Capalbio ⑭

Road map D5. 👥 4,049. 🚌 Wed.

Capalbio is another village which is popular with wealthy Italians. The hilltop town has several restaurants and hotels and is busy all year round. Summer tourists come for the beaches, and winter visitors flock to hunt deer and wild boar in the surrounding woodland, which is now managed as a game reserve. A game festival is held in September each year.

View across the rooftops of Capalbio

🌿 Giardino dei Tarocchi
Garavicchio, Pescia Fiorentina. **Tel** 0564 89 51 22. **Open** mid-May–mid-Oct: 2:30–7:30pm daily; mid-Oct–mid-May: group reservations only. **Adm charge.** At Pescia Fiorentina, southeast of Capalbio, is a modern sculpture garden created by the late French artist Niki de Saint-Phalle in 1982. It was inspired by the figures of the Tarot and was over ten years in the making. The bigger pieces each represent one card from the Tarot pack. Among the sculptures is *The Tower*, a glittering three-storey edifice made out of broken mirrors.

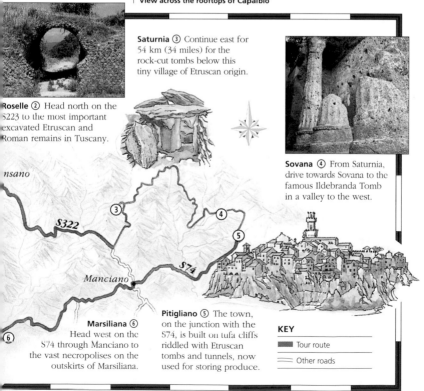

Saturnia ③ Continue east for 54 km (34 miles) for the rock-cut tombs below this tiny village of Etruscan origin.

Roselle ② Head north on the S223 to the most important excavated Etruscan and Roman remains in Tuscany.

Sovana ④ From Saturnia, drive towards Sovana to the famous Ildebranda Tomb in a valley to the west.

Marsiliana ⑥ Head west on the S74 through Manciano to the vast necropolises on the outskirts of Marsiliana.

Pitigliano ⑤ The town, on the junction with the S74, is built on tufa cliffs riddled with Etruscan tombs and tunnels, now used for storing produce.

KEY

▬ Tour route

═ Other roads

TRAVELLERS' NEEDS

WHERE TO STAY 244–263

RESTAURANTS, CAFES AND BARS 264–283

SHOPS AND MARKETS 284–289

ENTERTAINMENT 290–291

SPECIALIST HOLIDAYS AND
OUTDOOR ACTIVITIES 292–293

WHERE TO STAY

Sign showing
hotel rating

Of all Italy's regions, Tuscany has some of the most charming places to stay. Inland these range from ancient villas to elegant town houses. Smaller, family-run establishments excel in their cuisine and are sometimes filled with antiques. The major cities also offer B&B accommodation. Hotels on the riviera tend to be less distinctive, but the popularity of coastal resorts in summer means that standards are high. Many visitors opt for self-catering holidays Often the accommodation is a small flat or house on a farm, and the prices can prove very reasonable Other options include hostels and dormitories and, for walking enthusiasts, there are mountain huts throughout the region. For more information on hotels in Florence and Tuscany see the listings on pages 250–63.

Terrace at Hotel Continentale *(see p254)*

WHERE TO LOOK

Florence has a wide range of hotels, but prices can be high. The most attractive locations are along the north bank of the Arno, the historic centre and in nearby Fiesole. Parking is a problem in the city centre, so if you have a car it is best to choose a hotel which has parking facilities.

Accommodation in central Pisa is generally sub-standard but there are some lovely Tuscan villa hotels a short drive from the centre.

Though large, Arezzo has relatively few hotels and those in the centre are mostly geared for business people. If you can, stay outside the town and travel in to visit the centre.

The hill towns of central Tuscany offer a number of quality villa hotels, manor houses and even former palaces. The Chianti region is rich in converted villa hotels, with excellent regional restaurants, particularly around Radda and Gaiole. Siena's more attractive options are outside the city, such as the tiny hamlet of Strove.

Street sign showing the direction and location of hotels

HOTEL PRICES

During the low season (November to March) prices are cheaper and often negotiable. Florence is less busy than other parts of Tuscany in July and August, but this is the peak holiday season on the coast. Avoid the city during certain weeks of January and July when fashion shows fill the top hotels, raising low-season prices.

Single room rates are higher than individual rates for two people sharing a double room. Prices include tax and service. Bear in mind that accommodation in Florence and Siena is more expensive than elsewhere in the region.

HIDDEN EXTRAS

Before making a reservation, establish whether breakfast is included in the price. Garage parking, laundry and snacks in the hotel or from the minibar may be pricey and telephone charges from your hotel room can be phenomenal. Check the rates first if you are concerned. Some hotels may expect you to take full- or half-board during the high season.

HOTEL GRADINGS AND FACILITIES

Hotels in Italy are classified by a star-rating system, from one to five stars. However, each province sets its own levels for grading; consequently, standards for each category may vary from one area to another. Some hotels may not have a restaurant but those that do will welcome non-residents to stop by and eat.

Some of the converted castles and ancient villas are not air-conditioned, but as the stone walls are thick the

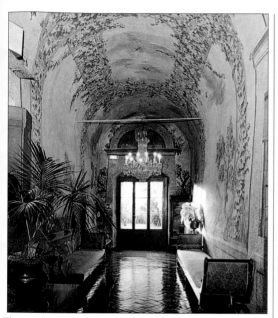

The marvellous gallery entrance of Hotel Villa Villoresi *(see p255)*

midsummer heat barely penetrates the buildings.

Children are welcome but the smaller hotels generally have limited facilities. Often, the more up-market hotels will arrange a baby-sitting service. Sometimes the proprietor of a smaller hotel, or a member of the family, will mind your children, if they are not busy.

WHAT TO EXPECT

In Florence, street numbers can be confusing *(see p298)*, so refer to the map references in the listings.

Hotel proprietors are obliged by law to register you with the police, so they will ask for your passport when you arrive. Make sure you take it back, as you will need some form of identification to change money or travellers' cheques.

Even a humble *pensione* should have a reasonably smart bathroom. Rooms without a bathroom will usually have wash basins and towels.

As far as hotel decoration goes, you may sometimes have to sacrifice smart decor for the charm of an old establishment.

The Italian breakfast is light – a cappuccino and a pastry

(brioche). Most hotels serve a continental breakfast of coffee, tea or hot chocolate, bread rolls and jam. However, it may be cheaper to go to a local bar or a *pasticceria*.

Florence can be very noisy. Top-class hotels usually have some form of soundproofing, but ask for a room facing away from the street if you are easily disturbed by noise.

Check-out time is usually noon in four- and five-star hotels and between 10am and noon in other establishments. If you stay longer you will be asked to pay for an extra day. However, many hotels will store your baggage if you plan on leaving the city several hours after check-out time.

BOOKING AND PAYING

Book at least two months in advance if you want to stay in a particular hotel in high season or at Easter. The local tourist office will have listings of all the hotels in the area and will be able to advise you on the best hotels for each category. Most hotels take credit cards, but check which ones when booking. You can usually pay the deposit by credit card, or send an international money order. Confirm your reservation by fax or e-mail including the dates of your stay and your credit card details.

Under Italian law, a booking is valid as soon as the deposit is paid and confirmation is received. As in restaurants, you are required by law to keep your hotel receipt until you leave Italy.

DISABLED TRAVELLERS

Facilities for the disabled are usually limited. The hotel listings on pages 250–63 indicate which hotels have these facilities.

HOTELS IN HISTORIC BUILDINGS

The Tuscany regional tourist board publishes a leaflet which lists hotels in historic buildings and those of artistic interest. Some of the best are included in the listings here. The booklet is also available from national Italian tourist offices worldwide. **Relais & Châteaux** produces a guide that includes a number of fine Tuscan hotels and hotel restaurants of historic interest, all of high quality.

Villa San Michele, a former monastery, in Fiesole *(see p256)*

Garden terrace at Villa La Massa *(see p256)*

Generally, a four-person villa within a complex in the low season will cost around €450 per week, while an individual villa in its own grounds can cost as much as €1,750 per week during the peak season.

STAYING IN PRIVATE HOMES

Rooms in private homes can usually be rented through one of the recreational associations such as **AB&BA** (Associazione Bed & Breakfast Affittacamere) in Florence. Meals are not provided but can sometimes be arranged on request.

RESIDENTIAL HOTELS

Throughout Tuscany there are former palaces or villas that have been converted into complexes of small apartments, often with facilities

SELF-CATERING

Farm and villa holiday accommodation abounds in Tuscany. There is an **Agriturist** office in each region with information on self-catering holidays, often on a farm that is still working.

An international agency dealing with self-catering holidays around Florence is the **American Agency**. Other agents include **Casaclub** in Siena, **Cuendet** in Monteriggioni and **Prima Italia** in Grosseto. **Solemar** has agents throughout the world, such as **Tailor Made Tours** in the UK and **Interhome** offices in the UK, the US and Australia.

Prices for self-catering vary enormously depending on the season and location.

DIRECTORY

HISTORIC HOTELS

Relais & Châteaux
5 Dovedale Studios,
465 Battersea Park Road,
London SW11 4LR.
Tel 00800 2000 0002.
Fax 020 7228 5483.
www.relaischateaux.com

SELF-CATERING AGENCIES

Agriturist Ufficio Regionale
Via degli Alfani 6/7,
50122 Florence.
Tel 055 28 78 38.
@ agritosc@
confagricoltura.it

American Agency
Via del Ponte Rosso 33r,
50129 Florence.
Tel 055 47 50 53.
www.americanagency.it

Casaclub
Viale Vittorio Veneto 41,
53100 Siena.
Tel 0577 440 41.
www.casaclub.it

Cuendet
Strada di Strove 17,
53035 Monteriggioni.
Tel 0577 57 63 30.
www.cuendet.com

Prima Italia
Viale Tirreno 19, 58046
Principina a Mare
(Grosseto). *Tel* 0564 300
09. www.primaita.it

Solemar
Tel UK: 020 8891 1294.
Tel US: 305 940 2299.
www.solemar.it

Tailor Made Tours
22 Church Rise,
London SE23 2UD.
Tel 020 8291 9736.
www.tailormadeitaly.com

PRIVATE HOMES

AB&BA
Via Pietro Mastri 26,
50135 Florence.
Tel 055 654 08 60.
www.abbafirenze.it

RESIDENTIAL HOTELS

Mini Residence
Via Giulio Caccini 20,
50141 Florence.
Tel 055 41 08 76.

Palazzo Ricasoli
Via delle Mantellate 2,
50129 Florence. **Map** 2
D3. *Tel* 055 35 21 51.
www.ricasoli.com

Residence Da-al
Via dell'Ariento 3,
50123 Florence.
Map 1 C4 (5 C1).
Tel 055 21 49 79.

La Valle
Via Sanminiatese,
Loc. La Valle, 50050
Montaione (Florence).
Tel 0571 69 80 59.
www.agricolalavalle.it

HOTEL COOPERATIVES

Chianti Slow Travel
Tel 055 854 62 99.
www.chianti
slowtravel.it

Family Hotels
Viale Fratelli Rosselli 39r,
50144 Florence.
Map 1 A4.
Tel 055 33 40 41.
www.familyhotels.com

Florence Promhotels
Viale Alessandro Volta 72,
50100 Florence.
Map 2 F2.
Tel 055 55 39 41.
www.promhotels.it

BUDGET ACCOMMODATION

Associazione Italiana Alberghi per la Gioventù
Viale Augusto Righi 2–4,
50137 Florence.
Tel 055 60 03 15.
www.ostellionline.org

Europa Villa Camerata
Viale Augusto
Righi 2–4, 50137
Florence.
Tel 055 60 14 51.

MOUNTAIN REFUGES AND CAMP SITES

Touring Club Italiano
Corso Italia 10, 20122
Milan.
Tel 02 852 61.
www.touringclub.it

Club Alpino Italiano
Via Fonseca Pimental 7,
20127 Milan.
Tel 02 205 72 31.

such as swimming pools or bars. The minimum period of stay in these residential hotels is usually a week, but there is more flexibility in low season.

Residential hotels in Florence include **Residence Da-al** and **Palazzo Ricasoli**. The local tourist office keeps a list of others in the region.

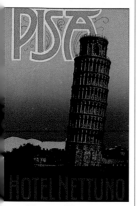

Poster (about 1918) for a Pisan hotel

HOTEL COOPERATIVES

These are not chains but consortiums of different hotel types. **Family Hotel** specializes in small, intimate family hotels and B&Bs, while **Florence Promhotels** provides a wider range of accommodation. **Chianti Slow Travel** books rooms in villas, castles and farmhouses in the Chianti region.

BUDGET ACCOMMODATION

One- and two-star budget hotels have recently increased in price, charging from €30 to €50 per person per night. They are generally small, family-run establishments that were originally known as *pensioni*. The term is no longer in use; however, many places retain the name and personal character that has made them so popular. Most offer breakfast and some have rooms with private bathrooms, but do not expect particularly high standards of service.

Hostel and dormitory accommodation can often be found in convents and religious institutions. Dormitory

accommodation can be arranged through the local tourist office. The **Associazione Italiana Alberghi per la Gioventù** (Italian Youth Hostel Association) in Rome has lists of youth hostels in Italy. The main youth hostel in Florence is **Europa Villa Camerata**.

Full lists and booking facilities for youth hostels are available through the Italian tourist board (ENIT) worldwide or from the local tourist offices *(see p296)*. Also, log on to www.ostellionline.org.

MOUNTAIN REFUGES AND CAMP SITES

If you are likely to be trekking, backpacking or walking, there are mountain refuges and huts dotted throughout Tuscany. The Garfagnana in the north west of Tuscany is worthy of note for these outdoor activities. This area caters for tourists well and is renowned for its outstanding natural beauty. There are also camp sites on the fringes of most towns. A list of camp sites and mountain refuges is available from ENIT *(see p297)* or local

tourist offices. **Club Alpino Italiano** in Milan owns most of the huts in the mountain districts of Italy, including Tuscany. The **Touring Club Italiano** publishes a list of camp sites in *Campeggi e Villaggi Turistici in* Italy.

USING THE LISTINGS

The hotels on pages 250–63 are listed according to area and price category. The symbols summarize the facilities at each hotel.

- No credit cards
- Lift
- Restaurant
- Swimming pool
- Caters for children
- Fitness facilities
- Air-conditioning

Price categories for a standard double room per night, including breakfast, tax and service:

- € under 100 euros
- €€ 100–150 euros
- €€€ 150–200 euros
- €€€€ 200–250 euros
- €€€€€ over 250 euros

Vaulted entrance hall of Hotel Porta Rossa *(see p252)*

Florence's Best Hotels

In a city renowned for its splendid architecture, it is hardly surprising that many of Florence's hotels are favoured by visitors for their charm and individual character. Former palazzi, monasteries such as Villa San Michele, and town villas offer a range of accommodation, though usually at a high price. Original features are sometimes preserved at the expense of modern comforts: among the older establishments listed on pages 250-56 we try to include those that combine both. The hotels shown here are a selection of the best.

Hotel Beacci Tornabuoni
This family-run former palace is particularly welcoming and furnished with fine antiques. (See p252.)

Hotel Excelsior
On a 13th-century square near the river Arno, this beautiful hotel epitomizes luxury, with well-appointed bedrooms and 19th-century fittings. (See p253.)

Torre di Bellosguardo
Vast, ancient and individual, this hill-top tower and villa lives up to its name: beautiful view. (See p256.)

Hotel Villa Belvedere
This 1930s hillside hotel is set in 11 acres (4 ha) of landscaped gardens and has excellent views of the city. Inside, the décor is impeccable. (See p255.)

| 0 metres | 1,000 |
| 0 yards | 1,000 |

Villa San Michele
This peaceful monastery in Fiesole is said to have been designed by Michelangelo. (See p256.)

Pensione Bencistà
A haven in the hills behind the city, this lovingly kept pensione has luxurious period furniture. (See p255.)

CITY CENTRE NORTH

CITY CENTRE EAST

Hermitage Hotel
The drawing room overlooks the Ponte Vecchio in this comfortable and quiet hotel housed on the top floors of a tall medieval building. (See p252.)

Villa La Massa
Surrounded by parkland, this former country home is one of Florence's most elegant hotels (See p256.)

Choosing a Hotel

Many hotels in Florence and Tuscany, even budget ones, offer very charming decor and environs. The best among them are reviewed on the following pages. For more information on other types of accommodation, see pages 244–9. Map references are either to the Street Finder on pages 140–7, or the road map on the inside back cover.

PRICE CATEGORIES
For a double room per night, including breakfast, tax and service:

€ under 100 euros
€€ 100–150 euros
€€€ 150–200 euros
€€€€ 200–250 euros
€€€€€ over 250 euros

FLORENCE

FLORENCE Hotel Cestelli
€

Borgo Santi Apostoli 25, 50123 **Tel/Fax** *055 21 42 13* **Rooms** *8*   **Map** *3 C1*

Proprieter Alessio Lotti and his Japanese wife Asumi add to the charm of this affordable eight-room hotel housed in 12th-century palazzo. Only three rooms have private baths. Despite much refurbishing, the hotel retains its original 16th-century floors. All rooms non-smoking. No breakfast served. **www.hotelcestelli.com**

FLORENCE Hotel Locanda Orchidea
€

Borgo degli Albizi 11, 50122 **Tel/Fax** *055 248 03 46* **Rooms** *10*   **Map** *6 F3*

Value-for-money accommodation at its best, the Locanda is a ten-minute walk from the heart of the city. Situated inside a 12th-century building, the hotel prides itself on its old-fashioned simplicity. Fans instead of air conditioning, and no en suite bathrooms. All rooms are refreshingly unique. **www.hotelorchideaflorence.it**

FLORENCE Istituto Gould
€

Via dei Serragli 49, 50100 **Tel** *055 21 25 76* **Fax** *055 28 02 74* **Rooms** *41*   **Map** *3 B2*

The combination of unbelievably low rates with their contribution to a good cause (disadvantaged children), makes it easier to fully appreciate this sparsely furnished hostel-like outfit. The rooms are spotless, and the gardens make for very attractive view. Ideal for those who want safety and basic comfort on a tight budget. **www.istitutogould.it**

FLORENCE Soggiorno Battistero
€

Piazza San Giovanni 1, 50129 **Tel** *055 29 51 43* **Fax** *055 26 81 89* **Rooms** *6*   **Map** *6 D2*

On the third floor of a 14th-century palazzo, this modest *pensione* is reasonably priced and excellently located. Most of the rooms have a splendid view of the Duomo and the Baptistery. The Museo del Bigallo is located on the ground floor. The decor is unremarkable but pleasant. Wi-fi in rooms. **www.soggiornobattistero.it**

FLORENCE Bellettini
€€

Via dei Conti 7, 50123 **Tel** *055 21 35 61* **Fax** *055 28 35 51* **Rooms** *27*   **Map** *1 C5*

Refurbished in 2003, this family-run hotel lies between the station and the Medici Chapels. Some rooms afford view of the Duomo or the inner courtyard through double-glazed windows. Rooms in the annexe are lovely. Free internet access in the bar. **www.hotelbellettini.com**

FLORENCE Dei Mori B&B
€€

Via Dante Alighieri 12, 50122 **Tel** *055 21 14 38* **Fax** *055 238 22 16* **Rooms** *5*   **Map** *6 3E*

This clean and cosy establishment is a very popular haunt, so book early. Don't be fooled by the dimly-lit stairway since it leads into a spacious lounge, and tastefully decorated rooms. The hosts are charming and helpful. All rooms in this gay-friendly inn overlook the tranquil courtyard. **www.bnb.it**

FLORENCE Hotel Alessandra
€€

Borgo Santi Apostoli 17, 50123 **Tel** *055 28 34 38* **Fax** *055 21 06 19* **Rooms** *27*   **Map** *5 C3*

Located on the second and third floors of a 16th-century building, this central hotel, with its vaulted ceilings, retains an aura of grandeur. Rooms overlooking the Arno are larger and more expensive. The Piazzetta del Limbo and the church of Santi Apostoli can be glimpsed from other rooms. **www.hotelalessandra.com**

FLORENCE Hotel Firenze
€€

Piazza Donati 4, 50133 **Tel** *055 21 42 03* **Fax** *055 21 23 70* **Rooms** *57*   **Map** *6 E3*

Tucked into a tiny side street off the pedestrianized Via del Corso, the Firenze is a quiet and efficiently managed hotel. The rooms have all the essentials, although the decor is simple. There are also several large rooms that can accommodate up to four people – ideal for families on a limited budget. **www.hotelfirenze-fi.it**

FLORENCE Piccolo Hotel
€€

Via San Gallo 51, 50129 **Tel** *055 49 29 25* **Fax** *055 47 45 15* **Rooms** *10*   **Map** *2 D4*

Among its special features, this wonderfully located hotel offers bicycles for hire as well as Internet access – both free of charge. The staff go out of their way to ensure that you have a pleasant stay. The decor is rather ordinary but the rooms are very comfortable. **www.piccolohotelfirenze.com**

Key to Symbols *see back cover flap*

FLORENCE Residenza il Villino

▤   €€

Via della Pergola 53, 50121 **Tel** *055 200 11 16* **Fax** *055 200 11 01* **Rooms** *9*   **Map** *2 E5*

The centrally located but soothingly quiet Residenza il Villino is very close to the Duomo, galleries and museums. This small and utterly delightful establishment is a recently refurbished 19th-century townhouse villa. One of the rooms offers an amazing view of the Duomo's cupola. **www.ilvillino.it**

FLORENCE Davanzati Hotel

▦▤   €€€

Via Porta Rossa 5, 50123 **Tel** *055 28 66 66* **Fax** *055 265 82 52* **Rooms** *21*   **Map** *6 C3*

This imposing 14th-century building was renovated in 2004, and combines the old and the new magnificently. The service in this family-run outfit is impeccable, and good English is spoken. Competitively-priced for a central location, there is free Internet access in all rooms and a complimentary *aperitivo* every evening. **www.hoteldavanzati.it**

FLORENCE Della Signoria

▦▤   €€€

Via delle Terme 1, 50123 **Tel** *055 21 45 30* **Fax** *055 21 61 01* **Rooms** *27*   **Map** *6 D4*

Run by the same family for over 50 years, the hotel is located on the corner of Por Santa Maria, a great central location, if a little bit noisy. Ask for a room on the side street Via delle Terme, or one overlooking the rear of the building. **www.hoteldellasignoria.com**

FLORENCE Hotel Annalena

▤   €€€

Via Romana 34, 50125 **Tel** *055 22 24 02* **Fax** *055 22 24 03* **Rooms** *20*   **Map** *3 B2*

Opposite the Boboli Gardens, and on the second floor of a 15th-century palazzo (once a convent), this *pensione* has a fascinating history. The single and double rooms come with their own little terrace. Rooms are decorated with antique pieces. The atmospheric hotel prides itself on its Florentine authenticity. **www.hotelannalena.it**

FLORENCE Hotel Casci

▦▤   €€€

Via Cavour 13, 50129 **Tel** *055 21 16 86* **Fax** *055 239 64 61* **Rooms** *29*   **Map** *6 E1*

The home of composer Gioacchino Rossini in the mid-1850s, the hotel is located on the second floor of a 15th-century building. In the bustling Via Cavour between the Duomo and San Lorenzo, this family-owned establishment has a great staff and offers large, clean rooms. Five non-smoking rooms. Free Internet access. **www.hotelcasci.com**

FLORENCE Hotel delle Arti

▦▤   €€€

Via dei Servi 38/a, 50122 **Tel** *055 260 87 68* **Fax** *055 29 01 40* **Rooms** *9*   **Map** *6 E1*

Originally an office building, this hotel is anything but impersonal; it is small, intimate and tastefully decorated. The service is flawless and the rooms are spacious and cheerful. The breakfast served here is delicious and substantial. You can relax on the charming terrace and gaze out at the city. **www.hoteldellearti.it**

FLORENCE Hotel Liana

▤   €€€

Via Vittorio Alfieri 18, 50121 **Tel** *055 24 53 03* **Fax** *055 234 45 96* **Rooms** *24*   **Map** *2 F4*

This wonderful hotel is just across the *viale* (boulevard) that marks the edge of the historic centre, but only a five-minute walk from Santa Croce. It was the British embassy for a few years in the 19th-century. The rooms are large and gorgeous with their frescoed ceilings and original floors. There is a deligtful garden to relax in. **www.hotelliana.com**

FLORENCE Hotel Ritz

▦▤   €€€

Lungarno della Zecca Vecchia 24, 50122 **Tel** *055 234 06 50* **Fax** *055 24 08 63* **Rooms** *30*   **Map** *4 E2*

Not affiliated to the other Ritz hotels worldwide, this three-star establishment opened in the 1950s. Almost all the rooms have stunning views of the city centre including Santa Croce, the city's rooftops, the river Arno and the surrounding hills. **www.hotelritz.net**

FLORENCE Hotel Silla

▦▤   €€€

Via de'Renai 5, 50100 **Tel** *055 234 28 88* **Fax** *055 234 14 37* **Rooms** *36*   **Map** *6 F5*

Located in a beautiful 16th-century building, this family-run hotel on the Oltrarno side of the river is reached through an elegant courtyard. A grand staircase leads to the first floor. The rooms and decor are a delight, and the staff are friendly. Guests can enjoy the terrace which overlooks the river. **www.hotelsilla.it**

FLORENCE Hotel Torre Guelfa

▦▤   €€€

Borgo Santi Apostoli 8, 50123 **Tel** *055 239 63 38* **Fax** *055 239 85 77* **Rooms** *29*   **Map** *5 C3*

On the third floor of a medieval palazzo, this hotel incorporates the tallest privately-owned tower in the city. This tower's terrace is a residents-only bar in summer. The hotel has a rustic, robust appeal. Book early to get the top-floor suite with its own terrace. The six newer rooms on the second floor are cheaper. **www.hoteltorreguelfa.com**

FLORENCE Orto de' Medici

▦▤   €€€

Via San Gallo 30, 50129 **Tel** *055 48 34 27* **Fax** *055 46 12 76* **Rooms** *31*   **Map** *2 D4*

Ten minutes on foot from the Duomo, and five from the Accademia, this mid-19th century building has large frescoes in its lounges and breakfast room. A delightful flower-filled terrace overlooks San Marco. The banqueting suites make the hotel popular with the locals for festive occasions. All rooms non-smoking. **www.ortodeimedici.it**

FLORENCE Palazzo Benci

▦▤   €€€

Piazza Madonna Aldobrandini 3, 50123 **Tel** *055 21 38 48* **Fax** *055 28 83 08* **Rooms** *35*   **Map** *1 C5*

Once belonging to the famous Benci family, this 16th-century palazzo has a breathtakingly beautiful courtyard-garden. Contemporary furnishings set off the original features of the carefully restored building. All rooms have double-glazed windows, and those at the back overlook the Medici Chapels. **www.palazzobenci.com**

FLORENCE Porta Rossa

Via Porta Rossa 19, 50123 **Tel** *055 28 75 51* **Fax** *055 28 21 79* **Rooms** *78*   **Map** *6 D3*

While the current building dates from 1500, documents confirm that a hotel stood here as early as 1386, making this one of Italy's oldest hotels. The vaulted entrance hall is decorated in the unique Italian Art Nouveau tradition (Liberty style) with beautiful stained glass. Rooms are large and furnished with antiques. **www.hotelportarossa.it**

FLORENCE Beacci Tornabuoni

Via de' Tornabuoni 3, 50123 **Tel** *055 21 26 45* **Fax** *055 28 35 94* **Rooms** *40*   **Map** *5 C2*

With a rich history of hospitality, this hotel takes up the top three floors of a 15th-century palazzo. Once a classic *pensione*, the hotel has been refitted so guests can now choose between junior suites, deluxe and standard rooms – all with antique furniture and tapestries. The rooftop terrace is lovely. **www.tornabuonihotels.com**

FLORENCE Hermitage Hotel

Vicolo Marzio 1, 50122 **Tel** *055 28 72 16* **Fax** *055 21 22 08* **Rooms** *28*   **Map** *6 D4*

Located on four floors of a medieval tower, the reception and common areas are on the fifth floor. Rooms are average in size but comfortable, and some have Jacuzzis. The terrace garden affords a panoramic view of the Vasari Corridor, the Ponte Vecchio and the Arno. Breakfasting in this garden is a treat. **www.hermitagehotel.com**

FLORENCE Hotel Balestri

Piazza Mentana 7, 50122 **Tel** *055 21 47 43* **Fax** *055 239 80 42* **Rooms** *46*   **Map** *6 E4*

Open for business since 1888, this hotel is located in a little piazza on the riverfront halfway between the Ponte Vecchio and Santa Croce. Extensively renovated, the rooms are clean, pretty and have all amenities. Thirty rooms face the Arno, while the rest overlook a quiet courtyard. **www.hotel-balestri.it**

FLORENCE Hotel De la Ville

Piazza Antinori 1, 50123 **Tel** *055 238 18 06* **Fax** *055 238 18 09* **Rooms** *75*   **Map** *5 C3*

This palazzo is located at the end of Via Tornabuoni and is ideal for those who want to shop till they drop, before settling into the lap of luxury. The rooms are spacious, elegant and soundproofed. The breakfast is exceptional. The bar is open until midnight and light meals are available throughout the day. **www.hoteldelaville.it**

FLORENCE Hotel Della Robbia

Via dei Della Robbia 7/9, 50132 **Tel** *055 263 85 70* **Fax** *055 246 63 71* **Rooms** *24*   **Map** *2 4F*

Just on the other side of the *viale* that marks the edge of the old city, the Della Robbia is housed in a recently restored late 19th-century villa. The rooms here have been decorated in Liberty style, which is quite a rarity in Renaissance-dominated Florence. **www.hoteldellarobbia.it**

FLORENCE Hotel Goldoni

Borgo Ognissanti 8, 50123 **Tel** *055 28 40 80* **Fax** *055 28 25 76* **Rooms** *20*   **Map** *1 B5*

Mozart was a guest in this hotel in 1770, and the Goldoni still retains the aura of an era gone by. Located on the second floor of an old palace, all but three rooms overlook a quiet private garden. The rooms are spacious and the decor elegant. Closed for two weeks every December. **www.hotelgoldoni.com**

FLORENCE Hotel Martelli

Via Panzani 8, 50129 **Tel** *055 21 71 51* **Fax** *055 26 85 04* **Rooms** *52*   **Map** *1 C5*

Located on the busy main street leading from the station to the Duomo, the Martelli is fairly quiet and comfortable. Four of the rooms are furnished in Florentine style and are the most in demand. The others have a more contemporary look. The building was originally a palazzo belonging to the Medici. **www.hotelmartelli.com**

FLORENCE Il Guelfo Bianco

Via Cavour 29, 50129 **Tel** *055 28 83 30* **Fax** *055 29 52 03* **Rooms** *40*   **Map** *6 E1*

A short walk from the Duomo, this impressive hotel comprises two adjacent 17th-century buildings. The rooms are very spacious, many resplendent with frescoed ceilings and period furniture. The view is always pleasant, regardless of whether you overlook the garden, rooftops or street. Free Internet access. **www.ilguelfobianco.it**

FLORENCE Loggiato dei Serviti

Piazza SS. Annunziata 3, 50122 **Tel** *055 28 95 92* **Fax** *055 28 95 95* **Rooms** *39*   **Map** *2 D4*

Built in the 16th-century by the Serviti order to house travelling priests, this hotel is the mirror-image of the Spedale degli Innocenti across the square. The opulent decor belies its monastic origins. Rooms either overlook the piazza or the Accademia di Belle Arti garden. Book well in advance. **www.loggiatodeiservitihotel.it**

FLORENCE Morandi alla Crocetta

Via Laura 50, 50121 **Tel** *055 234 47 47* **Fax** *055 248 09 54* **Rooms** *10*   **Map** *2 E4*

Once a convent, this small hotel has many admirers. Rooms are furnished in different styles, but all are equally delightful. Two have terraces and room 29 has a frescoed wall. Most of the rooms overlook the street, but the quaint interiors are the real attraction. It is essential to book in advance. **www.hotelmorandi.it**

FLORENCE Pitti Palace

Borgo San Jacopo 3, 50125 **Tel** *055 239 87 11* **Fax** *055 239 88 67* **Rooms** *72*   **Map** *3 C1*

As close to the Ponte Vecchio as you can get, this hotel is in a modernised 13th-century tower, with two terraces on the sixth floor. You can soak in the splendid vista of the city and the Boboli Gardens as you enjoy breakfast. Small and functional, but well-priced for such a good location. Try to book the top-floor suite. **www.vivahotels.com**

Key to Price Guide *see p250* **Key to Symbols** *see back cover flap*

FLORENCE Baglioni 🔲🍴🗐   €€€€€
Piazza Unità Italiana 6, 50123 **Tel** *055 235 80* **Fax** *055 235 888 95* **Rooms** *193*   **Map** *1 C5*

Ever since it opened its doors in 1903, this hotel has been charming guests with its plush interiors and lush gardens. Rooms are well-appointed, many with leaded glass windows. The beauty of the rooftop garden restaurant adds to the eating experience. Its full range of conference facilities are ideal for business travellers. **www.hotelbaglioni.it**

FLORENCE Berchielli 🔲🗐   €€€€€
Lungarno Acciaiuoli 14, 50123 **Tel** *055 26 40 61* **Fax** *055 21 86 36* **Rooms** *76*   **Map** *5 C4*

This Art Nouveau gem was once a 15th-century palazzo. The rooms have an understated, traditional elegance and are wonderful to relax in. About 25 of them overlook the river, while the rest either face Piazza del Limbo or the narrow side alleys. The service is excellent. **www.berchielli.it**

FLORENCE Bernini Palace 🔲🗐   €€€€€
Piazza San Firenze 29, 50122 **Tel** *055 28 86 21* **Fax** *055 26 82 72* **Rooms** *75*   **Map** *6 E4*

An ideal choice if easy access to the main sights is a priority. This hotel is on the road leading from Piazza del Duomo to the river, and is equidistant from Piazza della Signoria and Santa Croce. The double-glazed windows mute the street noise. The decor veers towards a shabby chic. Rooms are spacious. **www.hotelbernini.com**

FLORENCE Excelsior 🔲🍴🗐🗐   €€€€€
Piazza Ognissanti 3, 50123 **Tel** *055 271 51* **Fax** *055 21 02 78* **Rooms** *171*   **Map** *5 A2*

The Excelsior excels with its marble floors and columns, grand staircases, stained-glass windows, statues and period paintings. The rooms are equally opulent, while the staff add warmth to it all. On the downside, breakfast is not included in the price. Its restaurant, Il Cestello, is celebrated for its cuisine. **www.westin.com/excelsiorflorence**

FLORENCE Fenice Palace 🔲🗐   €€€€€
Via dei Martelli 10, 50129 **Tel** *055 28 99 42* **Fax** *055 21 00 87* **Rooms** *72*   **Map** *6 D1*

This 16th-century building, on the corner with Via de Pucci, is just a stone's throw from the Duomo. It is also a good base for shopping expeditions. Recently refurbished throughout, six rooms overlook the courtyard while two have terraces facing the street. Buses from the station stop outside. **www.hotelfenicepalace.it**

FLORENCE Gallery Hotel Art 🔲🍴🗐   €€€€€
Vicolo dell'Oro 5, 50123 **Tel** *055 272 63* **Fax** *055 26 85 57* **Rooms** *74*   **Map** *6 D4*

The lobby and library of this eight-storey boutique hotel also double as a contemporary art gallery. Fax and modem lines along with cutting-edge sound and video systems in every room. The penthouse suites feature linen sheets and cashmere blankets. The sushi bar offers a fusion of Italian, French and Japanese cuisine. **www.lungarnohotels.com**

FLORENCE Grand Hotel 🔲🍴🗐🗐   €€€€€
Piazza Ognissanti 1, 50123 **Tel** *055 28 87 81* **Fax** *055 21 74 00* **Rooms** *107*   **Map** *5 A2*

Crowned heads and other VIPs favour this classic hotel that lives up to its name. The rooms, furnished in Renaissance or Empire style, afford views either of the Arno or of a delightful courtyard filled with potted orange trees. This hotel is also home to a good restaurant. Sister to the Excelsior across the piazza. **www.starwood.com/grandflorence**

FLORENCE Grand Hotel Majestic 🔲🍴🗐   €€€€€
Via del Melarancio, 50123 **Tel** *055 26 40 21* **Fax** *055 26 84 28* **Rooms** *103*   **Map** *1 C5*

A short walk from the train station, tourists and business visitors alike find it convenient to stay here. With rooms on four floors, large tour groups are accommodated easily. Facilities include a piano bar, American bar and a restaurant serving international and regional cuisine. Private parking available. **www.panciolihotels.it**

FLORENCE Grand Hotel Minerva 🔲🍴🏊🗐   €€€€€
Piazza Santa Maria Novella 16, 50123 **Tel** *055 272 30* **Fax** *055 26 82 81* **Rooms** *102*   **Map** *1 B5*

With its rooftop swimming pool, the Grand Minerva does full justice to the romance of Florence. Watching the sunset from here or from the adjacent bar is a memorable experience. Recently refurbished, this hotel has welcomed many famous guests, including Henry James. Family suites have two bathrooms. **www.grandhotelminerva.com**

FLORENCE Grand Hotel Villa Medici 🔲🍴🏊🗐🗐   €€€€€
Via Il Prato 42, 50123 **Tel** *055 238 13 31* **Fax** *055 238 13 36* **Rooms** *103*   **Map** *1 A4*

This 18th-century villa conversion is the only hotel within the city limits to have an open-air pool in its own gardens. Located by Porta al Prato, it is within walking distance of the centre of town. The plush rooms are furnished with antiques. The fitness centre features a sauna and Turkish bath. **www.villamedicihotel.com**

FLORENCE Hotel Aprile 🔲🗐   €€€€€
Via della Scala 6, 50123 **Tel** *055 21 62 37* **Fax** *055 28 09 47* **Rooms** *28*   **Map** *1 B5*

Once owned by the Medici, this palazzo features frescoed ceilings, period paintings and spacious rooms. Traces of *The Triumph of David* can be seen on the interesting façade. Ask for a room overlooking the courtyard since the streets can be quite noisy. Breakfast is served in the colourful courtyard garden in summer. **www.hotelaprile.it**

FLORENCE Hotel Calzaiuoli 🔲🗐   €€€€€
Via Calzaiuoli 6, 50123 **Tel** *055 21 24 56* **Fax** *055 26 83 10* **Rooms** *45*   **Map** *6 D3*

Halfway down the pedestrianised street that links the Duomo and the Piazza della Signoria, this small hotel is located close to all the action. All the rooms are on the upper floors, and are large and comfortable. Some have views of Brunelleschi's dome. The buffet breakfast is excellent. Advance booking is essential. **www.calzaiuoli.it**

FLORENCE Hotel Continentale

Vicolo dell'Oro 6r, 50123   **Tel** *055 272 62*   **Fax** *055 28 31 39*   **Rooms** *43*   **Map** *6 D4*

Completely renovated in 2002, this trendy, contemporary hotel is designed to impress. The entrance lobby features installations by the leading Italian artist, Fabrizio Corneli. The rooms are chic and have good views – in most cases of the Ponte Vecchio. The fitness and wellness centre is housed in the medieval tower. **www.Lungarnohotels.com**

FLORENCE Hotel Degli Orafi

Lungarno Archibusieri 4, 50121   **Tel** *055 26 62 21*   **Fax** *055 266 21 11*   **Rooms** *42*   **Map** *6 D4*

Around the corner from the Uffizi and the Ponte Vecchio, both rooms and bathrooms are large. Some rooms have a view of the Arno, and some of the Vasari Corridor. Frescoed and coffered ceilings are offset by modern amenities. Specify a room with a view when booking. Pleasant rooftop bar/patio. **www.hoteldegliorafi.it**

FLORENCE Hotel Principe

Lungarno Amerigo Vespucci 34, 50123   **Tel** *055 28 48 48*   **Fax** *055 28 34 58*   **Rooms** *20*   **Map** *1 A5*

Apart from the addition of a lift, this hotel has maintained most of the characteristics it had as a private home built in the 1860s. Nonetheless, all modern amenities are provided. Most rooms have a balcony overlooking the river, or the beautifully maintained terraced garden which features parterres, palms and a fountain. **www.hotelprincipe.com**

FLORENCE Hotel Roma

Piazza Santa Maria Novella 8, 50123   **Tel** *055 21 03 66*   **Fax** *055 21 53 06*   **Rooms** *57*   **Map** *1 B5*

Restored in 1988, this large hotel flaunts many elegant touches such as marble floors, wood panelling and intriguing stained-glass works by Galileo and Tito Chini. Rooms facing the piazza are larger although they can be noisy. For a quieter stay, ask to be accommodated in a different part of the hotel. **www.hotelromaflorence.com**

FLORENCE Hotel Savoy

Piazza della Repubblica 7, 50123   **Tel** *055 273 51*   **Fax** *055 273 58 88*   **Rooms** *102*   **Map** *6 D3*

Architecturally magnificent with lavish interiors, the stylishly appointed rooms here are sleek and spacious. The sixth-floor gym affords spectacular views of the Duomo and Giotto's Campanile. L'Incontro bar on the piazza is a favourite rendezvous point for Florentines. Breakfast is not included in the price. **www.hotelsavoy.it**

FLORENCE J and J

Via di Mezzo 20, 50121   **Tel** *055 263 12*   **Fax** *055 24 02 82*   **Rooms** *20*   **Map** *2 E5*

A 16th-century convent is now this superb hotel. The large rooms, some of which are on two levels, are all decorated differently. All boast antique furniture and handwoven fabrics. Rooms either overlook the red-tiled rooftops or the cloister gardens, where breakfast and drinks can be enjoyed in the summer. **www.jandjhotel.com**

FLORENCE Lorenzo il Magnifico

Via Lorenzo il Magnifico 25, 50129   **Tel/Fax** *055 463 08 78*   **Rooms** *30*   **Map** *2 E2*

Lying between the station and Piazza Libertà, this recently converted villa offers exquisite bed and bath linens, as well as a Jacuzzi bath or shower in every room. One suite faces the luxuriant garden. Most major sights are walking distance but parking is available as is a convenient bus service. **www.lorenzoilmagnifico.net**

FLORENCE Lungarno

Borgo San Jacopo 14, 50125   **Tel** *055 272 61*   **Fax** *055 26 84 37*   **Rooms** *73*   **Map** *5 C4*

This boutique hotel sports a crisp and cool look that is refreshing to the eye. Many of the rooms have their own terraces jutting out over the river, offering great views of the Ponte Vecchio. Some rooms are in an adjacent medieval tower, while the Lungarno Suites across the river are available for longer stays. **www.lungarnohotels.com**

FLORENCE Monna Lisa

Borgo Pinti 27, 50121   **Tel** *055 247 97 51*   **Fax** *055 247 97 55*   **Rooms** *45*   **Map** *2 E5*

Close to Santa Croce, the hotel is in a 14th-century palazzo with terracotta floors, white stucco walls and *pietra serena* (a type of Italian sandstone) detailing. Some rooms are enormous, with old furniture and high ceilings. There are two more recent buildings in the courtyard but these, though quieter, have less character. **www.monnalisa.it**

FLORENCE Montebello Splendid

Via Garibaldi 14, 50123   **Tel** *055 274 71*   **Fax** *055 274 77 00*   **Rooms** *55*   **Map** *1 A5*

This 19th-century villa with its own *giardino all'Italiana* (Italian-style garden) was totally refurbished in 2004. Rooms are airy and bathrooms have marble fittings. There is no charge for children under six sharing a room with their parents. **www.hotel-florence-montebellosplendid.com**

FLORENCE Palazzo Magnani Feroni

Borgo San Frediano 5, 50124   **Tel** *055 239 95 44*   **Fax** *055 260 89 08*   **Rooms** *13*   **Map** *5 A3*

On the Oltrarno side of the river, this 16th-century palazzo features massive halls and a sweeping staircase. Large bedrooms and sitting rooms fitted with chandeliers and Renaissance-style furniture. The billiard room and rooftop terrace add to its appeal. Two apartments are available for rent by the week. **www.florencepalace.com**

FLORENCE Palazzo Niccolini al Duomo

Via dei Servi 2, 50122   **Tel** *055 28 24 12*   **Fax** *055 29 09 79*   **Rooms** *10*   **Map** *2 D5*

In a prime location facing the Duomo, this 16th-century palazzo is run by descendants of the original owners. Public rooms feature period paintings, antiques and chandeliers. Some rooms have frescoed walls or ceilings. Bathrooms are marbled. The suite upstairs offers a unique view of Brunelleschi's dome. **www.niccolinidomepalace.com**

Key to Price Guide *see p250*   **Key to Symbols** *see back cover flap*

FLORENCE Plaza Hotel Lucchesi
Lungarno della Zecca Vecchia 38, 50122 **Tel** *055 262 36* **Fax** *055 248 09 21* **Rooms** *97*   **Map** *4 E2*

A private home built in 1860, the building was converted into a hotel in the 1940s. Furnished in a warm and cosy style, the rooms have outstanding views of the Arno or Santa Croce. The restaurant, La Serra, specializes in Tuscan cuisine. **www.plazalucchesi.it**

FLORENCE Relais Santa Croce
Via Ghibellina 87, 50122 **Tel** *055 234 22 30* **Fax** *055 234 11 95* **Rooms** *24*   **Map** *4 F1*

This wonderful hotel, in an 18th-century palazzo, is just a short stroll from Michelangelo's house. Most of its luxurious rooms overlook the street. The music room and smoking room retain the splendour of their grand past. The restaurant serves Tuscan delicacies. **www.relaissantacroce.it**

FLORENCE Santa Maria Novella
Piazza Santa Maria Novella 1, 50123 **Tel** *055 27 18 40* **Fax** *055 27 18 41 99* **Rooms** *38*   **Map** *5 B2*

Furnished in Empire style, this superb hotel couples grandeur with tranquility. Standard doubles overlook Via delle Belle Donne, while the superiors face Santa Maria Novella and the Piazza. One junior suite has a roof terrace. The service is of a consistently high quality. The bar serves snacks and light meals. **www.hotelsantamarianovella.it**

FURTHER AFIELD Hotel Emma
Via A. Pacinotti 20, 50131 **Tel** *055 57 59 01* **Fax** *055 504 89 14* **Rooms** *9*

This two-star hotel has a laid-back, homely ambience. Two rooms overlook the street while the rest face the courtyard. TVs and private bathrooms add to the convenience. Enjoy breakfast or relax with a drink on the pretty rooftop terrace. This hotel is worth the 10-minute bus-ride from Piazza di San Marco. **www.hotelemma.net**

FURTHER AFIELD Villa Betania
Viale del Poggio Imperiale 23, 50125 **Tel/Fax** *055 22 22 43* **Rooms** *16*   **Map** *3 A4*

This family-run hotel has been warmly welcoming guests since 1945. Set in its own lush grounds, the southern city gate of Porta Romana is only a 10-minute walk downhill. The rooms are quiet, elegant and offer excellent value. Private parking and a regular bus service make it a convenient base. Superior breakfast. **www.villabetania.it**

FURTHER AFIELD Classic Hotel
Viale Machiavelli 25, 50125 **Tel** *055 22 93 51* **Fax** *055 22 93 53* **Rooms** *20*   **Map** *3 A3*

The shaded gravel driveway leading to this 19th-century villa, just minutes from Porta Romana, marks the end of the city bustle. The large rooms are simple yet elegant. The exposed beams in the attic rooms make them particularly attractive. The garden has an ancient sequoia, shrubs, flowers and wonderful niches to relax and read. **www.classichotel.it**

FURTHER AFIELD Pensione Bencistà
Via Benedetto da Maiano 4, 50014 **Tel/Fax** *055 591 63* **Rooms** *40*

Choose between full board, half board or just breakfast in this 1500s villa-turned-hotel. However, the place is so welcoming, and the views so lovely that people are usually happy to stick around all day. Watch the sun set over the Florentine countryside from the stone balcony. Advance booking is advisable. **www.bencista.com**

FURTHER AFIELD Hotel Villa Belvedere
Via Bernardo Castelli 3, 50124 **Tel** *055 22 25 01* **Fax** *055 22 31 63* **Rooms** *26*   **Map** *3 A5*

On the first hill outside Porta Romana to the south of the city, this spacious 1930s villa is set in immaculately landscaped gardens. The views of the hills and of the city are especially fine from the first floor terraces. Elegantly furnished rooms, swimming pool and a tennis court contribute to an enjoyable stay. **www.villa-belvedere.com**

FURTHER AFIELD Marignolle Relais & Charme
Via di San Quirichino a Marignolle 16, 50124 **Tel** *055 228 69 10* **Fax** *055 204 73 96* **Rooms** *6*

Located just off the Via Senese, this is an ideal location for those who want to explore the Chianti countryside, and perhaps play a little golf, while still being able to spend time in Florence. The large rooms are decorated impeccably, and the terrace offers breathtaking views of the city. The pool is set in a delightful garden. **www.marignolle.com**

FURTHER AFIELD Mediterraneo Grand
Lungarno del Tempio 42-44, 50121 **Tel** *055 66 02 41* **Fax** *055 67 95 60* **Rooms** *331*

One of the largest hotels in Italy, the Mediterraneo is situated on the banks of the Arno between the Ponte San Niccolò and the Ponte Verrazzano. A long walk from the centre, it is well-connected by bus. Rooms are comfortable, and there are three restaurants serving international and Tuscan cuisine. **www.hotelmediterraneo.com**

FURTHER AFIELD Villa le Rondini
Via Bolognese Vecchia 224, 50139 **Tel** *055 40 00 81* **Fax** *055 26 82 12* **Rooms** *42*

Set in a sprawling garden amid olive groves, this villa affords stunning views of the Arno valley. Book early to ensure a room in the main house that boasts quaint, traditional furnishings and beamed ceilings. Rooms with terraces are very popular and with good reason. The outdoor pool is available from June to September. **www.villalerondini.com**

FURTHER AFIELD Hotel Villa Villoresi
Via Ciampi 2, 50019 **Tel** *055 44 32 12* **Fax** *055 44 20 63* **Rooms** *28*

Halfway between the city and the countryside, this is an ideal hideaway. Built as a military stronghold in the 12th-century and then converted to a villa in the 1400s, it is now a national monument. Frescoes, murals and antique furniture perfect the atmosphere. Not all rooms are air conditioned. Garden with lemon trees. **www.villavilloresi.it**

FURTHER AFIELD Torre di Bellosguardo   ⬜🏊🍴   €€€€€
Via Roti Michelozzi 2, 50124 **Tel** *055 229 81 45* **Fax** *055 22 90 08* **Rooms** *16*

Far from the crowds, but with the city at its feet, the views from the 16th-century tower of this 14th-century villa are unparalleled. It is equally breathtaking indoors, with vast public areas and huge rooms decorated with antique furniture and Persian carpets. Two landscaped pools and a beautiful garden. **www.torrebellosguardo.com**

FURTHER AFIELD Villa la Massa   🛏️11🏊🛁🍴📋   €€€€€
Via della Massa 24, 50012 **Tel** *055 626 11* **Fax** *055 63 31 02* **Rooms** *37*

Perfect for a break from the city, this hotel is just a few kilometres downstream on the Arno and has been a luxury hotel since 1948. It is made up of three villas from different eras with period furniture and fabrics. Private chapel for weddings – David Bowie and Iman got married here. Open mid-March to October. **www.villalamassa.com**

FURTHER AFIELD Villa Montartino   🏊📋   €€€€€
Via Gherardo Silvani 151, 50125 **Tel** *055 22 35 20* **Fax** *055 22 34 95* **Rooms** *6*

The medieval origins of this villa can be seen in the main entrance door and the bastions, while the stone vaults of the windows are Renaissance. The rooms are large and you can have your run of the spacious public areas. The adjacent villa houses only suites, and has its own landscaped Italian-style gardens. **www.montartino.com**

FURTHER AFIELD Villa San Michele   11🏊🍴📋   €€€€€
Via Doccia 4, 50014 **Tel** *055 567 82 00* **Fax** *055 567 82 50* **Rooms** *45*

Once a monastery, the design of this hotel's façade is attributed to Michelangelo. Standing in sprawling 37-acre grounds, the views are spectacular, the best being from the loggia, where dinner is served in summer. Ask for a room overlooking the city. Closed end-November to mid-March. **www.villasanmichele.orient-express.com**

WESTERN TUSCANY

ARTIMINO Hotel Paggeria Medicea   11🏊🍴📋   €€€€
Viale Papa Giovanni XXIII 1, 59015 **Tel** *0558 751 41* **Fax** *0558 75 14 70* **Rooms** *37*   **Road map** *C2*

In the converted servant quarters of Artimino's famous Medici villa, La Ferdinanda, this hotel is complete with original furniture, terracotta floors and decorative frescoes. Adding to the experience are riding stables, the restaurant (Biagio Pignatta) and a farm shop that also sells local wines. There are 44 apartments for weekly rental. **www.artimino.com**

PISA Hotel Roseto   📋   €
Via Mascagni 24, 56100 **Tel/Fax** *050 425 96* **Rooms** *16*   **Road map** *B2*

This small two-star hotel is perfect for visitors on a tight budget. The Roseto makes a quiet, comfortable and attractive base in central Pisa. Rooms are airy with large windows, tiled floors and high ceilings. The green, leafy rooftop garden has great views over the city. **www.hotelroseto.it**

PISA Hotel Francesco   ⬜11📋   €€
Via Santa Maria 129, 56126 **Tel** *050 55 54 53* **Fax** *050 55 61 45* **Rooms** *13*   **Road map** *B2*

Within walking distance of the Leaning Tower of Pisa, the terrace of this small, welcoming hotel offers some beautiful views over the city. The rooms are clean, bright and minimally furnished. Non-smoking rooms available on request. Bike and moped hire organized by the hotel. **www.hotelfrancesco.com**

PISA Hotel Granduca   ⬜11🍴📋   €€
Via Statale del Brennero 13, 56017 **Tel** *050 81 41 11* **Fax** *050 81 88 11* **Rooms** *170*   **Road map** *B2*

In the heart of the spa town of San Giuliano Terme, this modern hotel is just a short drive from the Leaning Tower of Pisa. Set in a natural oasis, the emphasis here is on health and wellbeing, with a broad choice of spa and relaxation facilities. Facilities include a sporting centre with a tennis court and a jogging route. **www.hotelgranduca.it**

PISA Hotel La Pace   ⬜📋   €€
Viale Gramsci 14, 56126 **Tel** *050 293 51* **Fax** *050 50 22 66* **Rooms** *65*   **Road map** *B2*

This comfortable hotel is located within walking distance of Pisa's historical centre, and is close to the train station. The rooms are clean, tastefully furnished and outfitted with modern bathrooms. There is a generous buffet breakfast, and the concierge will recommend nearby restaurants. **www.hotellapace.it**

PISA Hotel Villa Kinzica   11📋   €€
Piazza Arcivescovado 2, 56126 **Tel** *050 56 04 19* **Fax** *050 55 12 04* **Rooms** *30*   **Road map** *B2*

In an imposing 18th-century villa, the Kinzica offers comfortable rooms with modern furnishings. The price is very reasonable given its central location. The best rooms retain many of the building's original features, including stone fireplaces and frescoed ceilings. Some have views over the Piazza dei Miracoli. **www.hotelvillakinzica.it**

PISA Royal Victoria Hotel   ⬜📋   €€
Lungarno Pacinotti 12, 56126 **Tel** *050 94 01 11* **Fax** *050 94 01 80* **Rooms** *48*   **Road map** *B2*

One of Pisa's most historic buildings, the hotel occupies a 10th-century tower built for the Winemakers' Guild. It became Pisa's first hotel in 1837, combining several medieval tower houses in the process. Run by the welcoming Piegaja family, the rooms are charming in their size and decor. Bike rental and private garage. **www.royalvictoria.it**

Key to Price Guide *see p250* **Key to Symbols** *see back cover flap*

PISA Grand Hotel Duomo   €€€

Via Santa Maria 94, 56126 **Tel** *050 56 18 94* **Fax** *050 56 04 18* **Rooms** *94*   **Road map** *B2*

Though it may not be the most exciting place to stay, this modern hotel is very well located. Within walking distance of the Leaning Tower of Pisa, it is a good base for exploring the Piazza dei Miracoli and its associated attractions. The restaurant's specialties offer an accessible insight into local cuisine. **www.grandhotelduomo.it**

PISA Hotel Relais dell'Orologio   €€€€€

Via della Faggiola 12/14, 56126 **Tel** *050 83 03 61* **Fax** *050 55 18 69* **Rooms** *25*   **Road map** *B2*

This five-star hotel is in a renovated manor house built near the remains of a 14th-century tower. Rooms are thoughtfully decorated with tartan rugs and curtains, antique furnishings and original fireplaces. Some have Jacuzzis. Breakfast is served in the manor garden, and the restaurant is very good. **www.hotelrelaisorologio.com**

RIGIOLI Hotel Villa di Corliano   €€

Via Statale 12, 56010 **Tel** *050 81 81 93* **Fax** *050 81 88 97* **Rooms** *12*   **Road map** *B2*

The former country residence of Italian nobility, this spectacular hotel is in a 16th-century Baroque building. It has been a hotel since 1980, and rooms are luxurious with frescoed ceilings and antique furnishings. You will also find a 1700s café and old church in the grounds. A large park surrounds this establishment. **www.corliano.it**

VOLTERRA Hotel La Locanda   €€

Via Guarnacci 24/28, 56048 **Tel** *0588 815 47* **Fax** *0588 815 41* **Rooms** *19*   **Road map** *C3*

A converted convent close to Volterra's Roman amphitheatre, this is a relatively new four-star hotel. Its former owner, Anton Filippo Giacchi, a historian, added excavated Etruscan relics to the building's façade. Rooms are elegant with antique furniture and private bathrooms. The restaurant enjoys a good reputation. **www.hotel-lalocanda.com**

VOLTERRA Hotel San Lino   €€

Via S. Lino 26, 56048 **Tel** *0588 852 50* **Fax** *0588 806 20* **Rooms** *43*   **Road map** *C3*

Within the medieval walls of Volterra, this 1400s convent was converted into a hotel in 1982. The rooms are modernly furnished, but in keeping with the building's illustrious past. Windows look out over the town's cobbled streets or into the hotel's garden. The small restaurant, La Monache, is very popular. **www.hotelsanlino.com**

VOLTERRA Hotel Villa Porta all'Arco   €€

Via Mazzini 2, 56048 **Tel** *0588 814 87* **Fax** *0588 929 29* **Rooms** *12*   **Road map** *C3*

In an early 20th-century villa surrounded by a large garden, this hotel is a short walk from Volterra's historical centre. The rooms are large, comfortable and well-furnished with some charming touches such as tiled floors and cosy sitting rooms. The buffet breakfast features Tuscan specialties. **www.villaportallarco.it**

VOLTERRA Albergo Villa Nencini   €€€

Borgo Santo Stefano 55, 56048 **Tel** *0588 863 86* **Fax** *0588 806 01* **Rooms** *35*   **Road map** *C3*

This family-run country house hotel in a magnificent location just outside of town has views as far as the Tuscany Archipelago. Rooms are airy with light furnishings. The hotel *enoteca* in the converted stables serves a range of local wines. You can swim in the pool next to a garden of luxuriant oak trees. **www.villanencini.it**

VOLTERRA Hotel le Fonti   €€€

Via di Fontecorrenti 8, 56048 **Tel** *0588 852 19* **Fax** *0588 927 28* **Rooms** *66*   **Road map** *C3*

Ten minutes' walk from the centre of Volterra, Hotel Le Fonti was renovated in 2002 to its current modern design. If you want to splash out, ask for the main suite, La Torre, with its lavish antiques and sumptuous fabrics. Large panoramic terrace. There are two pools and a lush, green park surrounds the hotel. **www.parkhotellefonti.com**

NORTHERN TUSCANY

BALBANO Villa Casanova   €

Via di Casanova 1004, 55050 **Tel** *0583 54 84 29* **Fax** *0583 36 89 55* **Rooms** *48*   **Road map** *B2*

A charming hotel in a converted 1600s farmhouse, Villa Casanova retains part of the walls of an older Lucchese military fortress. Just 12km (7 miles) from Lucca, the Villa is very suitable for hiking and cycling excursions. The restaurant serves traditional dishes using locally farmed ingredients. Tennis courts. **www.villacasanova.net**

LUCCA Locanda Vigna Ilaria   €

Via Per Pieve S.Stefano 967/C **Tel** *0583 33 20 91* **Fax** *0583 33 19 08* **Rooms** *4*   **Road map** *C2*

This small inn just outside of Lucca has modern and artfully decorated rooms with bright carpets, pastel walls and ceilings with wooden beams. Located on Lucca's Strada del Vino (wine road), the popular Tuscan restaurant has a list of over 300 wines. Booking recommended. **www.locandavignailaria.it**

LUCCA Piccolo Hotel Puccini   €

Via di Poggio 9, 55100 **Tel** *0583 554 21* **Fax** *0583 534 87* **Rooms** *14*   **Road map** *C2*

This friendly little hotel is in an attractive stone building, located just over the road from the house in which Giacomo Puccini was born (now a museum). It is also very close to the busy central square of San Michele. The rooms are small but reasonably priced considering the location. Courtesy car to airport and train station. **www.hotelpuccini.com**

LUCCA Albergo San Martino   €€

Via della Dogana 9, 55100 **Tel** *0583 46 91 81* **Fax** *0583 99 19 40* **Rooms** *9*   **Road map** *C2*

With a great location in Lucca's historical centre, just a brief stroll from the cathedral, this small three-star hotel offers large rooms at a reasonable price. The hotel prides itself on its personal touch and the service is exemplary. The breakfast is also a veritible feast. There is a car park, and bicycles can be rented. **www.albergosanmartino.it**

LUCCA Hotel Universo   €€

Piazza del Giglio 1, 55100 **Tel** *0583 49 36 78* **Fax** *0583 95 48 54* **Rooms** *60*   **Road map** *C2*

Located in the centre of town near the Palazzo Ducale, this 19th-century building houses 60 comfortable rooms, some with views over Lucca's cathedral. The recently restored restaurant serves delicious Tuscan fare in an elegant and tranquil setting. Parking is available. The hotel is open all year. **www.universolucca.com**

LUCCA Villa Romantica   €€

Via Barbaranti 246, 55100 **Tel** *0583 49 68 72* **Fax** *0583 95 76 00* **Rooms** *6*   **Road map** *C2*

In a quiet 1800s villa just outside Lucca's city walls, this hotel has only four double rooms, one suite and one junior suite. Each is furnished in consonance with the building's Liberty-style design. The suite has a lovely four-poster bed. The ample garden is shaded with trees and there are tennis courts as well. Bicycles for hire. **www.villaromantica.com**

LUCCA Grand Hotel Guinigi   €€€€

Via Romana 1247, 55100 **Tel** *0583 49 91* **Fax** *0583 49 98 00* **Rooms** *168*   **Road map** *C2*

This large four-star hotel is popular with both leisure and business travellers for its luxury rooms and conference facilities. Ideally placed in Lucca's ramparts, the many accoutrements include a gym and sauna. The cocktail bar and gourmet restaurant are advantages. Event and entertainment booking facilities available. **www.grandhotelguinigi.it**

LUCCA Locanda L'Elisa   €€€€€

Via Nuova per Pisa 1952, 55050 **Tel** *0583 37 97 37* **Fax** *0583 37 90 19* **Rooms** *10*   **Road map** *C2*

Five-star accommodation in a stately 18th-century home, this Relais & Chateaux chain hotel stands at the foot of a range of softly rolling hills. The luxury rooms are spacious with lounge areas full of antique furnishings, paintings and draperies. Understandably, it is a popular choice for couples on a romantic trip. **www.locandalelisa.com**

LUCCA Villa la Principessa   €€€€€

Via Nuova per Pisa 1616, 55050 **Tel** *0583 37 00 37* **Fax** *0583 37 91 36* **Rooms** *40*   **Road map** *C2*

The former home and court of Castruccio Castracani, Lord and Duke of Lucca at the turn of the 13th-century, Villa la Principessa stands at the base of the hills surrounding Lucca. The rooms are charmingly rustic, and the shared lounge has a fireplace and 13th-century furniture. The garden is tranquil and soothing. **www.hotelprincipessa.com**

PISTOIA Hotel Piccolo Ritz   €

Via A. Vannucci 67, 51100 **Tel** *0573 267 75* **Fax** *0573 277 98* **Rooms** *21*   **Road map** *C2*

This popular budget three-star hotel is near the city walls, and also conveniently close to the train station. The rooms are small but luxurious. The coffee bar has a stunning frescoed ceiling. Even though it is close to a busy and sometimes noisy road, this hotel is still an economical option given its proximity to the city's major sightseeing attractions.

PISTOIA Albergo Patria   €€

Via F.Crispi 8, 51100 **Tel** *0573 251 87* **Fax** *0573 36 81 68* **Rooms** *28*   **Road map** *C2*

Along an old cobbled street in the historical centre of Pistoia, this hotel is in an ancient building with modern fittings. Large, if slightly dishevelled, the 1970s-style rooms have views over Pistoia's Romanesque cathedral. Friendly bar and restaurant. The staff give helpful advice on sightseeing and restaurants in the city. **www.patriahotel.com**

PISTOIA Il Convento   €€

Via San Quirino 33, 51030 **Tel** *0573 45 26 51* **Fax** *0573 45 35 78* **Rooms** *32*   **Road map** *C2*

Once a 19th-century Franciscan monastery, this ambient hotel has simple but appealing rooms overlooking a picturesque courtyard and cloister. The rooms are in the monks' former cells, and the restaurant in the refectory. The garden, surrounded by woodlands, has views as far as Florence cathedral. **www.ilconventohotel.com**

PRATO Hotel Hermitage   €

Via Ginepraia 112, 59016 **Tel** *0558 772 44* **Fax** *0558 79 70 57* **Rooms** *59*   **Road map** *C2*

Located in a quiet residential area near the 15th-century Medicean Villa Ambra, this three-star hotel sits on top of a hill in a lush parkland. A great spot for touring the nearby vineyards. Rooms are unfussy and comfortable, and some come with stunning views over Florence. The restaurant serves Tuscan specialties. **www.hotelhermitageprato.it**

VIAREGGIO Hotel Liberty   €

Viale Manin 18, 55049 **Tel** *0584 462 47* **Fax** *0584 462 49* **Rooms** *50*   **Road map** *B2*

Close to the seafront, this three-star hotel is in the centre of town. The simply furnished rooms have views of the sea, the white Carraran marble mountains, or both. Comfortable modern lobby and sun terrace for guest use. The friendly and capable staff will help with restaurant recommendations. **www.hotelliberty.viareggio.it**

VIAREGGIO Hotel President   €€€€

Viale Carducci 5, 55049 **Tel** *0584 96 27 12* **Fax** *0584 96 36 58* **Rooms** *39*   **Road map** *B2*

This Liberty-style beachfront hotel, built in 1949, is typical of Viareggio's architecture. Its good reputation is justified by the comfortable, modern rooms with a real seaside feel. Restaurant Gaudì serves a generous buffet breakfast, and boasts an evening menu of Tuscan and international cuisine. Bicycle rental and playground. **www.hotelpresident.it**

Key to Price Guide *see p250* **Key to Symbols** *see back cover flap*

VIAREGGIO Hotel Astor ⏸🏊🛏🖥 €€€€€
Lungomare Carducci 54, 55049 **Tel** *0584 503 01* **Fax** *0584 551 81* **Rooms** *68* **Road map** *B2*

A luxury hotel alongside the white sand beaches of Viareggio, the Astor has a panoramic sundeck overlooking the town's Liberty-style promenade with its elegant shops and colourful attractions. The popular seafood restaurant, La Conchiglia, serves up a real treat with alfresco dining in the summer months. **www.astorviareggio.com**

EASTERN TUSCANY

AREZZO B&B Casa Bellavista ⏸🏊🖥 €€
Località Creti, 52044 **Tel** *0575 61 03 11* **Fax** *0575 61 07 49* **Rooms** *3* **Road map** *E3*

This family house on the hills outside Arezzo has only three guestrooms. The charming garden overlooks cypress-lined hills. You can be sure to get excellent, personalised service at this welcoming B&B. Breakfasts consist of delicacies made using great-grandmother Teresa's recipes. Cooking courses on request. **www.casabellavista.it**

AREZZO Casa Volpi B&B ⏸🖥 €€
Via Simone Martini 29, 52100 **Tel** *0575 35 43 64* **Fax** *0575 35 59 71* **Rooms** *15* **Road map** *E3*

In a lush green park in the hills above Arezzo, this family-run B&B accommodates guests in a 19th-century country house. The large bedrooms have high ceilings and wrought-iron furnishings. The breakfast terrace offers panoramic views over the Chiana valley. The garden is lovely. Well-placed for hiking. Bicycles for rent. **www.casavolpi.it**

AREZZO Castello di Gargonza ⏸🖥 €€
Località Monte San Savino, 52048 **Tel** *0575 84 70 21* **Fax** *0575 84 70 54* **Rooms** *30* **Road map** *E3*

This atmospheric castle-residence in the hills between Arezzo and Siena offers rooms by the night, and self-catering apartments by the week. Restaurant La Torre di Gargonza is just outside the main walls. Hiking and nature trails in the 600 acres of surrounding parkland.The frescoed chapel in the grounds is an added attraction. **www.gargonza.it**

AREZZO Hotel Continentale 🖥 €€
Piazza Guido Monaco 7, 52100 **Tel** *0575 202 51* **Fax** *0575 35 04 85* **Rooms** *73* **Road map** *E3*

A town house built in 1948 and within walking distance of the centre of Arezzo, this modern three-star hotel is a popular choice with business travellers thanks to its conference facilities and professional service. Rooms are spacious and luxurious with all amenities. Generous buffet breakfast. Family rooms. **www.hotelcontinentale.com**

AREZZO Hotel Il Patio 🖥 €€€€
Via Cavour 23, 52100 **Tel** *0575 40 19 62* **Fax** *0575 274 18* **Rooms** *7* **Road map** *E3*

Just a few meters from the Church of San Francesco, this charismatic hotel is in an 18th-century palazzo on the antique shop-lined Via Cavour. Each room is decorated to reflect the travels of author Bruce Chatwin (China, India, Morocco and so on). The effect, coupled with wood-beamed ceilings, is enchanting. **www.arezzoresorts.it**

AREZZO Relais la Commenda 🏊🖥 €€€€
Località Commenda 6, 52031 **Tel** *0575 72 33 56* **Fax** *0575 72 39 21* **Rooms** *7* **Road map** *E3*

This 11th-century monastery has been converted into apartments and suites by the Barboni family. The three buildings are surrounded by a glorious, ancient parkland. Rooms are striking with terracotta floors, exposed stone walls and Tuscan crafted furniture. Suites booked by night and apartments by week. **www.relaislacommenda.com**

CORTONA Hotel Italia ↕ €
Via Ghibellina 5-7-9, 52044 **Tel** *0575 63 02 54* **Fax** *0575 60 57 63* **Rooms** *26* **Road map** *E3*

Just off the main square of medieval Cortona, this hotel is located in an ancient palace dating back to the 1600s. Though no longer a family-run establishment, the service is exceedingly personalised and friendly. The large roof terrace has panoramic views over the Chiana valley and the Trasimeno lake. **www.planhotel.com**

CORTONA Hotel Oasi ↕⏸🖥 €€
Via delle Contesse 1, 52044 **Tel** *0575 63 03 54* **Fax** *0575 63 04 77* **Rooms** *63* **Road map** *E3*

This stunning three-star hotel is in a converted monastery just outside Cortona's Etruscan walls. The rooms are simple but comfortable. However, the main attractions are the surrounding walled garden and the monastery chapel, which has been standing here since 1235. The Renaissance-themed restaurant serves Tuscan cuisine. **www.hoteloasi.org**

CORTONA Hotel San Michele ↕🖥 €€€
Via Guelfa 15, 52044 **Tel** *0575 60 43 48* **Fax** *0575 63 01 47* **Rooms** *43* **Road map** *E3*

A beautifully restored Renaissance palazzo in the heart of Cortona, this hotel has fabulous bedrooms featuring exposed brickwork and wood-beamed ceilings. The rooms offer scenic views over the city and the hotel's interior courtyard. The hotel organizes excursions around town and into the countryside. **www.hotelsanmichele.net**

CORTONA Relais Villa Baldelli ↕🏊🖥 €€€€
San Pietro a Cegliolo 420, 52044 **Tel** *0575 61 24 06* **Fax** *0575 61 24 07* **Rooms** *15* **Road map** *E3*

Located in a restored 17th-century villa, Relais Villa Baldelli is surrounded by a tranquil parkland. The peaceful rooms are decorated with pastoral frescoes and vintage paintings. The shared lounge features an antique stone fireplace. Segments of 17th-century altars embellish the ground floor. **www.villabaldelli.com**

CENTRAL TUSCANY

CASTELLINA IN CHIANTI Colle Etrusco Salivolpi
Via Fiorentina 89, 53011 **Tel** *0577 74 04 84* **Fax** *0577 74 09 98* **Rooms** *19*   €€   **Road map** *D3*

An elegant country house surrounded by vineyards, olive groves and cypress trees, this hotel is within walking distance of Castellina in Chianti. The rooms are warmly decorated with authentic rustic Tuscan furniture including wrought-iron beds, terracotta floors and wooden beams. Large lounge room and garden. **www.hotelsalivolpi.com**

CASTELLINA IN CHIANTI Tenuta di Ricavo
Località Scotoni, 53011 **Tel** *0577 74 02 21* **Fax** *0577 74 10 14* **Rooms** *22*   €€€€€   **Road map** *D3*

This charming resort in a lovingly restored medieval hamlet rests in the middle of a natural park, offering a unique combination of history and nature. Bedrooms contain parts of the original furnishings, including terracotta tiles and wooden beams. The gourmet restaurant, Percora Nera, dishes out delicious meals. **www.ricavo.com**

GAIOLE IN CHIANTI Residence San Sano
Località San Sano 21, 53100 **Tel** *0577 74 61 30* **Fax** *0577 74 61 56* **Rooms** *14*   €€   **Road map** *D3*

The appealing rooms in this renovated 13th-century watchhouse show off whitewashed walls and wood-beamed ceilings. A three-course menu of Tuscan specialties is served under the well-known restaurant's stone arches. Meals can be enjoyed in the garden terrace during the summer months. **www.sansanohotel.it**

GAIOLE IN CHIANTI Castello di Spaltenna
Località Spaltenna, 53013 **Tel** *0577 74 94 83* **Fax** *0577 74 92 69* **Rooms** *38*   €€€€€   **Road map** *D3*

In an ancient feudal hamlet with a splendid medieval church and belltower, this beautiful converted monastery has fabulous views over the valley and its abundant vineyards. Rooms are luxurious with four-poster beds, large lounge areas and Jacuzzis. Gourmet restaurant. Horse riding by arrangement. **www.spaltenna.it**

PANZANO IN CHIANTI Villa le Barone
Via San Leolino 19, 50020 **Tel** *055 85 26 21* **Fax** *055 85 22 77* **Rooms** *28*   €€€€€   **Road map** *D3*

The home of the Della Robbia family since the 16th century, Villa le Barone has been renovated into a cheerful, welcoming hotel crammed full of antique furnishings, old prints and bright fabrics. The restaurant in the old winery serves typical Tuscan food and Chianti wines. The hotel also organizes sightseeing excursions. **www.villalebarone.it**

RADDA IN CHIANTI La Locanda
Località Montanino, 53017 **Tel** *0577 73 88 32* **Fax** *0577 73 92 63* **Rooms** *7*   €€€€€   **Road map** *D3*

This family-run hotel, in a converted 16th-century farmhouse, offers breathtaking views over the Chianti countryside. A nearby stone building houses a cosy drawing room with a bar and dining area. A large panoramic terrace beside the pool, along with a big garden are incentives to sit outdoors. Minimum stay of two nights. **www.lalocanda.it**

RADDA IN CHIANTI Relais Fattoria Vignale
Via Panigiani 9, 53017 **Tel** *0577 73 83 00* **Fax** *0577 73 85 92* **Rooms** *40*   €€€€€   **Road map** *D3*

Right in the middle of the Chianti Classico heartland, this hotel is the perfect stop for wine-loving tourists. The former manor house of a large wine estate, the hotel still has a busy wine shop, tavern and popular restaurant. Bedrooms are furnished with antiques. There is a wisteria and jasmine-covered breakfast terrace. **www.vignale.it**

SAN GIMIGNANO Albergo Leon Bianco
Piazza della Cisterna 13, 53037 **Tel** *0577 94 12 94* **Fax** *0577 94 21 23* **Rooms** *25*   €€   **Road map** *C3*

Overlooking the historical Piazza della Cisterna in the heart of San Gimignano, Hotel Leon Bianco boasts one of the best locations in town. It is also housed in an extremely interesting building – an 11th-century palazzo with exposed brickwork and wood-beamed ceilings in the bedrooms. **www.leonbianco.com**

SAN GIMIGNANO Casa de' Potenti
Piazza della Erbe 10, 53037 **Tel/Fax** *0577 94 31 90* **Rooms** *6*   €€   **Road map** *C3*

This unfussy B&B, in a private town house in the historic centre of the city, serves as one of the most economical options in the region. Located on the second floor of a 14th-century stone house, the rooms are small and simple, with views over the nearby Piazza della Cisterna. There is a cafè on the ground floor. **www.casadeipotenti.com**

SAN GIMIGNANO Hotel Villa Belvedere
Via Dante 14, 53037 **Tel** *0577 94 05 39* **Fax** *0577 94 03 27* **Rooms** *15*   €€   **Road map** *C3*

With a cypress-filled garden and comfortably refurbished rooms, this isolated medieval villa just outside San Gimignano is good value for money. The rooms are simple but intimate, with shared lounge areas and a breakfast terrace by the pool. Turn to the staff for helpful sightseeing advice on the area. **www.hotelvillabelvedere.net**

SAN GIMIGNANO La Cisterna
Piazza della Cisterna 23, 53037 **Tel** *0577 94 03 28* **Fax** *0577 94 20 80* **Rooms** *50*   €€   **Road map** *C3*

In a 14th-century palazzo in the centre of town, its rooms are furnished in traditional Florentine style and have great views over both the main square and the surrounding countryside. The restaurant, Le Terrazze (open since 1918) is split into two parts – one of which, Loggia Rustica, has gloriously high wooden ceilings. **www.hotelcisterna.it**

Key to Price Guide *see p250* **Key to Symbols** *see back cover flap*

SAN GIMIGNANO Albergo Relais Santa Chiara

Via Matteotti 15, 53037 **Tel** *0577 94 07 01* **Fax** *0577 94 20 96* **Rooms** *41*

Road map *C3*

An eclectic mix of historic and modern decor, this four-star hotel is situated on a hill just outside San Gimignano. The rooms are somewhat small, but clean and cheerful – try to book one with a balcony. A swimming-pool with Jacuzzi, garden and private parking add to its appeal. Wine-tasting and horse riding by arrangement. **www.rsc.it**

SAN GIMIGNANO La Collegiata

Località Strada 27, 53037 **Tel** *0577 94 32 01* **Fax** *0577 94 05 66* **Rooms** *20*

Road map *C3*

This outstanding Relais & Chateaux hotel in a converted Franciscan convent, offers stunning views of the towers of San Gimignano. The 16th-century *pietra serena* building is surrounded by ancient cypresses and Italian-style gardens. Indulge yourself in the restaurant and wine bar, or lounge in the spa and wellbeing centre. **www.lacollegiata.it**

SAN GIMIGNANO Villa San Paolo

Strada per Certaldo, 53037 **Tel** *0577 95 51 00* **Fax** *0577 95 51 13* **Rooms** *18*

Road map *C3*

Bounded by a rambling park, the isolated 18th-century country villa is now an exceptionally delightful four-star hotel just outside San Gimignano. It has recently been restored with plush double rooms that complement the architecture. Tennis courts and mountain bikes for hire. Three-night minimum stay. **www.hotelvillasanpaolo.com**

SAN GUSME Relais San Arceno

Località Castelnuovo Berardenga, 53100 **Tel** *0577 35 92 92* **Fax** *0577 35 92 76* **Rooms** *16*

Road map *D3*

In a stately, honey-coloured 17th-century villa, this hotel features large bedrooms with high vaulted ceilings and luxury reproduction antique furnishings. Views of the the surrounding park and lake. Many activities are on offer such as wine tasting and cookery courses. Excursions to Siena on foot, by bike and on horseback. **www.relaisvillarceno.com**

SIENA Antica Torre

Via di Fieravecchia 7, 53100 **Tel/Fax** *0577 22 22 55* **Rooms** *8*

Road map *D3*

Along Siena's southeast walls, this small hotel is in a stunning 16th-century tower. The rooms are quiet and romantic, while the old travertine stone staircase, stone arches, wooden beams and original brick vaults add lots of character. The breakfast room occupies a medieval potter's shop. Close to all the main sights. **www.anticatorresiena.it**

SIENA Hotel Arcobaleno

Via Fiorentina 32/40, 53100 **Tel** *0577 27 10 92* **Fax** *0577 27 14 23* **Rooms** *19*

Road map *D3*

A peaceful 19th-century country villa is now this friendly little hotel. The panoramic terrace and intimate rooms are very pleasant. Located at the city gates, the hotel is a short walk from Siena's historical centre. The restaurant, with its romantic alcoves, is accessed via a charming winding stairway. Baby-sitting facilities. **www.hotelarcobaleno.com**

SIENA Hotel Chiusarelli

Viale Curtatone 15, 53100 **Tel** *0577 28 05 62* **Fax** *0577 27 11 77* **Rooms** *49*

Road map *D3*

Within walking distance of Piazza del Campo, this tranquil villa is one of the oldest hotels in town. Built in 1870 by the Chiusarelli family, the rooms are furnished in Neo-Classical style with views over the church of San Domenico. Ask for a room with a balcony. Generous buffet breakfast served on the veranda. **www.chiusarelli.com**

SIENA Palazzo Bruchi di Masignani

Via Pantaneto 105, 53100 **Tel/Fax** *0577 28 73 42* **Rooms** *9*

Road map *D3*

In an 18th-century palazzo in the heart of Siena, this friendly B&B is within easy walking distance of Piazza del Campo. Lovely view of the palazzo garden and the ancient city walls. Luxury rooms come with frescoed ceilings and old-fashioned furnishings. Standard rooms are traditionally furnished with wall tapestries. **www.palazzobruchi.it**

SIENA Santa Caterina

Via Enea Silvio Piccolomini 7, 53100 **Tel** *0577 22 11 05* **Fax** *0577 27 10 87* **Rooms** *22*

Road map *D3*

An 18th-century villa lovingly converted into a cosy hotel, Santa Caterina is only a short distance from Siena's medieval walls. The rooms vary in size, but all are carefully decorated in ancient Tuscan style. Beautiful views can be enjoyed from the garden and veranda. Breakfast is served in a glass conservatory during summer. **www.hscsiena.it**

SIENA Villa Piccola Siena

Via Petriccio Belriguardo 7, 53100 **Tel** *0577 58 80 44* **Fax** *0577 58 95 10* **Rooms** *13*

Road map *D3*

Close to Siena's historic centre, this three-star hotel provides traditionally decorated rooms, small terrace garden, a gourmet restaurant, cookery courses, guided tours, bicycle rentals and horse riding by arrangement. The staff is friendly and baby-sitting can be arranged. **www.villapiccolasiena.com**

SIENA Hotel Athena

Via P Mascagni 55, 53100 **Tel** *0577 28 63 13* **Fax** *0577 481 53* **Rooms** *100*

Road map *D3*

Situated in a quiet residential area, this modern four-star hotel is just a short way from the Siena Duomo. Rooms are fairly large and comfortable though the decor is not very distinctive. The rooftop terrace has fantastic views over Siena and beyond. The fine restaurant serves authentic local cuisine. Private parking. **www.hotelathena.com**

SIENA Hotel Minerva

Via Garibaldi 72, 53100 **Tel** *0577 28 44 74* **Fax** *0577 433 43* **Rooms** *59*

Road map *D3*

A short walk from Piazza del Campo, Minerva may be a distinctly modern hotel, but many of its comfortable rooms have views over the historical centre. The bar serves breakfast and a range of cheeses, meats and Sienese patisserie items. Event and entertainment booking upon request. Air conditioning in most rooms. **www.albergominerva.it**

SIENA Pensione Palazzo Ravizza

Pian dei Mantellini 34, 53100 **Tel** *0577 28 04 62* **Fax** *0577 22 15 97* **Rooms** *30*　　**Road map** *D3*

This well-located, quiet *pensione* is in a renovated Renaissance palace. Rooms come with original terracotta floors, frescoed ceilings, carved doorways and antique furnishings. Suites have their own lounge areas. The gourmet restaurant and splendid terrace garden add to the Ravizza's considerable charm. **www.palazzoravizza.it**

SIENA Sangallo Park Hotel

Strada di Vico Alto 2, 53100 **Tel** *0577 33 41 49* **Fax** *0577 33 33 06* **Rooms** *50*　　**Road map** *D3*

Two kilometres (one mile) from Siena's historical centre, the Sangallo offers the perfect base for exploring the Chianti and Val d'Orcia countryside by car, bike or foot. The rooms are large with modern decor. The generous breakfast is served on the panoramic terrace, and there is also a pretty garden to relax in. **www.sangalloparkhotel.it**

SIENA Piccolo Hotel Oliveta

Via E.S.Piccolomini 35, 53100 **Tel** *0577 28 39 30* **Fax** *0577 27 00 09* **Rooms** *15*　　**Road map** *D3*

In a converted 18th-century farmhouse, this welcoming three-star hotel is within walking distance of Siena's major monuments and tourist attractions. Rooms have preserved all the original architectural features, including beamed ceilings, terracotta tiles and the original brickwork. The wine bar offers light snacks as well. **www.oliveta.com**

SIENA Villa Scacciapensieri

Via Scacciapensieri 10, 53100 **Tel** *0577 414 41* **Fax** *0577 27 08 54* **Rooms** *32*　　**Road map** *D3*

Located in a hilly parkland outside of Siena, this converted 19th-century villa overlooks the city walls and has a wonderful old-world charm. The lovely rooms have whitewashed walls and wood-beamed ceilings. Meals are served outside on one of the many atmospheric terraces with views over the Chianti hills. **www.villascacciapensieri.it**

SIENA Grand Hotel Continental

Via Banchi di Sopra 85, 53100 **Tel** *0577 560 11* **Fax** *0577 560 15 55* **Rooms** *51*　　**Road map** *D3*

Just off the Piazza del Campo, the Continental has quickly built up an impressive reputation since opening in 2002. In a majestic 1600s palazzo, the rooms are filled with priceless antiques, stunning fabrics and frescoed ceilings. A shuttle service links to the sister hotel (Park Hotel) with its golf, tennis and swimming facilities. **www.ghcs.it**

SIENA Hotel Certosa di Maggiano

Strada di Certosa 82, 53100 **Tel** *0577 28 81 80* **Fax** *0577 28 81 89* **Rooms** *17*　　**Road map** *D3*

Part of the Relais & Chateaux chain of luxury hotels, this converted monastery lies in the countryside just outside Siena. Built in 1314, the hotel is internationally renowned for its antique paintings and fine silk furnishings. The vast grounds include olive groves, vineyards and a helipad. **www.certosadimaggiano.it**

SIENA Palace Hotel Due Ponti

Viale Europa 12, 53100 **Tel** *0577 460 55* **Fax** *0577 24 79 07* **Rooms** *44*　　**Road map** *D3*

On the outskirts of Siena, the Palace Hotel Due Ponti is popular with business travellers since it is equipped with all mod-cons including a solarium, private parking and conference facilities. Rooms are clean and simply furnished. A large restaurant serves Tuscan fare and there is a very pleasant garden. **www.palacehoteldueponti.com**

SIENA Residence Bosco della Spina

Lupompesi, Murlo, 53016 **Tel** *0577 81 46 05* **Fax** *0577 81 46 06* **Rooms** *14*　　**Road map** *D3*

Fourteen apartments managed as a hotel, this residence-restaurant occupies the renovated barns, granaries, haylofts and stables of a medieval farmhouse outside Siena. Rooms have been renovated in antique style by using terracotta, stone, solid wood and wrought iron. The superb restaurant has a panoramic terrace. **www.boscodellaspina.com**

SIENA Villa Patrizia

Via Florentina 58, 53100 **Tel** *0577 504 31* **Fax** *0577 504 42* **Rooms** *33*　　**Road map** *D3*

A short walk from Siena's northernmost city walls, this converted villa offers a haven of tranquility in its garden and oak-filled park. Rooms are simply furnished and comfortable. The restaurant offers an authentic mix of local dishes including *pici* (hand-rolled pasta) with porcini mushrooms. The breakfast is also excellent. **www.villapatrizia.it**

SINALUNGA Locanda dell'Amorosa

Loc. L'Amorosa, 53048 **Tel** *0577 67 72 11* **Fax** *0577 63 20 01* **Rooms** *20*　　**Road map** *E3*

This idyllic 14th-century villa graces the rolling Sienese hills. Rooms are splendid with antique Tuscan furniture, prints and paintings. Visitors can enjoy the elegant restaurant which now occupies the ancient stables. The surrounding park, farm and vineyards capture the essence of the countryside and are ideal for long walks. **www.amorosa.it**

STROVE Albergo Casalta

Loc. Monteriggioni, 53035 **Tel/Fax** *0577 30 10 02* **Rooms** *10*　　**Road map** *D3*

A small hamlet in the centre of Strove is home to this welcoming, family-run hotel. The 1,000-year old stone building houses rooms that are beautifully furnished in a rustic style with simple antiques, exposed stone fireplaces and wood-beamed ceilings. An elegant restaurant serves traditional regional dishes. **www.chiantiturismo.it**

STROVE San Luigi Residence

Via della Cerreta 38, 53035 **Tel** *0577 30 10 55* **Fax** *0577 30 11 67* **Rooms** *73*　　**Road map** *D3*

Set in a vast park, the emphasis at San Luigi is on sport and relaxation. Accommodation is in a range of farm buildings (including 10 apartments) that are tastefully restored in rustic Tuscan style. The restaurant serves traditional local cuisine. Tennis, volleyball and basketball courts, as well as a cookery school. **www.borgosanluigi.it**

Key to Price Guide *see p250* **Key to Symbols** *see back cover flap*

SOUTHERN TUSCANY

ELBA Hotel Antares

🏠🏊♿📺🖥 €€

Lido di Capoliveri, 57031 **Tel** 0565 94 01 31 **Fax** 0565 94 00 84 **Rooms** 49   **Road map** B4

With the beach on one side, and a garden on the other, this hotel has a bright, cheerful look. Rooms are spacious and contemporary. The private beach has surfboards, sailing boards and motorboats for hire. Motorboat tours take visitors to the small quiet coves that dot the coast, and are inaccessible by land. **www.elbahotelantares.it**

ELBA Hotel Ilio

🏠🖥 €€

Via Sant'Andrea 5, 57030 **Tel** 0565 90 80 18 **Fax** 0565 90 80 87 **Rooms** 19   **Road map** B4

This fabulous "all nature" boutique hotel is located on the edge of a natural park. Quaintly, the rooms are named after the plants around them – you can stay in the Lemon, Oleander or Geranium room among others. The beach is close and the owners organize nature walks. The restaurant serves Elban dishes using local ingredients. **www.ilio.it**

ELBA Albergo Locanda del Volterraio

🏠🏊♿📺🖥 €€€€

Località Bagnaia, 57039 **Tel** 0565 96 12 19 **Fax** 0565 96 12 89 **Rooms** 18   **Road map** B4

Part of a holiday complex beside the tiny seaside village of Bagnaia, this exclusive four-star hotel shares 400 acres of private parkland with the apartments of Residenza Sant'Anna. The health conscious can enjoy the tennis courts and spa, and later relax at the beach bar. Baby-sitting facilities and the children's pool are also advantages. **www.volterraio.it**

ELBA Hotel Montecristo

🏊🏠🏊♿📺🖥 €€€€

Lungomare Nomellini 11, 57034 **Tel** 0565 97 68 61 **Fax** 0565 97 65 97 **Rooms** 43   **Road map** B4

This four-star hotel is simply furnished with a stunning poolside terrace and restaurant, with views across the bay of Marina di Campo. The sea can be viewed from some rooms. Steps from the hotel lead down to the sandy beach and to the adjacent pine forest. There is a spa and wellbeing centre. Diving by arrangement. **www.hotelmontecristo.it**

ELBA Hotel Hermitage

🏠🏊♿📺🖥 €€€€€

Località La Biodola, 57037 **Tel** 0565 97 40 **Fax** 0565 96 99 84 **Rooms** 30   **Road map** B4

The most luxurious hotel in Elba's most exclusive bay, the Hermitage has its own private beach, three pools, three restaurants, a piano bar, a six-hole golf course and nine tennis courts. Accommodation is split between the main building and smaller romantic cottages in the grounds. Three-day minimum stay. **www.hotelhermitage.it**

GIGLIO CAMPESE Hotel Campese

🏠🖥 €€€

Località Giglio Campese, 58012 **Tel** 0564 80 40 03 **Fax** 0564 80 40 93 **Rooms** 39   **Road map** C5

In the charming bay of Campese, northwest of the island of Giglio, Hotel Campese is simple but welcoming, with a private beach and an excellent restaurant that serves great seafood. The mountainous backdrop evokes a feeling of wild isolation. Terrace garden with glorious views over the quiet fishing bay at sunset. **www.hotelcampese.com**

GIGLIO PORTO Castello Monticello

🏊🏠♿📺🖥 €€

Via Provinciale, 58013 **Tel** 0564 80 92 52 **Fax** 0564 80 94 73 **Rooms** 29   **Road map** C5

Beautifully situated in the midst of Giglio's lush Mediterranean vegetation, this hotel was originally built as a private mansion. Rooms are tastefully decorated with superb views of the sea. A panoramic terrace, tennis court, and children's playground add to its appeal. Courtesy shuttle to the beach and ferry. **www.hotelcastellomonticello.com**

PITIGLIANO/SORANO Hotel della Fortezza

🖥 €€€

Piazza Cairoli 5, 58010 **Tel** 0564 63 20 10 **Fax** 0564 63 32 09 **Rooms** 16   **Road map** E5

A short drive from Pitigliano, this elegant three-star hotel is located within the walls of Sorano's most important medieval structure, the historical Fortezza Orsini. Room furnishings date from the 19th-century, but the ancient beams, tiled ceilings and winding pathways are much older. Closed in February. **www.fortezzahotel.it**

PORTO ERCOLE Hotel Don Pedro

🏊🏠🖥 €€

Via Panoramica 7, 58018 **Tel** 0564 83 39 14 **Fax** 0564 83 31 29 **Rooms** 44   **Road map** D5

The only hotel in town, the simply furnished rooms of the Don Pedro offer breathtaking views over Porto Ercole's yacht-filled port and Fortezza Spagnola. The hotel has its own private beach in the pebble-filled bay, with a bar and breakfast terrace. The restaurant serves a seasonal range of locally caught fish. **www.hoteldonpedro.it**

PUNTA ALA Piccolo Hotel Alleluja

🏠🏊♿📺🖥 €€€€€

Via del Porto, 58040 **Tel** 0564 92 20 50 **Fax** 0564 92 07 34 **Rooms** 38   **Road map** C4

This luxurious four-star seaside hotel is in the middle of the Punta Ala nature park, and boasts a private beach of fine white sand. Rooms are decorated in characteristic Tuscan-farmhouse style. Some double rooms have their own sitting rooms. Tennis courts on site and nearby golf club. Baby-sitting services on request. **www.baglionihotels.com**

TALAMONE Hotel Torre dell'Osa

🏊🏠♿🖥 €€€

SS Aurelia KM156, 58010 **Tel** 0564 88 49 53 **Fax** 0564 88 49 54 **Rooms** 14   **Road map** D5

South of the Parco della Maremma, this friendly hotel is on the Talamone promontory. The fabulous rural location is offset by classically furnished rooms with wood-beamed ceilings. Five minutes to the beach and golf course. An ideal choice for an isolated romantic break. Motorboat tours along the coast can be arranged. **www.torredellosa.it**

RESTAURANTS, CAFES AND BARS

F ood is one of the great Italian passions, and eating out on a balmy summer's evening can be a memorable experience. Few restaurants in Tuscany serve anything but Italian food, and most concentrate on the robust fare that typifies the region's cuisine. Most Tuscans take their lunch *(pranzo)* around 1pm, and have dinner *(cena)* from 8pm. Restaurants may shut for several weeks

Italian waiter at your service

during the winter and also during the holiday season in summer. If in doubt, phone first to check that the restaurant is open. Finding the restaurants in Florence can be confusing due to the dual numbering of the streets *(see p298)*, so use the map references. The restaurants listed on pages 270–281 have been selected from the best the city and region can offer across all price ranges

TYPES OF RESTAURANTS AND BARS

Italian restaurants have a bewildering variety of names, but in practice there's little difference between a *trattoria, osteria* or *ristorante* in terms of price, cooking or ambience. Both a *birreria* and *spaghetteria* are more down-market establishments, and sell beer, pasta dishes and snacks. A *pizzeria* is a cheap, informal restaurant with pasta, meat and fish on the menu as well as pizzas. It is usually open only in the evening, especially if it has wood-fired ovens.

At lunchtime you could visit a *tavola calda*, which will offer a range of hot and cold pasta dishes, vegetables and meats. A *rosticceria* offers spit-roast chicken to take away, often with other fast foods. Most bars sell filled rolls *(panini)* and sandwiches *(tramezzini)* and small pizza bars sell slices of pizza *(pizza taglia)* to eat on the street.

Old-fashioned wine bars *(vinaii* or *fiaschetterie)* are a dying breed, but they are atmospheric places to grab a snack or a glass of wine. Ice cream parlours *(gelaterie)*, by contrast, are thriving, and Florence has some of the best in Italy.

VEGETARIAN FOOD

Most Italians find it hard to understand vegetarianism, and Florence boasts only a couple of vegetarian restaurants. However, in the wake of mad-cow disease, restaurants

Il Latini, Florence *(see p271)*

are offering a wider vegetarian selection and you should have no trouble assembling a meat-free meal, particularly if you eat fish and seafood. Starters *(antipasti)* will usually include some suitable dishes. There are also vegetable-based soups and pasta sauces, but check that they have been cooked with vegetable stock *(brodo vegetariano)*.

HOW MUCH TO PAY

Prices are often higher in Florence than elsewhere. In the cheaper eating establishments and pizzerias you can have a two-course or a fixed-price *(menù turistico)* meal with half a litre of wine for around €15–€20. Average prices for a three-course meal are €20–€30, and in up-market restaurants you could easily pay as much as €40–€50.

Nearly all restaurants have a cover charge *(pane e coperto)* usually no more than €3. Many also add a 10 per cent service charge *(servizio)* to the bill *(il conto)*, so always establish whether or not this is the case. Where leaving a tip is a matter of your own discretion, 12–15 per cent is acceptable.

Restaurants are obliged by law to give you a receipt *(una ricevuta)*. Scraps of paper with an illegible scrawl are illegal, and you are perfectly within your rights to ask for a proper bill.

Outside the long-established Antico Fattore in Florence *(see p271)*

Cash is the preferred form of payment in most cafés and bars, but many restaurants, particularly the more expensive, will accept major credit cards. Check which cards are accepted when booking.

MAKING RESERVATIONS

Florence's best restaurants in all price ranges are well patronized. It is therefore advisable to try and reserve a table, even in the more down-market places. Where restaurants do not accept bookings, try to arrive early to avoid queuing.

DRESS CODE

Italians are relaxed about eating out, but nevertheless like to dress up to dine. The restaurant listings indicate where formal dress is required.

Trattoria Angiolino *(see p270)*

READING THE MENU

A meal in a restaurant will usually start with *antipasti*, or hors d'œuvres (hams, olives, salamis, crostini), followed by *primi* (soups, pasta or rice). Main courses – *secondi* – will be meat or fish, either served alone or accompanied by vegetables *(contorni)* or a salad *(insalata)*.

To finish, there will probably be a choice of fruit *(frutta)*, cheese *(formaggio)*, puddings *(dolci)*, or a combination of all three. Coffee – always espresso, never cappuccino – is ordered at the end of a meal, often with a *digestivo (see p269)*. In cheaper restaurants, the menu *(il menù* or *la lista)* may be written on a black

The 13th-century Il Pozzo in Monteriggioni *(see p279)*

board and in many establishments the waiter *(cameriere)* will recite the chef's daily specials at your table.

CHOICE OF WINE

House wines will usually be Chiantis or some close cousin. The cheaper establishments usually have only house wine, or a small choice of other Tuscan wines. Those in the €40–€50 price range will have a fuller selection of regional wines, as well as wines from other parts of Italy. At the top of the scale, there should be a wide range of Italian and local wines, and, as at the Enoteca Pinchiorri *(see p272)*, a selection of French and other foreign vintages. *(See also pp268–9.)*

CHILDREN

Children are generally welcome in restaurants, but less so in the evening and in more up-market places. Special facilities such as high chairs are not commonly provided.

The dark wood interior of Osteria le Logge in Siena *(see p280)*

Check the menu for the option of a small portion *(una porzione piccola)*: most restaurants will prepare a half portion *(mezza porzione)* if requested.

SMOKING

In 2005 new legislation came into force and now restaurants and bars throughout Italy must provide separate no-smoking areas or they will be fined. At cafés and restaurants that do not provide sealed-off areas, smoking is limited to outside tables.

WHEELCHAIR ACCESS

Few restaurants make special provision for wheelchairs, though a word when you are booking should ensure a conveniently situated table and assistance on arrival.

USING THE LISTINGS

Key to the symbols in the listings on pp270–81.

- 🚫 No credit cards
- 🧍 Caters for children
- 📋 Air conditioning
- 🎵 Live music
- ♿ Wheelchair access
- 🪑 Outdoor tables

Price categories for a three-course meal for one including a half-bottle of house wine, cover charge, tax and service.

- € under 20 euros
- €€ 20–30 euros
- €€€ 30–40 euros
- €€€€ 40–50 euros
- €€€€€ over 50 euros

Flavours of Florence and Tuscany

Tuscany is the orchard and vegetable garden of Italy, a vision of rolling, vine-clad hills and silvery grey olive groves, while the Ligurian sea yields a fabulous bounty of fish and seafood. The cuisine is rustic and simple, but always using the finest ingredients. It is said that Tuscany is where Italian cooking was born, thanks to Catherine de'Medici, an accomplished gourmet. Tuscans are known as *mangiafagioli* (bean eaters), because pulses are used so much in soups and robust stews. Juicy steaks from prized Valdichiana cattle, pork and game all feature strongly. Fungi are highly prized; even more so are truffles – "black gold".

Black truffles

Freshly harvested Tuscan olives, for pressing into olive oil

FIRST AND FOREMOST

Tuscan olive oil is simply outstanding in quality. This "liquid gold" has countless uses and is an integral part of *crostini*, slices of toasted bread smeared with olive oil on which are spread different toppings, such as *crostini alla Toscana*, topped sautéed with chickens livers. *Salumi* producers are an important feature of the region and *prosciutto di cinghiale* (wild boar ham) is a rich, gamey delicacy. Soups and minestrones are also very popular, often made with beans, especially the white kidney beans known as *cannellini*. The most typical pasta is papardelle, broad noodles that are often served with a rich hare sauce, called *papardelle alla lepre*.

EARTH AND WATER

The shining star of meat dishes is tender, succulent beef steak, *bistecca alla fiorentina*. The best is from cattle raised in Valdichiana, south of Arezzo, delicious marinated with extra virgin olive oil and herbs, grilled over an open fire and usually served very rare. Tuscans are passionate hunters and

6 months old, washed in wine
3 weeks old
6 months old
2 months old, rolled in sun-dried tomatoes
18 months old

Some of the varieties of ewe's milk Pecorino cheese found in Tuscany

REGIONAL DISHES AND SPECIALITIES

The olive is the staple ingredient – even the branches of the tree are used for grilling. Soups vary from those enriched with beans such as *ribollita* ("boiled again"), a rich soup of beans, herbs and vegetables whose second boiling makes it thicker and intensifies the flavour, to the simple, thin vegetable *acquacotta* (literally meaning "cooked water") to which an egg is added before serving. The vast array of salamis and cold cuts includes *finocchiona*, salami flavoured with wild fennel. Robust stews include *lepre in dolce e forte*. This hare stew is cooked with citrus fruits, cocoa, garlic, rosemary, vegetables and red wine. For the sweet-toothed, Tuscany offers *ricciarelli* (diamond-shaped almond cakes), *cantucci* (above) and *torta di riso* – a golden, rich rice cake that is mouthwateringly delicious.

Minestrone alla fiorentina
This thick vegetable and bean soup may also contain chicken and pork giblets.

Picture changed new caption needed

everything from the smallest songbird to the largest wild boar features on menus. Hare is a special favourite.

Seafood and fish includes especially good red mullet *(triglie)* from Livorno and *cacciucco* soup, claimed as the ancestor of *bouillabaisse*.

FUNGI FORAYS

From late August to early October Tuscans are seized by fungi fever. Armies of people with baskets make an annual pilgrimage to the Garfagna, Mugello and Maremma for prize pickings. The most sought-after are *porcini* (boletus or cep). Picking tends to be limited by licence and is certainly only advisable to those who know their edible fungi. Out of season, dried wild mushrooms accompany

many dishes. But the star and most highly prized fungi hide underground, waiting to be sniffed out by hunters with their keen-scented dogs – the truffle *(tartufo)*. The location of truffle troves is a closely-guarded secret as they are, literally, worth their

An array of beans on display in a Tuscan market square

weight in gold. San Miniato produces about a quarter of Italy's truffle crop, including the prized white truffle.

SWEET DELIGHTS

Chestnuts are plentiful and have many uses. They, with almonds and honey, are the main ingredients in some favourite and famous recipes. Castelnuovo della Garfagnana produces a superb chestnut cake, called *torta garfagnana*. Panforte, the Christmas cake originating from Siena, is a rich mix of fruits, nuts and spices. For something a little less rich, almond *cantucci* biscuits are sublime dipped into sweet *vin santo* wine.

TUSCAN TREATS

Cacciucco di Livorno Rich tomatoey fish soup served over toasted garlic bread.

Cantucci Sweet, very hard almond biscuits.

Cheeses Ricotta, Mucchino, (cow's milk made near Lucca), Pecorino, and Cacciotte (made with ewe, cow and goat milk).

Chestnuts Made into flour, pancakes, soup and sweet cakes like *castagnaccio*, flavoured with rosemary.

Chianti The fine Tuscan red wine, used in many recipes.

Crostini Toasted bread which is smeared with olive oil and rubbed with garlic.

Papardelle alla Lepre *Thick noodles are served with a sauce of hare cooked with herbs and red wine.*

Arista alla Fiorentina *Pork loin is roasted with rosemary in a recipe dating from the 15th century.*

Zuccotto *In this Tuscan speciality, sponge cake is filled with almonds, hazelnuts, chocolate and cream.*

What to Drink in Florence and Tuscany

Medieval engraving of a grape crusher

Tuscany is a major wine-producing region whose wines make ideal partners for the robust local food. Both reds and whites are made here, ranging from light, house wine (*vino della casa*) to the very best Europe can produce. The most famous reds, notably Brunello di Montalcino, Vino Nobile di Montepulciano and Chianti, are made from the Sangiovese grape and are produced inland, on the hills of Tuscany. A number of estates, particularly in Chianti Classico, also experiment with non-Italian grape varieties with considerable success. Throughout Tuscany, bars and cafés are open all day serving drinks from wine to beer and coffee. See also *A Day Out in Chianti* on page 229.

Il Poggione is an excellent producer of Brunello di Montalcino.

RED WINE

Solaia   **Chianti produced by Ruffino**

Chianti is made in seven defined zones, but the best wines generally come from the hilly areas of Classico and Rufina. Brunello, from further south, needs ageing and can be expensive but Rosso di Montalcino, made for younger drinking, often offers better value. Tuscan table wine can be cheap or expensive – the top-priced wines may not fit the traditional Chianti regulations, but are likely to be extremely good. Sassicaia, made from the French Cabernet Sauvignon grape, is an example. Other fine reds include Fontalloro, Cepparello and Solaia.

Carmignano, a good dry red, is made north of Florence.

Sassicaia is made from Cabernet Sauvignon grapes.

WHITE WINE

Galestro

Tuscany's white wines are less interesting than the reds, although some producers are experimenting with a handful of quality whites from grapes such as Chardonnay and Sauvignon. Most Tuscan white wine is made from the Trebbiano grape, at its lightest in the spritzy style called Galestro, but usually sold as plain dry Bianco della Toscana. Vernaccia di San Gimignano, from the Vernaccia grape, is sometimes good and Montecarlo, from near Lucca, a blend of grapes, offers more interesting drinking. Most Tuscan whites need to be drunk young.

VIN SANTO

Vin Santo

Vin Santo, or "Holy Wine", is a traditional wine once made on farms throughout the region and now seeing a revival of interest from modern producers. The best versions are sweet, though it can be found as a dry wine. It is often offered with *cantucci*, small almond biscuits, in Tuscan restaurants and homes. Vin Santo is made from Trebbiano and Malvasia grapes which are semi-dried, made into wine and then aged in small barrels for a number of years before bottling. The best are very concentrated in flavour. Quality varies, but superb versions are made by Avignonesi and Isole e Olena.

HOW CHIANTI IS MADE

Chianti is made as soon as possible after the October harvest. The quality of the wine can be very high, as wineries have combined the best of traditional and modern techniques.

Crushing and De-stemming
The Sangiovese grapes are separated from the stalks. The tannin from the skins preserves the wine, but the stalk tannin is too harsh for fine wine.

De-stemmer

Fermentation
The juice and grape skins go into the vat where a pump circulates wine over the floating "cap" of skins to extract colour, tannin and flavour. Fermentation may take up to 15 days or more.

Fermentation vat

Pressing the Residue
Once the new wine has been drained off, the remaining skins and pips are pressed, producing dark and sometimes harsh press wine. Stored separately, this may be used in the final blend.

Press

Wooden cask

The barrels
are topped up to prevent air from reaching the wine.

Harvest at the Brolio estate in Gaiole in Chianti

Maturation
A second fermentation, the malolactic, occurs in the spring, softening the wine, which is then run into wooden barrels to mature.

Cinzano, a popular early evening *aperitivo*

APERITIFS AND DIGESTIFS

Pre- and post-meal tipples include Campari, Cinzano and the artichoke-based Cynar, as well as Crodino, the best-known of several non-alcoholic drinks. The herb-flavoured *amaro* or a *grappa* commonly round off a meal; otherwise try a *limoncello*, a sweet, lemon-based liqueur, the aniseed-scented Sambuca or almond-flavoured Amaretto.

BEER

Beer can be a great thirst-quencher, especially in the summer heat. Draught beer *(birra alla spina)* is less expensive than bottled beer, and is sold by the measure. Good Italian lager-style beers include Peroni and Moretti.

OTHER DRINKS

Fruit juices are sold in small bottles *(succo di frutta)* or freshly squeezed *(spremuta)*. In summer, iced tea or coffee can be refreshing. Italian coffee is drunk with frothy milk for breakfast *(cappuccino)* or black after meals *(espresso)*. An *espresso* with a spot of milk is called a *macchiato*.

Espresso

Cappuccino

Choosing a Restaurant

These restaurants have been selected across a wide price range for their exceptional food, good value and location. They are listed by area and within these by price, for Florence and Tuscany, and the areas surrounding them. Map references refer either to the Street Finder, pages 138–147, or the road map on the inside back cover.

PRICE CATEGORIES
For a three-course meal for one, including a half-bottle of house wine, cover charge, tax and service.

€ under 20 euros
€€ 20–30 euros
€€€ 30–40 euros
€€€€ 40–50 euros
€€€€€ over 50 euros

FLORENCE

FLORENCE Da Mario
€

Via Rosina 2r, 50123 **Tel** *055 21 85 50*   **Map** *1 C4*

This lively trattoria is always packed with a mix of stall owners, business people and tourists who all come for the good, traditional, homely food at very reasonable prices. The daily handwritten menu is posted on the wall near the kitchen and features hearty soups, simple pastas and a number of meat and side dishes.

FLORENCE Il Pizzaiuolo
€

Via de' Macci 113r, 50122 **Tel** *055 24 11 71*   **Map** *4 E1*

Be sure to book a table at this lively pizzeria/restaurant; there aren't many of them and it's always full. The pizzas come Neapolitan-style with puffy bases and real mozzarella. There's also a great selection of antipasti (grilled vegetables and seafood salad) and excellent pasta dishes from Southern Italy.

FLORENCE Il Vegetariano
€

Via delle Ruote 30r, 50129 **Tel** *055 47 50 30*   **Map** *2 D3*

One of Florence's few vegetarian restaurants, this place has been around for a long time, but continues to be popular. The decor is rustic and the food wholesome and cheap; choose from the menu written on a blackboard, pay at the desk and take your receipt to the counter to collect your food. There's a great salad bar.

FLORENCE 4 Leoni
€€

Via dei Vellutini 1r, 50125 **Tel** *055 21 85 62*   **Map** *3 B2*

This restaurant is conveniently situated five minutes from the city centre, near the Ponte Vecchio. In warm weather, tables at this revamped trattoria are set out on the pretty Piazza della Passera, but the ambience is pleasant inside too. Though no longer the simple, traditional place it once was, the service is always friendly and the setting charming.

FLORENCE Alla Vecchia Bettola
€€

Viale Vasco Pratolini 3/7, 50124 **Tel** *055 22 41 58*   **Map** *3 A1*

This popular, noisy trattoria is a reliable place to eat traditional Florentine food at affordable rates. Flasks of house wine are quaffed from marble-topped tables by a regular, local clientèle. The house *penne* (with tomato, chilli, cream and a dash of vodka) is delicious, as is the *bistecca alla fiorentina*, a thick rare steak.

FLORENCE Angiolino
€€

Via Santo Spirito 36r, 50125 **Tel** *055 239 89 76*   **Map** *3 B1*

Modernization has compromised the old-world atmosphere that used to prevail at this Oltrarno trattoria. Nonetheless, it retains a certain neighbourhood bustle, even if standards are not always consistent. Specialities on the menu include *penne* with porcini mushrooms and *arista* (roast pork) served with garlicky spinach.

FLORENCE Aquacotta
€€

Via dei Pilastri 51r, 50121 **Tel** *055 24 29 07*   **Map** *2 E5*

This inexpensive restaurant is named after the house speciality, *acquacotta*, a Florentine vegetable soup served over toast. The food is very traditional and homely; the menu includes dishes such as pig's trotters and *bollito misto* (mixed boiled meats) served with *salsa verde*.

FLORENCE Baldovino
€€

Via San Giuseppe 22r, 50122 **Tel** *055 24 17 73*   **Map** *4 E1*

Big, noisy and lively, Baldovino is one of those places where you can eat anything, from a salad or a plate of cheese to a full meal. In between there are excellent pizzas, good pasta dishes, a choice of fish or meat main courses and a number of vegetarian options. Puddings are particularly good and there's a long wine list.

FLORENCE Boccadama
€€

Piazza Santa Croce 25–26r, 50122 **Tel** *055 24 36 40*   **Map** *6 F4*

This wine bar/restaurant enjoys a superb position on Piazza Santa Croce with a handful of outside tables; shelves of wine line the walls of the cosy interior. Wine can be ordered by the glass or the bottle from a long list. You can either nibble on a selection of cheese or cold meats or go for a full meal; the food is good and quite imaginative.

Key to Symbols *see back cover flap*

FLORENCE Cantinetta Antinori
€€

Piazza Antinori 3, 50123 **Tel** *055 235 98 27* **Map** 5 C2

More than just a wine bar, yet not a full-blown restaurant, this room on the ground floor of one of Florence's finest Renaissance palaces makes a lovely place to eat. There are traditional Florentine dishes such as tripe and pasta with duck sauce, and a fine selection of Antinori wines.

FLORENCE Coquinaros
€€

Via delle Oche 15r, 50122 **Tel** *055 230 21 53* **Map** 6 E2

A convenient, cosy little place, just behind the Duomo, where you can eat at almost any time of the day or evening. There are some delicious pasta dishes (try the ravioli with pecorino and pears). You can also order a salad, a plate of cheese or cured meats or a toasted open sandwich. There are good wines by the glass and bottle too.

FLORENCE Da Sergio
€€

Piazza San Lorenzo 8r, 50129 **Tel** *055 28 19 41* **Map** 1 C4

A popular, family-run eatery in the San Lorenzo area, Sergio's trattoria is hidden behind the market stalls. Big tables (you may end up sharing) are laid with white cloths in two airy rooms. The food is quintessentially Tuscan *casalinga* (traditional) cooking and very good; there's always tripe on Mondays and Thursdays and fresh fish on Fridays.

FLORENCE Fuori Porta
€€

Via Monte alle Croci 10r, 50125 **Tel** *055 234 24 83* **Map** 4 E3

One of Florence's classic *enoteche*, this is a popular place where you can go for a glass of wine or settle down to something more substantial. Choose wine from a list featuring over 600 labels. The *crostini* (toasted open sandwiches) make a particularly good accompaniment, but there are also excellent pastas and salads.

FLORENCE Il Santo Bevitore
€€

Via Santo Spirito 64/66r, 50125 **Tel** *055 21 12 64* **Map** 5 A4

Housed in an ex-stable, this relaxed restaurant/wine bar features delicately-flavoured, innovative dishes. The menu changes seasonally, but there is always a selection of soups and home-made pastas, fish and grilled meat. Or you can choose from a selection of well-sourced cheese and cured meats. The wine list is interesting too.

FLORENCE La Casalinga
€€

Via del Michelozzo 9r, 50125 **Tel** *055 21 86 24* **Map** 5 B5

In spite of the high numbers of tourists that flock to this no-frills trattoria, it is still very much a family-run eatery where the food is wholesome and plentiful. Go for the local dishes – *ribollita* (bread and vegetable soup), *arista* (roast pork) or *bollito misto* (mixed, boiled meats), served with a tangy *salsa verde*. Try the home-made *tiramisù*.

FLORENCE Trattoria Za Za
€€

Piazza del Mercato 26r, 50129 **Tel** *055 21 54 11* **Map** 1 C4

Though a bit touristy, with wooden stools and tressle tables, this old-style trattoria is great value. Soups, such as *ribollita*, *pappa al pomodoro* (thick soup of bread and tomato) and *pasta e fagioli* (bean soup with pasta), are a speciality. The *arista*, roast pork spiked with garlic or rosemary, is reliable. Finish with apple tart *alla zaza*.

FLORENCE Antico Fattore
€€€

Via Lambertesca 1/3r, 50123 **Tel** *055 28 89 75* **Map** 6 D4

This trattoria, a favoured haunt of the Florentine literati, was founded in 1908. Though it has lost some of its old charm, having been badly damaged by the 1993 Uffizi bomb, the food and service are still of a refreshingly old-fashioned kind. Try the pasta with wild boar and the *involtini* (meat wraps) with artichoke hearts.

FLORENCE Borgo Antico
€€€

Piazza Santo Spirito 6r, 50125 **Tel** *055 21 04 37* **Map** 3 B2

This restaurant/pizzeria is particularly busy on warm summer nights when tables on the terrace, overlooking Piazza Santo Spirito, are at a premium. It is perennially popular with a young crowd who enjoy its prime locatin for people-watching. Go for lunch; it's more relaxed.

FLORENCE Cavolo Nero
€€€

Via dell'Ardiglione 22, 50125 **Tel** *055 29 47 44* **Map** 3 B1

This small little Oltrarno restaurant, with elegant decor, is popular with an arty crowd who come for the sunny Tuscan cooking with the odd twist. Specialities include spaghetti with clams, roasted sea bass with aubergines and cherry tomatoes or, for meat-eaters, pigeon stuffed with *foie gras*.

FLORENCE Frescobaldi Wine Bar
€€€

Via dei Magazzini 2/4r, 50122 **Tel** *055 28 47 24* **Map** 6 E3

This wine bar and restaurant is owned by one of Tuscany's foremost wine producers. Lunch is a casual affair while dinner is a little more formal, with white cloths and gleaming crystal. Creative, elegant food is accompanied by some fine, in-house wines; if you just want a snack and a glass, pop into Frescobaldino next door.

FLORENCE I Latini
€€€

Via dei Palchetti 6r, 50123 **Tel** *055 21 09 16* **Map** 5 B3

There is always a crowd of both foreigners and locals clamouring for a table outside I Latini's large, noisy trattoria, where huge hams hang from the ceiling. The food is traditional and portions are enormous. Bypass the pasta and try the succulent grilled and roasted meats; *bistecca alla fiorentina* (broiled T-bone steak) is an experience.

FLORENCE Il Guscio

Via dell'Orto 49, 50125 **Tel** *055 22 44 21*

€€€

Map *3 A1*

This lively San Frediano restaurant is often full. The food is based on Tuscan traditions, but is a little more refined than an average trattoria and there is a good wine list too. First courses might include gnocchi with asparagus *crespelle* (thin pancakes) while the delicious mixed seafood *al guazzetto* (in tomato sauce) is a fixture.

FLORENCE Buca Mario

Piazza degli Ottaviani 16r, 50123 **Tel** *055 21 41 79*

€€€€

Map *5 B2*

One of Florence's traditional cellar restaurants, Buca Mario is a staple among foreign tourists. In spite of its popularity, it maintains its genuinely unpretentious Florentine atmosphere and offers local standards such as *ribollita, osso buco* (medallions of marrow bone surrounded with meat), grilled meats and *arista*.

FLORENCE Garga

Via del Moro 48r, 50123 **Tel** *055 239 88 98*

€€€€

Map *5 B2*

A Florentine classic presided over by Giuliano, one of the city's great characters, Garga is fun and often full. The walls are daubed in garish frescoes and you eat in one of a series of cosy rooms. Some dishes are better than others but *taglierini del Magnifico* (pasta with a creamy orange-and-mint flavoured sauce) is superb.

FLORENCE Osteria del Caffè Italiano

V Isola delle Stinche 11/13r, 50122 **Tel** *055 28 93 68*

€€€€

Map *6 F3*

You can eat at any time of the day in this beautifully appointed restaurant; at mealtimes there is a full menu of mainly Tuscan dishes, but in between times, you can snack on excellent cheeses or cured meats and choose from a selection of Tuscan wines. The next door pizzeria is under the same ownership.

FLORENCE Ristorante Ricchi

Piazza Santo Spirito 8r, 50125 **Tel** *055 21 58 64*

€€€€

Map *3 B2*

With elegant, modern decor and a lovely terrace, this small fish restaurant is situated on one of Florence's most beautiful squares. Oriental influences are evident in dishes such as pasta with shrimps and mint, sword fish with sichuan pepper and salt cod in a spice crust. There's a limited choice for carnivores too.

FLORENCE San Jacopo

Borgo San Jacopo 62r, 50125 **Tel** *055 28 16 61*

€€€€

Map *5 C4*

One of the city's newer restaurants, the San Jacopo enjoys a fabulous setting on the south bank of the Arno. Ask for one of the coveted tables on the tiny terrace. The chic and breezy atmosphere suits the unpretentious but beautifully-served food very well. Fish fans should try *brodetto* (fish soup), an Adriatic speciality.

FLORENCE Beccofino

Piazza degli Scarlatti 1r, 50125 **Tel** *055 29 00 76*

€€€€€

Map *5 B4*

Trendy and bustling, Beccofino has a sleek, modern look that wouldn't be out of place in London or New York. The imaginative food, however, is firmly rooted in Italian traditions and is generally very good. The menu, featuring both fish and meat, changes regularly and there is an interesting wine list.

FLORENCE Cibreo

V Andrea del Verrocchio 8r, 50122 **Tel** *055 234 11 00*

€€€€€€

Map *4 F1*

This restaurant offers superbly prepared traditional Tuscan dishes in an elegant and airy setting. There is no pasta, but an array of sublime soups and thoroughly Florentine dishes such as tripe, cockscomb or kidneys. Safer options include lamb with artichokes or stuffed pigeon. Desserts are fabulous.

FLORENCE Enoteca Pinchiorri

Via Ghibellina 87, 50122 **Tel** *055 24 27 57*

€€€€€€

Map *4 E1*

Pinchiorri is frequently described as Italy's finest restaurant and it has one of Europe's best stocked cellars with over 80,000 bottles. On the ground floor of a 15th-century palazzo, the ambience is very special too, but the food (ultra-refined Tuscan/French) and the fussy service will not please all.

FLORENCE La Taverna del Bronzino

Via delle Ruote 25–27r, 50129 **Tel** *055 49 52 20*

€€€€€

Map *2 D3*

The 15th-century palazzo housing this restaurant was designed by the Florentine painter Bronzino, hence the name. Businessmen on expense account lunches and well-heeled tourists make up the clientele. The atmosphere in the airy, vaulted room is reserved and the food (elegant Tuscan) is of the highest quality.

FLORENCE Oliviero

Via delle Terme 51r, 50123 **Tel** *055 21 24 21*

€€€€€

Map *5 C3*

A vaguely retro atmosphere prevails at this elegant restaurant in the centre of town, but the food is up-to-the-minute creative Tuscan and delicious too. Choose between interesting fish and meat dishes – try galantine of rabbit or seared tuna steak with ginger and white beans. Service is professional and there's an excellent wine list.

FLORENCE Onice

Viale Michelangelo 78, 50125 **Tel** *055 68 16 31*

€€€€€

Map *4 F3*

Glowing from its recently acquired Michelin star, this restaurant is part of the smart Villa La Vedetta hotel that overlooks the city from near Piazzale Michelangelo. The ambience is elegant and contemporary, while the food is superb and prepared with minimum fuss. Menu changes with the season.

Key to Price Guide *see p270* **Key to Symbols** *see back cover flap*

FURTHER AFIELD Da Burde

Via Pistoiese 6r, 50145 **Tel** *055 31 72 06*

It's worth trekking 6 km (4 miles) from the city centre to this family-run trattoria, to soak up an air of a time gone by. All the classics of traditional Florentine cooking are to be found on the menu – *fettunta* (Tuscan garlic bread), *ribollita* (Tuscan bread soup), *trippa alla fiorentina* (tripe) and *spezzatino* (meat stew).

FURTHER AFIELD Bibè

V delle Bagnese 1r, Galluzzo, 50124 **Tel** *055 204 90 85*

This pleasant, farmhouse restaurant is just a short distance from Porta Romana. The menu features traditional local dishes with the odd refinement (the porcini mushroom and chickpea soup is delicious). Deep-fried chicken and rabbit is a speciality of the house, and bread is home-made at weekends. The puddings are a real treat.

FURTHER AFIELD Omero

Via Pian dei Giuliari 11r, 50125 **Tel** *055 22 00 53*

Situated in the hamlet of Pian dei Giuliari just behind Piazzale Michelangelo and enjoying a wonderful rural setting, Omero occupies a large, sunny room at the back of a grocer's shop. The food is standard Tuscan and unexceptional, but the lovely views make for a great lunch experience.

FURTHER AFIELD Targa

Lungarno C Colombo 7, 50136 **Tel** *055 67 73 77*

Background jazz and a warm wood-and-glass interior, softened by lots of greenery, make for a relaxed setting in this bistro, set 2 km (1 mile) from the city centre on the Arno. The food is understated and based on seasonal local traditions; crêpes with artichokes and *taleggio* (cheese), rack of lamb with asparagus and broad beans. Fantastic wine list.

FURTHER AFIELD Fuor d'Acqua

Via Pisana 37r, 50143 **Tel** *552 2222 99*

Many locals say that this is the best fish restaurant in Florence – and one of the most expensive. The fish is very fresh indeed, coming straight off the boats in Versilia and cooked with the minimum of fuss. Some crustaceans are served raw. Try the black *tagliolini* (pasta) with calamari and sage.

WESTERN TUSCANY

ARTIMINO da Delfina

Via della Chiesa 1, 59015 **Tel** *055 871 80 74*   **Road map** *C2*

Surrounded by vineyards and some interesting historic villas, this delightful restaurant is located in a walled medieval village just 22 km (14 miles) from Florence. Owner Carlo Cioni renews the culinary traditions of his mother, Delfina. The rabbit galantine and *maccheroni* (pasta) with duck sauce are simply exquisite.

CASCIANA TERME Il Merlo

Piazza Minati 5, 56034 **Tel** *0587 64 40 40*   **Road map** *C3*

Bean soup, mushrooms, chestnuts and wild boar are the main ingredients for winter dishes in this friendly little eatery. In the summer, fish comes to the fore: anchovies, seafood salad, linguine with squid ink and fish soup. There is a good selection of local cheeses, and a discerning wine list, with a few contributions from smaller producers.

CASTAGNETO CARDUCCI Nettare degli Dei

Salita San Lorenzo, 57022 **Tel** *0565 76 51 18*   **Road map** *C3*

This small eatery on two levels offers dishes based on fish from the morning's catch. A classic that usually features is *crudités di mare* (raw seafood dressed with lemon, excellent local oil, herbs and pepper). Try the gnocchetti with scorpionfish sauce. Interesting wine list and desserts.

LIVORNO Cantina Nardi

Via Leonardo Cambini 6/8, 57100 **Tel** *0586 80 80 06*   **Road map** *B3*

Friendly, family-run tavern open only for lunch. The day's menu, written on a blackboard, offers tasty local dishes such as fish soup, octopus and potatoes, spelt with vegetables, salt cod with mushrooms. The desserts include excellent fruit tarts. This is also a good place for a glass of wine and a snack.

LIVORNO La Barcarola

Viale Carducci 39, 57122 **Tel** *0586 40 23 67*   **Road map** *B3*

Though Livorno may not be Tuscany's prettiest city, it is not without gastronomic charm. Fish-based dishes abound, including the hearty *cacciucco* (fish stew), for which this friendly restaurant is renowned. Much of your future meal can be seen swimming in ample tanks. Pleasantly comprehensive wine list.

LIVORNO Da Galileo

Via della Campana, 57122 **Tel** *0586 88 90 09*   **Road map** *B3*

For two generations the Piagneri family has been delighting diners with authentic local cuisine in this reassuringly simple restaurant. Even after five decades, Da Galileo's passion for gastronomy has not waned. Fish prevails, including various soups, seafood fettuccine and salt cod cooked with onions, Livorno-style.

MONTOPOLI VAL D'ARNO Trattoria dell'Orcio Interrato

Piazza San Michele 2, 56020 **Tel** *0571 46 68 78*   **Road map** *C2*

Those with a taste for history will find a palatable welcome at this trattoria, in the converted wine cellars of what is now the Albergo Quattro Gigli. The restaurant specializes in medieval and Renaissance recipes, interpreted with inventive flair: cockerel cooked with pomegranate or tripe with egg and saffron.

PISA Vineria di Piazza

Piazza delle Vettovaglie 13, 56100   **Road map** *B2*

Located under the portico of this central square, a trattoria much frequented by university students and faculty members who are drawn by the good food and reasonable prices. Tasty soups, including *pappa al pomodoro*, and simple but substantial *secondi*, both meat and fish. Quaffing wine on tap.

PISA Osteria dei Cavalieri

Via San Frediano 16, 56126 **Tel** *050 58 08 58*   **Road map** *B2*

This friendly tavern occupies the ground floor of a medieval tower-house halfway between Pisa's two most prestigious centres of further education. It's common to find a scholarly-looking crowd enjoying the special all-in-one lunch dishes. The menu expands in the evening. Try the beef with beans and mushrooms.

PISA Al Ristoro dei Vecchi Macelli

Via Volturno 49, 56126 **Tel** *050 204 24*   **Road map** *B2*

Classic, yet stylish, this Tuscan restaurant serves specialities such as ravioli stuffed with sausage meat and cauliflower, or chicken oven roasted with tomato and fennel. Game dishes are also available, and there's usually fish on the menu too. Enticing wine list. Leave room for the home-made desserts.

SAN MINIATO Il Convio

Via San Maiano 2, 56028 **Tel** *0571 40 81 14*   **Road map** *C2*

Just outside town, a fine, old 19th-century farmhouse has been converted into a restaurant serving classic local cuisine. Many of the dishes are made with home-grown ingredients, including the olive oil. Since San Miniato is renowned for its truffles, in November this "food of the gods" also features prominently on the menu.

SAN MINIATO L'Antro di Bacco

Via IV Novembre 5, 56027 **Tel** *0571 433 19*   **Road map** *C2*

This friendly eatery focuses on locally raised meats, and of course the Tuber Magnatum Pico truffle during its glorious autumnal season. Try the roast lamb, the beef *tagliata alle erbe aromatiche* (meat strips with aromatic herbs), or the fillet of pork cooked in red wine. The house desserts include a creamy *tortino* (patty-cake) served warm.

SAN VINCENZO Gambero Rosso

Piazza della Vittoria 13, 57027 **Tel** *0565 70 10 21*   **Road map** *C4*

This Michelin-starred restaurant is a must for the true foodie. Chef Fulvio Pierangelini's style is highly individual, and always spot on. His silky chickpea soup with sweet shrimp tails is superb; so is the seafood lasagna. For those on a brief visit, try the five-course set menu to appreciate his culinary art to the full.

SANTA CROCE SULL'ARNO da Beppe

Via Livornese 35–37, località Staffoli, 56020 **Tel** *0571 370 02*   **Road map** *C2*

An inventive menu, largely based on fish in an elegantly modern setting, is a feast for both the eye and the palate. The fish antipasto is magnificent, and the clam risotto with scampi ice cream a surprising treat. When the season permits, truffles also feature to a delectable effect. A good wine list complements the food.

VOLTERRA Etruria

Piazza dei Priory 6–8, 56048 **Tel** *0588 860 64*   **Road map** *C3*

Situated on Volterra's main square, Etruria has an interior decorated in a 19th-century style. In summer there are plenty of tables ouside to dine alfresco and soak up the ambience of this ancient town. Try the Etrutia antipasti, truffles, or their speciality – sweet and sour wild boar.

VOLTERRA Trattoria del Sacco Fiorentino

Piazza XX Settembre 18, 56048 **Tel** *0588 885 37*   **Road map** *C3*

Located in a nicely restored 17th-century palazzo, this restaurant focuses on seasonal fare such as the delectable savoury flan with courgettes, lard and porcini mushrooms, or the fettuccine pasta with spelt, beans and pecorino. There's a good selection of cheeses as well as an enticing wine list.

VOLTERRA Del Duca

Via del Castello 2, 56048 **Tel** *0588 815 10*   **Road map** *C3*

A charming 16th-century palazzo houses this small restaurant with its ancient wine cellar and secret garden. Try the fried pumpkin flowers stuffed with ricotta and tomato. The pigeon breast cooked with locally grown saffron and olives is another speciality. There's a good cheese platter.

VOLTERRA Il Vecchio Mulino

Via del Molino, Località Saline, 56047 **Tel** *0588 440 60*   **Road map** *C3*

This old mill complex in the countryside, just outside Volterra, now also comprises a hotel. The well-run restaurant serves inventive Tuscan cuisine. Besides the classic porcini risotto, try the ricotta flan with truffles, or the duck breast in a creamy bellpepper sauce. There's live music on Saturdays from October to April.

Key to Price Guide *see p270* **Key to Symbols** *see back cover flap*

NORTHERN TUSCANY

CASTELNUOVO DI GARFAGNANA Vecchio Mulino   €
Via Vittorio Emanuele 12, 55032 **Tel** *0583 621 92*   **Road map** *B1*

This traditional wine bar has changed little in aspect since the early 1900s. Run by Andrea Bertucci and his family, it now offers a fine choice of wines, plus some of Italy's best (and rarest) salamis, cold cuts and cheeses. The home-made quiches and steaming pots of polenta are a further delight. Only one table outside.

LUCCA Da Giulio in Pelleria   €
Via delle Conce 47, 55100 **Tel** *0583 559 48*   **Road map** *C2*

You must book ahead and enter into the spirit of this bright, boisterous and extremely busy neighbourhood restaurant. This is the reign of hearty local dishes such as *zuppa di farro* (Tuscan white bean and spelt soup) and polenta, so expect no gastronomic surprises. The prices are remarkably reasonable.

LUCCA Locanda Buatino   €
Via Borgo Giannotti 508, 55100 **Tel** *0583 34 32 07*   **Road map** *C2*

The eatery attached to this traditional inn also caters to locals who appreciate good food at extremely reasonable prices. So don't be alarmed at the lack of a menu with prices. Choose from the great soups, various pasta dishes, and *secondi* such as salt cod, pig's liver, sausages and beans. Good house wine and home-made desserts.

LUCCA Vecchia Trattoria Buralli   €€
Piazza Sant'Agostino 10, 55100 **Tel** *0583 95 06 11*   **Road map** *C2*

Exceptionally vegetarian-friendly, this trattoria provides a complete vegetarian menu on Friday evenings. Try the vegetable-based *zuppa alla frantoiana*. For dessert, go for *buccellato di Lucca*, a warm pudding of fried bread, anise and raisins soaked in Vin Santo. The wine list features Luccan recipes and wines.

LUCCA Buca di Sant'Antonio   €€€
Via della Cervia 3, 55100 **Tel** *0583 558 81*   **Road map** *C2*

This duly restored 19th-century tavern, with an excellent location, serves classic local fare with the occasional innovative touch. The stuffed rabbit *en croute* with mushrooms is excellent. In winter, several dishes feature locally-grown chestnuts. Try *buccellato*, the tasty local pudding. Interesting wines.

LUCCA La Mora   €€€
Via Sesto di Moriano 1748, Località Ponte Moriano, 55029 **Tel** *0583 40 64 02*   **Road map** *C2*

Situated 9 km (5.5 km) from Lucca, this nicely appointed restaurant focuses on local cuisine, using prime produce, much of it home-grown. Start with the exquisite ravioli with a hint of marjoram, best followed by the pigeon casserole. The desserts usually comprise *cialda garfagnanina*, a sort of creamy pancake.

LUCCA Ristorante Puccini   €€€
Corte San Lorenzo 1–3, 55100 **Tel** *0583 31 61 16*   **Road map** *C2*

Tucked away in a quiet courtyard with a secluded terrace, this attractive restaurant gets its daily catch from the Viareggio market. Seafood risotto and baked turbot with tomatoes, capers and olives feature regularly on the menu. It's also an ideal venue for a snack of pecorino with a glass of wine.

LUCCA Vipore   €€€
Pieve Santo Stefano 44–69, 55100 **Tel** *0583 39 40 65*   **Road map** *C2*

Located 8 km (5 miles) from Lucca in the surrounding hills, this 18th-century farmstead offers amazing views and an excellent opportunity to explore the Tuscan landscape. Seasonal produce is used to create dishes such as *tagliata di manzo alla erbe aromatiche* (strips of beef with aromatic herbs). Wide range of Tuscan wines.

MONTECATINI TERME Le Prunecce   €€
Via Montaccolle 14, 51016 **Tel** *0572 673 01*   **Road map** *C2*

The Macchini family has run this trattoria since 1910, never wavering from authentic traditional fare in favour of culinary fashions. All the pasta is hand-made, and the sauces tend to be rich and meaty. Fried vegetables feature from spring to autumn, while game takes pride of place in winter.

MONTECATINI TERME Enoteca Giovanni   €€€€€
Via Garibaldi 27, 51016 **Tel** *0572 716 95*   **Road map** *C2*

Chef Giovanni Rotti's approach to local cuisine is both innovative and winningly in keeping with the fine collection of wines in his cellar. This memorable dining experience is further enhanced by superb service. Try his pigeon with grapes and pine nuts, and seek his assistance in choosing what to drink with it.

PESCIA Cecco   €€
Via Francesco Forti 96/98, 51017 **Tel** *0572 47 79 55*   **Road map** *C2*

This quiet, easy-going restaurant is the best place to sample Pescia's famous *asparagi* (asparagus). Other examples of traditional fare include *pollo al mattone* (chicken cooked under a brick) and *fagioli al fiasco* (beans cooked in a flask). On cold days, try the pudding – *cioncia* – a delicious house speciality.

PIETRASANTA La Giudea 🕴🍽🏬 €€

Via Barsanti 4, 55045 **Tel** *0584 715 14* **Road map** *B2*

Located on the corner of Piazza Duomo, this simple, family-run trattoria has a menu that reveals the influence of neighbouring Liguria. Specialities include *tortelli di magro* topped with pesto sauce; seafood linguine; *baccalà* (salt cod) al forno. Delicious home-made desserts. Local wines come from the hillsides of Lucca.

PISTOIA La Bottegaia 🕴🍽♿🏬 €€

Via del Lastrone 17, 51100 **Tel** *0573 36 56 02* **Road map** *C2*

Looking onto the old market square to one side and the cathedral to the other, this cheerful, unpretentious wine bar boasts 300 of Italy's best wines. The food menu features cheeses, cold cuts and other toothsome delicacies, such as fish carpaccio, to go with the wines. Superb desserts. Service is friendly.

PRATO La Fontana 🕴🏬 €€

Via di Canneto 1, Località Filettole, 59100 **Tel** *0574 272 82* **Road map** *D2*

Located 3 km (2 miles) out of town, this nice little restaurant specializes in simple, authentic Tuscan food. Whet the appetite with an antipasto of local hams and sausage, then try the fresh *maccheroni* with duck sauce followed by a platter of grilled meats. To conclude, there are usually fragrant home-baked desserts.

PRATO Osteria Cibbè 🕴🍽🏬 €€

Piazza Mercatale 49, 59100 **Tel** *0574 60 75 09* **Road map** *D2*

Housed in a medieval building in the city centre, this cosy little family-run eatery serves good local cold cuts and crostini for antipasto, followed by classic Tuscan fare such as pappardelle with game sauce. The desserts are home-made too: try the apple and spelt tart. Interesting wine list.

PRATO Enoteca Barni 🍽 €€€€€

Via Ferrucci 22, 59100 **Tel** *0574 60 78 45* **Road map** *D2*

This minimalist eatery, related to the family-run deli next door, offers quick, informal lunches at very reasonable prices. The dinner menu, much more elaborate, features a range of choices such as pheasant tortelli with pig's cheek, onions and rosemary; spelt timbale with kale and shellfish; lamb in almond crust with *foie gras* sauce.

PRATO Il Pirana 🕴🍽 €€€€€

Via G. Valentini 110, 59100 **Tel** *0574 257 46* **Road map** *D2*

Take the Prato Est exit coming from Florence, and you'll find this comfortable, elegant restaurant on a street corner of an otherwise nondescript area. There's a variety of appetizing fish dishes, including bass-stuffed ravioli in a creamy scampi and pine nut sauce. The lovely light puddings are irresistible.

VIAREGGIO La Darsena 🕴🍽♿🏬 €€€

Via Virgilio 150, 55049 **Tel** *0584 39 27 85* **Road map** *B2*

Located in the lively docks area, this friendly trattoria offers excellent fish dishes at reasonable prices. The antipasti comprise little samples of all sorts of things based on the morning's catch. For a dish of pasta, try the tagliolini with fresh anchovies. Good desserts and some fine Italian white wines.

VIAREGGIO Cabreo 🕴🍽♿ €€€

Via Firenze 14, 55049 **Tel** *0584 546 43* **Road map** *B2*

The main focus of this pleasant restaurant, located in a little side street, is seafood simply cooked and served in the way that best enhances its natural aromas. Specialities include spaghetti with clams, gnocchi with lobster sauce, and baked fish. It is advisable to leave enough room for the delicious home-made desserts.

VIAREGGIO Romano 🕴🍽♿ €€€€€

Via Mazzini 122, 55049 **Tel** *0584 313 82* **Road map** *B2*

Although Romano is expensive, few other places give such value for money. Wines are fairly priced and the fixed-price menu has ten full courses. The owner, Romano, at the front of house is unfailingly courteous, and his wife, Franca, prepares dishes that are simple, immaculately presented and often inventive.

EASTERN TUSCANY

ANGHIARI Da Alighiero 🕴🍽 €€€

Via Garibaldi 8, 52031 **Tel** *0575 78 80 40* **Road map** *E3*

Anghiari is a gastronomic crossroads between Tuscany and Umbria. Suitably surrounded by thick stone walls of a 15th-century origin, this restaurant pays homage to that mixed, historic tradition. Try fresh pasta with porcini mushrooms, followed by roast breast of duck, and enjoy the discerning wine list.

AREZZO Antica Osteria l'Agania 🕴🍽🎵 €€

Via Mazzini 10, 52100 **Tel** *0575 29 53 81* **Road map** *E3*

This typical family-run tavern serves local dishes among plenty of noisy chatter and laughter. Home-made pasta, *ribollita* soup, tripe, roast meats are on offer. No-frills service but good value for money. This is not the place for an intimate *diner à deux*, but ideal for a quick, lively lunch with friends.

Key to Price Guide *see p270* **Key to Symbols** *see back cover flap*

AREZZO La Torre di Gnicche

Piaggia S. Martino 8, 52100 **Tel** *0575 35 20 35* **Road map** *E3*

Looking out over the beautiful Piazza Vasari, this is first and foremost a place for wine-lovers, with its great list of Tuscan wines, and some from other regions. The freshly-cooked food is as good, and uses ingredients depending on the season. There's no menu, so just be adventurous and try anything.

AREZZO Buca di San Francesco

Via San Francesco 1, 52100 **Tel** *0575 232 71* **Road map** *E3*

Set alongside the church of San Francesco in the historic centre, the Buca is ideal for those who have been sight-seeing in the frescoed church. The restaurant is found in the basement of a 14th-century building. Here, you can sample the famous Tuscan *ribollita* (cabbage and bread soup), or try the Chianti beef stew.

AREZZO Logge Vasari

Via Vasari 19, 52100 **Tel** *0575 29 58 94* **Road map** *E3*

In the frescoed rooms of a 16th-century building, Logge Vasari serves dishes based on local recipes revisited with creative flair. Try *tortelli del casentino* with partridge sauce, or fillet of Chianina beef cooked in Brunello. All the bread is home-made. There's an enticing choice of desserts and a good selection of wines.

AREZZO Ristorante I Tre Bicchieri

Piazzetta Sopra i Ponti 3, 52100 **Tel** *0575 265 57* **Road map** *E3*

Brothers Sefano and Lionello put great care and inventive spirit into this refined but unpretentious restaurant. Superb ingredients are handled with flair. Try the ravioli – two black and two white – stuffed with lobster and served in an exquisite flame-coloured tomato reduction. There's a fantastic wine list.

BORGO SAN LORENZO Ristorante degli Artisti

Piazza A. Romagnoli 1, 50032 **Tel** *055 845 77 07* **Road map** *D2*

Opened in 1997, this pleasant restaurant is located in a charming, old building in the historic centre. The menu boasts Tuscan cuisine interpreted with flair. Try the pheasant terrine with black truffles and larded croutons, or *strappati* pasta with duck sauce. Good cheeses too. The wine list offers plenty of choice.

CAMALDOLI Il Cedro

Via di Camaldoli 20, Località Moggiona, 52010 **Tel** *0575 55 60 80* **Road map** *E2*

One of the most popular restaurants in the region, Camadoli is known for its finely-cooked specialities such as venison and boar, no doubt hunted in the thickly forested Casentino Mountains that provide breathtaking views. In spring and summer, delicate fried vegetables are also a treat. Booking advised.

CASTELNUOVO BERARDENGA Del Pellegrino

Via del Paradiso 1, 53019 **Tel** *0577 35 52 82* **Road map** *D3*

Located in what was once a barn, this elegantly rustic eatery serves both meat and fish in a selection of well-presented dishes: John Dory mousse with scampi and tomato sauce; or green and white pasta dressed with lobster, squid and broad beans. There's an excellent wine list to match the inventive fare.

CASTELNUOVO BERARDENGA La Bottega del 30

Via Santa Caterina 2, Località Villa a Sesta, 53019 **Tel** *0577 35 92 26* **Road map** *D3*

This is a serious, award-winning restaurant run by Franco Camelia and his French wife Hélène. The menu inlcudes a renowned *petto di anatra con il finocchio selvatico* (breast of dusk with wild fennel). Pasta dishes are cooked with a difference. There's also superb home-made spaghetti with nettle, wild mint and porcini. Fine wine list.

CORTONA Osteria del Teatro

Via Maffei 2, 52044 **Tel** *0575 63 05 56* **Road map** *E3*

This classic trattoria serves well prepared traditional dishes. Apart from the excellent soups, try the risotto with porcini and saffron, or *caramelle al radicchio rosso* (pasta stuffed with red chicory and ricotta). The guinea fowl with mushrooms is also good. There are some nice wines to wash it all down.

CORTONA Preludio

Via Guelfa 11, 52044 **Tel** *0575 63 01 04* **Road map** *E3*

Cheese soufflé with pears and truffles: this creative combination of flavours is typical of a restaurant that uses unusual combinations of local ingredients to gratify the taste buds. Succulent meat dishes are based on Chianina beef, the renowned local breed. The menu also offers children-friendly dishes.

LUCIGNANO La Rocca

Via Matteotti 15–17, 52046 **Tel** *0575 83 67 75* **Road map** *E3*

While this easy-going restaurant serves all the classics of local cuisine, it also boasts something a bit different to the usual fare. One of the specialities is the delicious *zuppa dei tarlati* (chicken soup made with wild fennel and served with croutons). For a taste of the sublime, try the fried eggs topped with truffle shavings.

LUCIGNANO Il Goccino

Via Matteotti 88/90, 52046 **Tel** *0575 83 67 07* **Road map** *E3*

The tasting menu greets you with a sparkling *aperitivo* and then leads you through four excellent courses. There's also an option to choose from an inventive menu: in spring, there may be maltagliati pasta with asparagus, pears and pecorino. Good wine list, with many bottles that can be tasted by the glass.

POPPI Antica Cantina   €€

Via Lapucci 2, 52014 **Tel** *0575 52 98 44*   **Road map** *E2*

A stone's throw from the imposing Castello dei Conti Guidi, this restaurant is located in the cellar dating back to the 12th century. Chestnut ravioli, *tagliata di manzo con porcini* (beef strips with porcini mushrooms) and delectable desserts are among the temptations on the menu. A good wine list with bottles from various Italian regions.

SANSEPOLCRO Enoteca Guidi   €€

Via Luca Pacioli 44, 52037 **Tel** *0575 73 65 87*   **Road map** *E3*

Enoteca Guidi is a small eatery with a big wine list. You can enjoy your chosen bottle matched with an interesting cheese tasting. Alternatively, select from primi such as potato ravioli with cured lard, rosemary and cherry tomatoes. The carpaccio of wild Alaskan salmon with fennel slices is also delicious.

SANSEPOLCRO Il Convivio   €€

Via Traversari 1, 52037 **Tel** *0575 73 65 43*   **Road map** *E3*

Located in the historic Palazzo Bourbon del Monte, this restaurant provides a pleasant showcase for the local culinary tradition. Mushrooms and truffles prevail, and meats range from succulent steaks to game. The antipasti include a tasty game terrine. Good soups as well as pasta dishes can also be found on the menu.

SANSEPOLCRO Osteria in Aboca   €€€

Frazione Aboca 11, 52037 **Tel** *0575 74 91 25*   **Road map** *E3*

With a rustic-chic decor, this restaurant specializes in local cuisine interpreted and revisited. The outcome is lighter than the usual fare. Try the ravioli stuffed with potato and Crescenza cheese, served with a buttery spinach sauce. There are home-made cold cuts, an impressive cheese board and an excellent wine list.

SANSEPOLCRO Ristorante da Ventura   €€€

Via Aggiunti 30, 52037 **Tel** *0575 74 25 60*   **Road map** *E3*

Run by the same family for over 50 years, this charming restaurant serves delectable *agnolotti al tartufo* (stuffed pasta with truffles). Another of their classic dishes is the veal cooked slowly in Chianti. Mushrooms often feature too. Even the cantucci biscuits for dipping in Vin Santo are home-made.

TERRANUOVA BRACCIOLINI Il Canto del Maggio   €€

Località Penna 30/D, 52028 **Tel** *055 970 51 47*   **Road map** *D3*

In a tiny hamlet between Terranuova and Loro Ciuffenna you'll find this gem of a restaurant restored and run by Mauro Quirini and his family. Surrounded by blossoms and aromatic herbs, enjoy the rare, peppery beef dish known as *peposo alla fornacina*, along with a wine from the excellent cellar.

CENTRAL TUSCANY

BAGNO VIGNONI Hotel Terme   €€€

Piazza delle Sorgenti 13, 53027 **Tel** *0577 88 71 57*   **Road map** *D4*

A fantastic location and an injection of youthful energy have turned an average hotel restaurant into a cool eatery offering good food well matched with fine wines. You don't have to eat the whole three-course lunch, and the opening times are less rigid than most restaurants. A must-try is the delicious *carabaccia* (sweet onion soup).

BUONCONVENTO I Poggioli   €€€

Via Tassi 6, 53022 **Tel** *0577 80 65 46*   **Road map** *D4*

Even if the building is a bit uninspiring, the food is good here and the people delightful. Written up on a board, the menu changes regularly, offering both fish and meat dishes prepared with prime ingredients. The trio running it have far-flung restaurant experience, so they bring a fresh touch to Tuscan cuisine.

CHIANCIANO Patry   €€€

Viale G. di Vittorio 80, 53042 **Tel** *0578 630 14*   **Road map** *E4*

Unprepossessing though Chianciano may be, it is worth a visit for its Archeological Museum and for Patry, an impressive fish restaurant. The menu depends on the day's catch, so let yourself be guided by Danilo, the affable restaurateur. The cooking style is simple, and the flavours speak for themselves.

COLLE VAL D'ELSA Arnolfo   €€€€€

Via XX Settembre 50/52A, 53034 **Tel** *0577 92 05 49*   **Road map** *D3*

French-trained chefs have earned this intimate three-roomed restaurant one of Tuscany's few Michelin stars. The wines, food and service are all impeccable, though the reverential hush feels a bit odd for Italy. Typical dishes include a sublime *ribollita* (Tuscan bread soup), and pigeon cooked with wine, prunes and pine nuts.

COLLE VAL D'ELSA L'Antica Trattoria   €€€€€

Piazza Arnolfo 23, 53034 **Tel** *0577 92 37 47*   **Road map** *D3*

This well-run family restaurant features classic Tuscan fish and meat dishes as well as some more inventive fare. For instance, the saddle of venison is cooked in grape must and juniper. There are also some inviting desserts such as orange *semifreddo*. The cheese board is extensive and the wine list decent.

Key to Price Guide *see p270* **Key to Symbols** *see back cover flap*

GAIOLE IN CHIANTI Il Carlino D'Oro

Via Brolio, località San Regolo, 53013 **Tel** *0577 74 71 36*   **Road map** *D3*

Eating here is a bit like being invited to Sunday lunch at the home of your Tuscan neighbours. *Crostini neri* (toast with black olive paste) will be followed by panzanella bread salad in summer, or a bean soup in winter. The *pappardelle* with hare sauce is also delicious. Leave room for fried chicken and rabbit, or calves' liver with sage.

GAIOLE IN CHIANTI Castello di Spaltenna

Località Pieve di Spaltenna, 53013 **Tel** *0577 74 94 83*   **Road map** *D3*

This lovely stone-walled, flower-filled restaurant forms part of a peaceful hotel in a castle just outside Gaiole in Chianti. Popular with expatriates, it offers refined versions of Tuscan classics such as pigeon cooked in Chianti, fresh porcini mushrooms, chickpea soup and, occasionally, more offbeat innovations.

MONTALCINO Il Grappolo Blu

Scale di Via Moglio 1, 53024 **Tel** *0577 84 71 50*   **Road map** *D4*

A few steps down a steep alley off the main drag, this restaurant can be relied on for a perfectly decent meal: neither heavily traditional nor pretentious revisitations. Fresh pasta, some enjoyable *secondi* such as shin of beef in balsamic vinegar, home-made desserts and, of course, a good wine list.

MONTALCINO Il Boccon Divino

Località Colombaio, 53024 **Tel** *0577 84 82 33*   **Road map** *D4*

Perfect for summer dining alfresco, this restaurant offers some interesting dishes and a magnificent view. The *carabaccia* (onion soup) is a must, and the *scottiglia di cinghiale* (wild boar stew) is excellent. Not exclusively local, the cheese board is also interesting. Excellent wine list, as befits the town.

MONTEPULCIANO La Grotta

Località San Biagio, 53045 **Tel** *0578 75 76 07*   **Road map** *E4*

A restaurant for discerning diners, La Grotta is located right opposite one of the foremost expressions of Renaissance architecture in Tuscany: Sangallo the Elder's Church of San Biagio. Specialities include the excellent *pici* (local pasta strips) with duck and saffron sauce. Also good is the fillet of Chianina beef with asparagus and truffles.

MONTEPULCIANO Le Loggie del Vignola

Via delle Erbe 6, 53045 **Tel** *0578 71 72 90*   **Road map** *E4*

An *aperitivo* greets diners at this attractive, small restaurant, where cover and service charges have been abolished. Some traditional items on the menu are pecorino and vegetable tartlet with a cheese sauce; pigeon with red onions stewed in Vino Nobile. There are also tempting desserts and cheeses.

MONTERIGGIONI Il Pozzo

Piazza Roma 20, 53035 **Tel** *0577 30 41 27*   **Road map** *D3*

Occupying 13th-century stables, Il Pozzo is an ideal place for lunch. The food is rigorously Tuscan, essentially simple, but never banal. Try the truffle-fragrant *tortelli al cartoccio* (tortelli cooked in tinfoil), which comes wrapped up like a packet to conserve the aromas. Equally delicious is the stuffed pigeon.

PIENZA La Pergola

Via dell'Acero 2, 53026 **Tel** *0578 74 80 51*   **Road map** *E4*

Unpretentious but inventive, La Pergola is the best restaurant in the area. Chef Emanuele injects a little of his Abruzzo origins into Tuscan fare, conjuring up dishes that have real flair. Try the *sformato di verdura con crema di porri e patata*, a vegetable flan with a leek and potato sauce. Excellent wine list.

SAN GIMIGNANO Osteria delle Catene

Via Mainardi 18, 53037 **Tel** *0577 94 19 66*   **Road map** *C3*

This small restaurant specializes in regional cooking enhanced with its own special touch. You could start off with cold cuts made from wild boar, then continue with a saffron soup made according to a medieval recipe. The hare cooked in local wine is also good, and the home-made desserts are worth leaving room for.

SAN GIMIGNANO Dorandò

Vicolo dell'Oro 2, 53037 **Tel** *0577 94 18 62*   **Road map** *C3*

This restaurant is small and very select, so booking is advised. Impressive wine list, and dishes to go with it. The pasta with pigeon sauce on a bed of creamed mushrooms is delicious. There are various fish specialities, including angler fish in a nutty crust served with leeks. Take your time to enjoy it all.

SANT'ANGELO IN COLLE SCALO Il Marrucheto

Località Sant'Angelo in Colle Scalo, 53020 **Tel** *0577 80 80 00*   **Road map** *D4*

Il Marrucheto is known for its simplicity, warmth and good value: a combination that's becoming increasingly rare in Tuscany. The focus is fish, or pizza, though there are meat dishes too. Try the seafood spaghetti, which is very filling. The *zuppa di cozze*, or clam soup, is also good. Finish up with a simple salad.

SARTEANO Da Gagliano

Via Roma 5, 53047 **Tel** *0578 26 80 22*   **Road map** *E4*

Da Gagliano is a tiny eatery, almost opposite Sarteano's gem of an Archeological Museum. You sit at wooden tables with paper place mats, and Giuliano plies you with anchovies in pesto, excellent gnocchi, a steaming plate of tripe, or rabbit cooked with herbs. The menu is written on a blackboard.

SARTEANO Santa Chiara
Via Costa S. Chiara 30, 53047 **Tel** *0578 26 54 12*   **Road map** *E4*

A small hotel with a good restaurant, Santa Chiara is located in an old convent with lovely views across the valley. Home-made pasta, including exquisite ravioli stuffed with dandelion and borage leaves, is a speciality. Mushrooms also feature on the menu when they're in season. The rabbit with wild fennel makes a perfect *secondo*.

SEGGIANO Silene
Località Pescina, 58038 **Tel** *0564 95 08 05*   **Road map** *D4*

A little distance up the road from Seggiano, just past Daniel Spoerri's sculpture garden, you will come to this mountain hamlet with an inn serving excellent food, prepared and presented to perfection. The pigeon ravioli and small gnocchi with truffles are exquisite. Great wines and memorable desserts.

SIENA Enoteca I Terzi
Via dei Termini 7, 53100 **Tel** *0577 443 29*   **Road map** *D3*

This restaurant has a nice vaulted space and a friendly atmosphere in which to enjoy a good bottle of wine accompanied by a wide range of premium cold cuts, *carpaccio*, smoked meats, steak tartare, and cheeses from all over Italy. In addition, each day there are three cooked dishes which change with the seasons.

SIENA La Taverna del Capitano
Via del Capitano 6/8, 53100 **Tel** *0577 28 80 94*   **Road map** *D3*

Located up near the Duomo, this restaurant with vaulted ceilings and dark wood furnishings is quintessentially Sienese. The *ribollita* soup; *pici* with pecorino and pepper, stewed rabbit and tasty beef tagliata, all speak for unbroken tradition. What's more, the house wine is good too.

SIENA L'Osteria
Via d' Rossi 79–81, 53100 **Tel** *0577 28 75 92*   **Road map** *D3*

This informal haunt is a favourite among faculty members from the neighbouring university. It serves simple, well-cooked Tuscan food at wooden tables. The pasta with truffles is consistently exquisite, and the beef tagliata always succulent. You can choose a bottle or go for a carafe of quaffing wine.

SIENA La Compagnia dei Vinattieri
Via delle Terme 79, 53100 **Tel** *0577 23 65 68*   **Road map** *D3*

An impressive underground, vaulted space with a magnificent wine cellar and some interesting food to go with it. You can sip by the glass, with a platter of cheese and salami, or enjoy a bottle with a hot meal such as salt cod soup. of Good desserts and unusual sweet wines. Only one table outside.

SIENA La Sosta di Violante
Via di Pantaneto 115, 53100 **Tel** *0577 437 74*   **Road map** *D3*

Close to Piazza del Campo, La Sosta di Violante provides two small rooms in which you can relish local seasonal ingredients cooked with imagination: aubergine rolls containing Scamorza cheese and pine nuts, for instance, or *pici* (pasta) with duck sauce. Great care is taken in matching the meat dishes with suitable wines.

SIENA Osteria Le Logge
Via del Porrione 33, 53100 **Tel** *0577 480 13*   **Road map** *D3*

Siena's prettiest, and often full, restaurant has a dark wood and marble interior. The tables are laid with crisp linen cloths and decorated with plants. Home-produced oils and Montalcino wines accompany dishes that wander slightly from mainstream Tuscan cooking. The stuffed guinea fowl is delicious.

SOUTHERN TUSCANY

CAPALBIO Da Maria
Piazza Carlo Giordano 3, 58011 **Tel** *0564 89 60 14*   **Road map** *D5*

Capalbio's holiday population of Roman politicians and media types sit down with locals in this pleasant eatery to enjoy genuine Maremma cuisine. Dishes include stuffed pasta with truffles, spelt soup, *cinghiale alla cacciatora* (rich, spicy wild boar) and an enticing warm apple and pear tart.

CASTIGLIONE DELLA PESCAIA Pierbacco
Piazza Repubblica 24, 58043 **Tel** *0564 93 35 22*   **Road map** *C4*

Located in a building dating back to the 1500s, this restaurant largely serves seafood: the little potato gnocchi with lobster sauce is just one example. The mixed seafood platter varies in content daily but is alway excellent. To further enhance your enjoyment, there is an impressive wine list.

ELBA Rendez-Vous da Marcello
Piazza della Vittoria 1, Marciana Marina, 57033 **Tel** *0565 992 51*   **Road map** *B4*

Outdoor tables on the harbour front at this noted fish restaurant make a pleasant retreat from the summer crowds of Marciana Marina. Clearly, the dishes reflect the morning's catch. Most dishes are pleasantly simple, but on occasions the menu also embraces the fashionable culinary fads of the moment.

Key to Price Guide *see p270* **Key to Symbols** *see back cover flap*

ELBA Publius
🚶 ♿ 🍴 €€€

Piazza del Castagneto, Località Poggio Marciana, 57030 **Tel** *0565 992 08* **Road map** *B4*

Food with a view. Not only does this historic trattoria have perhaps the best cellar on the island, but it also provides an alternative to the seafood that prevails elsewhere. In addition to fish, you can eat poultry, game, lamb roasted in herbs and a choice of pecorino and other cheeses.

GROSSETO Il Pescatore
🚶 ☰ ♿ 🍴 €€€

Via Orcagna 62, 58100 **Tel** *0564 49 10 35* **Road map** *D4*

In the unprepossessing southern suburbs of Grosseto, follow signs towards the airport. You'll be rewarded by the discovery of a well-appointed restaurant offering beautifully prepared fish dishes at reasonable prices. The menu depends on the morning's catch. Decent wine list.

MAGLIANO IN TOSCANA Da Sandra
🚶 ☰ 🍴 €€€

Via Garibaldi 20, 58051 **Tel** *0564 59 21 96* **Road map** *D5*

This quietly classy establishment showcases some of the best wines, now made in this promising area. The menu reflects the changing seasons. Pasta with truffles or mushrooms, wild asparagus (growing abundantly in the spring sun), game, including beautifully cooked wild boar. Good desserts.

MAGLIANO IN TOSCANA Antica Trattoria Aurora
🚶 ♿ 🍴 €€€€

Chiasso Lavagnini 12/14, 58051 **Tel** *0564 59 27 74* **Road map** *D5*

With its lovely hanging gardens for summer eating, this attractive restaurant serves dishes that add flair to local traditions. The tortelli with duck cooked in Morellino wine is excellent. Likewise, the delectable breast of goose is perfectly offset by a slightly tart bilberry sauce. Wine is also served by the glass.

MASSA MARITTIMA Da Tronca
🚶 ☰ €€

Vicolo Porte 5, 58024 **Tel** *0566 90 19 91* **Road map** *C4*

Da Tronca has a rustic ambience befitting the well-cooked, simple fare. The *zuppa dell'osteria* (kale and cannellini beans on garlic-rubbed bread drizzled with oil) is delicious. There's also a good chickpea soup, served hot. Otherwise try the tripe, or the rabbit baked with potatoes. Good local wine list.

MASSA MARITTIMA Taverna Vecchio Borgo
🚶 €€

Via Norma Parenti 12, 58024 **Tel** *0566 90 39 50* **Road map** *C4*

Ancient barrel-vaulted rooms with an enticingly well-stocked wine cellar. The menu usually features pasta stuffed with ricotta and dressed with a sauce of nuts and herbs as well as *acquacotta* bread soup. The wild boar cooked with olives and the pheasant breast done in Vin Santo are also recommended.

MASSA MARITTIMA Bracali
☰ ♿ €€€€€

Via di Perolla 2, Località Ghirlanda, 58020 **Tel** *0566 90 23 18* **Road map** *C4*

If you drive a small distance north out of Massa Marittima, you will come across this attractive family-run restaurant, where local culinary traditions are revisited with flair. The aubergine flan, served with a potato and anchovy sauce, is a case in point; likewise the hare cooked with fennel and juniper.

ORBETELLO Osteria del Lupacante
🚶 ☰ 🍴 €€€

Corso Italia 103, 58015 **Tel** *0564 86 76 18* **Road map** *D5*

This pleasant osteria sticks to old ways in a place increasingly overrun by affluent out-of-towners. Based on seafood, the cooking is light in touch and quite adventurous. The *zuppa di pesce* (fish soup) is excellent. The risotto with prawns and pine nuts and the sole with almonds and onions are also good.

PITIGLIANO Il Tufo Allegro
🚶 ☰ €€€

Vicolo della Costituzione 5, 58017 **Tel** *0564 61 61 92* **Road map** *E5*

This little restaurant features local Maremma cuisine with a subtle difference. There are *pappardelle* with a lamb ragout, and lasagne with artichokes, mature cheese and rabbit ragout. The saddle of rabbit with wild fennel is excellent, as is the courgette and goat's cheese flan.

PORTO ERCOLE Osteria dei Nobili Santi
🚶 ☰ ♿ €€€€

Via dell'Ospizio 8, 58018 **Tel** *0564 83 30 15* **Road map** *D5*

There aren't many bargains to be had in Porto Ercole. Nonetheless, this little fish restaurant offers value for money and the food is delicious. The amazing *antipasti della casa* (the house antipasti) will leave you almost satiated. It's worth making an effort to leave some room to try the main courses.

SATURNIA Bacco e Cerere
🚶 ☰ 🎵 🍴 €€€

Via Mazzini 4, 58050 **Tel** *0564 60 12 35* **Road map** *D5*

The wide range of antipasti at this small, friendly place is a great introduction to the traditional Maremma cuisine. The *zuppa di ricotta* makes a delectable change from the traditional *acquacotta* (vegetable soup served over toast). The enoteca of the same name offers an interesting range of wines. Occasional live music in summer. Closed on Wed.

SCANSANO Osteria Il Rifrullo
🚶 🎵 🍴 €€

Via Marconi 3, 58054 **Tel** *0564 50 71 83* **Road map** *D5*

Be warned – the portions are so generous in this informal eatery that you may not manage the full three courses. There are excellent giant tortelli filled with ricotta; and the gnocchi are good too. Wild boar usually features among the *secondi*, cooked slowly with plenty of herbs. Good wine list with many local labels.

Light Meals and Snacks in Florence

The traditional pavement café is not as much a part of local life in Florence as in other Italian cities. However, small, hole-in-the-wall bars can be found on most of the city's streets. Here, you can have alcoholic and soft drinks, as well as a range of tempting breakfast and lunch-time snacks. Old-fashioned wine bars provide alternative eating and drinking venues, and the city has plenty of take-away establishments, especially near Santa Maria Novella station, if you want to eat on the move.

Sitting down at a bar or café can be expensive, as there is a charge for taking a table. If you only want a quick snack, it may be cheaper to eat at the stand-up counter. It is also worth noting that some cafés and bars may close during August.

BARS

Locals generally use bars as stop-offs for a coffee, quick snack, an early morning apéritif, to make a phone call or to use the toilet (il bagno). Some bars may stay open late, particularly during the summer, but most are busiest during the day. Most of them have a stand-up counter rather than tables.

Some bars also double as a pastry shop (pasticceria) and virtually all serve filled rolls (panini) or sandwiches (tramezzini) for lunch.

Breakfast is usually un caffè (a short espresso) or un cappuccino (milky coffee) with a plain jam or custard-filled croissant (una brioche or un cornetto).

The cheapest way to buy beer at a bar is from the keg (una birra alla spina) either as a piccola, media or grande measure. Italian bottled beers such as Peroni are also reasonably priced but foreign beers are expensive. Other drinks available are freshly squeezed fruit juice (una spremuta), grappa and wine by the glass (un bicchiere di vino).

Once you have chosen what to eat or drink, you must first pay at the cash desk (la cassa), and then take your receipt (lo scontrino) to the bar, where you will be served. A small tip on the counter will usually ensure quicker service.

There are numerous bars dotted around Florence, and many are convenient for the sights. For example, **Il Caffè** is opposite the Palazzo Pitti.

WINE CELLARS

Though wine cellars of the rustic style (vinaii or fiaschetterie) are a dying breed, they are quickly being replaced by modern, upscale versions, where you can sample from a wide range of Tuscan and Italian wines, accompanied by antipasti, often featuring local salamis, cheeses, and a variety of crostini and other light snacks.

CAFES

Four of Florence's handful of old-world cafés stand around the dour perimeter of Piazza della Repubblica. **Gilli**, renowned for its cocktails, dates back to 1733. It has two rear panelled rooms still redolent of an earlier age. **Giubbe Rosse**, once the haunt of the city's turn-of-the-century literati, also evokes its former glory with dazzling chandeliers. However, like the neighbouring cafés, it is over-priced and likely to be filled with wealthy foreigners rather than elegant Florentines. Instead, locals head for the **Rivoire**, also expensive, but with more genuine class and a beautiful marble interior. Bars which offer Manaresi, a locally roasted coffee, are usually worth a stop. This coffee is considered by many to be the best in Italy.

The young and fashionable hang out at **Capocaccia**, an elegant bar/bistrot along the river, or at **Procacci**, renowned for its delicious truffle rolls (tartufati).

TAKE-AWAY FOOD

Traditional street food includes tripe and lampre-dotto (pig's intestines) sandwiches, sold from the stalls at the Mercato Centrale (see p88), around the Mercato Nuovo (see p112), as well as in the Piazza dei Cimatori. The Mercato Centrale is a great place to buy picnic provisions if you are planning a day's excursion out of the city.

In the same areas there are often vans selling porchetta, crispy slices of suckling pig in bread rolls. Small shops selling pizza by weight or slice (al taglio) are found all over the city, especially around Santa Maria Novella station.

As well as bread, bakeries sell schiacciata, a focaccia sold plain, with oil and salt, or with herbs and spices. Bars offer other take-away options including panini, tramezzini and ice cream. Some vinaii, notably in Via dei Cimatori and Piazza dell'Olio, serve crostini and sandwiches to eat out on the pavement.

Snack bars, such as **Gastronomia Vera**, selling burgers, chips and flavoured milk shakes, are becoming increasingly popular.

ICE-CREAM PARLOURS

Florentines often round off a meal or the evening passeggiata (walk) with an ice cream (gelato). No day in the city is complete without one visit to an ice-cream parlour (gelateria). You can choose between a cone (un cono) and a cup (una coppa) and pay by size, usually starting at €1 and working up in 50-cent stages to enormous multi-scoop offerings at €5.

It's best to avoid bars where the selection is limited and the ice cream is made off the premises. Make instead for **Bar Vivoli Gelateria** (see p71), thought by many to make the best ice cream in Italy, or to **Badiani**, famed for its egg-rich Buontalenti. **Carabè** is well known for its Sicilian ice granitas, made with coffee or fruit.

DIRECTORY

CITY CENTRE EAST

Bars and Cafés
Caffè Caruso
Via Lambertesca 14 –16r.
Map 6 D4.

Chiaroscuro
Via del Corso, 36r.
Map 4 E1.

Dolci Dolcezze
Piazza Cesare Beccaria 8r.
Map 4 F1.

Galleria degli Uffizi
Piazzale degli Uffizi 6.
Map 6 D4.

Red Garter
Via de' Benci 33.
Map 4 D2 (6 E4).

Rivoire
Piazza della Signoria 5.
Map 4 D1 (6 D3).

Robiglio
Via de' Tosinghi 11.
Map 6 D2.

Scudieri
Piazza di San Giovanni 19.
Map 1 C5 (6 D2).

Trattoria Santa Croce
Borgo Santa Croce 31r.
Map 4 D1 (6 F4).

Wine Cellars
Boccadama
Piazza Santa Croce 25–26r.
Map 4 E1 (6 F4).

Bottiglieria Torrini
Piazza dell'Olio, 15r.
Map 6 D2

Cantinetta del Verrazzano
Via dei Tavolini 18–20r.
Map 4 D1 (6 D3).

Enoteca Baldovino
Via San Giuseppe, 18r.
Map 4 E1.

Enoteca De' Giraldi
Via De' Giraldi 4r.
Map 4 D1 (6 E3).

Fiaschetteria Balducci
Via de' Neri 2r.
Map 4 D1 (6 E4).

Giovacchino
Via de' Tosinghi 34r.
Map 6 D2.

Vini del Chianti
Via dei Cimatori.
Map 4 D1 (6 D3).

Vini e Panini
Via dei Cimatori 38r.
Map 4 D1 (6 D3).

Take-Away Food
La Ghiotta
Via Pietrapiana 7r.
Map 4 E1.

Ice-Cream Parlours
Bar Vivoli Gelateria
Via Isola delle Stinche 7r.
Map 6 F3.

Gelateria de' Ciompi
Via dell'Agnolo 121r.
Map 4 E1.

Gelateria Veneta
Piazza Cesare Beccaria.
Map 4 F1.

Perchè No!
Via dei Tavolini 19r.
Map 4 D1 (6 D3).

CITY CENTRE NORTH

Bars and Cafés
Da Nerbone
Mercato Centrale.
Map 1 C4 (5C1).

Rex Café
Via Fiesolana 23–25r.
Map 2 E5.

Wine Cellars
Casa del Vino
Via del Ariento.
Map 1 C4.

Take-Away Food
Forno Pugi
Piazza San Marco 10.
Map 2 D4.

Lì Per Lì
Via XXVII Aprile 42r.
Map 1 C4.

Ice-Cream Parlours
Badiani
Via dei Mille 20.
Map 2 F2.

Carabè
Via Ricasoli 60r.
Map 2 D5.

Vestri
Borgo Albizi 11r.
Map 2 D5.

CITY CENTRE WEST

Bars and Cafés
Alimentari
Via Parione 12r.
Map 3 B1 (5 B3).

Caffè Amerini
Via della Vigna Nuova 61– 63.
Map 3 B1 (5 B3).

Caffè Strozzi
Piazza degli Strozzi 16r.
Map 3 C1 (5 C3).

Caffè Voltaire
Via della Scala 9r.
Map 1 A4 (5 A1).

Capocaccia
Lungarno Corsini 12r.
Map 3 B1 (5 B3).

Donnini
Piazza della Repubblica 15r.
Map 1 C5 (6 D3).

Gilli
Piazza della Repubblica 39r.
Map 1 C5 (6 D3).

Giubbe Rosse
Piazza della Repubblica 13–14r.
Map 1 C5 (6 D3).

Il Barretto Piano Bar
Via Parione 50r.
Map 3 B1 (5 B3).

La V igna
Via della Vigna Nuova 88.
Map 3 B1 (5 B3).

Paszkowski
Piazza della Repubblica 6r.
Map 1 C5 (6 D3).

Procacci
Via de' Tornabuoni 64r.
Map 1 C5 (5 C2).

Rose's Bar
Via Parione 3.
Map 3 B1 (5 B3).

Ice-Cream Parlours
Banchi
Via dei Banchi 14r.
Map 1 C5 (5 C2).

OLTRARNO

Bars and Cafés
Café Ricchi
Piazza di Santo Spirito 9r.
Map 3 B2 (5 A5).

Caffè La Torre
Lungarno Cellini 65r.
Map 4 F2.

Caffè Santa Trinita
Via Maggio 2r.
Map 3 B2 (5 B5).

Caffeteria Henry
Via dei Renai 27a.
Map 4 D2 (6 E5).

Cennini
Borgo San Jacopo 51r.
Map 3 C1 (5 C4).

Dolce Vita
Piazza del Carmine.
Map 3 A1 (5 A4).

Gastronomia Vera
Piazza de' Frescobaldi 3r.
Map 3 B1 (5 B4).

Il Caffè
Piazza de' Pitti 11–12r.
Map 3 B2 (5 B5).

Il Rifrullo
Via di San Niccolò 55r.
Map 4 D2.

La Loggia
Piazzale Michelangelo 1.
Map 4 E3.

Marino
Piazza Nazario Sauro 19r.
Map 3 B1 (5 A3).

Pasticceria Maioli
Via de' Guicciardini 43r.
Map 3 C2 (5 C5).

Tiratoio
Piazza de' Nerli.
Map 3 A1.

Wine Cellars
Enoteca Fuoriporta
Via Monte alle Croci 10r.
Map 4 E3.

Le Volpi e l'Uva
Piazza de' Rossi 1r.
Map 5 C5.

Take-Away Food
Gastronomia Vera
Piazza de' Frescobaldi 3r.
Map 3 B1 (5 B4).

Ice-Cream Parlours
Fa Chi Sa
Via San Miniato 5r.
Map 4 E2.

Il Innocenti
Piazza Sauro 25r.
Map 3 B1 (5 A3).

SHOPS AND MARKETS

Protective bag with designer label

Shopping in Florence can be a unique experience as you wander through its ancient and medieval streets, exploring the city's renowned tradition of crafts and family-run businesses. Few cities of comparable size can boast such a profusion and variety of high-quality goods. Walking around the city you will find shops selling Italian fashion, antiques and jewellery as well as typical Florentine crafts. Tuscany is dwarfed by Florence when it comes to shopping possibilities. However, the rich traditions of many outlying towns and villages boast a variety of local crafts and specialities. These range from ceramics, hand-woven materials to the region's many gastronomic delicacies. (*See also pp30–31*.)

A colourful shop display of elegant handbags

WHEN TO SHOP

Generally, shops open around 9am and close at 1pm. In the afternoon they re-open from 3:30pm to 7:30pm, though food shops tend to open earlier in the morning and remain closed from 1pm to 5pm. Most shops are shut on Monday morning but food stores are closed on Wednesday afternoon.

Almost all shops close on Saturday afternoon in summer, and shops and markets tend to close for two or three weeks around 15 August, the national holiday (*ferragosto*).

HOW TO PAY

Major credit cards are usually accepted in larger shops, but smaller ones prefer cash. Travellers' cheques are widely accepted for payment of goods, though the rate is less favourable than at a bank.

Shopkeepers and market stallholders should by law give you a receipt (*ricevuta fiscale*). If a purchased item is defective, most shops will change the article or give you a credit note, as long as you show the till receipt. Cash refunds are uncommon.

VAT EXEMPTION

Visitors from non-EU countries can reclaim the 20 per cent sales tax (IVA) on purchases from the same shop exceeding €160. Ask for an invoice (*la fattura*) when you buy the goods and inform the shop of your intention to reclaim the tax. You will need to show your passport and the shop will fill out and stamp a form which can be taken to the relevant office at the airport.

SHOPPING IN FLORENCE

The centre of Florence is packed with shops selling everything from designer clothes to second-hand books. It is compact and easy to get around, as many streets are pedestrianized. It is also worth exploring the streets away from the centre around Piazza di Santa Croce, Piazza

Window shopping in the Via de' Tornabuoni, Florence

dei Ciompi and Piazza di Santo Spirito for furniture and gift shops where craftsmen are busy at work. The best time for bargains is during the January and July sales (*saldi*).

DEPARTMENT STORES

The main chain store in Florence is **Coin**, a popular independent department store with branches in Montecatini Terme and Livorno. This store stocks mid-range casual clothing, shoes, toiletries, children's clothing and toys, and a huge range of fashion accessories, including hosiery, sunglasses, bags and scarves. It also has an extensive home collection, with many lines imported from India and China.

Rinascente in Piazza della Repubblica has designer clothing, lingerie, household items and a rooftop bar with direct views of the Duomo. **Principe** has classic menswear and women's and children's clothes as well as upmarket home accessories.

CLOTHING

In Florence the big names in Italian fashion, **Gucci**, **Armani**, **Ferragamo**, **Versace**, **Prada** and **Enrico Coveri** are mostly found in Via de' Tornabuoni (*see p105*). This elegant street is also home to the French designer **Yves Saint Laurent** and, at the top of the street in Piazza Antinori, is **Hermes**. Opposite the imposing Palazzo Strozzi is **Louis Vuitton**, with impressive collections of footware, clothing and luggage.

In Via della Vigna Nuova (*see p105*), you'll find **Dolce & Gabbana** and **Valentino**.

La Perla, specializing in sophisticated lingerie, is also here while younger and more affordable styles can be found at **Intimo Tre** and **Intimissimi**.

Luisa Via Roma and **Raspini** are both emporia for top-designer clothing and shoes, while **Eredi Chiarini** and **Matucci** have more casual styles. Make an appointment to visit the showroom at the family palace of **Emilio Pucci** *(see p88)*, famous for his extravagant 1960s' print clothes, or visit the shop in Via de' Tornabuoni.

There are opulent hand-woven fabrics and fine silks at **Rubelli** and embroidered linen can be found at **Taf**. Those looking for discounts on Italian designer clothing and shoes can venture out to **The Mall**, an outlet centre about 30 minutes away from Florence.

Classic leather goods at Beltrami

SHOES

Italy is renowned worldwide for its shoes and, with the local Tuscan tanneries, there is nowhere better than Florence to find footwear for all tastes. Some shops design and make classic shoes by hand in-store, while others stock huge collections of new styles for each season.

At the top end, the refined finishing and elegance of **Ferragamo's** shoes are sought-after by Hollywood stars, and **Gucci** and **Prada** are both meccas for admirers of designer Italian shoes. If you prefer more classic styles then head across the Arno to **Francesco**, a tiny shop that sells simple handmade

Trendy sandals at Ferragamo

shoes and sandals. The mid-priced range is well represented by **Romano**, which stocks collections of shoes and boots in good-quality leather. For more casual and sporty styles, try the reasonably-priced **Peppe Peluso** or the chain store, **Bata**, for a huge range of fashionable footwear. Alternatively stroll down Via de' Cerretani, which houses many affordable shoe shops including **Divarese**.

LEATHER GOODS

Piazza di Santa Croce *(see pp72–3)* and the adjoining streets are filled with leather shops and workshops. Inside the cloisters of the church itself is the **Scuola del Cuoio**, where leather craftsmen work in front of the customers. Classic leather bags and gifts are sold at **Bojola**, **Il Bisonte** and **Beltrami**, and more contemporary styles can be found at **Coccinelle** and **Furla**. **Peruzzi** stocks leather clothing and accessories for men and women. The best place to buy gloves is **Madova**. For good value bags, belts and leather jackets try the **Mercato di San Lorenzo** or the market stalls in Via Pellicceria *(see p287)*.

TOILETRIES

For toiletries and beauty products head to a *profumeria* (perfumery), such as **Aline**, **Profumeria Inglese** or **Le Vanita'**, which also has a beauty centre and solarium. *Erboristerie* (herbalists) sell a range of natural products. Try the **Erboristeria di Palazzo Vecchio** *(see p75)* for unique handmade perfumes. The **Erboristeria Inglese** on Via de' Tornabuoni dispenses natural remedies and tisanes, and stocks natural beauty products, perfumes and gifts. Also worth a visit is the **Farmacia di Santa Maria Novella**, a frescoed apothecary, selling products from the elixirs of the Camaldoli monks to perfumes, herbal remedies and sweets.

JEWELLERY

Florence has always been noted for its gold and sliver-smiths. Go to **Torrini**, whose family has produced jewellery for six centuries, and to **Pommellato's** stunning shop on Via de' Tornabuoni, for its famous chunky white gold rings with huge semi-precious gems. **Bulgari** is on the same street, and so is **Parenti**, which has beautiful Baccarat rings and unique antique jewels. Try **Aprosio & Co.** for decorative jewellery made from precious metals and tiny glass stones.

The tiny wooden shops on the Ponte Vecchio *(see pp106-7)* are all jewellery shops, some with antiques from Italy and abroad, others with high-quality new Italian gold pieces.

A vibrant display of soaps in the busy shopping street Via del Corso

Typical antiques shop in Florence

ART AND ANTIQUES

Florence has always been a centre of artistic excellence. This heritage has translated into a wealth of antiques and fine art shops. The antiques shops are mostly clustered around Via dei Fossi *(see pp112-3)*, Via Maggio *(see p118)* and Via dei Serragli.

For top-quality antiques go to **Neri** or the nearby **Cei**. **Romanelli** has bronze statuary and works encrusted in semi-precious stones, while **Ducci** has an exquisite selection of handmade boxes, prints and sculpture in marble and wood. For lovers of Art Nouveau and Art Deco there is **Fallani Best**, and for modern art objects and gifts go to **Armando Poggi**. **Ugo Poggi** has a selection of household objects including elegant porcelain.

Ugolini and **Mosaico di Pitti** create tables and framed pictures using the age-old technique of marble inlay. **Arredamenti Castorina** has a wonderful selection of picture frames, mouldings, brassware and intricate intarsias. More contemporary styles are at **Mirabili**, which showcases furniture and interior designers.

GIFTS

Florence is a treasure trove for unusual gifts and souvenirs. Via de' Guicciardini and the area between Piazza di Santa Croce and Piazza della Signoria are good places to look for gifts.

Housed in a converted wine cellar, **Signum** has postcards, posters and prints, and items such as miniature shop models and tiny packs of cards. **Mandragora** in Piazza del Duomo has a wide choice of gifts based on famous artworks in the city, while the renowned **Pineider** has upmarket stationery and office gifts in leather, linen and paper.

For locally made terracotta and decorative glazed ceramics visit **Sbigoli Terracotte**. **La Bottega dei Cristalli** has Murano glass kitchenware, chandeliers and decorative objects. **Passamaneria Valmar** sells decorative key and curtain tassels, tapestries and soft furnishings in silks and wools, while **Rosa Regale** has eccentric pieces of furniture and furnishings, clothing and accessories all with a rose theme, in a delightful shop at the end of a decorative passageway.

BOOKS AND PAPER

The main bookshops in Florence are **Feltrinelli International**, which sells publications in various languages, and **Edison**, which stocks magazines, maps, books in English as well as coffee-table photography books, and also houses a café. **Paperback Exchange** has an extremely wide selection of new and second-hand books in English.

Typical Florentine crafts include bookbinding and handmade marbled paper, used to decorate a variety of gift objects. These are easily available at **Giulio Giannini**, **Il Papiro** and **Il Torchio**, where bookbinding can be seen in action on the balcony workshop.

Feltrinelli International bookshop

FOOD AND WINE

Those shopping for food should go to **Pegna**, a mini-supermarket in the heart of Florence that stocks fresh, as well as vast selection of gourmet, foods. The **Bottega dell'Olio** has shelves of extra virgin Tuscan olive oils, spice-flavoured oils and gifts. For typically British items such as teas and speciality foods go to **Old England Stores**.

Dolceforte sells chocolate souvenirs in the shape of the Duomo and the statue of David. A huge selection of biscuits and chocolates fills the front half of **Alessi**, while at the back and in the cellar are fine wines, spirits and liqueurs. Another good place to buy wine is **Zanobini**,

Fresh vegetables at a Florentine market stall

where you can mix with the locals and sample the wines. At **Procacci** in Via de' Tornabuoni, shoppers can stop for a glass of wine and a canapé while choosing between pots of black or white truffles and other delicacies to take away.

FLORENCE'S MARKETS

Florence's central street market is the **Mercato di San Lorenzo**, which caters mostly for tourists *(see p88)*. Nearby, in Via dell'Ariento, is the covered

Mercato Centrale, the city's main food market *(see p88)*. The **Mercato di Sant'Ambrogio** also has fresh fruit and vegetable stalls, as well as clothing and household goods. Beneath the 16th-century Loggia del Porcellino, is the **Mercato Nuovo**, or Straw Market, which sells leather goods and souvenirs *(see p112)*. On Tuesday mornings, there is an enormous market at the **Parco delle Cascine** with cheap clothing, shoes and food. The **Mercato delle Pulci**

is a flea market, selling antiques and bric-à-brac. Garden enthusiasts might want to check out the **Mercato delle Piante** held on Thursday mornings under the porticoes of Via Pellicceria, selling flowers, houseplants and herbs.

Occasional markets spring up in Piazza Santa Croce and Piazza Santa Maria Novella, notably the German gift market in the weeks before Christmas and the monthly antiques market in **Piazza Santo Spirito**.

DIRECTORY

DEPARTMENT STORES

Coin
Via dei Calzaiuoli 56r.
Map 6 D3.
Tel 055 28 05 31.

Principe
Piazza Strozzi 1.
Map 1 C5 (5 C3).
Tel 055 29 27 64.

Rinascente
Piazza della Repubblica 1.
Map 1 C5 (6 D3).
Tel 055 21 91 13.

CLOTHING

Armani
Via de' Tornabuoni 48/50r.
Map 1 C5 (5 C2).
Tel 055 21 90 41.

Dolce & Gabbana
Via della Vigna Nuova 27.
Map 3 B1 (5 B3).
Tel 055 28 10 03.

Emilio Pucci
Via de' Tornabuoni 20r.
Map 1 C5 (5 C3).
Tel 055 265 80 82.

Enrico Coveri
Via de' Tornabuoni 81r.
Map 1 C5 (5 C3).
Tel 055 21 12 63.

Eredi Chiarini
Via Roma 16r.
Map 3 C1 (6 D2).
Tel 055 28 44 78.
Also: Via Porta Rossa 39r.
Map 1 C5 (5 C3).
Tel 055 21 22 79.

Ferragamo
Via de' Tornabuoni 14r.
Map 1 C5 (5 C2).
Tel 055 29 21 23.

Gucci
Via de' Tornabuoni 73r.
Map 1 C5 (5 C2).
Tel 055 26 40 11.

Hermes
Piazza Antinori 6r.
Map 1 C5 (5 C2).
Tel 055 238 10 04.

Intimissimi
Via dei Calzaiuoli 99r.
Map 3 C1 (6 D3).
Tel 055 230 26 09.

Intimo Tre
Via del Corso 27.
Map 3 C1 (6 D3).
Tel 055 21 24 15.

Louis Vuitton
Piazza degli Strozzi 1.
Map 3 C1.
Tel 055 26 69 81.

Luisa Via Roma
Via Roma 19r-21r.
Map 3 C1 (6 D2).
Tel 055 21 78 26.

The Mall
Via Europa 8,
Leccio Reggello.
Tel 055 865 77 75.

Matucci
Via del Corso 71r.
Map 3 C1 (6 D3).
Tel 055 239 64 20.
Also: Via del Corso 46r.
Map 3 C1 (6 D3).
Tel 055 21 20 18.

La Perla
Via della Vigna
Nuova 17-19.
Map 3 B1 (5 B3).
Tel 055 21 70 70.

Prada
Via de' Tornabuoni 67r.
Map 1 C5 (5 C2).
Tel 055 28 34 39.

Raspini
Via Roma 25r-29r.
Map 3 C1 (6 D2).
Tel 055 21 30 77.

Rubelli
Via dei Fossi 45r.
Map 1 B5 (5 B3).
Tel 055 21 24 30

Taf
Via Por Santa Maria 17r.
Map 3 C1 (6 D4).
Tel 055 239 60 37.

Valentino
Via della Vigna Nuova 47r.
Map 3 B1 (5 B3).
Tel 055 29 31 42.

Versace
Via de' Tornabuoni 13-15r.
Map 1 C5 (5 C2).
Tel 055 28 26 38.

Yves Saint Laurent
Via de' Tornabuoni 29r.
Map 1 C5 (5 C2).
Tel 055 28 40 40.

SHOES

Bata
Via dei Calzaiuoli 110r.
Map 3 C1 (6 D2).
Tel 055 21 16 24.

Divarese
Piazza del Duomo 55r.
Map 3 C1 (6 D2).
Tel 055 21 31 68.

Francesco
Via di Santo Spirito 62r.
Map 3 B1 (5 A4).
Tel 055 21 24 28.

Peppe Peluso
Via del Corso 5-6r.
Map 3 C1 (6 D3).
Tel 055 26 82 83.

Romano
Via Porta Rossa 14r.
Map 1 C5 (5 C3).
Tel 055 28 96 88.

LEATHER GOODS

Beltrami
Via de' Tornabuoni 48r.
Map 1 C5 (5 C2).
Tel 055 28 77 79.

Il Bisonte
Via del Parione 31r.
Map 1 C5 (5 C3).
Tel 055 21 57 22.

Bojola
Via de' Rondinelli 25r.
Map 1 C5 (5 C2).
Tel 055 21 11 55.

Coccinelle
Via Por S. Maria 49r
Map 3 C1 (6 D4).
Tel 055 239 87 82.

Furla
Via de' Calzaiuoli 47r
Map 3 C1 (6 D3).
Tel 055 238 28 83.

Madova
Via dei Giucciardini 1r.
Map 3 B1 (5 C4).
Tel 055 239 65 26.

Mercato di San Lorenzo
See Markets.

Peruzzi
Borgo de' Greci 8–20r.
Map 4 D1 (6 E4).
Tel 055 28 90 39.

Scuola del Cuoio
Piazza di Santa Croce 16.
Map 3 C1 (6 F4).
Tel 055 24 45 33.

DIRECTORY

TOILETRIES

Aline
Via dei Calzaiuoli 53r.
Map 3 C1 (6 D3).
Tel 055 21 54 36.

Erboristeria Inglese
Via de' Tornabuoni 19.
Map 1 C5 (5 C2).
Tel 055 21 06 28.

Erboristeria di Palazzo Vecchio
Via Vacchereccia 9r.
Map 3 C1 (6 D3).
Tel 055 239 60 55.

Farmacia di Santa Maria Novella
Via della Scala 16.
Map 1 A4 (5 A1).
Tel 055 21 62 76.

Profumeria Inglese
Piazza dell'Olio 4.
Map 3 C1 (6 D2).
Tel 055 260 88 01.

Le Vanita'
Via Porta Rossa 55r.
Map 1 C5 (5 C3).
Tel 055 29 01 67.

JEWELLERY

Aprosio & Co.
Via di Santo Spirito 11.
Map 3 B1 (5 B4).
Tel 055 29 05 34

Bulgari
Via de' Tornabuoni 61r.
Map 1 C5 (5 C3).
Tel 055 21 24 69.

Parenti
Via de' Tornabuoni 67r.
Map 1 C5 (5 C2).
Tel 055 28 34 39.

Pommellato
Via de' Tornabuoni 89r–91r.
Map 1 C5 (5 C2).
Tel 055 28 85 30.

Torrini
Piazza del Duomo 10r.
Map 2 D5 (6 D2).
Tel 055 230 24 01.

ART AND ANTIQUES

Armando Poggi
Via dei Calzaiuoli 103–116r. **Map** 6 D3.
Tel 055 21 65 28.

Arredamenti Castorina
Via di Santo Spirito 15r.
Map 3 B1 (5 A4).
Tel 055 21 28 85.

Cei
Via dei Fossi 17.
Map 1 B5 (5 B3).
Tel 055 239 60 39.

Ducci
Lungarno Corsini 24r.
Map 3 B1 (5 B3).
Tel 055 21 91 37.

Fallani Best
Via San Niccoló 79r.
Tel 055 24 18 61.

Mirabili
Lungarno Giucciardini 24r.
Map 3 B1 (5 A4).
Tel 055 294 257.

Mosaico di Pitti
Piazza de' Pitti 16–18r.
Map 3 B2 (5 B5).
Tel 055 28 21 27.

Neri
Via dei Fossi 55–57r.
Map 1 B5 (5 B3).
Tel 055 29 21 36.

Romanelli
Lungarno degli Acciaiuoli 74r. **Map** 3 C1 (5 C4).
Tel 055 239 66 62.

Ugo Poggi
Via degli Strozzi 26r.
Map 1 C5 (5 C3).
Tel 055 21 67 41.

Ugolini
Lungarno degli Acciaiuoli 66–70r.
Map 3 C1 (5 C4).
Tel 055 28 49 69.

GIFTS

La Bottega dei Cristalli
Via dei Benci 51r
Map 3 C1 (6 F4).
Tel 055 234 48 91.

Mandragora
Piazza del Duomo 50r.
Map 3 C1 (6 D2).
Tel 055 29 25 59.

Passamaneria Valmar
Via Porta Rossa 53r.
Map 1 C5 (5 C3).
Tel 055 28 44 93.

Pineider
Piazza della Signoria 13r.
Map 3 C1 (6 D3).
Tel 055 28 46 55.

Rosa Regale
Via Tosinghi Volta Mazzuconi 3r.
Map 3 C1 (6 D2).
Tel 055 267 03 13.

Sbigoli Terracotte
Via Sant'Egidio 4r.
Map 6 F2.
Tel 055 247 97 13.

Signum
Borgo dei Greci 40r.
Map 3 C1 (6 E4).
Tel 055 28 06 21.

BOOKS AND PAPER

Edison
Piazza della Repubblica 27r.
Map 1 C5 (6 D3).
Tel 055 21 31 10.

Feltrinelli International
Via Cavour 12–20r.
Map 2 D4.
Tel 055 21 95 24.

Giulio Giannini
Piazza de' Pitti 37r.
Map 3 B2 (5 B5).
Tel 055 21 26 21.

Paperback Exchange
Via Fiesolana 31r.
Map 2 E5.
Tel 055 247 81 54.

Il Papiro
Piazza del Duomo 24r.
Map (6 D4).
Tel 055 28 16 28.

Il Torchio
Via de' Bardi 17.
Map 3 C2 (6 D5)
(6 D4). *Tel 055 234 28 62.*

FOOD AND WINE

Alessi
Via delle Oche 27r.
Map 3 C1 (6 D2).
Tel 055 21 49 66.

Bottega dell'Olio
Piazza del Limbo 2r.
Map 3 C1 (6 D4).
Tel 055 267 04 68.

Dolceforte
Via della Scala 21.
Map 1 C5 (5 B2).
Tel 055 21 91 16.

Old England Stores
Via de' Vecchietti 28r.
Map 1 C5 (5 C2).
Tel 055 21 19 83.

Pegna
Via dello Studio 26r.
Map 6 E2.
Tel 055 28 27 01.

Procacci
Via de' Tornabuoni 64r.
Map 1 C5 (5 C2).
Tel 055 21 16 56.

Zanobini
Via Sant'Antonino 47r.
Map 1 C5 (5 C1).
Tel 055 239 68 50.

FLORENCE'S MARKETS

Mercato Centrale
Via dell' Ariento 10–14
Map 1 C4 (5 C1).

Mercato Nuovo
See p112.
Map 3 C1 (6 D4).
Open 9am–7pm daily
(Nov–Mar: Tue–Sat).

Mercato delle Piante
Via Pellicceria.
Map 6 D3.
Open Thu am.

Mercato delle Pulci
Piazza dei Ciompi.
Map 4 E1.
Open 8am–7:30pm
daily (Nov–Mar: Mon–Sat).

Mercato di San Lorenzo
Piazza di San Lorenzo.
Map 1 C5 (6 D1).

Mercato di Sant'Ambrogio
Piazza Sant'Ambrogio.
Open 7am–2pm Mon–Sat.

Parco delle Cascine
Piazza Vittorio Veneto.
Open Tue am

Piazza Santo Spirito
Map 1 C5 (B4).
Open 8am–12.30pm
Mon–Fri. Antiques market
2nd Sun of month.

Shopping in Tuscany

Small towns throughout Tuscany have a multitude of shops selling a range of handicrafts, foods and some of the best wine in Italy. These are invariably displayed in small shops or at the frequent markets, seasonal fairs and local celebrations (*see pp34–9*), which are such an integral part of Tuscan rural life.

A Tuscan delicatessen

For textiles, Lucca lays claim to a rich tradition of silk manufacture, as well as embroidery and hand-woven fabrics, reflecting the strong rural craft tradition of the nearby Garfagnana area. Rustic crafts are common in the Mugello and Casentino.

FOOD AND WINE

Excursions into Tuscany should be accompanied by visits to a local vineyard where wine is sold directly from the cellars. The Chianti region is studded with farms producing their own wines (*see p229*). Greve has several good wine outlets, and during the third week of September there is the annual wine festival, the Rassegna del Chianti Classico (*see p38*).

The excellent Vernaccia, a white wine, is typical of the San Gimignano area. The vineyards around Montalcino produce some of the best wine in Italy (*see p224*).

Tuscany's rich gastronomic tradition is reflected in the profusion of local products. The main streets of towns such as Greve, Montalcino, San Gimignano and Pienza have a range of food shops.

Sheep's cheese (*pecorino*), produced around the area of Crete, can be bought directly from the farm or from shops in local towns. In Pienza, shop shelves are laden with local cheeses (*see p226*), cured meats, wines and grappas. In Grosseto you will find truffles.

Siena is renowned for its *panforte*, a dark cake spiced with cloves and cinnamon, which has been produced since the Middle Ages. Biscuits include *cavallucci* (ground walnuts and aniseed) and *ricciarelli*, made from almonds, orange peel and honey.

MARKETS IN TUSCANY

Markets are aplenty throughout the region. Particularly famous is the Mercato dell'Antiquariato, which sells goods from antique furniture to bric-à-brac. It takes place in Arezzo on the Piazza Grande on the first weekend of each month, in Pisa on the Ponte di Mezzo on the second weekend, and in Lucca in Piazza San Martino on the third weekend.

Display of local pottery

GIFTS AND SOUVENIRS

Characteristic ceramics are found throughout the region, from the famed raw terracotta of Impruneta to the decorated glazed pottery of Montelupo and Siena. In San Gimignano, look out for shops selling artistic ceramics (*see p30*) and hand-woven fabrics.

The best in marble can be found in Pietrasanta and Carrara (*see p172*). The famous white marble of the Alpi Apuane still serves local crafts-men, who make busts and replicas of sculpted works of art, as in Michelangelo's day.

The Etruscans mastered the art of working alabaster, and today the tradition lives on in Volterra, where many shops sell a range of souvenirs (*see p166*). The Etruscans also had knowledge of the minerals and precious stones typical of the volcanic Colline Metallifere, Maremma and Elba, the latter famous for its quartz and opals (*see pp234–5*).

The Mercato dell'Antiquariato on the Piazza Grande in Arezzo

ENTERTAINMENT

There is plenty going on in Florence and Tuscany by way of entertainment throughout the year. The warm summer months see a concentration of events from traditional festivals, classical concerts and dance performances to open-air films and live music in alfresco bars. The areas of Santo Spirito

Puccini Opera Festival poster

in the Oltrarno and Santa Croce are home to lively bars and restaurants, while clubs tend to be situated on the edge of town. Opera lovers will not be disappointed; Florence's Teatro del Maggio, one of Italy's best, hosts some fine operas and concerts, while Tuscany plays host to the celebrated Puccini Opera Festival.

PRACTICAL INFORMATION

Local newspapers, such as *La Nazione* and the Florence section of *La Repubblica*, carry entertainment listings. The monthly magazine *Firenze Spettacolo*, with a short section in English, lists local events, entertainment venues and places to eat and drink. Look out too for the bi-lingual, *Concierge Information*, which is free and is a useful source of listings. There is also a host of websites detailing events in the region: www.firenze.net, www.comune.firenze.it, and www.turismo.toscana.it, to name a few.

BOOKING TICKETS

Box Office is a ticket agency for concerts, opera and ballet nationwide. Tickets for performances at the **Teatro del Maggio** can also be purchased at their box office and online. It is advisable to buy tickets for opera in advance, but for other events, tickets are generally available on the door.

FACILITIES FOR THE DISABLED

Most major concert halls and music venues in Tuscany are now fully wheelchair accessible. However, churches, villas and gardens, which hold occasional performances, are unlikely to be so well equipped. If in doubt, always check in advance. There is a booklet published by the Province of Florence available at tourist offices, which details the accessibility of many outdoor venues in the area.

OPERA AND CLASSICAL MUSIC

The most important musical event in Tuscany is the annual Maggio Musicale festival *(see p32)*, held at **Teatro del Maggio** in Florence between late April and late June, and features opera, concerts and ballet. The theatre also puts on a year-round programme, while Orchestra della Toscana gives several concerts a month at its base in **Teatro Verdi**. From October to April the wonderful 18th-century **Teatro della Pergola** in Florence hosts world-class chamber music concerts. **Estate Fiesolana** organizes opera, dance and music events from July to August in Fiesole's atmospheric amphitheatre.

The rest of Tuscany also celebrates the arts. Puccini's lakeside villa on the shores of Lago di Massaciuccoli makes a spectacular setting for the **Puccini Opera Festival**, held

every July to August. The Opera Barga festival showcases little-known works in the restored **Teatro dei Differenti** *(see p174)*. In July and August, Siena hosts the **Estate Musicale Chigiana** in the magnificent abbeys of San Galgano, Monte Oliveto Maggiore and Sant' Antimo. The **Incontri in Terra di Siena** festival is known for its excellent chamber music, and the recently-established **Tuscan Sun Festival** is based in Cortona.

FILM, THEATRE AND DANCE

Films in English are shown three times a week at the **Odeon Original Sound** in Florence, and several other Tuscan towns now cater for the huge number of foreign visitors by screening English-language films.

Theatre has a long and distinguished history in Tuscany, but performances in

Fiesole's Roman amphitheatre is the setting for opera and dance events

Contemporary dance performance

English are rare, and as such, the genre attracts few non-Italian speaking visitors. However, Tuscany's 300 local theatres – many of them now restored – are worth a visit.

Dance is popular throughout the region and several festivals, including the Florence Dance Festival, feature classical and contemporary dance.

JAZZ, BLUES AND ROCK

Florence will not disappoint jazz fans. A great season of progressive jazz concerts, often featuring international names,

is staged in the **Sala Vanni**, while several bars regularly hold live jazz sessions.

Big-name rock concerts are mostly held at the 7,000-seater **Palasport** or, occasionally, at the city's football stadium. For smaller, more intimate venues go to clubs such as **Auditorium Flog**, **Tenax** or **Saschall**. *Firenze Spettacolo* has a detailed list of bars and clubs hosting live music.

In summer, Florence's piazzas and gardens become the venues for alfresco bars and live music. Summertime also sees open-air jazz and rock concerts taking place all over the region.

Blues fans should look out for **Pistoia Blues**, a mid-July weekend jamboree of open-air blues concerts, which attracts well-known names.

OPEN-AIR ENTERTAINMENT

Unique to Tuscany are the many traditional festivals celebrated through the year, the most famous being the Palio in Siena *(see p222)*. The others range from large events attended by thousands of spectators to tiny little village

sagre. Commonly defined by food, drink and music, these events are a great way to see the Tuscans at play.

CHILDREN'S ENTERTAINMENT

While Florence and Tuscany are extremely child-friendly, child-orientated entertainment is lacking so parents need to be inventive. As far as museums are concerned, only the Museo dei Ragazzi in Palazzo Vecchio *(see pp78-9)* has a specific programme for children, but several other museums, such as Museo di Storia della Scienza *(see p74)* and Museo "La Specola" *(see p119)*, are fun too. For children below ten years, **Mondobimbo Inflatables Parterre** has bouncy castles and **Giordino di Boboli** is good for a run-around.

Outside Florence, there's a small zoo in Pistoia *(see p187)* and **Parco Preistorico**, with its gigantic model dinosaurs, is near Pisa. **Pinocchio Park** at Collodi *(see 183)*, is dedicated to one of Tuscany's most loved characters, and **Parco Giochi Cavallino Matto** is a huge funfair with plenty of rides to keep the kids amused.

DIRECTORY

OPERA AND CLASSICAL MUSIC

Box Office
Via Alamanni 39.
Map 1 B4.
Tel 055 210 804.
www.boxol.it

Estate Fiesolana
Tel 055 597 8308.
www.estatefiesolana.it

Estate Musicale Chigiana
Via di Città 89, Chigiana.
Tel 057 722 091.
www.chigiana.it

Incontri in Terra di Siena
La Foce, Chianciano Terme.
Tel 057 869 101.

Puccini Opera Festival
Torre del Lago.
Tel 0584 35 93 22.
www.puccinifestival.it

Teatro dei Differenti
Piazza Angelo 8, Barga.
Tel 0583 72 32 50.

Teatro del Maggio
Corso Italia 16.
Map 1 A5.
www.maggio
fiorentino.com

Teatro della Pergola
Via della Pergola 12–32.
Map 2 E5.
Tel 055 226 43 16.

Teatro Verdi
Via Ghibellina 99.
Map 4 D1.
Tel 055 21 23 20.

Tuscan Sun Festival
www.tuscansun
festival.com

FILM, THEATRE AND DANCE

Florence Dance Festival
Borgo Stella 23r.
Map 3 B1.
Tel 055 28 92 76.

Odeon Original Sound
Via de' Sassetti 1.
Map 5 C3.
Tel 055 21 40 68.

JAZZ, BLUES AND ROCK

Auditorium Flog
Via Michele Mercati 24B.
Tel 055 48 71 45.

Palasport
Viale Paoli.
Tel 055 678 841.

Pistoia Blues
Tel 057 321 622.
www.pistoiablues.com

Sala Vanni
Piazza del Carmine 14.
Map 3 A1.
Tel 055 287 347.

Saschall
Lungarno Aldo Moro 3.
Tel 055 65 04 11 12.

Tenax
Via Pratese 46.
Tel 055 308 160.

CHILDREN'S ENTERTAINMENT

Giordino di Boboli
Piazza de' Pitti.
Map 3 B2.
Tel 055 229 87 32.

Mondobimbo Inflatables Parterre
Piazza della Libertà.
Map 2 E2.
Tel 055 553 29 46.

Parco Giochi Cavallino Matto
Via Po 1, Marina di Castagneto Donoratico.
Tel 0565 74 57 20.

Parco Preistorico
Via Cappuccini 20, Peccioli.
Tel 0587 63 60 30.

Pinocchio Park
Collodi.
Tel 0572 42 93 42.

SPECIALIST HOLIDAYS
AND OUTDOOR ACTIVITIES

Nowhere is the Italian motto for good living, *la dolce vita*, more in evidence than in Tuscany. Sitting outside a café in a Tuscan village you can glimpse original Renaissance art or take in the sight of well-tended olive groves and vineyards terraced into the steep hillsides. No wonder the

Olives and olive oil

gentle pace of an activity holiday here, which in many cases means painting the stunning countryside or sipping vintage wines, is so appealing. Those more interested in energetic pursuits will not be disappointed as the region has plenty of sporting activities on offer, ranging from horse riding to water sports.

ART

Those of an artistic persuasion can enrol at art school and try their hand at sculpture, art restoration or painting the beautiful countryside. **Centro d'Arte Verrocchio**, a residential art school in the hilltop village of Casole d'Elsa offers courses in drawing, painting and sculpture. Students can work on the terrace in stunning surroundings. For city-based courses try **Lorenzo de' Medici Art Institute of Florence**. The semester and summer school programmes include sketching, watercolour, fine art, painting, print-making, restoration and art history.

COOKERY AND WINE TASTING

Tuscany offers many gastronomic delights from pecorino cheese to porcini mushrooms. The regional cuisine values quality of ingredients rather than complex technique, and recipes are handed down from one generation to the next.

There are plenty of cookery courses where you can learn Italian food traditions – some of which are listed on **Nonna Lina's Kitchen** website.

Originally a medieval Benedictine abbey, **Badia a Coltibuono** *(see p229)* is a prestigious Chianti wine-producing estate. Courses on offer here range from brief wine and olive oil tastings, to five-day residential cookery courses with tours of the vineyards, olive mills and wine-making cellars at Monti in Chianti.

Apicius Culinary Institute in Florence is affiliated to Lorenzo de' Medici Art Institute. The duration of the cookery courses range from one-week to year-long diplomas.

La Cucina del Garga cookery school and restaurant, also in Florence, teaches recipes with a modern flourish. It holds one-day classes in the city and four to eight-day gastronomic excursions in Tuscany.

Vineyards offer wine tastings by appointment. **Chianti Classico** promotes stays at

Students learning Italian recipies

vineyards in the Chianti Classico region, while **Consorzio del Vino Brunello di Montalcino** has information on visits to the Brunello region. Specialist *enoteca* (wine bars) and shops, including **Millesimi** near Santa Spirito, also arrange wine tastings by appointment.

WALKING, CYCLING AND HORSE RIDING

Tuscany's scenery can be best enjoyed at walking pace. Several holiday companies offer walking itineraries, some through the landscape of forested hills and olive groves, while others wend their way through the medieval hilltop towns, taking in cultural landmarks along the way. **Ramblers Holidays** and **Sherpa Expeditions** are two such companies, and **Club Alpino Italiano** runs guided mountain treks.

Another great way to see the Tuscan countryside is by bike. For cycling holidays contact **Cicloposse**, which deals in both guided and self-guided bike tours.

Painting the beautiful Tuscan countryside

The Maremma in southern Tuscany is famous for its wild horses and *butteri* (cowboys), and there are plenty of riding schools in the region. **Vallebona** in Pontassieve organizes trekking holidays and guided tours on horseback and **Rendola Riding Stables** at Montevarchi offers riding lessons.

SPA HOLIDAYS

Spa holidays are enjoying a renaissance with many hotels offering a pool, gym and massage treatments, but Tuscany has the real thing. Try the thermal pools at **Terme di Saturnia** in the Maremma, or bathe in the warm sulphurated waters of Cascate del Gorello *(see p238)* close by. You can purchase a day pass to experience the therapeutic waters of

Montecatini Terme *(see pp184–5)*, with its nine spas. A vast array of health and beauty treatments is also available.

WATER SPORTS

Tourists on the Ponte Vecchio *(see pp106–7)* can watch canoes gliding through the inky waters of the River Arno. **Societa Canottieri Firenze** offers keen rowers visitor membership for a nominal sum.

In summer, many locals travel to the coast to escape the city heat. Those who can't head for one of the open air swimming pools. **Costoli** is open summer and winter, and **Piscina Bellariva** has indoor and outdoor pools.

For the more adventurous there is diving off the coast of Elba *(see pp234–5)* through **Spiro Sub Diving Club**.

MOUNTAIN SPORTS

Skiing in the Appennines is a possible day trip from Florence because, rather than being isolated in Alpine resorts, the slopes at **Abetone** near Pistoia are only 80 km (50 miles) away. Weekly as well as daily ski passes are available.

Ufficio Guides organise summer mountaineering courses, but single-minded climbers can go rock climbing independently at **Le Cave di Maiano** at Fiesole.

GOLF

Combine a few rounds of golf at **Ugolino Golf Course** with sightseeing in Florence, or enjoy a golfing holiday at **Punta Ala Golf Club** overlooking the coast, at Grosseto *(see p238)*, an hour from Pisa airport.

DIRECTORY

ART

Centro d'Arte Verrocchio
Casole d'Elsa.
www.verrocchio.co.uk

Lorenzo de' Medici Art Institute of Florence
Via dell' Alloro 14R.
Map 5 C1.
Tel 055 28 31 42.

COOKERY AND WINE TASTING

Apicius Culinary Institute
Via Guelfa 85.
Map 1 C4.
Tel 055 265 81 35.
www.apicius.it

Badia a Coltibuono
Gaiole in Chianti.
Tel 0577 74 48 32.
www.coltibuono.com

Chianti Classico
Via Scopeti 155, Florence.
Tel 055 822 85.
www.chianticlassico.com

Consorzio del Vino Brunello di Montalcino
Costa del Municipio 1, Montalcino.
Tel 0577 84 82 46.
www.consorziobrunellodi montalcino.it

La Cucina del Garga
Via del Moro 48R.
Map 5 B2.
www.garga.it

Millesimi
Borgo Tegolaio 33R.
Map 5 A5.
Tel 055 265 46 75.
www.millesimi.it

Nonna Lina's Kitchen
www.nonnalinaskitchen. com

WALKING, CYCLING AND HORSE RIDING

Club Alpino Italiano
Via del Mezzetta 2.
Tel 055 612 04 67.
www.caifirenze.it

Cicloposse
Via I Maggio 27, Pienza.
Tel 0578 749 983.
www.cicloposse.com

Ramblers Holidays
Tel 01707 33 11 33.
www.ramblersholidays. co.uk

Rendola Riding Stables
Montevarchi.
Tel 055 970 70 45.
www.rendolariding. freeweb.org

Sherpa Expeditions
Tel 020 857 7 27 17.
www.sherpa-walking-holidays.co.uk

Vallebona
Via di Grignano 32, Pontassieve.
Tel 055 839 72 46.

SPA HOLIDAYS

Terme di Saturnia
Saturnia (Grosseto).
Tel 0564 60 01 11.
www.termedisaturnia.it

Montecatini Terme
Viale Verdi 41, Montecatini Terme.
Tel 800 132 538.
www.termemontecatini.it

WATER SPORTS

Costoli
Viale Paoli, Florence.
Tel 055 623 60 27.

Piscina Bellariva
Lungarno Aldo Moro 6, Florence.
Tel 055 677 521.

Societa Canottieri Firenze
Lungarno Luisa dei Medici 8. **Map** 6 D4.
Tel 055 28 21 30.
www.canottierifirenze.it

Spiro Sub Diving Club
La Foce 27, Marina di Campo, Elba.
Tel 0565 97 61 02.

MOUNTAIN SPORTS

Abetone
Tel 0573 602 31 *(tourist info)*.
Tel 0573 600 01 *(ski info)*.

Le Cave di Maiano
Via delle Cave 16, Fiesole.

Ufficio Guide
Libreria Stella Alpina via Corridoni 14b/r.
Tel 055 41 16 88.
www.ufficioguide.it

GOLF

Punta Ala Golf Club
Punta Ala, Grosseto.
www.puntaala.net/golf

Ugolino Golf Course
Via Chiantigiana 3, Grassina.
Tel 055 230 10 09.
www.golfugolino.it

SURVIVAL
GUIDE

PRACTICAL INFORMATION 296–305
TRAVEL INFORMATION 306–315

PRACTICAL INFORMATION

ENTE NAZIONALE ITALIANO PER IL TURISMO
Tourist board logo

Visitors have been coming to Tuscany for centuries, drawn by its magnificent art and architecture, landscape and cuisine. These may all seem overwhelming at first, so try to plan your stay to make the most of this beautiful region. Start your day early and take time over lunch: most sights and shops close for several hours and reopen in the late afternoon.

Try to have a relaxed attitude to your sightseeing – opening hours can be erratic and may vary depending on the season. Bear in mind that most Italians take their holiday in August, so some places may be shut. If your stay in Florence is limited, you could take a city tour. You can also combine your stay with a study course, offered throughout the year by colleges.

MUSEUMS AND MONUMENTS

Museums in Italy often have irregular opening times, so it may be worth your while to plan ahead by visiting a few relevant websites (see p297) prior to your trip and the local tourist office once you arrive. Most museums open in the morning and close all day Monday. Privately owned museums have various opening hours and often open later in the afternoon. There is usually an admission charge but some museums offer concessions. Churches sometimes charge admission to view particularly precious works of art. For a small fee, **Firenze-musei** offers an advanced booking service for entry to some museums. This could save you hours of queuing for popular sites and can be done by phone or at booking desks in the Uffizi and Palazzo Pitti. Note that many ticket offices often close half an hour before the museum closes. The

Evening concert in Piazza del Campo in Siena

booklet *City Guide*, available at most tourist offices, lists the different museums.

TOURIST INFORMATION

Florence, Pisa and Siena have several **Uffici Informazioni Turistiche** (tourist offices) offering information about tourist sites in the entire province. Tourist offices in small towns tend to give details only on their particular town. Travel agents, such as **CIT Viaggi** and **American Express**, have information on local tours and offer guidance on rail and coach travel in Italy. If you want to plan ahead, contact **ENIT** (the Italian Tourist Board) in your country before you leave for Italy. There is a complaint desk at the tourist office in via Cavour.

ENTERTAINMENT INFORMATION

The best guide for entertainment is the monthly magazine *Firenze Spettacolo*, which has restaurant and café guides, as well as details of concerts, exhibitions, museums and sporting events. Another useful booklet is *Concierge Information*, which is written in Italian and English and is available from most hotels. Tourist offices often have a selection of leaflets on local entertainment and events. During the summer evenings, fêtes with local bands are held throughout Tuscany. Most of the nightspots are found in the cities and beach resorts, although you are likely to find a bar just about anywhere you go.

Sign for tourist information

A busker with an accordion entertaining outside the Uffizi

Listings magazines for Florence

GUIDED TOURS

Tours around Florence can be arranged through **American Express**. For guided walks around the city, contact **Walking Tours of Florence**. Guides for private groups can be hired from **CAF. Citysightseeing Firenze** offers a hop-on hop-off bus service (complete with audioguide) to all the major sites in the city. Information on these services is available in the tourist office.

Tourist offices and travel agents throughout Tuscany have lists of authorized guides for both city and regional tours. In Florence, visit the **Tourist Guide Association** for further information.

A guided tour of Florence

ETIQUETTE

Efforts to speak a few words of Italian will be appreciated, although most of the big hotels have multilingual staff.

Italians drink in moderation, and in spite of a law banning smoking in public spaces it is common almost everywhere

VISITING CHURCHES

Italians are strict on dress code in churches and you may be refused entry if you are wearing shorts or vests. Some churches charge an entrance fee, and several close during mass. Most are dark, so make sure you carry plenty of small change for the automatic metered lighting.

TIPPING

Service in restaurants is included in the price, unless otherwise stated (see p264). However, foreigners are expected to tip. Keep a few euros handy for taxi drivers, porters, doormen and sacristans.

DISABLED TRAVELLERS

Facilities for the disabled traveller in Tuscany are limited. If you book a package tour, representatives can assist in organizing help at airports and ensure the most convenient hotel room.

Some intercity trains have special facilities for wheelchair users. There is a lift at some stations, such as Santa Maria Novella, to help those with wheelchairs on and off trains, but it must be booked 24 hours in advance.

RESTROOMS

There are few public toilets in Tuscany. Many galleries and museums have toilets, otherwise most bar and café owners will let you use theirs.

USEFUL ADDRESSES

American Express
Via Dante Alighieri 22r, Florence.
Map 4 D1 (6 E3). **Tel** 055 509 81.

CAF
Via Sant'Antonino 6r, Florence.
Map 1 C5. **Tel** 055 28 32 00.

CIT Viaggi
Piazza della Stazione 51r,
Florence. **Map** 1 B5 (5 B1).
Tel 055 28 41 45.

Citysightseeing Firenze
Stazione Santa Maria Novella,
Florence. **Map** 1 B4 (5 B1).
Tel 055 565 04 60.
www.ataf.net

ENIT UK
1 Princes Street, London W1B 2AY.
Tel 020 7408 1254.
www.enit.it

Firenzemusei
Tel 055 29 48 83.
www.firenzemusei.it

Tourist Guide Association
Via Ghibellina 110, Florence.
Map 4 D1 (6 E3).
Tel 055 28 84 48.
www.webcom97.com/
centroguide

Ufficio Informazioni Turistiche
Via Cavour 1r, Florence.
Map 2 D4 (6 D1). **Tel** 055 29 08
32. **www**.firenzeturismo.it
Piazza del Campo 56, Siena.
Tel 0577 28 05 51.
Piazza del Duomo, Pisa.
Tel 050 56 04 64.

Walking Tours of Florence
Piazza Santo Stefano 2, Florence.
Tel 055 264 50 33.
www.artviva.com

HORSE-DRAWN CARRIAGES

This is a very pleasant way to spend an hour seeing the historic part of Florence. Carriages carry up to five people and can be hired in Piazza della Signoria and Piazza del Duomo. They can be expensive so try to negotiate a price depending on the duration of the ride. Establish whether the price is per person, or for the whole carriage.

Carriage at the Piazza della Signoria

IMMIGRATION AND CUSTOMS

European Union (EU) residents and visitors from the US, Canada, Australia and New Zealand do not need visas for stays of up to three months. However, all visitors need to bring a valid passport. A visa is needed for stays longer than three months. However, it is advisable to check with the Italian consulate before departure. Vaccination certificates are not necessary.

All visitors to Italy should by law register with the police within three days of arrival. Most hotels will register visitors when they check in. If in doubt, contact a local police department or phone the **Questura.**

Duty-free allowances are as follows: non-EU residents can bring in either 200 cigarettes, 50 cigars, 100 cigarillos or 250 grams of tobacco; 1 litre of spirits and 2 litres of wine; 50 grams of perfume. Goods such as watches and cameras may be imported as long as they are for personal or professional use. EU residents no longer have to declare goods, but random checks are often made to guard against any drugs traffickers.

The refund system for Valued Added Tax (IVA in Italy) for non-EU residents is complicated and slow and is only worth reclaiming if you have spent at least €160 in a single establishment (*see p284*).

SELF-CATERING HOLIDAYS

If you are travelling with a family, self-catering accommodation is usually cheaper than hotels (*see p246*), but be prepared for the odd hiccup, such as a shortage of water.

Italy has retained the small shops culture, so you may have to go to several different shops to get your necessities. Fortunately, even the smallest

Student relaxing in the sun in Gaiole in Chianti

village usually has a grocery store *(alimentari)*. Shops may shut for a couple of hours at lunchtime (*see p284*). Launderettes *(lavanderie)* will offer service washes.

ADDRESSES

Red street number

Blue street number

Florence has a confusing dual address system. Each street has a double set of numbers: a red number indicates a shop, restaurant or business, while a blue or black number refers to a hotel or domestic residence. When writing to a business, insert an "r" after the number to distinguish it from a residential address. Each set of numbers has its own sequence, so business premises at, say, No. 10r may well be next to a residential address at No. 23.

STUDENT INFORMATION

An international student Identity Card (ISIC) or a YIEE (Youth International Educational Exchange Card) will usually get reductions on museum and other charges. For discount air and rail travel, go to the **Centro Turistico Studentesco (CTS).** Discount rail tickets, such as InterRail passes, can be bought at Santa Maria Novella station in Florence or at the CTS.

Villa Europa Camerata youth hostel provides listings of hostels in Tuscany. **Student Point** provides information on housing.

EDUCATIONAL COURSES

There are many language and art schools in Tuscany. **The British Institute** in Florence is one of the better known, as is the **Centro di Cultura per Stranieri dell'Università di Firenze.** The **Istituto per l'Arte e il Restauro** offers courses on art, restoration, upholstery, drawing, ceramics and painting. The **Centro Internazionale Dante Alighieri** or the **Università per Stranieri** in Siena has courses on Italian culture, history and cooking. A list of schools in Tuscany is available from the **Ufficio Promozione Turistica, Turismo Sociale e Sport.**

NEWSPAPERS, TV, RADIO

Most major newspapers, like *La Repubblica* and *La Nazione*, carry regional supplements. European and American newspapers and magazines are also available. *USA Today*, the *International Herald Tribune* and the *Financial Times* are available on the day of issue.

Newspaper stall selling national and international publications

La Nazione with supplement

The state TV channels are RAI Uno, RAI Due and RAI Tre. Satellite and cable TV transmit European channels in many languages, as well as CNN news in English. BBC World Service is broadcast on radio on 15.070 MHz (short wave) in the mornings and 648 KHz (medium wave) at night.

EMBASSIES AND CONSULATES

If you lose your passport or need other help, contact your national embassy or consulate as listed below.

ELECTRICAL ADAPTORS

Electrical current in Italy is 220V AC, with two-pin, round-pronged plugs. It is probably better to buy an adaptor before leaving for Italy. Most hotels with three stars and above have electrical points for shavers and hair-dryers in all bedrooms.

Standard Italian plug

TUSCAN TIME

Tuscany is one hour ahead of Greenwich Mean Time (GMT). The time difference between Tuscany and other cities is as follows: London: -1 hour; New York: -6 hours; Perth: +7 hours; Auckland: +11 hours; Tokyo: +8 hours.

These figures may vary for brief periods in the summer with local changes. For all official purposes the Italians use the 24-hour clock (eg 10pm = 22.00 hrs).

RELIGIOUS SERVICES

The Florence Duomo has a mass in English at 5:30pm every Saturday (*see pp64–5*). See below for other services.

CONVERSION TABLE

Imperial to Metric
1 inch = 2.54 centimetres
1 foot = 30 centimetres
1 mile = 1.6 kilometres
1 ounce = 28 grams
1 pound = 454 grams
1 pint = 0.6 litres
1 gallon = 4.6 litres

Metric to Imperial
1 centimetre = 0.4 inches
1 metre = 3 feet, 3 inches
1 kilometre = 0.6 miles
1 gram = 0.04 ounces
1 kilogram = 2.2 pounds
1 litre = 1.8 pints

DIRECTORY

IMMIGRATION INFORMATION

Questura
Via Zara 2, Florence. **Map** 2 D3. *Tel* 055 497 71.
Via del Castoro, Siena. *Tel* 0577 20 11 11.
Via Lalli 4, Pisa. *Tel* 050 58 35 11.

STUDENT INFORMATION

Centro Turistico Studentesco
Via de' Ginori 25r, Florence. **Map** 2 D4 (6 D1). *Tel* 055 28 95 70.
www.cts.it
Via Bandini 21, Siena. *Tel* 0577 28 50 08.

Student Point
Viale Gramsci 9a, Florence.
Tel 055 24 31 40. @
info@studentpointfirenze.it

Villa Europa Camerata
Viale Augusto Righi 2–4, Florence. *Tel* 055 60 14 51.

EDUCATIONAL COURSES

Centro di Cultura per Stranieri dell'Università di Firenze
Via di Boldrone 2, 05141 Florence.
Tel 055 45 40 16.

Centro Internazionale Dante Alighieri
Via Tommaso Pendola 36, 53100 Siena.
Tel 0577 495 33.

Istituto per l'Arte e il Restauro
Palazzo Spinelli Borgo Santa Croce 10, 50122 Florence. **Map** 4 D1 (6 F4). *Tel* 055 24 60 01.
www.spinelli.it

The British Institute Library
Lungarno Guicciardini 9, 50125 Florence.
Map 3 B1 (5 B3).
Tel 055 267 78 270.
www.britishinstitute.it

Ufficio Promozione Turistica, Turismo Sociale e Sport
Via di Novoli 26, 50127 Florence.
Tel 055 438 21 11.
www.turismo.toscana.it

Università per Stranieri
Piazzetta Grassi 2, 53100 Siena.
Tel 0577 192 60.

EMBASSIES AND CONSULATES

Australia
Via Alessandria 215, Rome. *Tel* 06 85 27 21.
www.italy.embassy.gov.au

New Zealand
Via Zara 28, Rome.
Tel 06 441 71 71.
www.nzembassy.com

UK
Lungarno Corsini 2, Florence. **Map** 3 B1 (5 B3). *Tel* 055 28 41 33.
www.britain.it

US
Lungarno Amerigo Vespucci 38, Florence.
Map 1 A5 (5 A2).
Tel 055 26 69 51.
www.italyemb.it

RELIGIOUS SERVICES

American Episcopal
Via Bernardo Rucellai 9, Florence. **Map** 1 A4.
Tel 055 29 44 17.

Chiesa Evangelica Valdese
Study Centre, Via Manzoni 21, Florence. **Map** 2 D3.
Tel 055 247 78 00.

Church of England
Via Maggio 16, Florence.
Map 3 B2 (5 B5).
Tel 055 29 47 64.

Jewish
Tempio Israelitico, Via Luigi Farini 4, Florence.
Map 2 F5.
Tel 055 24 52 52.

Methodist
Via de' Benci 9, Florence.
Map 4 D2 (6 E4).
Tel 055 28 81 43.

Personal Security and Health

Tuscany and its cities are generally safe as long as a few simple precautions are taken. As in many European cities, pickpockets are a common problem, especially around Florence and Pisa. Take extra care in crowded areas, particularly around popular tourist spots, and on buses. Leave valuables and any important documents in the hotel safe, and carry only the minimum amount of money necessary for the day. Make sure you take out adequate travel insurance before leaving for Italy, as it is very difficult to obtain once you are in the country.

Florentine policewoman helping a tourist with directions

LOOKING AFTER YOUR PROPERTY

Travellers' cheques are the safest way to carry large sums of money. Try to keep your receipts and travellers' cheques separate, together with a photocopy of vital documents, in case of loss.

Be wary of pickpockets, especially around the Duomo and Santa Maria Novella in Florence, and around the Leaning Tower in Pisa. They are mainly children, operating in small groups, usually carrying newspapers or cardboard as a cover for their hands. "Bum bags" or money belts are their favourite target, so try to keep them hidden. Thefts from cars are particularly common. Buses are

notorious for pickpockets. Be aware if someone bumps into you – they may be trying to distract you while somebody else takes your wallet. Buses No. 12/13 to Piazzale Michelangelo in Florence and No. 7 to Fiesole are prime targets, as are the buses to and from Pisa station.

To make an insurance claim you must report the theft to the police within 24 hours and obtain a statement *(denuncia)*.

PERSONAL SAFETY

Although there is a fair amount of petty crime in the cities, such as pickpocketing and car theft, violent crime is rare. The streets are busy until late evening and women travelling alone are rarely harassed, and usually not very persistently. However, try to avoid badly lit areas late at night. Always use the official taxis, with the licence number clearly displayed. When you call for a taxi, make sure you are given the code name of the driver, for example, Napoli 37.

POLICE

The Vigili Urbani, or municipal police, wear blue uniforms in winter and white during the summer. They are most often seen in the streets regulating the traffic. The *carabinieri* are the military police. They dress in red striped trousers and

A team of *carabinieri* in traffic police uniform

deal with a variety of offences from theft to speeding. *La polizia* (the state police) wear blue uniforms, with white belts and berets. They specialize in serious crimes. Any of these should be able to help you.

PERSONAL PRECAUTIONS

Visitors from the European Union (EU) are officially entitled to reciprocal state medical care in Italy. Before you travel, pick up a European Health Insurance Card (EHIC), which covers you for emergency medical treatment.

Municipal policeman

EMERGENCY NUMBERS

Ambulance
Tel 118.

Automobile Club d'Italia
Tel 116. Car accidents and breakdowns. www.aci.it

Fire
Tel 115.

General SOS
Tel 113.

Medical Emergencies
Tel 118.

Police (Carabinieri)
Tel 112.

Traffic Police
Florence *Tel* 055 227 69.
Pisa *Tel* 050 31 39 21.
Siena *Tel* 0577 24 62 11.

You may want to take out additional medical insurance, as the EHIC does not cover repatriation costs or additional expenses, such as accommodation, food and flights for anyone travelling with you. Visitors from outside the EU should take out a comprehensive travel insurance policy which covers against emergency medical treatment.

Inoculations are not necessary for Tuscany, but take mosquito repellent, especially for the rural areas. One effective solution to rid mosquitos is a small electrical machine which burns a tablet on a tiny hotplate. It repels insects for up to 12 hours and is available in grocery stores and small houseware shops. Also, do not underestimate the strength of the sun – drink plenty of water and use a high factor sunscreen. You can drink the water from the taps but most Italians prefer bottled water.

MEDICAL TREATMENT

Outside a Florentine pharmacy with a green cross sign

If you are in need of urgent medical attention, go to the *Pronto Soccorso* (outpatients) department of the nearest main hospital. Patients staying in hospitals are expected to supply their own cutlery, crockery, towels and toilet paper, but not bed linen. The nursing staff will also expect either friends or

A volunteer for the Misericordia dressed in traditional black cassock

relatives to help feed and wash hospital patients.

In Florence and Siena, the **Associazione Volontari Ospedalieri** has interpreters who can help with medical matters. The service is free and available in English, French, German and Spanish. The **Tourist Medical Centre** in Florence has English- and French-speaking doctors, and offers a 24-hour on-call service.

Dentists are expensive in Italy. You can find the nearest one in the yellow pages *(pagine gialle)*, or ask for a recommendation at your hotel.

Pharmacies in Tuscany have a night rota *(servizio notturno)* and a Sunday rota posted on their doors. The **Farmacia Comunale 13** at Florence's Santa Maria Novella station is open 24 hours a day, as is the **Farmacia Molteni** in Via dei Calzaiuoli. Pharmacies do not usually accept prescriptions made in other countries.

The Misericordia *(see p197)*, one of the world's oldest charitable lay institutions, arranges many ambulance services in Tuscany. Most of the staff are volunteers, but there is also a fully qualified medical team. Volunteers do not wear the traditional black cassock when out on a medical emergency.

Ambulance run by the Misericordia, on the streets of Florence

USEFUL INFORMATION

Associazione Volontari Ospedalieri
Florence **Tel** 055 234 45 67.
Siena **Tel** 0577 58 63 62.

Tourist Medical Centre
Via Lorenzo Il Magnifico 59, Florence. **Map** 1 C3.
Tel 055 47 54 11.

Farmacia Comunale 13
Santa Maria Novella station, Florence. **Map** 1 B4 (5 B1).
Tel 055 21 67 61.

Farmacia Molteni
Via dei Calzaiuoli 7r, Florence.
Map 6 D3.
Tel 055 28 94 90.

Florence Hospital
Arcispedale di Santa Maria Nuova. Piazza di Santa Maria Nuova 1.
Map 6 F2.
Tel 055 275 81.

Meyer Children's Hospital
Via Luca Giordano 13.
Map 2 F2. **Tel** 055 566 21.

Siena Hospital
Policlinico Le Scotte, Viale Bracci 16. **Tel** 0577 58 61 11.

Pisa Hospital
Ospedale di Santa Chiara, Via Roma 67. **Tel** 050 99 21 11.

Questura (Police Offices)
Via Zara 2, Florence. **Map** 2 D3.
Tel 055 497 71.
Via del Castoro, Siena.
Tel 0577 20 11 11.
Via Lalli, Pisa.
Tel 050 58 35 11.

Missing Credit Cards
American Express.
Tel 06 722 82.
Diners Club.
Tel 800 86 40 64 (freephone).
VISA.
Tel 800 87 72 32 (freephone).

Missing Travellers' Cheques
American Express.
Tel 800 87 20 00 (freephone).
Thomas Cook.
Tel 800 87 20 50 (freephone).
VISA.
Tel 800 87 41 55 (freephone).

Banking and Local Currency

Visitors to Tuscany have a number of options available to them for changing money. Banks tend to give more favourable rates than bureaux de change, hotels and travel agents, but the paperwork is usually more time consuming. Alternatively, credit cards can be used for purchasing goods. When changing money you will need to show some form of identification, such as a passport. Try to keep a few coins in reserve for telephones, tips and for coin-operated lights which illuminate works of art in churches.

Exchange office at one of the Italian national banks

CHANGING MONEY

Banking hours can be erratic, especially the day before a bank holiday, so bring some euros with you. Exchange rates will vary from place to place, so you may want to shop around. Main post offices exchange currency commission free.

For the best rates, change money at a bank (look for the sign *cambio*). Hotels tend to give poor rates, even if they charge modest commissions. The American Express office *(see p297)* offers good rates.

A convenient way to change money is to use electronic exchange machines. These are found at Florence and Pisa airports, in Florence and Siena, as well as in some smaller towns, such as San Gimignano. There are multilingual instructions and the exchange rate is displayed on the screen. You simply feed in notes of the same foreign currency, and you will get euros back.

CREDIT CARDS

Credit cards are widely accepted throughout Italy, and it is worth bringing one with you. VISA and Access (MasterCard) are the most popular, followed by American Express and Diners Card.

Most banks and cash dispensers in Florence and throughout Tuscany accept VISA or Access cards for cash advances, but be aware that interest is payable as soon as the money is withdrawn.

Some restaurants, cafés or shops may require a minimum expenditure to accept credit card payment. Always make sure you have some cash in case your credit card is not accepted.

TRAVELLERS' CHEQUES

Travellers' cheques are probably the safest way to carry large sums of money. Choose a well-known, reputable name such as Thomas Cook, American Express or cheques issued through a major bank. There is a minimum commission charge, which may make changing small sums of money uneconomical. Some establishments will charge you for each cheque.

You should check the exchange rates before you travel and decide whether sterling, dollar or euro travellers' cheques are more appropriate for your trip.

Bear in mind that it may be more difficult to cash euro travellers' cheques, especially in hotels, because it is not very profitable for the exchanger.

BANKING HOURS

Banks are usually open between 8:30am–1:20pm, Mon–Fri. Most branches also open for an hour in the afternoon from about 2:45pm till 4pm. They close at weekends and for public holidays *(see p37)*, and they also close early the day before a major holiday. Exchange offices stay open longer but in general the rates are less favourable.

In Florence, the exchange office behind the station is open from 8am till late evening, depending on the season. In Pisa, the exchange offices in Piazza del Duomo and at the railway station stay open until the evening and at weekends.

USING BANKS

Changing money at a bank can at times be a frustrating process, as it inevitably involves endless form-filling and queuing. You must apply first at the window displaying the *cambio* sign, then go to the *cassa* to obtain your euros. It is a good idea to take some form of identification with you, such as a passport.

For security reasons, most Italian banks have electronic double doors. Press the button to open the outer door, then wait for it to close behind you. The inner door then opens automatically. Metal objects may set off emergency detectors as you enter.

Entering and leaving a bank through an electronic double door

THE EURO

Twelve countries have replaced their traditional currencies, such as the Italian lire, with the euro. Austria, Belgium, Finland, France, Germany, Greece, Ireland, Italy, Luxembourg, Netherlands, Portugal and Spain chose to join the new currency; the UK, Denmark and Sweden stayed out, with an option to review their situation. The euro was introduced on 1 January 1999, but only for banking purposes. Notes and coins came into circulation on 1 January 2002. A transition period allowed euros and lire to be used simultaneously, and the lire was phased out on 28 February 2002. All euro notes and coins can be used anywhere inside the participating member states.

Banknotes

Euro banknotes have seven denominations. The 5-euro note (grey in colour) is the smallest, followed by the 10-euro note (pink), 20-euro note (blue), 50-euro note (orange), 100-euro note (green), 200-euro note (yellow) and 500-euro note (purple). All notes show the stars of the European Union.

5 euros

10 euros

20 euros

50 euros

100 euros

200 euros

500 euros

2 euros

1 euro

50 cents

20 cents

10 cents

Coins

The euro has eight coin denominations: 1 euro and 2 euros, 50 cents, 20 cents, 10 cents, 5 cents, 2 cents and 1 cent. The 2- and 1-euro coins are both silver and gold in colour. The 50-, 20- and 10-cent coins are gold. The 5-, 2- and 1-cent coins are bronze.

5 cents

2 cents

1 cent

Using Tuscany's Telephones

There are plenty of public phones throughout Tuscany but telephoning, especially abroad, can at times be frustrating. Do not be surprised if you get a crossed line or if you get cut off in mid-conversation. There are phone kiosks on the streets of all main towns, and public phones can also be found in bars, tobacconists and post offices.

Telephone company logo

PUBLIC TELEPHONES

The growing use of mobile phones in Italy has caused a cutback in certain public telephone services. Florence has a single telephone office *(Telefono)* centre run by Telecom Italia at via Cavour 21/r. Here you can buy phonecards from a machine and use the directories covering the whole of Italy. The centre is open daily until 11pm, and there is no attendant on duty. Similar services are at Pisa train station, open until 9:45pm, and at Pisa airport. The Telecom Italia office in Siena is at Via dei Termini 40. Telecom Italia phone boxes can still be

Telephone sign

found in train stations, airports, and in restaurants and bars displaying a telephone sign.

There are several privately operated phone centres offering economical rates, especially around Florence's train station. These centres also sell international phonecards that can be used with any telephone. Faxes can be sent from post offices, copy centres and Internet points.

CALL CHARGES

Calls within Italy are cheapest between 10pm and 8am from Monday to Saturday and all day Sunday. They are also cheap between 6:30pm and 10pm weekdays and after

1pm on Saturdays. Calls within Europe are cheapest between 10pm and 8am and all day Sunday. Calls to Canada and the US are cheapest from 11pm to 8am weekdays, and 11pm to 2pm at weekends. For Australia, call between 11pm and 8am Monday to Saturday and all day Sunday.

Hotels will charge a higher rate to call from your room. Also, calls from Italy cost more than the equivalent call from the US or the UK.

E-MAIL

Access to e-mail and the Internet is very convenient in Florence. Some hotels allow guests to check their e-mails at the front desk, while others offer in-room modem connections. Privately run Internet points can be found in the most popular areas of

USING A TELECOM ITALIA CARD TELEPHONE

3 The display shows how much credit is left.

1 Lift the receiver and wait for the dialling tone.

4 Dial the number and wait to be connected.

2 Insert a phonecard in the slot.

5 If you still have credit and want to make a second call, press the "follow-on call" button.

To use a card, break off the marked corner and insert, arrow first.

Florence. These offer particularly good deals for tourists, selling Internet time in 15- and 30-minute segments. The most widely established of these services is **Internet Train**, which has 13 centres operating in Florence. Internet Train issues a magnetic card on which clients place credit and which can be used in any Internet Train centre in any of the 22 Italian cities in which the company is located.

Internet Train
Santa Maria Novella station, Piazza Stazione 14/38, Florence.
Map 1 B5 (5 B1). *Tel 055 239 97 20.*
www.internettrain.it

USING PUBLIC TELEPHONES

You can make long-distance and international calls from Telecom Italia telephones. When making long-distance calls, have plenty of change ready. If you don't put enough coins in to start with, the telephone disconnects you and retains your money. Coin-operated telephones are being phased out and replaced with phones that take pre-paid phonecards *(carta or scheda*

REACHING THE RIGHT NUMBER

- Dialling codes are: Florence 055; Siena 0577; Pisa 050; Viareggio 0584; Arezzo 0575; Lucca 0583; and Pistoia 0573.
- For international directory enquiries, dial 4176 followed by 187 upon reply.
- International operator assistance is on 170. You can place reverse charge
- and credit card calls on this number.
- For direct access to operators in other countries, dial: 800 172 440 (UK); 800 172 444 (AT&T, US); 800 172 401 (MCI, US); 800 172 405 (US Sprint); 800 172 213 (Canada); 800 172 610 (Telstra, Australia); 800 172 611 (Optus, Australia); 800 172 641 (New Zealand).
- *See also* Emergency Numbers, *p300.*

telefonica). You can buy these from bars, newsagents and tobacconists displaying the black-and-white T sign.

Some older-style phones in remote villages only accept tokens *(gettoni)*, which are now being withdrawn from circulation. Find a metered phone for long-distance calls; ask a bar owner if you can use the phone and the meter will be set. You pay when you have finished your call.

When dialling local numbers always remember to include the area code, such as 055 for Florence or 050 for Pisa.

Telephone cards and stamps are available from here

Sending Letters

Letters can be sent either by ordinary post or by priority mail. The ordinary post is the most economical, with a fixed rate for letters sent within Italy and the rest of Europe. Postcards inside a regular stamped envelope arrive faster than a stamped postcard. Given the delays of regular service, *poste priorità*, priority mail, is now the preferred way to send mail. Priority mail requires a special stamp and a sticker and should be placed in the blue collection boxes, or in traditional red boxes marked *poste priorità*. You can buy stamps *(francobolli)* and stickers from

Post Office sign

any tobacconist with the black-and-white T sign and from post offices. Sub-post office hours are usually 8:30am – 2pm Mon–Fri and 8:30am– noon on Saturday and the last day of the month. Main offices stay open until early evening.

SENDING PARCELS

Certain rules must be adhered to when sending parcels. The package must be placed in a rigid box, wrapped in brown paper and bound with string and a lead seal. You may also need to fill in a simple customs declaration form. Often a stationery or gift shop in the major towns will, for a fee, wrap your package. Very few post offices offer this service. Parcels sent inter-

nationally arrive most quickly if mailed via *postacelere*, available at most major post offices.

POSTE RESTANTE

Letters and parcels should be sent care of (c/o) Fermo Posta, Ufficio Postale Principale, then the name of the town in which you wish to pick them up. Print the surname clearly in block capitals and underline it to make sure the letters are filed correctly. To collect your post you need to show some form of identity (such as a passport) and pay a small fee.

MAIN POST OFFICES

Pellicceria 3, Florence. **Map** 6 D3.
Tel 055 273 61.

Piazza Matteotti 37, Siena.
Tel 0577 20 22 73.

Piazza Vittorio Emanuele II, Pisa.
Tel 050 450 80.

City letters   Other destinations

Italian post box

TRAVEL INFORMATION

Tuscany is most easily reached by air, but although planes arrive from European airports, there are no direct intercontinental flights, and visitors from outside Europe have to transfer. The nearest intercontinental airports are Milan and Rome. Tuscany's main airport is in Pisa; it receives both domestic and European flights as well as most charter traffic. Florence's airport is smaller and is located slightly north

Alitalia aircraft

of the city, a short bus ride away from the centre. Almost exclusively, it deals with scheduled flights. Florence is also the main arrival point for the far-reaching European train and coach network, and Pisa has good international rail connections. However, overland travel to Tuscany is much slower than flying, and the savings on cost are negligible. It is only worthwhile if you have particular reasons for doing so.

The main entrance hall at Pisa airport

ARRIVING BY AIR

Daily flights between London and Pisa are operated by **Alitalia, British Airways** and low-cost airline **Ryanair** (from Stansted). Pisa also serves Florence from Munich and Frankfurt.

There are no direct intercontinental flights to Pisa or Florence, but it is easy to fly direct to Rome or Milan and connect to these cities from there. Alitalia has good connections from Los Angeles, Chicago, Vancouver, and Sydney and many other airlines can offer good worldwide connections via Rome and other European capitals. Transfers to Pisa and Florence from Milan and Rome can also easily be made by road or rail.

Italian airline **Meridiana** serves Florence with direct flights from Amsterdam, Barcelona, Paris and London Gatwick, and has a wide

range of domestic flights to Pisa and Florence from points all over Italy.

Generally speaking, the further you are able to book your ticket in advance, the lower will be the available fare. However, many of the best fares are non-refundable so it is vital to take out the necessary travel insurance at or before the time of booking. Also, remember that the lowest fares are often only

The train station at Pisa's Galileo Galilei airport

made available on the Internet, so check the airlines' websites.

The Italian travel agency **CIT Viaggi** has offices worldwide; to book or change flights during your stay in Tuscany, try their local office or the **American Express** office in Florence.

USEFUL NUMBERS

Alitalia
National Flights
📞 *8488 65 641.*
International Flights
📞 *8488 65 642.*
Information
📞 *8488 65 643.*
www.alitalia.it

British Airways
Tel 199 71 22 66.
www.britishairways.com

Meridiana
Tel 0552 30 23 34.
www.meridiana.it

Ryanair
Tel 050 50 37 70.
www.ryanair.com

CIT Viaggi
Florence *Tel 055 28 41 45.*
London *Tel 020 8686 0677.*
Sydney *Tel (2) 267 12 55.*

American Express
Via Dante Alighieri 22r,
Florence *Tel 055 509 81.*

Airport Information
Florence *Tel 055 31 58 74.*
www.aeroporto.firenze.it
Pisa *Tel 050 84 93 00.*
www.pisa-airport.com

PACKAGE HOLIDAYS

Package holidays are almostalways cheaper than travelling independently, unless you are travelling on a very tight budget and prefer camping and youth hostels. Florence is often offered as part of a two- or three-centre holiday with Rome and Venice, or with a stay in the Tuscan countryside. Different tour operators may use the same hotels in Florence, so it is worth looking around for the best deal. Transfer from the airport on arrival is usually included in the holiday price, and saves both money and effort.

PISA AIRPORT

Sign to the trains at Pisa airport

Trains run directly from Pisa's Galileo Galilei airport to Florence's Santa Maria Novella station. To reach the trains, turn left as you leave the airport arrivals hall. Train tickets can be bought from the information kiosk at the airport. The journey to Florence takes an hour and the service runs once an hour, but is less regular or frequent in the early morning and evening. There is also an infrequent train serving Lucca and Montecatini.

The through train to Florence stops at Pisa Centrale, and Empoli, where you can change on to

Trolley attendant at Pisa airport

the local line that serves Siena.

The No. 3 bus runs from Pisa airport to the town centre. Buy tickets before you get on the bus from the airport information kiosk. There is also a taxi rank at the front of the airport.

There are baggage trolleys at the airport, but you must have cash ready to hand over to the attendant. Buy some euros before landing, as there are no money-changing facilities in the baggage-reclaim hall.

FLORENCE AIRPORT

Florence's Amerigo Vespucci airport, often known as Peretola, is very small. The "Vola in Bus" goes to and from the airport every 30 minutes between 6am and 8pm and hourly between 9pm and 11pm. The bus to the city centre leaves from the front of the airport building, while the bus to the airport

departs from the SITA station (Via di Santa Caterina da Siena 15r). The evening buses (from 9pm) leave from Piazza dell'Unità. The journey takes 20 minutes. Tickets may be purchased from the driver.

Only take a taxi from the official rank. They will charge a supplement for coming from the airport plus a supplement for the luggage. There is also an extra charge on Sundays and holidays. Most drivers are honest, but check that the meter is switched on and showing the minimum fare before you begin your journey.

CAR RENTAL

All the major car rental firms have rental offices at both airports. However, it is wise to make rental arrangements before your departure (see p314), as it will cost you far less than renting after you arrive in Italy.

Leaving Pisa airport by car, it is straightforward to get on to the dual carriageway linking Pisa and Florence. At Florence airport, it might be easier to take public transport into the centre and pick up your car there (see p315).

AIRPORT CAR RENTAL

Avis
Florence Airport **Tel** 055 31 55 88.
Pisa Airport **Tel** 050 420 28.

Hertz
Florence Airport **Tel** 055 30 73 70.
Pisa Airport **Tel** 050 432 20.

Maggiore
Florence Airport **Tel** 055 31 12 56.
Pisa Airport **Tel** 050 425 74.

Florence's Amerigo Vespucci airport, which has only recently started accepting international flights

Travelling by Train

Travelling overland can be a very pleasurable way of getting to and travelling around Tuscany. Italy's state railway (Ferrovie dello Stato, or FS) has a train for every type of journey, from the quaintly, maddeningly slow *locali* (stopping trains) through various levels of rapid intercity service to the luxurious, superfast Eurostar, which rushes between Italian cities at a speed to match its ticket price. The network between large cities is very good, but journeys to towns on branch lines may be quicker by coach (bus) *(see p311)*.

An FS train at Florence station

ARRIVING BY TRAIN

Florence and Pisa are the main arrival points for trains from Europe. The Galilei from Paris and the Italia Express from Frankfurt travel direct to Florence. Passengers from London have to change in Paris or Lille.

From Florence, there is also a direct train link with Pisa's Galileo Galilei airport, which can be very useful.

Europe-wide train passes, such as EurRail (US) or InterRail for those under 26 (Europe), are accepted on the FS network. You may have to pay a supplement, however, to travel on fast trains. Always check first before using any private rail lines.

Eurostar high-speed train

TRAIN TRAVEL IN ITALY

Trains from all over Italy arrive at and depart from Pisa Centrale and Florence's Santa Maria Novella station *(see p310)*. Eurostars (Italy's high-speed trains) also use Santa Maria Novella.

If you are planning to travel around the country, the Trenitalia pass is valid from four to ten consecutive or non-consecutive days in a two-month period for unlimited travel on Italian trains. There are discounts for young people and groups of two to five people. Available only

to non-residents, the pass can be purchased from the train station.

There are facilities for disabled travellers on some intercity services *(see p297)*. Assistance can be arranged by calling the railway's call centre (89 20 21) in advance.

BOOKING AND RESERVATIONS

Booking is obligatory on the Eurostar and on some other intercity services, indicated on the timetable by a black R on a white background. The booking office is at the front of Florence station. Alternatively you can book on the FS website (www.trenitalia.com). Users must first register on the site, then follow the instructions on how to book and pay for seats. Tickets booked online can be delivered by courier for an additional charge, or picked up for free at a self-service ticket machine in stations offering this service. Do not forget to bring the booking code (PNR) you receive via e-mail after completing the transaction

online. Travel agents can book your railway tickets free of charge.

Booking is advisable if you wish to travel at busy times: during the high season or at weekends. Buying your intercity ticket at least five hours before travelling entitles you to a free seat reservation. For a small fee, you can reserve a seat on any train, except local trains.

BOOKING AGENTS

CIT Viaggi
Piazza della Stazione 51r, Florence.
Map 1 B5 (5 B1).
Tel 055 28 41 45.

Palio Viaggi
Piazza Gramsci, Siena.
Tel 0577 28 08 28.

TICKETS

Always buy a ticket before you travel. You can also purchase your ticket on the train, but you will be

Ticket machines at Florence's Santa Maria Novella station

charged the price of a full-fare ticket, plus a 25 fine. You can upgrade to first class or sleeper by paying the conductor.

If the ticket office is busy, try one of the self-service ticket machines found at most stations. They accept coins, notes and credit cards. The instructions are easy to follow and come in six European languages.

If you are travelling no more than 200 km (124 miles) within the region, you can buy a short-range ticket *(biglietto a fasce chilometriche)* from a station newsstand. The name of your station of departure will usually be stamped on the ticket, but if it is not, write it on the back. You must then validate the ticket by stamping it in one of the gold-coloured machines situated at the entrance to most platforms. These machines must also be used to timestamp the return portion of a ticket.

Both the outward and return portions of a return (round-trip) ticket must be used within three days of purchase. Singles (one-way tickets) are issued in 200-km (124-mile) bands and are valid according to band: for example, a ticket for 200 km lasts for a day, a ticket for 400 km (248 miles) lasts for two days, and so on.

All intercity trains charge a supplementary fee *(supplemento)* even if you have an InterRail card. This includes the Eurostar and Eurocity services. The cost depends on how far you are travelling.

Stamp ticket here

Machine for validating tickets

MACHINES FOR FS RAIL TICKETS

These machines are easy to use, and most have instructions on screen in a choice of six languages. They accept coins, notes and credit cards.

1 Select your destination.

2 The price is shown on the display.

3 Insert coins, notes, or an American Express, VISA or Diners Club card.

4 Take your ticket and change.

5 You must insert your ticket here to validate it for your journey.

ITALY'S PRINCIPAL FS NETWORK

KEY

● Main stations

O Other stations

— Principal rail route

-- Route over water

The Italian State Rail Network operates seven types of service. Study a timetable before buying your ticket and choose a service to suit both your pocket and agenda.

SANTA MARIA NOVELLA STATION, FLORENCE

Santa Maria Novella station is Florence's central railway station. The station is always busy; however, like most major termini, it can attract some unsavoury characters and it is not a place where one would want to linger. There is a taxi rank at the front, and local buses *(see p312)* depart from the sides of the station.

During the summer months, long queues often form at the station's main ticket office, so it is worth tackling the self-service ticket machines *(see p309)* or booking a ticket through a travel agent.

The left-luggage office *(deposito bagagli)* is on platform 16, as is the *Polfer*, the railway police.

For timetable information, you will need to queue at the staffed information booths. Take a ticket and wait for your number to be shown. There are usually some staff available who can speak English and French. Alternatively, you can consult the electronic timetable on the automated ticket machines, or the train company's user-friendly website (www.trenitalia.com).

Other facilities in the foyer of Santa Maria Novella include a 24-hour pharmacy, an office with a hotel-booking service, and stalls selling international magazines, newspapers and city bus tickets. The international telephone office is near platform 5. A bank and a bureau de change are also inside the

View of Santa Maria Novella railway station, Florence

station. There is a tourist information office located in Piazza della Stazione 4, across the street.

Entrance to Santa Maria Novella station, with departure board

SIENA STATION

Situated outside the city walls on Piazzale Carlo Roselli, Siena station is quite small and is about a 20-minute walk from the centre. Any bus from opposite the station goes to the city centre.

Train information is available at the ticket office and there are also automatic help points with information available in English, French

and German. Other facilities include a left luggage office, a snack bar and a newspaper stand. In addition to services leaving from the city centre, the TRA-IN bus company runs coaches to Montepulciano, Montalcino and Buonconvento. These depart from the front of the station. Tickets must be bought from the bus ticket window or self-service machines in the station foyer before you board.

PISA CENTRALE

Pisa's central station is quite large, with most facilities situated either in the foyer or on platform 1: a restaurant and bar, newspaper kiosks which sell bus tickets and telephone cards, and several self-service information and ticket machines.

An exchange booth, open until 7pm, is on the left of the foyer, along with the train information and booking office. The international telephone office, which is open until 9:45pm, is on the right. The left luggage office and the *Polfer* (railway police) are on platform 1.

Tourist information is at the front of the station, near the Banca Nazionale del Lavoro. Most local buses, including that for the Campo dei Miracoli *(see pp158–9)* and that for the airport, stop in front of the station. A bus information and ticket office are close to the bus stops, on your right as you leave the station. There is also a machine selling tickets.

There is another station at Pisa airport *(see p307)*.

Concourse of Santa Maria Novella station

Travelling by Coach (Bus)

Lazzi coach, for travel all over Italy

Florence is linked by coach (bus) to most major European cities and local companies operate an extensive network of services within Tuscany. Coaches are quicker where there is no direct train link, particularly in the countryside. Although the train is faster for long journeys, the coach may be cheaper. To plan trips by coach, maps and timetables are available from all the coach companies' offices, which are usually situated near city railway stations.

ARRIVING BY COACH (BUS)

Santa Maria Novella railway station in Florence is Tuscany's main arrival and departure point for all long-distance coach (bus) journeys, and the hub of the extensive local coach network. The **Lazzi** company runs coach links with major European cities from Florence and sells tickets for Eurolines coaches (buses). Book tickets at their office by Santa Maria Novella station. Express services to Rome are run by Lazzi from Florence and **TRA-IN** from Siena.

FLORENCE

Florence has four main coach (bus) companies. **Lazzi** serves the region north and west of Florence and **SITA** serves the southern and eastern region. The **COPIT** bus company connects the city with the Abetone/Pistoia region and **CAP** links it to the Mugello area north of the city. All these have ticket and information offices near Santa Maria Novella railway station.

SIENA

Siena's main bus and coach company is TRA-IN, which runs urban, local and regional services. Local services leave from Piazza Antonio Gramsci and regional buses from Piazza San Domenico. There is an information/ticket office in both squares. TRA-IN runs buses to most of Tuscany, including a direct coach to Rome twice daily.

Lazzi office in Florence

PISA

The city bus company **CPT** also serves the surrounding area, including the towns of Volterra, Livorno, San Miniato and Pontedera. These buses leave from Piazza Sant'Antonio. **Lazzi** runs a service to Viareggio, Lucca and Florence from Pisa, departing from Piazza Vittorio Emanuele II, which has a Lazzi ticket office.

DIRECTORY

FLORENCE

CAP & COPIT of Florence
Largo Fratelli Alinari 9. **Map** 1 C4 (5 B1). *Tel 055 21 46 37.*
www.capautolinee.it

COPIT of Pistoia
Piazza San Francesco.
Tel 0573 36 30.

Lazzi
Piazza della Stazione. **Map** 1 B5 (5 B2). *Tel 055 21 51 55 (all services).* **www**.lazzi.it

SITA
Via di Santa Caterina da Siena 15r. **Map** 1 B5 (5 A1). *Tel 800 37 37 60 (Tuscany); 055 29 49 55 (national).* **www**.sita-on-line.it

SIENA

TRA-IN
Piazza Antonio Gramsci.
Tel 0577 20 42 46 (local).
Piazza San Domenico.
Tel 0577 20 42 45 (regional).

PISA

CPT
Piazza Sant'Antonio 1.
Tel 050 50 55 11.

Lazzi
Piazza Vittorio Emanuele II.
Tel 050 462 88. **www**.lazzi.it

A Florence coach (bus) line

SITA coach arriving at the station in Florence

Getting Around on Foot and by Bus

Pedestrian zone sign

Tuscan cities are compact enough to get around reasonably comfortably on foot, and the city buses are relatively cheap, regular and wide-ranging. A one-way ticket takes you 15 km (10 miles) out of town, making the bus ideal for trips from the city centre to outlying areas of Florence, Pisa or Siena. The buses get very hot in the summer and are popular with pickpockets (especially Florence's No. 7 bus), so take care when they're crowded.

WALKING

Sightseeing on foot in Tuscan cities is made all the more pleasurable by the fact that there are plenty of squares in which to rest and watch the world go by, or cool churches to pop into when the heat gets too much. Moreover, there are limited-traffic zones in the centre of most towns, which makes life slightly easier for pedestrians.

Signs for sights and landmarks are usually quite clear, especially those in Siena. In Florence it is easy to pick out the Duomo and the river and orientate yourself in relation to them. A gentle stroll around the main sights of Florence can take just a couple of hours. The Duomo, Santa Maria Novella, Ponte Vecchio and the Accademia are all within ten minutes' walk of each other. The main sights in Pisa are all in the same square. Siena is also compact but hilly, so be sure to wear comfortable shoes.

The cities can, however, be unbearably hot in summer. Plan your day so that you are inside for the hottest part. Recuperate Italian-style with a

Stay on the pavement at all costs

It is marginally less dangerous to cross

leisurely lunch followed by a siesta. Shopping is more pleasant in the early evening when it is cooler, and the streets start to come alive.

CROSSING ROADS

Use the *sottopassaggio* (underpass) wherever possible. The busiest roads also have signals to help you cross: the green *avanti* sign gives you right of way, in theory, but *never* expect drivers to recognize this as a matter of course. Seize your opportunity and walk out slowly and confidently, glaring at the traffic and maintaining a determined pace: the traffic should stop, or at least swerve. Take extra care at night: traffic lights are switched to flashing amber and crossings become free-for-alls.

CITY BUSES

Florence's city bus company is called **ATAF**, Pisa's is **CPT**, and Siena's **TRA-IN**. All the buses are bright orange. Most lines run until at least 9:30pm, with the most popular running until midnight or 1am in Florence.

In Pisa and Florence, buses run near all the main sights. Among the most useful Florentine routes for visitors are the No. 12 and No. 13, which make hour-long clockwise/anticlockwise circuits of the city, the No. 7 to Fiesole, and the new "eco-routes" A, B, C and D which are electric or eco-diesel fuelled minibuses.

Bus stop displaying the route

One of Florence's ATAF buses, heading back to depot

USING LOCAL SERVICES

Florence does not have a main terminus, but most buses can be picked up alongside Santa Maria Novella station. In Pisa, most buses stop at the railway station and Piazza Vittorio Emanuele II; in Siena, at Piazza Antonio Gramsci and Piazza San Domenico. There are bus information kiosks at all these points, but they are not always open. Tourist information offices can usually help.

Enter the bus at the front or back and get off through the middle doors. The four low seats at the front of the bus are meant for the elderly, the disabled and people with children. Fare dodging is common, but so are inspectors. The fine is at least 40 times the cost of a ticket. To validate a ticket, feed it through a ticket machine on the bus.

BUS TICKETS

Tickets for city buses must be bought before you get on, from newsstands, bars displaying the bus company sign (ATAF, APT, TRA-IN) or tobacconists, or at the bus termini. If you are likely to make a few trips, buy several tickets at once; they become valid when you timestamp them

Signposting for pedestrian routes to sights in Florence

in the machine at the front or rear of the bus. There are also ticket vending machines in the streets, but they are often out of order.

Ticket prices and validity vary from town to town. You can usually buy a ticket valid for one, two or sometimes four hours' unlimited travel. The time limit starts when you stamp your ticket on the first bus. You can also buy daily passes, or a ticket for *quattro corsi*, valid for four trips. You must stamp the ticket for each of the four trips. A *quattro corsi* is slightly cheaper than the same number of single tickets. You just stamp it as and when needed until you have made the permitted number of trips.

LONG-TERM PASSES

If you are staying for a long time in one town, a pass for unlimited travel is a good idea. Anyone can buy a regular monthly pass (*abbonamento mensile ordinario*), but for student rates, you will need a photocard. In Florence, these are available for a small fee from the **ATAF Ufficio Abbonamenti**; in Siena, from the **TRA-IN** office in Piazza San Domenico. Monthly passes can be bought wherever bus tickets are on sale.

In Florence, the best bus ticket is the *plurigiornale*, available from the ATAF office, bars, tobacconists and newsstands. These are valid for 2, 3 or 7 days. The ATAF

Main bus stop at Florence's Santa Maria Novella station

also sells an *abbonamento plurigiornaliero*, valid for between 2–25 days. These are non-transferable.

You can also buy a *carta arancio*, valid for 7 days on trains and bus lines within the province of Florence. You can buy it from any train, coach or bus company ticket office.

USEFUL ADDRESSES

ATAF
Ufficio Informazioni & Abbonamenti, Piazza della Stazione, Florence. **Map** 1 B5 (5 B1). **Tel** *800 424 500.* www.ataf.net

CPT
Ufficio Informazioni, Piazza Sant'Antonio 1, Pisa. **Tel** *050 505 511.* www.cpt.pisa.it

TRA-IN
Piazza Antonio Gramsci, Siena. **Tel** *0577 20 42 46.*

Ticket inserted here

Stamping machine

Ticket valid for 4 rides of 1 hour

Ticket valid for 1 hour

Ticket valid for 3 days

Validating Tickets
Bus tickets are bought in advance and only become valid when stamped in special machines on the bus.

TAXIS IN TUSCANY

Official taxis are white in Tuscan cities, with a "Taxi" sign on the roof. Only take taxis at official ranks, not offers from touts at the stations. There are supplements for baggage, for rides between 10pm and 7am, on Sundays and on public holidays, and for journeys to and from the airport. If you phone for a taxi, the meter starts to run from the moment you book the taxi; by the time it arrives there could already be several euros clocked up. Generally, travelling by taxi is costly. Taxi drivers are usually honest, but make sure you know what any supplements are for. Italians give very small tips or nothing at all, but 10 per cent is expected from visitors.

In Florence, there are ranks at Via Pellicceria, Piazza di Santa Maria Novella and Piazza di San Marco. In Siena, taxis can be found in Piazza Matteotti and Piazza della Stazione, and in Pisa at the Piazza del Duomo, Piazza Garibaldi and Piazza della Stazione.

BOOKING NUMBERS

Florence Radiotaxi
Tel *055 47 98* or *055 42 42* or *055 43 90.*

Siena Radiotaxi
Tel *0577 492 22.*

Pisa Radiotaxi
Tel *050 54 16 00.*

Taxi waiting for a fare at an official rank in Florence

Motoring in Florence and Tuscany

The classic Fiat 500

A motoring tour through Tuscany makes a memorable holiday, if you are prepared for high fuel costs and erratic Italian driving. But if you are staying in Siena or Florence, with no plans to travel around, there is little point in having a car: both cities are small enough to walk around and parking can be difficult and expensive. If you are staying in the countryside and visiting towns by car, it is best to park on the outskirts and walk or take a bus into the centre.

ARRIVING BY CAR

Drivers from Britain need a Green Card for insurance purposes and the vehicle's registration document. EU nationals who intend to stay for more than six months and do not have the standard pink licence will need an Italian translation of their licence, available from most motoring organizations and Italian tourist offices.

The **ACI (Automobile Club d'Italia)** provides excellent maps and invaluable help. It will tow anyone free, and offers free repairs to members of affiliated associations, such as the AA or RAC in Britain, the ADAC in Germany, the AIT in France, the RACE in Spain and ANWB in Holland. SOS columns on motorways allow instant, round-the-clock access to the emergency services.

CAR RENTAL

Car rental in Italy is expensive and, ideally, should be organized through a tour operator before leaving for Tuscany. Cars can be pre-booked through any rental firm with branches in Italy. If you rent a car when in Tuscany, a local firm such as **Maggiore** may be cheaper. Book in advance, especially for weekend outings.

To rent a car you must be over 21, and have held a licence for at least a year. Visitors from outside the EU need an international licence. Make sure the rental package includes collision damage waiver, breakdown service and insurance against theft.

Getting around Florence by scooter

BIKE AND MOPED RENTAL

A day spent cycling in the countryside can be a healthy and relaxing pastime, and a moped or scooter helps

Rules of the Road

Drive on the right and, generally, give way to the right. Seat belts are compulsory in the front and back, and children should be properly restrained. You must also carry a warning triangle in case of breakdown. In town centres, the speed limit is 50 km/h (30 mph); on ordinary roads 90 km/h (55 mph); and on motorways 110 km/h (70 mph) for cars up to 1099cc, and 130 km/h (80 mph) for more powerful cars. Penalties for speeding include spot fines and licence points, and there are drink-driving laws as elsewhere in the EU.

One-way street

make swifter work of the Tuscan hills.

Bicycles can be rented for around €3 per hour; moped prices start at about €25 per day. Helmets are mandatory on mopeds.

DRIVING IN TOWN

City centres are usually fraught with one-way systems, limited traffic zones and erratic drivers, and are only recommended to the confident driver. In Lucca, Siena and San Gimignano, only residents and taxis may drive inside the city walls. Visitors may go in to unload at their hotel but must then park outside the walls.

Pisa has limited traffic zones around the Arno, and the rule for tourists unloading also applies in Florence, with its *zona traffico limitato* or *zona blu*, which covers most of the centre. There is a pedestrian zone around the Duomo, although pedestrians here should be prepared, nevertheless, to step aside for taxis, mopeds and bicycles. The latter two often do not comply with traffic light instructions.

Speed limit (on minor road)

End of speed restriction

Pedestrianized street – no traffic

Give way to oncoming traffic

320 m

Give way 320 m (350 yd) ahead

Danger (often with description)

Automatic tollbooths on the motorway outside Florence

PARKING

Street parking in the centre of Florence is closed to non-residents, and visitors must park in designated areas. These are marked by blue lines, usually with a meter or an attendant nearby. For metered parking, insert the amount of money necessary for the time you need, and leave the receipt visible on your dashboard. Many metered parking areas have two-hour limits.

There are three large underground car parks in Florence: at Santa Maria Novella station; at the Parterre, northeast of Piazza della Libertà; and below the Central Market. These car parks are open 24 hours a day, but rates can be exorbitant. The car park in Piazza della Calza offers good rates for long-term parking. Some hotels offer their own parking or have agreements for reduced rates with private garages.

In Tuscany, one day a week is set aside for street cleaning, when parking is forbidden. This is indicated by signs saying *zona rimozione* with the day and time. Beware of residents-only parking areas, marked *riservato ai residenti*.

If you park illegally, your car could be towed away. If this happens, phone the **Vigili**, the municipal police, to find out where it has been taken.

DRIVING IN THE COUNTRYSIDE

Driving on the quiet Tuscan country roads can be a pleasure. However, distances can be deceptive. What may look like a short trip on the map, could take much longer because of winding roads. Some back roads may not be surfaced, so beware of punctures. You may also find driving at night disorientating as roads and signs are generally poorly lit.

TOLLS AND FUEL

Tolls operate on all motorways, although there are some free dual carriageways. Tollbooths take cash or pre-paid magnetic "swipe" cards called Viacards, available from tobacconists and ACI.

Motorway service stations occur at irregular intervals, and there are fewer fuel stations in the countryside than in the cities. Hardly any outside the cities take credit cards. Many close at noon and reopen about 3:30pm until about 7:30pm; few open on Sundays. Many in the countryside close in August.

At fuel stations with self-service pumps, put notes or credit cards in the machine. Lead-free fuel is *senza piombo*.

Official parking area patrolled by attendant

DIRECTORY

CITY CAR RENTAL

Avis
Borgo Ognissanti 128r, Florence.
Map 1 A5 (5 A2).
Tel 055 21 36 29.
c/o de Martino Autonoleggi,
Via Simone Martini 36, Siena.
Tel 0577 27 03 05.

Hertz
Via Maso Finiguerra 33r, Florence.
Map 1 B5 (5 A2).
Tel 055 239 82 05.

Maggiore
Via Maso Finiguerra 31r, Florence.
Map 1 B5 (5 A2).
Tel 055 21 02 38.

CYCLE AND MOPED RENTAL

Florence by Bike
Via San Zanobi 91r.
Map 1 C4. *Tel 055 48 89 92.*
www.florencebybike.com

Happy Rent
Bargo Ognissanti 153r.
Map 1 A5. *Tel 055 239 96 96.*
www.happyrent.com

DF Bike
Via Massetana Romana 54, Siena.
Tel 0577 27 19 05.

DF Moto
Via dei Gazzani 16, Siena.
Tel 0577 28 83 87.

BREAKDOWN

Automobile Club d'Italia
Viale G. Amendola 36, Florence.
Map 4 F1. *Tel 055 248 61.*
Via Cisanello 168, Pisa.
Tel 050 95 01 11.
Viale Vittorio Veneto 47, Siena.
Tel 0577 490 01.

Emergencies *Tel 116.*

TOWING AWAY

Vigili (Municipal Police)
Florence *Tel 055 78 38 82.*
Pisa *Tel 050 91 03 78.*
Siena *Tel 0577 29 25 58.*

24-HOUR FUEL STATIONS, FLORENCE

AGIP
Viale dei Mille. **Map** 2 F2.
Tel 055 58 70 91.
Via Senese. **Map** 3 A5.
Tel 055 204 97 85.

General Index

Page numbers in **bold** type refer to
main entries

A

AB&BA 246
Abbadia di San Salvatore 37
Abbazia di San Rabano 237
Abetone 293
Accademia delle Arte del Disegno
(Florence) 98
Accademia di Belle Arti (Florence)
92, 135
Accademia del Cimento (Florence)
74
Addresses 298
Admission charges 296
Adoration of the Magi (Botticelli)
51, 83
AGIP 315
Agriturist Ufficio Regionale 246
Air travel **306–7**
Airports
  Amerigo Vespucci (Florence) 307
  Galileo Galilei (Pisa) 21, 153,
  306, 307
Albany, Countess of 136
Alberese 35
Alberti, Leon Battista
  Palazzo Rucellai (Florence) 104,
  226
  San Pancrazio (Florence) 104
  Santa Maria Novella (Florence)
  110, 135
Alberti family 74
Aldobrandesca family 238
Alessi (Florence) 288
Alfano, Franco 179
Alfieri, Vittorio 136
Alimentari (Florence) 283
Alinari brothers 104
Aline (Florence) 288
Alitalia 306
Alpi Apuane (Apuan Alps) 169, 174
Amati 95
Ambulances 300, 301
American Agency 246
American Episcopal Church 299
American Express 297, 306
Amerigo Vespucci Airport 307
Amici della Musica (Florence) 36
Ammannati, Bartolomeo 27
  Biblioteca Mediceo-Laurenziana
  (Florence) 90
  Neptune Fountain (Florence) 76
  Palazzo Ducale (Lucca) 176
  Palazzo Pitti (Florence) 120
  Palazzo Pucci (Florence) 88
  Ponte Santa Trinità (Florence) 108
  San Giovannino degli Scolopi
  (Florence) 87
Angelico, Fra 27
  The Annunciation 97, 204

Angelico, Fra (cont.)
  The Crucifixion 97, 133
  The Deposition 96
  The Entombment 97
  Madonna with Angels 133
  The Mocking of Christ 96
  San Marco frescoes (Florence) 92,
  96–7, 135
  Virgin and Child 85
Anghiari **197**
Annigoni, Pietro
  *St Joseph and Christ in the
  Workshop* 91
  San Michele frescoes (Ponte
  Buggianese) 185
The Annunciation (Fra Angelico)
97, 204
The Annunciation (Leonardo da
Vinci) 83
The Annunciation (Pietro da
Cortona) 204
The Annunciation (Pontormo) 119
Ansedonia **240–41**
Antinori family 112
Antiques shops 286, 288
Aperitifs 269
Apicius Culinary Institute 293
Aprosio & Co. (Florence) 288
Apuan Alps 169, 174
Architecture **24–5**
  Tuscan town squares **22–3**
Aretino, Spinello 198
Arezzo 21, 191, **198–201**
  Anfiteatro Romano e Museo
  Archeologico 199
  Casa del Vasari 199
  Duomo 198
  festivals 36, **39**
  Fortezza Medicea e Parco il Prato
  41, 198
  map 199
  Museo del Duomo 198
  Museo Statale d'Arte Medioevale
  e Moderna 199
  Piazza Grande 198
  Pieve di Santa Maria 198
  San Francesco **200–201**
  Santa Maria delle Grazie 199
  Visitors' Checklist 199
Ariosto, Ludovico 173
Armando Poggi (Florence) 288
Armani (Florence) 287
Arno, river 191, 196
  estuary 153, 161
  floods 56, 57
Arno Corridor, Uffizi (Florence)
83
Arnoldi, Alberto 62
Arnolfo di Cambio 26
  Cloister, Santa Croce (Florence) 72
  Colle di Val d'Elsa 210
  Duomo (Florence) 65, 67

Arnolfo di Cambio (cont.)
  Madonna of the Glass Eyes 67
Arredamenti Castorina (Florence) 288
Arringatore (Etruscan bronze) 99
Art **26–7**
  holidays 292, 293
  Renaissance frescoes **28–9**
  shops 286, 288
  see also Museums and galleries
Arte di Calimala 130–31
Artichoke Fountain, Palazzo Pitti
(Florence) 120
Artimino **165**
Asciano **211**
Aspertini, Amico 182
Associazione Italiana Alberghi per
la Gioventù 246
Associazione Volontari Ospedalieri
301
Assumption of the Virgin triptych
(Taddeo di Bartolo) 227
ATAF 313
Auditorium Flog (Florence) 291
Augustinian order 99
Automobile Club d'Italia 300, 315
Autumn in Tuscany 36–7
Avis 307, 315

B

Il Baccanale (Montepulciano) 35
Bacchus (Michelangelo) 68
Bacchus Fountain (Cioli) 124
Baccio d'Agnolo 131, 210
Baciocchi, Elisa 55
  rules Lucca 176, 179
Badia a Coltibuono 293
  Day out in Chianti 229
Badia Fiesolana (Fiesole) 133
Badia Fiorentina (Florence) **70**, 134
  Street-by-Street map 63
Badiani (Florence) 283
Bagni di Lucca **174–5**, 185
  Day out around Lucca 183
Bagno Vignoni 11, **226**
Balestro del Girifalco (Massa
  Marittima) 34, **39**
Banchi (Florence) 283
Bandinelli, Baccio 65
  Hercules and Cacus 77
  Orpheus 89
  statue of Giovanni delle Bande
  Nere 87, 88
Bandini, Angelo 133
Bandini, Giovanni
  Monumento dei Quattro Mori 162
Banking **302**
Banknotes 303
Baptistries 22
Baptistry (Florence) **64–6**
  Street-by-Street map 62
Bar Vivoli Gelateria (Florence) **71**,
283

Barbino, Pietro 124
Bardi Chapel, Santa Croce (Florence) 73
Bardini, Stefano 119
Barga **174**
Bargello (Florence) **68–9**, 134
  Street-by-Street map 63
Baroncelli, Bernardo 69
Baroncelli Chapel, Santa Croce (Florence) 73
Baroque architecture 25
Il Barretto Piano Bar (Florence) 283
Bars 264, 282, 283
Bartolini, Lorenzo 95
Bartolo di Fredi 210
  The Creation 212
  Sant'Agostino 212
  San Gimignano frescoes 215
Bartolomeo, Fra 94, 167
Bata (Florence) 287
The Battle of Anghiari (Leonardo da Vinci) 197
The Battle of San Romano (Uccello) 48, 82
Beccafumi, Domenico 219
Becket, St Thomas à 178
Beer 269
Before the Proconsul (Lippi) 127
Bellariva (Florence) 11
Beltrami (Florence) 287
Benedetto da Maiano
  bust of Onofrio di Pietro 214
  Palazzo Strozzi (Florence) 105
  Sant'Agostino altar (San Gimignano) 215
  Santa Maria delle Grazie (Arezzo) 199
Benedict, St 211
Benedictine order 191
Berardi, Piero 113
Berlinghieri, Bonaventura 184
Berlinghieri, School of 182
Bernardino of Siena, St 221
Betti, Niccolo 95
Bianchi faction 186
Bibbiena 191, **196**
Biblioteca Mediceo-Laurenziana (Florence) 90
Biblioteca Riccardiana (Florence)
  Street-by-Street map 87
Bicci di Lorenzo 196
  St Nicholas of Tolentino 164
  The Virgin with St George and St Leonard 130
Bicycles *see* Cycling
Bigarelli, Guido 174
Birds **33**
  Lago di Burano 241
  Museo Ornitologico (San Gimignano) 215
The Birth of Venus (Botticelli) 49, 81, 82–3

The Birth of the Virgin (Andrea del Sarto) 98
Il Bisonte (Florence) 287
Black Death 47, 207, 218
Blues music 291
Boboli Gardens (Florence) 10, 115, 120, **124–5**, 291
  Street-by-Street map 117
  walk to San Miniato al Monte 130
Boccaccio, Giovanni 46
  Badia Fiorentina (Florence) 70
  The Decameron 47, 111
Boccadama (Florence) 283
Bojola (Florence) 287
Boldini, Giovanni 123
Bonaguida
  Tree of the Cross 92, 94
Book shops 286, 288
Borgo San Frediano (Florence) 137
Borgo San Lorenzo **194**
La Bottega dei Cristalli (Florence) 288
Bottega dell'Olio (Florence) 288
Botticelli, Sandro 19, 27, 122, 136
  Adoration of the Magi 51, 83
  The Birth of Venus 49, 81, 82–3
  Madonna del Mare 94
  Pallas and the Centaur 27
  Primavera 34, 49, 82, 83
  St Augustine 113
  tomb of 113, 137
  Uffizi collection 82–3
Bottiglieria Torrini (Florence) 283
Boy Removing a Thorn from his Foot 81
Brancacci, Felice 126
Brancacci Chapel (Florence) **126–7**, 137
Breakdown services 315
Breakfast 244, 245
Bridges
  Ponte Amerigo Vespucci (Florence) 137
  Ponte della Maddalena (Bagni di Lucca) 174, 183
  Ponte Santa Trinità (Florence) 108
  Ponte Vecchio (Florence) 103, **106–7**, 134
British Airways 306
British Institute Library (Florence) 299
Bronzino, Agnolo 27, 83, 94, 179
  Badia Fiorentina fresco 70
  Cappella di Eleonora frescoes, Palazzo Vecchio (Florence) 79
  The Martyrdom of St Lawrence 27, 90
  Portrait of Bia 83
  Santa Felicità frescoes 119

Browning, Elizabeth Barrett 116, 118
Browning, Robert 116, 118
Brunelleschi, Filippo 25, 26, 186, 204
  Baptistry doors competition 66, 69
  Capella de' Pazzi, Santa Croce (Florence) 73
  Cloister, Santa Croce (Florence) 72
  Duomo (Florence) 48, 62, **65**, 67, 135
  Loggia degli Innocenti (Florence) 136
  Palazzo Medici Riccardi (Florence) 89
  Palazzo di Parte Guelfa (Florence) 109
  Palazzo Pitti (Florence) 120
  Piazza della Santissima Annunziata (Florence) 98
  Rotonda di Santa Maria degli Angeli (Florence) 135
  San Lorenzo (Florence) 10, 87, 90
  Santo Spirito (Florence) 116, 118
  Spedale degli Innocenti (Florence) 48, 93, 95, 135
Bruni, Leonardo
  tomb of 73
Bucelli, Pietro 227
Budget accommodation 246, 247
Bulgari (Florence) 288
Buontalenti, Bernardo
  Forte di Belvedere (Florence) 130
  Palazzo Nonfinito (Florence) 70, 134
  Piazza de' Frescobaldi fountains 117
  Piazza Grande (Livorno) 162
  San Lorenzo (Florence) 90
  Tribune, Uffizi (Florence) 83
  Villa di Artimino (Artimino) 165
Burano, Lago di 241
Bureaux de change 302
Buscheto
  tomb of 159
Buses
  city buses 312–13
  coaches **311**
  crime on 300
Byron, Lord 95

C

Caccini, Giovanni 118
Cacialli, Giuseppe 122
CAF 297
Café Ricchi (Florence) 11, 283
Cafés, Florence 282, 283
Il Caffè (Florence) 283
Caffè Amerini (Florence) 283

Caffè Caruso (Florence) 283
Caffè Santa Trinita (Florence) 283
Caffè Strozzi (Florence) 283
Caffè La Torre (Florence) 283
Caffè Voltaire (Florence) 283
Caffeteria Henry (Florence) 283
Calcio in Costume (Florence) 35
Camaldoli 191, **195**
Camaldolite order 89
Camp sites 246, 247
Campanile (Florence) **64–5**, 135
  Street-by-Street map 62
Campaniles 22, 23
Campo dei Miracoli (Pisa) **158–9**
Canoes 293
Canova, Antonio
  Venus Italica 122
Cantagallina 162
Cantiere Internazionale d'Arte
  (Montepulciano) 35
Cantinetta del Verrazzano
  (Florence) 283
CAP & COPIT of Florence 311
Capalbio **241**
Capocaccia (Florence) 283
Capodanno 37
Capoliveri
  Day out on Elba 235
Cappella de' Pazzi, Santa Croce
  (Florence) 73
Cappella dei Principi, San Lorenzo
  (Florence) 90–1
Cappelle Medicee, San Lorenzo
  (Florence)
  Street-by-Street map 86
Cappello, Bianca 165
  Palazzo di Bianca Cappello
  (Florence) 116
Capponi family 119
Capraia **163**
Caprese Michelangelo **196**
Carabè (Florence) 283
Caravaggio 83, 122
Carmelite order 99
Carnevale (Viareggio) 34, 37, **38**
Carrara 169, **172**
Carretto, Ilaria del
  tomb of 180
Carriage Museum, Palazzo Pitti
  (Florence) 121
Cars
  breakdowns 315
  driving in Florence and Tuscany
  314–15
  parking 315
  renting 307, 314, 315
  see also Tours by car
Carthusian order 162
Casa Buonarroti (Florence) **71**
Casa di Dante (Florence) **70**
  Street-by-Street map 63

Casa Guidi (Florence)
  Street-by-Street map 116
Casa del Vino (Florence) 283
Casaclub 246
La Casalinga (Florence) 10
Cascate del Gorello 238
The Casentino 191, 193, **196**
Casole d'Elsa 19
Cassioli, Amos
  Museo Amos Cassioli (Asciano) 211
Cassone Adimari (Scheggia)
  94
Castagno, Andrea del
  The Last Supper 89, 92
Castellina in Chianti
  Day out in Chianti 229
Castello di Brolio
  Day out in Chianti 229
Castello di Romena 45
Castelnuovo di Garfagnana **173**
Cathedral *see* Duomo
Catherine of France 50
Catherine of Siena, St 185
  Bagno Vignoni 226
  birthplace 216
  Casa di Santa Caterina (Siena) 219
  San Domenico (Siena) 223
Cattani, Count Orlando 196
Cavaliere (Marini) 104
Le Cave di Maiano 293
Cavo
  Day out on Elba 235
Cei (Florence) 288
Cellini, Benvenuto 27, 63
  Autobiography 54
  bust of 106, 134
  Perseus 77
  tomb of 98
Cenacolo di Sant'Apollonia
  (Florence) **89**
  Street-by-Street map 92
Cenacolo di Santo Spirito (Florence)
  118
  Street-by-Street map 116
Cennini (Florence) 283
Central Tuscany **207–29**
  Exploring Central Tuscany 208–9
Centro d'Arte Verrocchio 293
Centro di Cultura per Stranieri
  dell'Università di Firenze
  (Florence) 299
Centro Internazionale Dante
  Alighieri (Siena) 299
Centro Turistico Studentesco
  (Florence) 299
Ceramics
  What to Buy in Tuscany 30
Certosa di Pisa **162**
Charlemagne, Emperor 44
  Sant'Antimo 45, 228
  Santi Apostoli (Florence) 102, 109
Charles I, King of England 51

Charles V, Emperor 52
Charles VIII, King of France 52
Charles IX, King of France 50
Cherubini, Luigi 95
Chianti Classico 207, 293
Chianti region
  Day out in Chianti **229**
  wine 21, 207, 269
Chianti Slow Travel 246
Chiaroscuro (Florence) 283
Chiesa Evangelica Valdese 299
Children
  entertainment 291
  in hotels 245
  Pinocchio Park (Collodi) 183, 184
  in restaurants 265
Chimera (Etruscan bronze) 99
Chini, Galileo 175, 194
Chiusi **228**
Christmas 37
Church of England 299
Churches 20
  admission charges 296, 297
  visiting 297
  see also individual towns
Churches in Florence
  Badia Fiorentina 134
  Duomo 62–3, 134–5
  Ognissanti **113**, 137
  Orsanmichele 62, **67**
  Santissima Annunziata 93, **98**
  Santi Apostoli 102, **109**
  Santa Felicità **119**
  San Filippo Neri 134
  San Frediano in Cestello **119**
  San Gaetano 136
  San Giovannino degli Scolopi
  87
  San Lorenzo 10, 87, **90–91**, 135
  Santa Margherita de' Cerchi 63, 70
  Santa Maria del Carmine 126–7,
  137
  Santa Maria Maddalena dei Pazzi
  99
  Santa Maria Novella **110–11**, 135,
  136
  San Miniato al Monte 129, 130–31
  San Pancrazio 104, 136
  Santo Spirito 116, **118**
  Santo Stefano al Ponte **74–5**, 134
  Santa Trinità 102, **108–9**
Cicero 26, 48
Cicloposse 293
Cigarettes, duty-free allowances 298
Cigoli 70
Cimabue 26
  Crucifixion 72
Cina da Pistoia 186
Cinema *see* Film
Cioli, Valerio
  Bacchus Fountain 124
Cistercian order 99, 224

CIT Viaggi 297, 306, 308
Citysightseeing Firenze 297
Ciuffagni, Bernardo 67
Civitali, Matteo 176, 180, 182
Clement VII, Pope 50, 52, 53
Climate 35–7
Clothes
  in churches 297
  in restaurants 265
  shops 284–5, 287
  see also Fashion
Club Alpino Italiano 246, 293
Coach travel **311**
Coccinelle (Florence) 287
Coffee 269
Coin (Florence) 287
Coins 303
Colle di Val d'Elsa 20, **210**
Collodi **184**
Collodi, Carlo 184
Columbus, Christopher 75, 113
Conservatorio Musicale Luigi
  Cherubino (Florence) **95**
  Street-by-Street map 92
Consorzio del Vino Brunello di
  Montalcino 293
Constantine I, Emperor 43, 200
Consulates 299
Convento di Montesenario 194
Conversion table 299
Cook, Captain 70
Cookery holidays 292, 293
Cooperatives, hotel 246, 247
COPIT of Pistoia 311
Corridoio Vasariano, Ponte Vecchio
  (Florence) 75, **106**, 107, 134
Corsa del Palio (Siena) 35
Corsi, Nera 108–9
Corsini family 136
Cortiles (arcaded courtyards) 22
Cortona 21, 24, 192, **204–5**
  festivals 35
  map 205
Cortona, Pietro da
  The Annunciation 204
  Palazzo Pitti frescoes (Florence)
  120, 122
Cosimo I, Grand Duke of Tuscany
  50, 51, 54
  Chimera 99
  Fortezza (Montalcino) 224
  Fortezza Medicea (Arezzo) 198
  Fortezza Medicea (Siena) 223
  Giardino dei Semplici (Florence) 89
  Livorno 162
  Montepulciano 227
  Palazzo dei Cavalieri (Pisa) 156
  Palazzo Vecchio (Florence) 78, 79
  Piazza di Santa Trinità (Florence)
  108
  Piazza della Signoria (Florence) 77
  portrait of 123

Cosimo I, Grand Duke of Tuscany
  (cont.)
  Rocca (San Gimignano) 215
  statues of 55, 76, 156, 157
  Uffizi (Florence) 80
  Valdichiana 203
Cosimo II, Grand Duke of Tuscany
  51, 54, 55
  Four Seasons statues 102
Cosimo III, Grand Duke of Tuscany
  51, 54, 99
Cosimo il Vecchio *see* Medici,
  Cosimo (il Vecchio)
Costoli (Florence) 293
Covatti, Bernardino 205
Coveri 57
CPT 311, 313
The Creation (Bartolo di Fredi) 212
Credit cards 302
  in hotels 245
  lost 301
  in restaurants 265
  in shops 284
The Crete 32, 207, 209, 211
Crime 300
Cristofanello 204
Cristofori, Bartolomeo 95
Cronaca (Simone del Pollaiuolo)
  Palazzo Guadagni (Florence) 118
  Palazzo Strozzi (Florence) 105
  Santo Spirito (Florence) 118
The Crucifixion (Fra Angelico) 97
La Cucina del Garga 293
Cuendet 246
Currency **302–3**
Customs allowances 298
Cycling
  bike rental 314, 315
  holidays 292, 293

D
Da Mario (Florence) 10
Da Nerbone (Florence) 283
Daddi, Bernardo
  Madonna 74
  The Story of the Holy Girdle
  188
  Virgin and Child 67
Daelli 57
Dance 290–91
D'Annunzio, Gabriele 166
Dante Alighieri
  baptism 64
  bust of 70
  Casa di Dante (Florence) 62, 63,
  70
  Castello di Romena 195
  The Divine Comedy 47, 70, 87,
  111
  Duomo (Florence) 134
  Inferno 46, 211
  Monteriggioni 210–11

Dante Alighieri (cont.)
  Santa Margherita de' Cerchi
  (Florence) 63, 70
Datini, Francesco di Marco 188
David (Donatello) 69, 89
David (Michelangelo) 52, 77, 135
  Piazza della Signoria 61, 94
  Piazzale Michelangelo 94, 131
David (Verrocchio) 49
Decius, Emperor 130
Della Quercia, Jacopo 26
  Madonna 197
  San Frediano altarpiece (Lucca)
  182
  Siena fountain 218
  tomb of Ilaria del Carretto 180
Della Robbia, Andrea
  The Assumption 198
  Madonna and Child 195
  Santa Maria delle Carceri
  roundels (Prato) 189
  Santa Maria delle Grazie altar
  (Arezzo) 199
  Spedale degli Innocenti reliefs
  (Florence) 48, 93, 95, 135
Della Robbia, Giovanni 187
Della Robbia, Luca 27, 47
  Barga tabernacle 174
  Capella de' Pazzi roundels 73
  choir loft 67
  San Miniato al Monte roundels
  131
  terracotta panels in Duomo
  (Florence) 67
Della Robbia family 48
  La Verna sculptures 196
  Santi Apostoli tabernacle 109
  Santa Maria delle Grazie
  (Anghiari) 197
Demidoff, Prince 235
Dentists 301
Department stores 284, 287
The Deposition (Fra Angelico) 96
The Deposition (Rosso Fiorentino)
  166
"Devil's Bridge" (Borgo a Mozzano)
  174–5
  Day out around Lucca 183
DF Bike 315
DF Moto 315
Dialling codes 305
Digestifs 269
Disabled travellers 297
  entertainments 290
  in hotels 245
  in restaurants 265
Discounts
  bus tickets 313
  student 298
Divarese (Florence) 287
Diving 293
Doctors 301

Dodecapolis 42
Dolce & Gabbana (Florence) 287
Dolce Vita (Florence) 283
Dolceforte (Florence) 288
Dolci Dolcezze (Florence) 283
Domenico di Bartolo 219
Dominican order 92, 96, 110
Donatello 26, 126, 204
  Baptistry doors competition 66
  choir loft 67
  Crucifix 73
  David 69, 89
  La Maddalena 27, 67
  Marzocco 76
  Prato Duomo frieze 188
  St George 48
  St John 67
  San Lorenzo (Florence) 90, 91
  San Rossore 157
Donati, Gemma 63
Donnini (Florence) 283
Drinks
  What to Drink in Florence and
    Tuscany 268–9
  see also Wine
Ducci (Florence) 288
Duccio di Buoninsegna
  The Life of Christ 219
  Madonna and Child 211
  Maestà 26, 219
Dudley, Sir Robert 74, 162
The Duke and Duchess of Urbino
  (Piero della Francesca) 81, 82
Duomo (Florence) 23, **64–5**, 134–5
  clock 61
  Museo dell'Opera del Duomo **67**
  Street-by-Street map 62–3
Duomo (Siena) 11, 216, **220–21**
Duomo of San Romolo (Fiesole)
  132
Dürer, Albrecht 83
Duty-free allowances 298

E

E-mail 304–5
Eastern Tuscany **191–205**
  Exploring Eastern Tuscany 192–3
Edison (Florence) 288
Educational courses 298, 299
Edward III, King of England 47
Elba
  Day out on Elba **234–5**
  Napoleon's exile 234, 235
Electrical adaptors 299
Eleonora di Toledo
  Palazzo Pitti (Florence) 115
  Palazzo Vecchio (Florence) 79
  portrait of 83
  Santa Maria Novella (Florence) 110
Elias, Brother 204
Elisabetta, Queen of Spain 51
Embassies 299

Emergencies 300
Empoli **164**
ENIT UK 297
Enoteca Baldovino (Florence) 283
Enoteca Fuoriporta (Florence) 283
Enoteca De' Giraldi (Florence) 283
Enrico Coveri (Florence) 287
Entertainment **290–91**
  tourist information 296
The Entombment (Fra Angelico) 97
Erboristeria (Florence) **75**
Erboristeria Inglese (Florence) 288
Erboristeria di Palazzo Vecchio
  (Florence) 288
Eredi Chiarini (Florence) 287
Estate Fiesolana (Fiesole) 35, 291
Estate Musicale Chigiana 291
Etiquette 297
Etruscan Canal 240–41
Etruscans 19, **42–3**
  Chiusi 228
  Cortona 204
  Etruscan tour **240–41**
  Fiesole 132–3
  Maremma 231
  Museo Archeologico (Florence)
    99
  Museo Civico Archeologico
    (Marciana) 235
  Museo Etrusco (Pitigliano) 239
  Museo Etrusco Gasparri
    (Piombino) 235
  Museo Etrusco Guarnacci
    (Volterra) 166
  Necropoli Etrusca (Sovana) 238
  Necropoli di Poggio Pinci
    (Asciano) 211
  Volterra 166
Euro 303
Europa Villa Camerata 246
Europe, map 12
The Expulsion of Adam and Eve
  (Masaccio) 126

F

Fa Chi Sa (Florence) 283
Falcon Contest (Massa Marittima)
  39
The Fall (Cappella del Tau, Pistoia)
  186
Fallani Best (Florence) 288
Family Hotels 246
Fantastici, Agostino 225
Farmacia Comunale 13, 301
Farmacia di Santa Maria Novella
  (Florence) 288
Farmacia Molteni 301
Fascism 56
Fashion 57
  shops 284–5, 287
  What to Buy in Tuscany 31
Fattori, Giovanni 163

Fattori, Giovanni (cont.)
  *The Italian Camp after the Battle
    of Marengo* 123
  The Tuscan Maremma 121
Feltrinelli International (Florence)
  288
Ferdinand, King of Spain 75
Ferdinando I, Grand Duke of
  Tuscany 51
  and Jews 99
  Monumento dei Quattro Mori 162
  Ponte Vecchio (Florence) 106
  statues of 93, 98
  Villa di Artimino (Artimino) 165
Ferdinando II, Grand Duke of
  Tuscany 51, 95, 161
Ferragamo, Salvatore 57, 287
  Palazzo Spini-Ferroni (Florence)
    102, 108
Ferragamo Shoe Museum
  (Florence) 10, 105
Ferri, Antonio Maria 119, 184
Ferri, Ciro 99, 122
Ferri, Simone 210
Festa degli Aquiloni (San Miniato)
  34
Festa della Bistecca (Cortona) 35
Festa del Grillo (Florence) 34
Festival dei Popoli (Florence) 37
Festival Pucciniano (Torre del Lago
  Puccini) 35
Festa della Rificolona (Florence) 36
Festival of the Thrush (Montalcino)
  36, **39**
Festivals **34–9**
Fiaccole di Natale (Abbadia di San
  Salvatore) 37
Fiaschetteria Balducci (Florence)
  283
Fibonacci, Leonardo 46
Fiesole
  festivals 35
  walk through Fiesole 132–3
Film 290, 291
Fiorentino, Pier Francesco 210
Fire services 300
Firenze Nuova 21, 56
Firenzemusei 297
Florence 13, 21, **59–147**
  airport 307
  Baptistry doors 66
  Bargello **68–9**
  bars and cafés 283
  Boboli Gardens **124–5**
  Brancacci Chapel **126–7**
  City Centre East **61–83**
  City Centre North **85–99**
  City Centre West **101–13**
  coach travel 311
  Duomo, Campanile and Baptistry
    64–6
  festivals 34–7, 38

Florence (cont.)
floods (1966) 56, 57
Florence's Best Hotels 248–9
great days out **10–11**
history **41–57**
hospital 301
maps 14–15, 16–17
markets 287, 288
Oltrarno **115–27**
Palazzo Pitti **120–23**
Palazzo Vecchio **78–9**
Piazza della Repubblica **102–3**
Piazza della Signoria **76–7**
Ponte Vecchio **106–7**
railway station 57
Republic **52–3**
San Lorenzo 86–7
San Marco **96–7**, 135
Santa Croce (Florence) **72–3**
shops 284
siege of (1530) 52–3, 131
Street Finder **138–47**
Street-by-Street maps
Duomo 62–3
Oltrarno 116–17
Piazza della Repubblica 102–3
San Lorenzo 86–7
San Marco 92–3
trains 308, 310
Uffizi **80–83**
walks 129–37
Florence by Bike 315
Florence Dance Festival 291
Florence Promhotels 246
Florence Radiotaxi 313
Flowers **33**
Foggini, Giulio 72
Fondazione Salvatore Romano 118
Food and drink
breakfast 244, 245
ice-cream parlours 282, 283
light meals and snacks 282
markets 88
mushrooms **202**
shops 286–7, 288, 289
specialist holidays 292, 293
take-away food 282, 283
vegetarian food 264
What to Buy in Tuscany 31
What to Drink in Florence and
Tuscany 268–9
What to Eat in Florence and
Tuscany 266–7
see also Restaurants
Football in Costume (Florence)
38
Forno Pugi (Florence) 283
Forte di Belvedere (Florence) 130
Fortezza Medicea (Arezzo) 41
Fountains
Artichoke Fountain (Florence) 120
Bacchus Fountain (Florence) 124

Fountains (cont.)
Chimera Fountain (Arezzo) 198
Neptune Fountain (Florence) 76,
124
Oceanus Fountain (Florence) 125
Piazza de' Frescobaldi (Florence)
117
Il Porcellino (Florence) 112, 134
Putto Fountaín (Florence) 78
Four Seasons, statues of (Florence)
102, 108
Francavilla, Pietro 156
statue of Cosimo I 55
Francesco I, Grand Duke of
Tuscany 51, 54
Palazzo di Bianca Cappello
(Florence) 116
Poggio a Caiano 165
Uffizi 82, 83
Francesco (Florence) 287
Franciabigio 165
Francis, St **47**
Berlinghieri's frescoes of 184
La Verna 191, 196
"stigmata" 46
Francis II, King of France 50
Franciscan order 47, 108–9
François Vase 99
Frederick II, Emperor 46
Castello dell'Imperatore (Prato)
189
San Miniato Rocca 163, 164
Frederick Barbarossa, Emperor 45
Frescobaldi family 137
Frescoes, Renaissance **28–9**
Frieze of Papier Mâché (Florence)
117
Fuel stations 315
Furla (Florence) 287
Futurists 112

G

Gabinetto Vieusseux (Florence) 105
Gaddi, Agnolo 108
Gaddi, Taddeo
Ponte Vecchio (Florence) 103
Santa Croce frescoes 72, 73
Gaiole in Chianti
Day out in Chianti 229
Galgano, St **224**
Galileo Galilei 41, **54–5**, 130
Museo di Storia della Scienza
(Florence) 74
portrait of 74
tomb of 72
Galileo Galilei airport (Pisa) 21,
153, 306, 307
Galleria dell'Accademia (Florence)
94–5, 135
Street-by-Street map 92
Galleria d'Arte Moderna, Palazzo
Pitti (Florence) 121, 123

Galleria del Costume, Palazzo Pitti
(Florence) 121, 123
Galleria degli Uffizi (Florence) 283
Galleries *see* Museum and galleries
Game of the Bridge (Pisa) 38
Gardens *see* Parks and gardens
The Garfagnana 32, 169, 173, **174**
Garibaldi, Giuseppe
statue of 132
Gastronomia Vera (Florence) 283
Gelateria de' Ciompi (Florence) 283
Gelateria Veneta (Florence) 283
Gentile da Fabriano 157
Ghibellines 46, 109
Ghiberti, Lorenzo 26
Baptistry doors 65, **66**
stained glass in the Duomo
(Florence) 65
tomb of 72
Ghiberti, Vittorio 72
La Ghiotta (Florence) 283
Ghirlandaio, Domenico 10, 27, 118
The Adoration of the Magi 95
The Adoration of the Shepherds 109
The Annunciation 215
Christ in Majesty 166
The Last Supper 113, 137
The Life of John the Baptist 111
The Life of St Fina 215
The Life of St Francis 102
The Life of the Virgin 111
The Madonna and Saints 180
Madonna della Misericordia 113
Ognissanti frescoes (Florence) 137
St Jerome 113
Sala dei Gigli frescoes (Florence)
78
Santa Trinità frescoes (Florence)
108–9
Ghirlandaio, Ridolfo del 94
Giambelli, Pietro 98
Giambologna 27
Mercury 68
Oceanus Fountain 125
The Rape of the Sabine Women 77
statue of Appennino 194
statue of Grand Duke Cosimo I 76
statue of Grand Duke Ferdinando
I 93, 98
tomb of 98
Venus Bathing 124
Giardino di Boboli (Florence) *see*
Boboli Gardens
Giardino dei Semplici (Florence) **89**
Street-by-Street map 93
Giardino dei Tarocchi (Pescia
Fiorentina) **241**
Gift shops
Florence 286, 288
Tuscany 289
Gilli (Florence) 283
Gioco del Ponte (Pisa) 35, **38**

Giordano, Luca 89
Giostra del Saracino (Arezzo) 36, **39**
Giottino 82
Giotto di Bondone 26, 82
    Bardi Chapel frescoes 73
    birthplace 86
    Campanile (Florence) 62, **64**, 65, 135
    Ognissanti Madonna 80, 82
    St Stephen polyptych 74
    Santa Croce frescoes 72, 73
Giovacchino (Florence) 283
Giovanni di Stefano 223
Giubbe Rosse (Florence) 283
Giugni, Bernardo
    tomb of 70
Giuliano da Maiano 136, 210
Giulio Giannini (Florence) 288
Goldoni, Carlo
    statue of 136
Golf 293
Gombo 161
Good Government (Lorenzetti) 46–7, 164, 218
Gorgona 163
Gothic architecture 24
Gothic art 82
Gozzoli, Benozzo 10, 27, 135
    The Life of St Augustine 215
    The Procession of the Magi 56–7, 89
Grand Duchy **54–5**
Grand Tour 55, 83, 207
Greater Florence, map 14–15
Gregory I, Pope 164
Gregory XI, Pope 219
Greve in Chianti 36
Grosseto **238**
    Etruscan tour 240
Grotta Giusti (Monsummano Terme) 185
La Grotta Grande, Boboli Gardens (Florence) 124
Gucci
    fashion 57
    shops 287
    What to Buy in Tuscany 31
Guelphs
    conflict with Ghibellines 46, 109
    Palazzo di Parte Guelfa (Florence) 103, **109**
Guglielmo da Pisa 186–7
Guided tours 297
Guidi family 195
Guido d'Arezzo 45
Guido da Como 187
Guidoriccio da Fogliano (Martini) 218, 219
Guinigi, Paolo 178, 180
Guinigi family 178

H

Happy Rent 315
Hawkwood, Sir John 47, 224
Health **300–301**
Helena, Empress 200
Henri II, King of France 50
Henri III, King of France 50
Henri IV, King of France 51
Henrietta Maria, Queen of England 51
Henze, Hans Werner 35, 227
Hercules and Cacus (Bandinelli) 77
Hermes (Florence) 287
Hermitage Hotel
    Florence's Best Hotels 249
Hertz 307, 315
History **41–57**
Hogarth, William 106
Holidays, public 37
The Holy Family (Michelangelo) 27, 81, 83
Homem, Lopo 74
    map 75
Honorius III, Pope 109
Horne, Herbert Percy
    Museo Horne (Florence) **74**
Horses
    horse-drawn carriages 297
    Palio (Siena) 19, 39, **222**
    riding 292–3
Hospitals 301
Hotel Beacci Tornabuoni
    Florence's Best Hotels 248
Hotel Excelsior
    Florence's Best Hotels 248
Hotel Villa Belvedere
    Florence's Best Hotels 248
Hotels **244–63**
    booking and paying 245
    budget accommodation 246, 247
    cooperatives 246, 247
    disabled travellers 245
    Florence's Best 248–9
    gradings and facilities 244–5
    hidden extras 244
    in historic buildings 245, 246
    prices 244
    residential 246–7
    what to expect 245
    where to look 244
Humanists 48, 49

I

Ice-cream parlours 71, 282, 283
Immigration and customs 298, 299
Incontri in Terra di Siena 291
Incontro di Teano (Fiesole) 132
Il Innocenti (Florence) 283
Inoculations 301
Inquisition 99

Insurance
    cars 314
    medical 301
    travel 300
Internet access 304–5
Intimissimi (Florence) 287
Intimo Tre 287
Isola Capraia
    map 154
L'Isolotto, Boboli Gardens (Florence) 125
Istituto per l'Arte e il Restauro (Florence) 299
The Italian Camp after the Battle of Marengo (Fattori) 123
Italy, map 12–13

J

Jazz 291
Jewellery
    Ponte Vecchio (Florence) 106–7
    shops 285, 288
Jews
    Tempio Israelitico (Florence) **99**
    religious services 299
Joanna of Austria 51
John XVIII, Pope 161
Jones, Inigo 162
Joust of the Saracen (Arezzo) **39**
Julius II, Pope
    Florentine Republic 52
    tomb of 79, 94

K

Kaffeehaus, Boboli Gardens (Florence) 124
Kite festival (San Miniato) 34

L

La Valle 246
La Verna 191, **196**
Lady with a Posy (Verrocchio) 69
Lanci, Baldassarre 223
Landscape **32–3**
The Last Supper (Castagna) 89, 92
Lavatories, public 297
Lazzi 311
Leaning Tower (Pisa) 153, 158, 159, **160**
Leather goods
    shops 285, 287
    What to Buy in Tuscany 31
The Legend of the True Cross (Piero della Francesca) 49
Leo X, Pope 50
    coronation 52
    Palazzo Vecchio (Florence) 79
    Poggio a Caiano 165
Leonardo da Vinci 27, 69, 83, 197
    The Adoration of the Magi 83
    The Annunciation 83
    birthplace 164

Leonardo da Vinci (cont.)
Lady with a Posy 69
Museo Leonardiano (Vinci) 153,
164, 165
Palazzo Vecchio (Florence) 78
Leopold II, Emperor of Austria 54
Leopoldo I, Grand Duke of Tuscany
55, 184–5
Lì Per Lì (Florence) 283
Libraries
Biblioteca Mediceo-Laurenziana
(Florence) 90
Biblioteca Riccardiana (Florence)
87
Gabinetto Vieusseux (Florence)
105
San Marco (Florence) 97
The Life of Christ (Pisano) 220
The Life of John the Baptist
(Ghirlandaio) 111
The Life of Pope Pius II
(Pinturicchio) 220
The Life of St Augustine (Gozzoli)
215
The Life of St Francis (Ghirlandaio)
102
The Life of St Peter (Masaccio) 48,
126–7
The Life of St Peter (Masolino) 126–7
Linus, St 167
Lippi, Filippino 27, 94, 137
Before the Proconsul 127
Madonna and Child 118
St Lucy 188
*Saints Helena, Jerome, Sebastian
and Roch* 182
*The Virgin Appearing to St
Bernard* 70
Lippi, Fra Filippo 27
Crucifixion 164
The Life of John the Baptist 188
Madonna and Child 27
Madonna and Child with Angels
82
Madonna del Ceppo 188
Listings magazines 290, 296
Liszt, Franz 95
Livorno 21, 54, 153, 155, **162–3**
La Loggia (Florence) 283
Loggia del Bigallo (Florence) 134–5
Street-by-Street map 62
Loggia dei Lanzi (Florence) 77, 134
Loggia di San Paolo (Florence) 136
Loggias 22, 23
Lorentino d'Arezzo 199
Lorenzetti, Ambrogio 11, 26
Bad Government 46, 218
Good Government 46–7, 164, 218
Life of St Galgano 224
Presentation in the Temple 82
St Michael the Archangel 211
Two Views 219

Lorenzetti, Pietro 204
Lorenzi, Stoldo
Neptune Fountain 117, 124
Lorenzo de' Medici Art Institute of
Florence 293
Lorraine, Dukes of 54, 55
Palazzo Pitti (Florence) 120, 122,
123
Louis XIII, King of France 51
Louis Vuitton (Florence) 287
Lucca 21, 169, **176–83**
Anfiteatro Romano 178
Casa di Puccini 179
Day out around Lucca **183**
festivals 34, 36
Giardino Botanico 178
Museo della Cattedrale 178–9
Museo Nazionale di Palazzo
Mansi 179
Palazzo dei Guinigi 178
Palazzo Pfanner 179
Piazza del Giglio 179
Piazza Napoleone 179
Ramparts 179
San Frediano 182
San Martino **180–81**
San Michele in Foro 182
Street-by-Street map 176–7
Via Fillungo 182
Villa Bottini 182
Lucignano 47, **203**
Luisa Via Roma (Florence) 287
Luminara di Santa Croce (Lucca)
36
The Lunigiana 169, **172**
Lusitania, Cardinal Iacopo di 131

M

Macchiaioli School 123, 163, 199
Machiavelli, Niccolò 53
The Prince 53
tomb of 72
La Maddalena (Donatello) 27
Madonna and Child (Lippi) 27
Madonna and Child with Angels
(Lippi) 82
Madonna and Saints 95
Madonna del Ceppo (Lippi) 188
Madonna del Mare (Botticelli) 94
Madonna della Misericordia
(Ghirlandaio) 113
Madonna del Parto (Piero della
Francesca) 28–9
Madonna of the Chair (Raphael)
122, 123
Madonna of the Goldfinch
(Raphael) 83
Madova (Florence) 287
Maestà (Duccio) 26
Magazines, listings 290, 296
Maggio Musicale (Florence) 34
Maggiore 307, 315

Mail services 305
Malaspina, Dukes of 169, 172
The Mall (Florence) 287
Mandragora (Florence) 288
Manetti 90
Mannelli family 107
Mannelli Tower, Ponte Vecchio
(Florence) 107
Mannerist art **27**
Uffizi collection 83
Maps
ancient **75**
Arezzo 199
Central Tuscany 208–9
Cortona 205
Day out around Lucca 183
Day out in Chianti 229
Day out on Elba 234–5
Eastern Tuscany 192–3
Etruscan tour 240–41
Europe 12
Fiesole walk 132–3
Florence 16–17
Florence: Around the Duomo
62–3
Florence: City Centre East 61
Florence: City Centre North 85
Florence: City Centre West 101
Florence: Greater Florence 14–15
Florence: Oltrarno 115, 116–17
Florence: Piazza della Repubblica
102–3
Florence: San Lorenzo 86–7
Florence: San Marco 92–3
Florence: Street Finder 138–47
Florence's Best Hotels 248–9
Isola Capraia 154
Italy 12–13
Lucca 176–7
Northern Tuscany 170–71
Piazza Santo Spirito walk 136–7
Pisa 157
Pistoia 187
Prato 189
railways 309
Renaissance Florence walk 134–5
San Gimignano 212–13
San Miniato al Monte walk
150–51
Siena 216–17, 223
Southern Tuscany 232–3
Tuscany 150–51
Volterra 167
Western Tuscany 154–5
Marble, Carrara 172
Marbled paper 30
Marciana Alta **235**
Day out on Elba 234
Marciana Marina **235**
Day out on Elba 234
Marcillat, Guillaume de 198, 205
The Maremma 231, **236–7**

Margaritone di Arezzo 198
Maria of Austria 108
Marie Louise de Bourbon
  statue of 176, 179
Marina di Campo
  Day out on Elba 234
Marina di Pisa **161**
Marini, Marino
  Cavaliere 104
  Centro Marino Marini (Pistoia) 186
  Museo Marino Marini (San
  Pancrazio, Florence) **104**, 136
  Pomona 186
Marino (Florence) 283
Markets
  in Florence 288
  Mercato Centrale (Florence) 10,
  86, **88**, 288
  Mercato Nuovo (Florence) 103,
  112, 134, 288
  Mercato delle Piante (Florence)
  288
  Mercato delle Pulci (Florence) 288
  Mercato di Sant'Ambrogio
  (Florence) 288
  Mercato di San Lorenzo
  (Florence) 19, 288
  in Tuscany 289
  see also Shopping
Marsiliana
  Etruscan tour 241
Martelli, Diego 123
Martin, St 180, 181
Martini, Francesco di Giorgio 205
Martini, Simone 26
  Guidoriccio da Fogliano 218, 219
  Madonna and Child 74
  Maestà 218
  Virgin and Child 157
The Martyrdom of St Lawrence
  (Bronzino) 27, 90
Mary Magdalene (Titian) 122
Marzocco (Donatello) 76
Masaccio 27, 89, 94
  The Expulsion of Adam and Eve
  126
  The Life of St Peter 48, 126–7, 137
  St Paul 157
  St Peter Heals the Sick 126
  The Tribute Money 126
  The Trinity 26, 110
  Woman in a Turban 127
Maso di Bartolommeo 188
Masolino
  The Life of St Peter 126–7, 137
  Pietà 164
  Temptation of Adam and Eve 127
Massa Marittima 231, 232, **234**
  festivals 34, **39**
Massaciuccoli, Lago di 170
Matilda, Countess 45, 163, 174
Matteo di Giovanni 197

Matucci (Florence) 287
Medical emergencies 300, 301
Medici, Alessandro de', Duke of
  Florence 50, 53
Medici, Anna Maria Lodovica de'
  51, 55
  Uffizi (Florence) 82
Medici, Cosimo (il Vecchio) 48, 50,
  85
  Castello del Trebbio (Borgo San
  Lorenzo) 194
  death of 49
  Palazzo Medici Riccardi
  (Florence) 89
  patronage of the arts 51
  San Lorenzo (Florence) 86
  San Marco (Florence) 49, 96–7
  tomb of 91
  Villa di Cafaggiolo (Borgo San
  Lorenzo) 194
  Villa Medici (Fiesole) 133
Medici, Elisabetta de' 51
Medici, Gian Gastone de' 51
Medici, Giovanni de' 51
Medici, Cardinal Giovanni de' *see*
  Leo X, Pope
Medici, Giovanni delle Bande Nere
  51
  statue of 87, 88
Medici, Giovanni di Bicci 50
Medici, Giuliano de' (1453–78) 50,
  51
Medici, Giuliano de', Duke of
  Nemours (1479–1516) 50
Medici, Giulio de' *see* Clement VII,
  Pope
Medici, Lorenzo de' (1394–1440) 51
Medici, Lorenzo de' (1463–1503) 51
Medici, Lorenzo de', Duke of
  Urbino 50
Medici, Lorenzo de' (the
  Magnificent) 50, 51, 109
  Bagno Vignoni 185, 226
  death of 49
  Pazzi conspiracy 49, 69
  pietre dure collection 123
  Poggio a Caiano 165
Medici, Lucrezia de' 104
Medici, Maria de' 51
Medici, Princess Maria Maddalena
  de' 99
Medici, Pierfrancesco de' (1431–77)
  51
Medici, Pierfrancesco de'
  (1487–1525) 51
Medici, Piero de' 50, 52, 75
Medici, Piero de' (the Gouty) 50
Medici family 21, 41, 48, **50–51**
  Bagno Vignoni 226
  Boboli Gardens (Florence) 124
  Corridoio Vasariano (Florence) 106
  Fortezza Medicea (Arezzo) 41

Medici family (cont.)
  Livorno 74
  and Lucca 178
  menagerie 92
  Oltrarno (Florence) 115
  Opificio delle Pietre Dure
  (Florence) **95**
  Palazzo Medici Riccardi
  (Florence) 87, **89**
  Palazzo Pitti (Florence) **120–23**
  San Lorenzo (Florence) 87,
  90–91, 135
  Santissima Annunziata (Florence)
  93
  Uffizi (Florence) 80, 82
Medici Tombs (San Lorenzo,
  Florence) 10, 53, 85, 90, 91
Medieval art **26**
Medieval Tuscany **44–7**
Mehta, Zubin 34
Meleto
  Day out in Chianti 229
Memmi, Lippo
  Life of Christ 215
  Maestà 213
  Virgin Enthroned 214
Memmo di Filippucci
  Wedding Scene 214, 215
Mengoni, Giuseppe 88
Menus 265
Mercato Centrale (Florence) 10, **88**,
  288
  Street-by-Street map 86
Mercato Nuovo (Florence) **112**,
  134, 288
  Street-by-Street map 103
Mercato delle Piante (Florence) 288
Mercato delle Pulci (Florence) 288
Mercato di Sant'Ambrogio
  (Florence) 288
Mercato di San Lorenzo (Florence)
  288
"Merchant of Prato" 21
Mercury (Giambologna) 68
Meridiana 306
Methodist Church (Florence) 299
Metric system 299
Metullus, Aulus 99
Meyer Children's Hospital 301
Michelangelo 27, 126
  Accademia di Belle Arti
  (Florence) 92
  Bacchus 68
  and Baptistry doors 66
  The Battle of the Centaurs 71
  Biblioteca Mediceo-Laurenziana
  (Florence) 90
  birthplace **196**
  Cappelle Medicee (Florence) 86
  Carrara marble 172
  Casa Buonarroti (Florence) **71**
  David 52, 61, 77, 94, 135

Michelangelo (cont.)
  Dawn and Dusk 85, 91
  Day and Night 85, 91
  Galleria dell'Accademia
    (Florence) 94
  The Holy Family 27, 81, 83
  Madonna della Scala 71
  Medici Tombs (Florence) 10, 53,
    85, 90, 91
  Palazzo Medici Riccardi
    (Florence) 89
  Palazzo Vecchio (Florence) 78
  Piazzale Michelangelo (Florence)
    131
  Pietà 67
  Ponte Santa Trinità 108
  Quattro Prigioni 94, 124
  San Lorenzo (Florence) 91
  siege of Florence 53
  tomb of 72
  Victory 79
  Villa San Michele (Fiesole) 249
Michelozzo 27
  Castello del Trebbio (Borgo San
    Lorenzo) 194
  Ospedale del Ceppo (Pistoia) 187
  Palazzo Comunale
    (Montepulciano) 227
  Palazzo Medici Riccardi
    (Florence) 89
  Sant'Agostino (Montepulciano) 227
  Santissima Annunziata (Florence)
    93, 98
  San Marco (Florence) 96, 97
  Villa di Cafaggiolo (Borgo San
    Lorenzo) 194
  Villa Medici (Fiesole) 133
Michelucci, Giovanni 57, 113
Millesimi 293
Milton, John 191, 194
Mini Residence (Florence) 246
Minias, St 43, 130–31
Mino da Fiesole 70, 166–7
Mirabili (Florence) 288
Misericordia 62
The Mocking of Christ (Fra
  Angelico) 96
Mondobimbo Inflatables Parterre
  (Florence) 291
Money **302–3**
  see also Credit cards; Traveller's
    cheques
Monsummano Terme 185
Montalcino **224–5**
  festivals 36, 39
Monte, Cardinal Antonio di 203
Monte Argentario 231, **240**
Monte Oliveto Maggiore **211**
Monte San Savino 193, **203**
Montecatini Terme **184–5**, 293
Montefegatesi 171
Montepulciano 11, **227**

Montepulciano (cont.)
  Duomo 227
  festivals 35
  Madonna di San Biagio 227
  Palazzo Bucelli 227
  Palazzo Comunale 227
  Palazzo Tarugi 227
  Sant'Agostino 227
  Santa Maria dei Servi 227
Monterchi 191, **197**
Monteriggioni 13, 207, **210–11**
Monteverdi, Claudio 95
Monticchiello 11
Monumento dei Quattro Mori
  (Bandini and Tacca) 162
Mopeds, renting 314, 315
Mosaico di Pitti (Florence) 288
Mosaics
  Opificio delle Pietre Dure
    (Florence) 92, **95**
Mosquitos 301
Mostra Mercato Internazionale
  dell'Antiquariato (Florence) 36
Mostra Mercato Internazionale
  dell'Artigianato (Florence) 34
Motorways 315
Mountain refuges 246, 247
Mountain sports 293
The Mugello 191, **194**
Museums and galleries
  admission charges 296
  advanced booking 296
  opening times 296
  Bargello (Florence) 63, **68–9**, 134
  Carriage Museum, Palazzo Pitti
    (Florence) 121
  Casa di Dante (Florence) 62, 63,
    70
  Casa di Leonardo (Vinci) 164,
    165
  Casa di Puccini (Lucca) 179
  Cenacolo di Santo Spirito
    (Florence) 116, **118**
  Centro per l'Arte Contemporaneo
    Luigi Pecci (Prato) 189
  Centro Marino Marini (Pistoia) 186
  Comune Casa Natale
    Michelangelo (Caprese
    Michelangelo) 196
  Ferragamo Shoe Museum
    (Florence) 10, 105
  Galleria dell'Accademia
    (Florence) 92, **94–5**, 135
  Museo dell'Accademia Etrusca
    (Cortona) 204
  Museo Alinari (Florence) 104
  Museo dell'Alta Valle del Tevere
    (Anghiari) 197
  Museo Amos Cassioli (Asciano)
    211
  Museo Archeologico (Arezzo) 199
  Museo Archeologico (Asciano) 211

Museums and galleries (cont.)
  Museo Archeologico (Colle di Val
    d'Elsa) 210
  Museo Archeologico (Florence)
    93, **99**
  Museo Archeologico Nazionale
    (Chiusi) 228
  Museo Archeologico and
    Pinacoteca (Massa Marittima) 234
  Museo Archeologico della
    Valdinievole (Pescia) 184
  Museo d'Arte Sacra (Asciano) 211
  Museo d'Arte Sacra (Colle di Val
    d'Elsa) 210
  Museo d'Arte Sacra (San
    Gimignano) 212, 214
  Museo d'Arte Sacra (Volterra) 167
  Museo Bandini (Fiesole) 133
  Museo Bardini (Florence) **119**, 131
  Museo del Cassero (Monte San
    Savino) 203
  Museo della Cattedrale (Chiusi) 228
  Museo Civico (Colle di Val d'Elsa)
    210
  Museo Civico (Livorno) 163
  Museo Civico (Pescia) 184
  Museo Civico (Pistoia) 186
  Museo Civico (Prato) 188
  Museo Civico (San Gimignano)
    212, 214
  Museo Civico (Sansepolcro)
    196–7
  Museo Civico Archeologico
    (Marciana) 235
  Museo Civico Archeologico e
    d'Arte della Maremma (Grosseto)
    238
  Museo Civico del Marmo
    (Carrara) 172
  Museo della Collegiata di
    Sant'Andrea (Empoli) 164
  Museo Comunale (Lucignano)
    203
  Museo di Cosa (Ansedonia) 240,
    241
  Museo Diocesano (Cortona) 204
  Museo Diocesano d'Arte Sacra
    (San Miniato) 164
  Museo del Duomo (Arezzo) 198
  Museo Etnografico (San
    Pellegrino in Alpe) 174
  Museo Etrusco (Pitigliano) 239
  Museo Etrusco Gasparri
    (Piombino) 235
  Museo Etrusco Guarnacci
    (Volterra) 166
  Museo Faesulanum (Fiesole) 132
  Museo della Figurina di Gesso
    (Coreglia Antelminelli) 173
  Museo di Firenze com'era
    (Florence) **71**
  Museo Horne (Florence) **74**

Museums and galleries (cont.)
Museo Leonardiano (Vinci) 164, 165
Museo Madonna del Parto (Monterchi) 197
Museo Marino Marini (San Pancrazio, Florence) **104**, 136
Museo dei Minerali (Rio Marina) 238
Museo della Miniera (Massa Marittima) 234
Museo della Misericordia (Anghiari) 197
Museo Nazionale di Palazzo Mansi (Lucca) 179
Museo Nazionale di San Matteo (Pisa) 157
Museo Nazionale Villa Guinigi (Lucca) 178–9
Museo dell'Opera della Cattedrale (Lucca) 177, 178
Museo dell'Opera del Duomo (Florence) 63, **67**
Museo dell'Opera del Duomo (Pisa) 156
Museo dell'Opera del Duomo (Prato) 188
Museo dell'Opera Metropolitana (Siena) 216, 219
Museo Ornitologico (San Gimignano) 215
Museo Palazzo Orsini (Pitigliano) 239
Museo di San Zeno (Pistoia) 186
Museo delle Sinopie (Pisa) 156
Museo "La Specola" (Florence) 10, **119**
Museo Statale d'Arte Medioevale e Moderna (Arezzo) 199
Museo delle Statue-Stele Lunigianesi (Pontremoli) 172
Museo di Storia Naturale (Certosa di Pisa) 162
Museo di Storia della Scienza (Florence) **74**
Museo del Tessuto (Prato) 189
Museo Villa Puccini (Torre del Lago Puccini) 175
Museo della Vita e del Vino della Val di Sieve (Rufina) 194
Palazzo Comunale (Montalcino) 225
Palazzo Datini (Prato) 188
Palazzo Davanzati (Florence) **109**
Palazzo Medici Riccardi (Florence) **89**
Palazzo Nonfinito (Florence) 70
Palazzo Pitti (Florence) 117, **120–23**
Palazzo Vescovile (Montalcino) 225
Piccolo Museo di Palazzo Strozzi (Florence) 105

Museums and galleries (cont.)
Pinacoteca e Museo Civico (Volterra) 166
Pinacoteca Nazionale (Siena) 11, 219
Polveriera Guzman (Orbetello) 239
Porcelain Museum (Florence) 125
Santa Maria della Scala (Siena) 219
Uffizi (Florence) **80–83**
Mushrooms **202**, 267
Music
festivals 34–5
jazz, blues and rock 291
opera and classical opera 290, 291
Mussolini, Benito 56

N
Nanno di Banco 67
Napoleon I, Emperor 41
bathroom at Palazzo Pitti 55, 122
exile on Elba 234, 235
Piazza Napoleone (Lucca) 176
Venus Italica 122
Nardo di Cione
The Crucifixion 118
Strozzi Chapel frescoes, Santa Maria Novella (Florence) 111
Necropoli Etrusca (Sovana) 238
Necropoli di Poggio Pinci (Asciano) 211
Neptune Fountain (Florence) 76
Neptune Fountain (Lorenzi) 117, 124
Neri (Florence) 288
Neri di Bicci 70
Neri faction 186
New Year's Day 37
Newspapers 298
Nigetti, Matteo 90
Nonna Lina's Kitchen 293
Northern Tuscany **169–89**
Exploring Northern Tuscany 170–71

O
Oceanus Fountain (Giambologna) 125
Odeon Original Sound 291
Ognissanti (Florence) **113**, 137
Ognissanti Madonna (Giotto) 80, 82
Old England Stores (Florence) 288
Olivetan order 211
Oltrarno (Florence) **115–27**
area map 115
Street-by-Street map 116–17
Ombra della Sera (Etruscan bronze) 166
Onofrio di Pietro 214
Open-air entertainment 291

Opening hours
banks 302
museums 296
shops 284
Opera 290, 291
Opificio delle Pietre Dure (Florence) **95**
Street-by-Street map 92
Orangery, Boboli Gardens (Florence) 125
Orbetello 232, **239**, 240
Orcagna, Andrea
The Crucifixion 118
Orsanmichele altar 67
Strozzi Chapel frescoes, Santa Maria Novella (Florence) 111
Origo, Iris 188
Orlandi, Deodato 161
Orrido di Botri 170–71, 174
Orsanmichele (Florence) 24, **67**
Street-by-Street map 62
Orto Botanico Pánia di Corfino (San Pellegrino in Alpe) 174
Osteria Le Logge (Siena) 11
Outdoor activities **292–3**

P
Package holidays 307
Palasport (Florence) 291
Palatine Gallery, Palazzo Pitti (Florence) 120, 122–3
Palazzi (town houses) 22
Palazzi del Comune (town halls) 23
Palazzo Antinori (Florence) **112**, 136
Palazzo Bartolini-Salimbeni (Florence) 108
Palazzo di Bianca Cappello (Florence)
Street-by-Street map 116
Palazzo dei Cavalieri (Florence) 55
Palazzo Comunale (Fiesole) 132
Palazzo Corsini (Florence) 108, 136
Palazzo Davanzati (Florence) **109**
Street-by-Street map 103
Palazzo Frescobaldi (Florence) 137
Palazzo Gondi (Florence) 134
Palazzo Guadagni (Florence) 118
Street-by-Street map 116
Palazzo Lenzi (Florence) 136–7
Palazzo Masetti (Florence) 136
Palazzo Medici Riccardi (Florence) **89**, 121, 135
Street-by-Street map 87
Palazzo de' Mozzi (Florence) 131
Palazzo Niccolini (Florence) 135
Palazzo Nonfinito (Florence) **70**, 134
Street-by-Street map 63
Palazzo Pandolfini (Florence)
Street-by-Street map 92
Palazzo di Parte Guelfa (Florence) **109**

Palazzo di Parte Guelfa (cont.)
Street-by-Street map 103
Palazzo Pazzi-Quaratesi (Florence) 134
Palazzo Pitti (Florence) 71, 115, **120–23**
Corridoio Vasariano 75, **106**, 107, 134
floorplan 120–21
Galleria d'Arte Moderna 123
Galleria del Costume 121, 123
Museo degli Argenti 120, 123
Napoleon's bathroom 55, 122
Palatine Gallery 122–3
Royal Apartments 121, 123
Street-by-Street map 117
Visitors' Checklist 121
Palazzo Pucci (Florence) **88**
Street-by-Street map 87
Palazzo Ricasoli (Florence) 118, 246
Palazzo Riccardi-Manelli (Florence)
Street-by-Street map 86
Palazzo Rottigiani (Florence) 119
Palazzo Rucellai (Florence) **104**, 226
Palazzo Salviati (Florence)
Street-by-Street map 63
Palazzo Spini-Ferroni (Florence) 108
Street-by-Street map 102
Palazzo Strozzi (Florence) 25, **105**
Street-by-Street map 102
Palazzo Vecchio (Florence) 11, **78–9**
Palazzo Vescovile (Fiesole) 133
Palio (Siena) 19, 39, **222**
Palio della Balestra (Sansepolcro) 36
Palio Viaggi 308
Pallas and the Centaur (Botticelli) 27
Pampaloni, Luigi 164
Paoletti, Gaspare Maria 123
Paper
marbled 30
shops 286, 288
Paperback Exchange (Florence) 288
Il Papiro (Florence) 288
Parco delle Cascine (Florence) 288
Parco Demidoff 194
Parco Giochi Cavallino Matteo 291
Parco Naturale delle Alpi Apuane **173**
Parco Naturale dell'Uccellina 236
Parco Naturale della Viriglia 229
Parco Preistorico 291
Parenti (Florence) 288
Parigi, Giulio 99
Parking 315
Parks and gardens
Boboli Gardens (Florence) 10, 115, 117, 120, **124–5**, 130

Parks and gardens (cont.)
Giardino Botanico (Lucca) 178
Giardino dei Semplici (Florence) **89**, 93
Giardino dei Tarocchi (Pescia Fiorentina) **241**
Horti Leonini (San Quirico d'Orcia) 11, 225
Orto Botanico Pánia di Corfino (San Pellegrino in Alpe) 174
Parco dell' Orecchiella (San Pellegrino in Alpe) 174
Parco il Prato (Arezzo) 198
Ramparts (Lucca) 179
Parmigianino 83
Parri di Spinello 199
Passamaneria Valmar (Florence) 288
Passeggiata (evening stroll) 21, 22
Passports 298, 299
Pasticceria Maioli (Florence) 283
Paszkowski (Florence) 283
Pazzi Chapel, Santa Croce (Florence) 73
Pazzi conspiracy 49, 69
Pazzi family 49, 134
Pedro, Don 51
Pegna (Florence) 288
Street-by-Street map 63
Pensione Bencistà
Florence's Best Hotels 249
Peppe Peluso (Florence) 287
Perchè No! (Florence) 283
Peretola Airport (Florence) 307
Perfume
duty-free allowances 298
What to Buy in Tuscany 30
La Pergola (Pienza) 11
La Perla (Florence) 287
Perseus (Cellini) 77
Perugino 83, 122
Crucifixion and Saints 99
Peruzzi Chapel, Santa Croce (Florence) 73
Peruzzi's (Florence) 287
Pescia 169, **184**
Peter, St 161
Petrarch 46, 47
statue of 198
Petrol 315
Pharmacies 301
Philip IV, King of Spain 51
Piazza Carlo Goldoni (Florence) 136
Piazza del Cestello (Florence) 137
Piazza de' Frescobaldi (Florence)
Street-by-Street map 117
Piazza Mino da Fiesole (Fiesole) 132
Piazza della Repubblica (Florence) **112**
Street-by-Street map 102–3
Piazza della Santissima Annunziata (Florence) **98**, 135

Piazza di San Firenze (Florence) 134
Piazza di San Giovanni (Florence) 134–5
Piazza di San Lorenzo (Florence) **88**
Piazza di San Marco (Florence) 135
Street-by-Street map 92
Piazza di Santa Maria Novella (Florence) 135, 136
Piazza di Santo Spirito (Florence) 10, **118**, 137, 288
walk to 136–7
Piazza di Santa Trinità (Florence) 101, **108**, 136
Piazza della Signoria (Florence) **76–7**, 134
Piazzale Michelangelo (Florence) 131
Piazzas **22–3**
Piccolomini family 219
Pickpockets 300
Pienza 11, 207, **226**
Duomo 49
Piero della Francesca 27, 191
birthplace 196–7
The Duke and Duchess of Urbino 81, 82
The Legend of the True Cross 49, 198, **200–201**
Madonna della Misericordia 197
Madonna del Parto 28–9, 197
The Resurrection 196–7
Pieroni 162
Pietà (Masolino) 164
Pietre Dure, Opificio delle (Florence) **95**
Pietro da Domenico 219
Pietro Leopoldo, Grand Duke of Tuscany 119
Pineider (Florence) 288
Pinocchio Park (Collodi) 184, 291
Day out around Lucca 183
Pinturicchio
The Life of Pope Pius II 220
The Madonna with Saints Gregory and Benedict 213, 214
Piombino **234–5**
Pisa 21, 153, **156–61**
airport 21, 153, 307
architecture 24
Campo dei Miracoli **158–9**
coach travel 311
festivals 35, **38**
hospital 301
Leaning Tower 153, 158, 159, **160**
map 157
Museo Nazionale di San Matteo 157
Museo dell'Opera del Duomo 156
Museo delle Sinopie 156
Piazza dei Cavalieri 156–7
San Paolo a Ripa d'Arno 161

Pisa (cont.)
  Santa Maria della Spina 161
  trains 308, 310
  Visitors' Checklist 157
Pisa Radiotaxi 313
Pisanino, Monte 173
Pisano, Andrea 26
  Baptistry doors (Florence) 65
  terracotta panels in Duomo
    (Florence) 67
Pisano, Bonanno
  Portale di San Ranieri 159
Pisano, Giovanni 26, 47
  Duomo (Siena) 216
  Pisa Cathedral pulpit 159
  Pistoia holy water basin 186
  Pistoia pulpit 187
  Simone 219
  Virgin and Child 156
Pisano, Guglielmo 167
Pisano, Nicola 26, 156
  The Deposition 180
  The Journey of the Magi 180
  The Life of Christ 220
  Pisa Baptistry pulpit 158
Pisano, Nino 157
Piscina Bellariva (Florence) 293
Pissarro, Camille 123
Pistoia 169, **186–7**
  festivals 35
  map 187
Pistoia Blues (Pistoia) 35, 291
Pitigliano **239**
  Etruscan tour 241
Pitti, Luca 120
Pitti Immagine Uomo (Florence) 37
Pius II, Pope 217
  coat of arms 226
  Pienza 11, 49, 226
Pius IV, Pope 108
Plato 26, 48
Poggi, Giuseppe 71, 131
Poggio a Caiano **165**
Police 300
  registration with 298
Politian (Agnolo Poliziano) 109
Pollaiuolo, Piero del 215
Pollaiuolo, Simone del *see* Cronaca
Pommellato (Florence) 288
Pomona (Marini) 186
Ponte Amerigo Vespucci (Florence)
  137
Ponte della Maddalena (Bagni di
  Lucca) 174
  Day out around Lucca 183
Ponte Santa Trinità (Florence) 108
Ponte Vecchio (Florence) **106–7**,
  134
  Street-by-Street map 103
Pontormo, Jacopo da 27, 83, 122,
  179
  The Annunciation 119

Pontormo, Jacopo da (cont.)
  Conette fresco 165
  The Deposition 119
  Santissima Annunziata frescoes
    (Florence) 98
  Venus and Cupid 94
  The Visitation 165
Poppi **195**
Porcelain Museum (Florence) 125
Il Porcellino (Tacca) 112, 134
Porsena, Lars 42
Porta, Orazio 203
Porta San Frediano (Florence) 137
Porta San Giorgio (Florence) 130
Porta San Miniato (Florence) 130
Porta San Niccolò (Florence) 131
Portale di San Ranieri (Bonanno
  Pisano) 159
Portinari, Beatrice 62, 70
Porto Azzurro
  Day out on Elba 235
Portoferraio **235**
  Day out on Elba 235
Portrait of Bia (Bronzino) 83
Postal services 305
Poste restante 305
Prada (Florence) 287
Prato 21, 169, **188–9**
  map 189
Praxiteles 83
Prima Italia 246
Primavera (Botticelli) 34, 49, 82,
  83
Principe (Florence) 287
Private homes, staying in 246
Procacci (Florence) 10, 283, 288
Procchio 233
The Procession of the Magi
  (Gozzoli) 56–7, 89
Profumeria Inglese (Florence) 288
Public holidays 37
Pucci, Antonio 109
Pucci, Emilio
  fashion 57, 88
  Palazzo Pucci (Florence) 87, **88**
  shops 287
Puccini, Giacomo
  birthplace 176, 179
  La Bohème 56
  Festival Pucciniano (Torre del
    Lago Puccini) 35, 291
  Lucca 179
  Museo Villa Puccini (Torre del
    Lago Puccini) 175
  portrait of 179
  Torre del Lago Puccini 169, **175**
Punta Ala Golf Club (Grosseto)
  293
Putto Fountain (Florence) 78
Putto with Dolphin (Verrocchio)
  79
Pythagoras 205

Q
Questura 299, 301
Quiricus, St 225

R
Raddia in Chianti
  Day out in Chianti 229
Radio 298–9
Railways *see* Trains
Rainfall 36
Ramblers Holidays 293
The Rape of the Sabine Women
  (Giambologna) 77
Raphael 27
  Madonna of the Chair 122, 123
  Madonna of the Goldfinch 83
  Palatine Gallery, Palazzo Pitti
    (Florence) 120
  Palazzo Pandolfini (Florence) 92
  Portrait of a Woman 122
Raspini (Florence) 287
Rassegna del Chianti Classico
  (Greve in Chianti) 36
Red Garter (Florence) 283
Regata di San Ranieri (Pisa) 35
Relais & Châteaux 246
Religion 20
Religious services 299
Rembrandt 83, 106
Renaissance
  architecture 25
  art **26–7**, 82, 83
  frescoes **28–9**
  history **48–9**
  walk in Renaissance Florence
    134–5
Rendola Riding Stables 293
Reni, Guido 83
Renting
  bikes and mopeds 314, 315
  cars 307, 314, 315
Residence Da-al (Florence) 246
Residential hotels 246–7
Restaurants **264–83**
  children in 265
  dress code 265
  menus 265
  prices 264–5
  reservations 265
  smoking in 265
  tipping 264
  types of 264
  vegetarian food 264
  What to Drink in Florence and
    Tuscany 268–9
  What to Eat in Florence and
    Tuscany 266–7
  wheelchair access 265
  wines 265
  see also Food and drink
The Resurrection (Piero della
  Francesca) 196–7

Rex Café (Florence) 283
Riccardi family 89
Il Rifrullo (Florence) 283
Rinaldo, Muccio and Francesco di 218
Rinascente (Florence) 287
Rio Marina **238**
  Day out on Elba 235
Risorgimento 54
Rivoire (Florence) 283
Road safety 312
Robiglio (Florence) 283
Rock music 291
Rodeo della Rosa (Albarese) 35
Romanelli (Florence) 288
Romanesque architecture 24
Romano (Florence) 287
Romans **42–3**
  Arezzo 199
  Cosa 240
  Fiesole 132–3
  Lucca 176, 178
  The Maremma 231, 236
  Piazza della Repubblica (Florence) 102
  spas 185
  Teatro Romano (Volterra) 167
Romualdo, San 195
Rosa, Salvatore 179
Rosa Regale (Florence) 288
Roselle
  Etruscan tour 241
Rose's Bar (Florence) 283
Rosselli, Cosimo 118
Rossellino, Antonio 131
Rossellino, Bernardo
  The Annunciation 198
  Badia Fiorentina (Florence) 70
  Palazzo Piccolomini (Siena) 217, 219
  Pienza 226
  Santo Stefano frescoes (Empoli) 164
  tomb of Leonardo Bruni 73
Rossi, Vincenzo de' 124
Rossini, Gioacchino 95
Rosso, Zanobi del 125
Rosso Fiorentino 27
  The Deposition 166, 197
  Santissima Annunziata frescoes (Florence) 98
Rotonda di Santa Maria degli Angeli (Florence) 135
Rubelli (Florence) 287
Rubens, Peter Paul 83, 122
  The Consequences of War 123
  Self-portrait 106
Rucellai, Bernardo 104
Rucellai, Giovanni 48
  Palazzo Rucellai (Florence) 104
  tomb of 104
Rucellai family 110

Rufina 194
Ruggeri 95
Ruggieri, Ferdinando 119
Rules of the road 314
Ruskin, John 55, 83, 182
Ryanair 306

S

Safety 300
Sagra Musicale Lucchese (Lucca) 34
Sagra del Tordo (Montalcino) 36, **39**
St George (Donatello) 48
St Joseph and Christ in the Workshop (Annigoni) 91
St Peter Heals the Sick (Masaccio) 126
Saint-Phalle, Niki de
  Giardino dei Tarocchi (Pescia Fiorentina) **241**
Sala dei Gigli frescoes (Ghirlandaio) 78
Sala Vanni (Florence) 291
Salone del Cinquecento, Piazza della Signoria (Florence) 76
Sant'Agostino (Bartolo di Fredi) 212
Sant'Alessandro (Fiesole) 133
Sant'Anna in Camprena 11
Santissima Annunziata (Florence) **98**
  Street-by-Street map 93
Sant'Antimo 44–5, **228**
Santi Apostoli (Florence) 45, **109**
  Street-by-Street map 102
Santa Croce (Florence) **72–3**
San Domenico 133
Santa Felicità (Florence) **119**, 130
San Filippo Neri (Florence) 134
San Francesco (Arezzo) **200–201**
San Francesco (Fiesole) 133
San Frediano (Lucca) 182
San Frediano in Cestello (Florence) **119**, 137
San Gaetano (Florence) 136
San Galgano **224**
San Gimignano 11, 41, 207, **212–15**
  Collegiata 214–15
  Museo d'Arte Sacra 214
  Museo Civico 214
  Museo Ornitologico 215
  Palazzo Vecchio del Podestà 214
  Rocca 215
  Sant'Agostino 215
  Street-by-Street map 212–13
San Giorgio
  Day out around Lucca 183
San Giovanni Battista (Florence) 57
San Giovannino degli Scolopi (Florence)
  Street-by-Street map 87
San Lorenzo (Florence) 10, **90–91**, 135

San Lorenzo (cont.)
  Cappella dei Principi 90–91
  Medici Chapels 90–1
  Medici Tombs 91
  Michelangelo's Staircase 90
  Street-by-Street map 86–7
San Lorenzo market (Florence) 19
San Marco (Florence) **96–7**, 135
  Cloisters 49, 96
  frescoes 96–7
  Library 97
  Street-by-Street map 92–3
Santa Margherita de' Cerchi (Florence) 70
  Street-by-Street map 63
Santa Maria del Carmine (Florence) 137
  Brancacci Chapel **126–7**, 137
Santa Maria del Fiore (Florence) *see* Duomo (Florence)
Santa Maria Maddalena dei Pazzi (Florence) **99**
Santa Maria Novella (Florence) **110–11**, 135, 136
Santa Maria Novella Station (Florence) **113**
  architecture 57
  coaches 311
  trains 310
  walk to Piazza Santo Spirito 136
Santa Maria della Spina (Pisa) 24
San Martino (Lucca) **180–81**
San Michele in Foro (Lucca) 182
San Miniato **163–4**
  festivals 34
San Miniato al Monte (Florence) 53, 129
  walk to 130–31
San Pancrazio (Florence) 104, 136
San Paolo a Ripa d'Arno (Pisa) 24
San Pellegrino in Alpe 174
San Piero a Grado **161**
San Quirico d'Orcia 11, 207, **225**
San Salvatore al Monte (Florence) 131
Santo Spirito (Florence) **118**
  Street-by-Street map 116
Santo Stefano dei Cavalieri (Florence) 25
Santo Stefano al Ponte (Florence) **74–5**, 134
Santa Trinità (Florence) 10, **108–9**
  Street-by-Street map 102
Sangallo, Antonio da the Elder 203, 227
Sangallo, Antonio da the Younger 198
Sangallo, Giuliano da
  Duomo (Cortona) 204
  Palazzo Gondi (Florence) 134
  Palazzo Strozzi (Florence) 105

Sangallo, Giuliano da (cont.)
Poggio a Caiano 165
Porta Nova (Colle di Val d'Elsa) 210
Santa Maria delle Carceri (Prato) 189
Santa Maria Maddalena dei Pazzi 99
Santo Spirito (Florence) 118
Temple of San Biagio (Montepulciano) 11
tomb of Francesco Sassetti 109
Sano di Pietro 219, 225
Sansepolcro **196–7**
festivals 36
Sansovino, Andrea 203
Sarto, Andrea del 27, 122, 179
The Birth of the Virgin 98
The Journey of the Magi 98
La Madonna del Sacco 98
Poggio a Caiano frescoes 165
Santissima Annunziata frescoes (Florence) 93
Saschall (Florence) 291
Sassetti, Francesco 108–9
Sassetti, Teodoro 109
Saturnia **238**
Etruscan tour 241
Savonarola, Girolamo
burned at the stake 53, 76
Florentine Republic 52
San Marco (Florence) 92, 96
Sbigoli Terracotte (Florence) 288
Scalza, Ippolito 227
Scheggia, *Cassone Adimari* 94
Scoppio del Carro (Florence) 34
Scudieri (Florence) 283
Scuola del Cuoio (Florence) 287
Security **300–301**
Self-catering accommodation 246, 298
Settimana Musicale Senese (Siena) 35
Severini, Gino 205
Shelley, Percy Bysshe 34
death 55, 161
Sherpa Expeditions 293
Shoes
Ferragamo Shoe Museum (Florence) 10, 105
shops 285, 287
What to Buy in Tuscany 31
Shopping **284–9**
art and antiques 286, 288
books and paper 286, 288
clothing 284–5, 287
department stores 284, 287
Florence 284
food and wine 286–7, 288, 289
gifts 286, 288
how to pay 284
jewellery 285, 288

Shopping (cont.)
leather goods 285, 287
self-catering holidays 298
shoes 285, 287
toiletries 285, 288
Tuscany 289
VAT exemption 284, 298
What to Buy in Tuscany **30–31**
when to shop 284
see also Markets
Siena 11, 21, 207, 208, **216–23**
architecture 24
coach travel 311
Duomo 216, **220–21**
festivals 35, **39**
Fortezza Medicea 223
hospital 301
map 223
Museo dell'Opera Metropolitana 219
Palazzo Piccolomini 219
Palazzo Pubblico 218–19
Palio 19, 39, **222**
Piazza del Campo 218
Pinacoteca Nazionale 11, 219
San Domenico 223
Santa Maria della Scala 219
Santuario e Casa di Santa Caterina 219
Street-by-Street map 216–17
Torre del Mangia 218
trains 310
Siena Radiotaxi 313
Siena School 203, 210, 211, 219, 227, 238
Signorelli, Luca 199
The Annunciation 166
The Crucifixion 197
The Deposition 204
Life of St Benedict 211
Madonna and Child 203
Madonna and Child with Saints 166
tomb of 204
Signum (Florence) 288
Simone (Pisano) 219
SITA 311
Skiing 293
Sloane, Francis 72
Smoking, in restaurants 265
Smollett, Tobias
grave of 163
Società Canottieri Firenze 293
Soderini, Chancellor 52
Sodoma 27, 179
The Deposition 219
frescoes of St Catherine of Siena 223
The Life of Saint Benedict 211
Sant'Anna in Camprena 11
Temptation of St Benedict 211

Solemar 246
Sorpasso 57
Sorri, Pietro 219
Southern Tuscany **231–41**
Exploring Southern Tuscany 232–3
Sovana 43, **238**
Etruscan tour 241
Spanish Chapel, Santa Maria Novella (Florence) 110
Spas **185**
Bagno Vignoni **226**
holidays 293
Monsummano Terme 185
Montecatini Terme **184–5**
Saturnia **238**
Specialist holidays **292–3**
Spedale degli Innocenti (Florence) **95**, 135
Renaissance architecture 25, 48–9
Street-by-Street map 93
Spinazzi, Innocenzo
monument to Machiavelli 72
Spiro Sub Diving Club 293
Spring in Tuscany 34
Squares **22–3**
Stationery
What to Buy in Tuscany 30
Statues in Florence
Cosimo I 76
Ferdinando I 93, 98
The Four Seasons 102, 108
Giovanni delle Bande Nere 87, 88
Incontro di Teano (Fiesole) 132
Stazione di Santa Maria Novella (Florence) *see* Santa Maria Novella Station
Stendhal 105
Stia **195**
Stilicho, Flavius 43
The Story of the Holy Girdle (Daddi) 188
Stradivari, Antonio 95
Straw Market (Florence) 112
Street numbers 298
Strozzi, Filippo 105
Strozzi Chapel, Santa Maria Novella (Florence) 111
Strozzi family 105
Student information 298, 299
Student Point (Florence) 299
Summer in Tuscany 35
Sunscreen 301
Sunshine 35
Susini, Francesco
Artichoke Fountain 120
Sustermans, Justus 123
Swimming 293
Synagogues
Tempio Israelitico (Florence) **99**

T

Tacca, Pietro
  Mannerist fountains 98
  Monumento dei Quattro Mori 162
  Il Porcellino 112
  statue of Ferdinando I 93
Taddeo di Bartolo 41
  Assumption of the Virgin triptych 227
  The Last Judgment 215
  The Life of the Virgin 218
  San Gimignano and his Miracles 214
  Virgin and Child 214
Taf (Florence) 287
Tailor Made Tours 246
Take-away food 282, 283
Talamone
  Etruscan tour 240
Tarlati, Guido
  tomb of 198
Tarquinia 240
Tax, Value Added (VAT) 284, 298
Taxis 313
  from Pisa airport 307
  safety 300
Teatro dei Differenti (Barga) 291
Teatro del Maggio (Florence) 291
Teatro del Pergola (Florence) 291
Teatro Romano (Fiesole) 132
Teatro Verdi (Florence) 291
Telephones 304–5
Television 298–9
Temperatures 37
Tempio Israelitico (Florence) 99
Temple of San Biagio
  (Montepulciano) 11
Temptation of Adam and Eve
  (Masolino) 127
Temptation of St Benedict (Sodoma) 211
Tenax (Florence) 291
Tenuta di San Rossore 161
Terme di Saturnia 293
Theatre 290–91
Theft 300
Theme parks
  Pinocchio Park (Collodi) 183, 184, 291
Tiburzi, Domenico 56
Tickets
  buses 312–13
  for entertainments 290
  trains 308–9
Time zone 299
Tintoretto 122, 179
Tipping 297
  in restaurants 264
Tiratoio (Florence) 283
Tirrenia 161
Titian
  La Bella 122

Titian (cont.)
  Mary Magdalene 122
  The Venus of Urbino 80, 83
Toiletries 30
  shops 285, 288
Toilets, public 297
Tolls, motorway 315
Tombs, Etruscan 42–3
  Etruscan tour 240–41
  melon tombs 205
  Necropoli Etrusca (Sovana) 238
  Necropoli di Poggio Pinci
    (Asciano) 211
Il Torchio (Florence) 288
Torre di Bellosguardo
  Florence's Best Hotels 248
Torre di Castelmarino 236
Torre del Lago Puccini 169, 170,
  175
  festivals 35
Torre de' Lanfredini (Florence) 137
Torrini (Florence) 288
Totila the Goth 44
Touring Club Italiano 246
Tourist Guide Association 297
Tourist Medical Centre 301
Tourist offices 296
Tours, guided 297
Tours by car
  Day out around Lucca 183
  Day out in Chianti 229
  Day out on Elba 234–5
  Etruscan tour 240–41
TRA-IN 311, 313
Traffic police 300
Trains 308–10
  from Pisa airport 307
  Stazione di Santa Maria Novella
    (Florence) 113
Trattoria Santa Croce (Florence)
  283
Travel 306–15
  air 306–7
  buses 312–13
  cars 314–15
  Central Tuscany 208
  coaches 311
  Eastern Tuscany 192
  horse-drawn carriages 297
  Northern Tuscany 171
  Southern Tuscany 232
  taxis 300, 313
  trains 308–10
  Western Tuscany 155
Travellers' cheques 300, 302
  lost 301
Tree of the Cross (Bonaguida) 92,
  94
Treves, Marco 99
Tribolo, Niccolò 89
Tribuna (Zoffani) 55
Tribune, Uffizi (Florence) 83

The Trinity (Masaccio) 26, 110
The Triumph of Death (frescoes)
  158
Tuscan Sun Festival 291
Tuscany
  architecture 24–5
  art 26–9
  Central Tuscany 207–29
  Eastern Tuscany 191–205
  festivals 34–9
  great days out 11
  history 41–57
  landscape 32–3
  markets 289
  shops 289
  Southern Tuscany 231–41
  town squares 22–3
  Tuscany at a Glance 150–51
  Western Tuscany 153–67
  What to Buy in Tuscany 30–31

U

Uberto, Count of Tuscany 70
Uccello, Paolo 27, 82
  The Battle of San Romano 48, 82
  Duomo clock 61
  Noah and the Flood 110
Ufficio Guide 293
Ufficio Informazioni Turistiche 297
Ufficio Promozione Turistica,
  Turismo Sociale e Sport
  (Florence) 299
Uffizi (Florence) 75, 80–83, 134
  Arno Corridor 83
  bomb damage 57
  Botticelli 82–3
  Corridoio Vasariano 75, 106, 107,
    134
  early Renaissance 82
  floorplan 80–81
  Gothic art 82
  High Renaissance and Mannerism
    83
  later paintings 83
  Leonardo da Vinci 83
  non-Florentine art 83
  The Tribune 83
  Visitors' Checklist 81
Ugo, Count of Tuscany
  tomb of 70
Ugo Poggi (Florence) 288
Ugolini (Florence) 288
Ugolino, Count 157
Ugolino Golf Course (Grassina) 293
Umbrian School 99
UNICEF 95
Università per Stranieri (Siena) 299
Urbino, Duchess of 81, 82
Urbino, Duke of 81, 82
Utens, Giusto 71
  Lunette of Boboli Gardens 125
  Villa di Poggio a Caiano 165

V

Vaccinations 298, 301
Vagli, Lago di 169, 173
Vagli di Sopra 173
Vagli di Sotto 169, 173
Valentino (Florence) 287
Vallebona 293
Vallombrosa 191, **194**
Vallombrosan order 108, 194
Value Added Tax (VAT) 284, 298
Van Dyck, Sir Anthony 83, 122
Le Vanita' (Florence) 288
Vanni, Andrea 223
Vanni, Francesco 219
Vanni, Lippo 203
Vanvitelli, Luigi 215
Vasari, Giorgio 27
  Arezzo arcade 198
  Arezzo frescoes 198
  The Assumption 203
  Casa del Vasari (Arezzo) 199
  Chimera 99
  Last Judgment frescoes 65
  Michelangelo's tomb 72
  Monte San Savino gate 203
  Palazzo dei Cavalieri (Pisa) 156
  Palazzo di Parte Guelfa
    (Florence) 109
  Palazzo Vecchio frescoes
    (Florence) 78
  Ponte Vecchio (Florence) 106
  Putto Fountain (Florence) 78
  Salone del Cinquecento frescoes
    76
  Santa Felicità (Florence) 119
  Santo Stefano dei Cavalieri (Pisa)
    157
  The Siege of Florence 52–3
  Uffizi (Florence) 80, 81
Vasari Corridor, Uffizi (Florence) 75,
  106, 107, 134
VAT exemption 284, 298
Vegetarian food 264
Venus Italica (Canova) 122
The Venus of Urbino (Titian) 80, 83
Veronese, Paolo 122
Verrocchio, Andrea del 27, 63
  bust of Christ 164
  David 49
  Lady with a Posy 69
  Putto Fountain (Florence) 78
  Putto with Dolphin 79
Versace (Florence) 287
The Versilia 169, **172–3**
Vespucci, Amerigo 75, 113
Vespucci family 113
Vestri (Florence) 283
Via dei Calzaiuoli (Florence)
  Street-by-Street map 62
Via dei Fossi (Florence) **112–13**
Via de' Ginori (Florence)
  Street-by-Street map 87

Via Maggio (Florence) **118**
Via de' Tornabuoni (Florence) **105**
Via della Vigna Nuova (Florence)
  105
Viareggio 169, **175**
  festivals 34, 37, **38**
Victory (Michelangelo) 79
Vieusseux, Gian Pietro 105
Vigili (municipal police) 315
La Vigna (Florence) 283
Viligiardi, Arturo 228
Villa Europa Camerata (Florence)
  299
Villa La Massa
  Florence's Best Hotels 249
Villa di Poggio a Caiano (Utens)
  165
Villa San Michele (Fiesole)
  Florence's Best Hotels 249
Villas
  Castello di Palagio (Stia) 191
  Castello di Poppi (Poppi) 191
  Castello di Porciano (Stia) 191
  Castello di Romena (Poppi) 191
  Fortezza Medicea (Arezzo) 41
  Museo Nazionale Villa Guinigi
    (Lucca) 178–9
  Poggio a Caiano 165
  Villa di Artimino (Artimino) 165
  Villa Bottini (Lucca) 182
  Villa di Cafaggiolo (Borgo San
    Lorenzo) 194
  Villa Garzoni (Collodi) 183, 184
  Villa Mansi (Lucca) 183
  Villa Medici (Fiesole) 133
  Villa San Martino (Portoferraio)
    235
  Villa Torrigiani (Lucca) 183
Vincenzo di Michele 178
Vinci 153, **164–5**
Vini del Chianti (Florence) 283
Vini e Panini (Florence) 283
Viottolone
  Boboli Gardens (Florence) 125
Virgin and Child (Fra Angelico)
  85
Virgin and Child (Martini) 157
The Virgin Appearing to St Bernard
  (Lippi) 70
Virgin's Girdle 188
Visas 298
Visdomini, St Giovanni Gualberto
  194
Vittorio Emanuele II, King 219
  statue of 132
Le Volpi e l'Uva (Florence) 283
Volterra 42, 43, 153, **166–7**
  Duomo 166–7
  map 167
  Museo Etrusco Guarnacci 166
  Pinacoteca e Museo Civico 166
Vulci 240

W

Walking Tours of Florence 297
Walks 312
  holidays 292, 293
  Renaissance Florence 134–5
  through Fiesole 132–3
  to Piazza Santo Spirito 136–7
  to San Miniato al Monte 130–31
Water, drinking 301
Water sports 293
WCs 297
Weather 35–7
Wedding Scene (Memmo di
  Filippucci) 214, 215
Western Tuscany **153–67**
  Exploring Western Tuscany 154–5
Wheelchair access *see* Disabled
  travellers
Wildlife **33**
  Ansedonia 241
  The Maremma 236–7
  Orbetello 239
  Parco dell' Orecchiella (San
    Pellegrino in Alpe) 174
  Parco Naturale delle Alpi Apuane
    173
  Parco Naturale dell'Uccellina 236
  Parco Naturale della Viriglia 229
  Tenuta di San Rossore **161**
Willa, Countess 70
Wine
  duty-free allowances 298
  in restaurants 265
  shops 286–7, 288
  What to Drink in Florence and
    Tuscany 268–9
  wine cellars 282, 283
  wine tasting 292, 293
Winter in Tuscany 37
Woman in a Turban (Masaccio)
  127
World War I 56
World War II 19, 41, 56
Worldwide Fund for Nature 239,
  241

Y

Yves Saint Laurent (Florence) 287

Z

Zaccaria da Volterra 167
Zanobini (Florence) 288
Zocchi 95
Zoffani, Johann
  Tribuna 55
Zoos
  Pistoia 187
  Zoo Fauna Europa (Poppi) 195
Zuccarelli, Francesco 239

Acknowledgments

Dorling Kindersley would like to thank the following people whose contributions and help have made the preparation of this book possible.

Main Contributor
Christopher Catling has been visiting Florence and Tuscany since his first archaeological dig there as a student at Cambridge University 25 years ago. He is the author of several guide books on the city and region.

Additional Photography
Jane Burton, Philip Dowell, Neil Fletcher, Steve Gorton, Frank Greenaway, Neil Mersh, David Murray, Ian O'Leary, Poppy, Clive Streeter, Linda Whitwam.

Additional Illustrations
Gillie Newman, Chris D Orr, Sue Sharples, Ann Winterbotham, John Woodcock, Martin Woodward.

Cartography
Uma Bhattacharya; Colourmap Scannning Limited; Contour Publishing; Cosmographics; European Map Graphics; Suresh Kumar; Kunal Singh. Street Finder maps: ERA Maptech Ltd (Dublin), adapted with permission from original survey and mapping by Shobunsha (Japan).

Cartographic Research
Caroline Bowie, Peter Winfield, Claudine Zante.

Design and Editorial Assistance
Louise Abbott, Gaye Allen, Douglas Amrine, Sam Atkinson, Rosemary Bailey, Tessa Bindloss, Hilary Bird, Lucia Bronzin, Ann-Marie Bulat, Carolyn Burdet, Julia Burdet, Jacob Cameron, Cooling Brown, Vanessa Courtier, Michelle Crane, Felicity Crowe, Joy FitzSimmons, Natalie Godwin, Jackie Gordon, Vinod Harish, Jacky Jackson, Annette Jacobs, Emma Jones, Roberta Kedzierski, Steve Knowlden, David Lamb, Neil Lockley, Siri Lowe, Georgina Matthews, Rebecca Milner, Helen Partington, Alice Peebles, Pamposh Raina, Sands Publishing Solutions, Baishakhee Sengupta, Shailesh Sharma, Asavari Singh, Kate Singleton, Ellie Smith, Nicky Swallow, Rachel Symons, Andrew Szudek, Dawn Terrey, Tracy Timson, Alka Thakur, Daphne Trotter, Nick Turpin, Glenda Tyrrell, Janis Utton, Alastair Wardle, Lynda Warrington, Fiona Wild, Stewart J. Wild.

Special Assistance
Antonio Carluccio; Sam Cole; Giuseppe de Micheli and Moira Barbacovi at the Museo dell'Opera di Santa Croce; Julian Fox, University of East London; Simon Groom; Signor Tucci at the Ministero dei Beni Culturali e Ambientali; Museo dell'Opificio delle Pietre Dure; Signora Pelliconi at the Soprintendenza per i Beni Artistici e Storici delle Province di Firenze e Pistoia; Prof. Francesco Villari, Direttore, Istituto Italiano di Cultura, London.

For special assistance in supplying the computer-generated image of the Gozzoli frescoes in the Palazzo Medici Riccardi: Dr Cristina Acidini, Head of Restoration, and the restorers at Consorzio Pegasus, Firenze; Ancilla Antonini of Index, Firenze; and Galileo Siscam SpA, Firenze, producers of the CAD Orthomap graphic programme.

Photographic Reference
Camisa I & Son, Carluccio's, Gucci Ltd.

Photography Permissions
Dorling Kindersley would like to thank the following for their permission to photograph:

Florence: Badia Fiorentina; Biblioteca Mediceo-Laurenziana; Biblioteca Riccardiana; Centro Mostra di Firenze; Comune di Firenze; Duomo; Hotel Continentale; Hotel Hermitage; Hotel Villa Belvedere; Le Fonticine; Museo Bardini; Museo di Firenze com'era; Museo Horne; Museo Marino Marini; Museo dell'Opera del Duomo di Firenze; Ognissanti; Palazzo Vecchio; Pensione Bencistà; Rebus; Santi Apostoli; Santa Croce; San Lorenzo; Santa Maria Novella; Santa Trinità; Soprintendenza per i Beni Ambientali e Architettonici delle Province di Firenze e Pistoia; Tempio Israelitico; Trattoria Angiolino; Ufficio Occupazioni Suolo Pubblico di Firenze; Villa La Massa; Villa Villoresi.
Tuscany: Campo dei Miracoli, Pisa; Collegiata, San Gimignano; Comune di Empoli; Comune di San Gimignano; Comune di Vinci; Duomo, Siena; Duomo, Volterra; Museo della Collegiata di Sant'Andrea, Empoli; Museo Diocesano di Cortona; Museo Etrusco Guarnacci, Volterra; Museo Leonardiano, Vinci; Museo dell'Opera del Duomo, Pisa; Museo dell'Opera del Duomo, Siena; Museo delle Sinopie, Pisa; Opera della Metropolitana di Siena; Opera Primaziale Pisana, Pisa; Soprintendenza per i Beni Ambientali e Architettonici di Siena; Soprintendenza per i Beni Artistici e Storici di Siena; Soprintendenza per i Beni Ambientali, Architettonici, Artistici e Storici di Pisa.

Picture Credits
t = top; tl = top left; tc = top centre; tr = top right; cla = centre left above; ca = centre above; cra = centre right above; cl = centre left; c = centre; cr = centre right; clb = centre left below; cb = centre below; crb = centre right below; bl = bottom left, b = bottom; bc = bottom centre; br = bottom right; (d) = detail.

Every effort has been made to trace the copyright holders and we apologize in advance for any unintentional omissions. We would be pleased to insert the appropriate acknowledgments in any subsequent edition of this publication

The publisher would like to thank the following individuals, companies and picture libraries for permission to reproduce their photographs:

AGENZIA PER IL TURISMO, FIRENZE: 72tr; ALAMY IMAGES: Gary Cook 267t; CuboImages srl/Nico Tondini 135t; ARCHIVI ALINARI, FIRENZE: 104b; THE ANCIENT ART AND ARCHITECTURE COLLECTION: 77tl; ANTICO FATTORE RESTAURANT: Walter Bellini 264b; ARCHIVIO FOTOGRAFICO ENCICLOPEDICO, ROMA: Giuseppe Carfagna 38t, 39b, 203t, 203c; Luciano Casadei 38b; Cellai/Focus Team 38c; Claudio Cerquetti 33bl; B. Kortenhorst/K & B News Foto 21t; B. Mariotti 39c; S. Paderno 23t, 39t; G. Veggi 34c.

THE BRIDGEMAN ART LIBRARY, LONDON: Archivio dello Stato, Siena 47clb; Bargello, Firenze 68t, 69t; Biblioteca di San Marco, Firenze/K & B News Foto 97t; Biblioteca Marciana, Venezia 44br; Galleria dell'Accademia, Firenze 94b; Galleria degli Uffizi, Firenze 27br, 45b, 47cla, 80b, 81tl, 81tr, 83t, 83b; Musée du Louvre, Paris/Lauros-Giraudon, 105t; Museo di San Marco, Firenze 52tl, 55t, 97cb; Museo Civico, Prato 188t; Palazzo Pitti, Firenze 121tr; Sant'Apollonia, Firenze 89t (d), 92c (d); Santa Croce, Firenze 72b; Santa Maria del Carmine, Firenze 127bl (d); Santa Maria Novella, Firenze 111cr; © THE BRITISH MUSEUM: 42b.

FOTO CARFAGNA & ASSOCIATI: 285cl, 285br, 286tr, 290tc, 308b, 310t; BRUCE COLEMAN: N. G. Blake 33br, Hans Reinhard 33cla, 33cra; CORBIS: Ric Ergenbright 267c; Owen Franken 266cla; Massimo Listri 285tc; JOE CORNISH: 32–33, 36t, 37, 129t, 205, 227t; GIANCARLO COSTA, MILANO:

34t, 45t, 55clb, 56ca, 56bl, 149 (inset), 268tl. IL DAGHERROTIPO: Salvatore Barba 135b, 137b; Marco Cerruti 136cla; Maurizio Leoni 136b; Paolo Marini 11t, 134tl; Marco Ravasini 134b; Giovanni Rinadli 137t.

MARY EVANS PICTURE LIBRARY: 46t, 48b, 50bl (Explorer), 55b, 56br, 74c, 179c, 196c.

FERROVIA DELLO STATO: B Di Giulio 308cl; FLORENCE DANCE FESTIVAL: Rambert Dance Company/Swamp 291tl.

JACKIE GORDON: 57cb, 285cl, 309, 314c.

ROBERT HARDING PICTURE LIBRARY: 58–9; ALISON HARRIS: Museo dell'Opera del Duomo, Firenze 27bl, 67t, 67c; Palazzo Vecchio, Firenze/Comune di Roma/Direzione dei Musei 4t, 52cb (Sala di Gigli), 53clb, 79t; San Lorenzo, Firenze/Soprintendenza per i Beni Artistici 91c; Santa Felicità, Firenze 119t (d); Santo Spirito, Firenze 118b; 116; HOTEL PORTA ROSSA, FIRENZE: 183b; PIPPA HURST: 183cr.

THE IMAGE BANK: 60t; C. Place 100, 108t; Guido Alberto Rossi 11t, 11b; IMPACT PHOTOS: Piers Cavendish 5b; Brian Harris 19b; INDEX, FIRENZE: 186t (d), 186b, 186c (d), 187t; Biblioteca Nazionale, Firenze 9 (inset); Biblioteca Riccardiana, Firenze 59 (inset); 243 (inset) 295 (inset); Galileo Siscam, S.p.A, Firenze 56–7; P. Tosi, 66cr; Gaetano Zumbo 10tr; ISTITUTO E MUSEO DI STORIA DELLA SCIENZA DI FIRENZE: 74b, 75t; WWW.ITALIANCOOKERYCOURSE.COM: 222cra.

WWW.LANDSCAPEPAINTING.COM: Daria Insalaco 292b; FRANK LANE PICTURE AGENCY: R. Wilmshurst 33crb.

THE MANSELL COLLECTION: 47b; MUSEO DELL'OPIFICIO DELLE PIETRE DURE, FIRENZE: 95c.

MARKA: F Pizzochero 31cla; Roberto Benzi 285cla; M Motta 301cl.

GRAZIA NERI, MILANO: R. Bettini 36b; Carlo Lannutti 57b; PETER NOBLE: 5t, 18, 172b, 222tr, 222cra, 300c.

OSTERIA LE LOGGE: 265b; OXFORD SCIENTIFIC FILMS: Stan Osolinski 236tr.

ROGER PHILLIPS: 202cra, 202crb; ANDREA PISTOLESI, FIRENZE: 224b, 290b, 301t; EMILIO PUCCI S.R.L, FIRENZE: 57cla.

RETROGRAPH ARCHIVE, LONDON: © Martin Breese 173c, 184b, 247t, 269bl; RESTAURANT IL POZZO: Mario Palma 265t; ROYAL COLLECTION: © HER MAJESTY QUEEN ELIZABETH II: 55t (d). SCALA, FIRENZE: Abbazia, Monte Oliveto Maggiore 211t; Galleria dell'Accademia, Firenze 92b, 94t, 95t; Badia, Fiesole 49clb; Badia, Firenze 70b; Bargello, Firenze 41t, 43bl, 46b, 49cla, 49b, 51cr, 54br, 66tr, 68b, 69cla, 69cra,

69clb, 108c; Battistero, Pisa 158b; Biblioteca Laurenziana, Firenze 90c; Camposanto, Pisa 156b; Cappella dei Principi, Firenze 50tl, 90t; Cappelle Medicee, Firenze 53crb, 91t; Casa del Vasari, Arezzo 199t (d); Chiesa del Carmine, Firenze 126–7, (126t, 126b, 127br all details); Cimitero, Monterchi 28c; Collegiata, San Gimignano 212cb; Corridoio Vasariano, Firenze 106t; Duomo, Lucca 180b; Duomo, Pisa 159t; Duomo, Prato 28t (d), 29t (d), 29c (d), 29b (d), 28–9; Galleria Comunale, Prato 188b; Galleria d'Arte Moderna, Firenze 54cb, 121tl; Galleria Palatina, Firenze 55crb, 122–3; Galleria degli Uffizi, Firenze 19t, 43cla, 43br, 48c, 50c, 50br, 51t, 51cl, 51b, 52cl, 52b (Collezione Giovanna), 80t, 81ca, 81cb, 81b, 82t, 82b, 83c (d); Loggia dei Lanzi, Firenze 77tr; Musée Bonnat, Bayonne 69b; Musei Civici, San Gimignano 40, 213b, 215b; Museo Archeologico, Arezzo 199c; Museo Archeologico, Firenze 42ca, 43clb, 43bl, 93cb, 99t, 99b, 240b; Museo Archeologico, Grosseto 240c; Museo Civico, Bologna 48tr; Museo degli Argenti, Firenze 53b, 54t, 54ca, 120b; Museo dell'Accademia Etrusca, Cortona 43t, 44ca; Museo dell'Opera del Duomo, Firenze 47t, 63t (d); Museo dell'Opera Metropolitana, Siena 26t; Museo di Firenze com'era, Firenze 71t, 125t, 165b; Museo Diocesano, Cortona 204b; Museo Etrusco Guarnacci, Volterra 42t; Museo di San Marco, Firenze 84, 96t (d), 96c, 96b, 97ca, 97b; Museo Mediceo, Firenze 50tr; Museo Nazionale di San Matteo, Pisa 157t; Necropoli, Sovana 241crb; Palazzo Davanzati, Firenze 103c (Sala dei Pappagalli); Palazzo Medici Riccardi, Firenze 2–3; Palazzo Pitti, Firenze 120c, 121bl; Palazzo Pubblico, Siena 46–7, 219t; Palazzo Vecchio, Firenze 52–53 (Sala di Clemente VII), 78t (Sala dei Gigli); Pinacoteca Comunale, Sansepolcro 197b; Pinacoteca Comunale, Volterra 166cr; San Francesco, Arezzo 200–1, (200t, 200b, 201t, 201b, 201cl all details); San Lorenzo, Firenze 27t; Santa Maria Novella, Firenze 26b, 46c (d), 49t (d), 110b; Santa Trinità, Firenze 102t; Santissima Annunziata, Firenze 98b; Tomba del Colle, Chiusi 42cb, 228t; Tribuna di Galileo, Firenze 54–5; Vaticano 41b (Galleria Carte Geographica); SUPERSTOCK: age fotostock 10cla; SYGMA: G. Giansanti 222cla, 222crb, 222bl; Keystone 57t.

THE TRAVEL LIBRARY: Philip Enticknap 94cr, 218t, 296c.

JACKET
Front - CORBIS: Jim Zuckerman main image; DK IMAGES: John Heseltine bl. Back - DK IMAGES: John Heseltine tl; Kim Sayer bl; PETER NOBLE: cla, clb. Spine - DK IMAGES: Alison Harris b; CORBIS: Jim Zuckerman t.

FRONT ENDPAPER
THE IMAGE BANK: tl; SCALA, FIRENZE: tr.

All other images © Dorling Kindersley. For further information see www.dkimages.com

SPECIAL EDITIONS OF DK TRAVEL GUIDES

DK Travel Guides can be purchased in bulk quantities at discounted prices for use in promotions or as premiums. We are also able to offer special editions and personalized jackets, corporate imprints, and excerpts from all of our books, tailored specifically to meet your own needs.

To find out more, please contact:
(in the United States) SpecialSales@dk.com
(in the UK) Sarah.Burgess@dk.com
(in Canada) DK Special Sales at general@tourmaline.ca
(in Australia) business.development@pearson.com.au

Phrase Book

In An Emergency

Help!	**Aiuto!**	eye-**yoo**-toh
Stop!	**Fermate!**	fair-**mah**-teh
Call a doctor.	**Chiama un medico**	kee-**ah**-mah oon **meh**-dee-koh
Call an ambulance.	**Chiama un' ambulanza**	kee-**ah**-mah oon am-boo-**lan**-tsa
Call the police.	**Chiama la polizia**	kee-**ah**-mah lah pol-ee-**tsee**-ah
Call the fire brigade.	**Chiama i pompieri**	kee-**ah**-mah ee pom-pee-**air**-ee
Where is the telephone?	**Dov'è il telefono?**	dov-**eh** eel teh-**leh**-foh-noh?
The nearest hospital?	**L'ospedale più vicino?**	loss-peh-**dah**-leh pee-**oovee**-**chee**-noh?

Communication Essentials

Yes/No	**Sì/No**	see/**noh**
Please	**Per favore**	pair fah-**vor**-eh
Thank you	**Grazie**	**grah**-tsee-eh
Excuse me	**Mi scusi**	mee **skoo**-zee
Hello	**Buon giorno**	bwon **jor**-noh
Good bye	**Arrivederci**	ah-ree-veh-**dair**-chee
Good evening	**Buona sera**	**bwon**-ah **sair**-ah
morning	**la mattina**	lah mat-**tee**-nah
afternoon	**il pomeriggio**	eel pob-meh-**ree**-joh
evening	**la sera**	lah **sair**-ah
yesterday	**ieri**	ee-**air**-ee
today	**oggi**	**oh**-jee
tomorrow	**domani**	doh-**mah**-nee
here/there	**qui/là**	kwee/**lah**
What?	**Quale?**	**kwah**-leh?
When?	**Quando?**	**kwan**-doh?
Why?	**Perchè?**	pair-**keh**?
Where?	**Dove?**	**doh**-veh

Useful Phrases

How are you?	**Come sta?**	**koh**-meh stah?
Very well, thank you.	**Molto bene, grazie.**	**moll**-toh **beb**-neh **grah**-tsee-eh
Pleased to meet you.	**Piacere di conoscerla.**	pee-ah-**chair**-eh dee coh-noh-shair-lah
See you soon.	**A più tardi.**	ah pee-**oo** tar-dee
That's fine.	**Va bene.**	va **beh**-neh
Where is/are ...?	**Dov'è/Dove sono ...?**	dov-**eh**/doveh **soh**-noh?
How long does it take to get to ...?	**Quanto tempo ci vuole per andare a ...?**	**kwan**-toh **tem**-poh chee voo-**oh**-leh pair an-**dar**-eh ah...?
How do I get to ...?	**Come faccio per arrivare a ...?**	koh-meh **fah**-choh pair arri-**var**-eh ah..?
Are you getting off?	**Scende?**	**Shen**-deh?
Do you speak English?	**Parla inglese?**	**par**-lah een-**gleb**-zeh?
I don't understand.	**Non capisco.**	non ka-**pee**-skoh
Could you speak more slowly, please?	**Può parlare più lentamente, per favore?**	pwoh par-**lah**-reh pee-**oo** len-ta-**men**-teh pair fah-**vor**-eh?
I'm sorry.	**Mi dispiace.**	mee dee-spee-**ah**-cheh

Useful Words

big	**grande**	**gran**-deh
small	**piccolo**	**pee**-koh-loh
hot	**caldo**	**kal**-doh
cold	**freddo**	**fred**-doh
good	**buono**	**bwoh**-noh
bad	**cattivo**	kat-**tee**-voh
enough	**basta**	**bas**-tah
open	**aperto**	ah-**pair**-toh
closed	**chiuso**	kee-**oo**-zoh
left	**a sinistra**	ah see-**nee**-strah
right	**a destra**	ah **dess**-trah
straight on	**sempre dritto**	**sem**-preh **dree**-toh
near	**vicino**	vee-**chee**-noh
far	**lontano**	lon-**tah**-noh
up	**su**	**soo**
down	**giù**	**joo**
early	**presto**	**press**-toh
late	**tardi**	**tar**-dee
entrance	**entrata**	en-**trah**-tah
exit	**uscita**	oo-**shee**-ta
toilet	**il gabinetto**	eel gab-ben-**net**-toh
free, unoccupied	**libero**	**lee**-bair-oh
free, no charge	**gratuito**	grah-**too**-ee-toh

Making a Telephone Call

I'd like to place a long-distance call.	**Vorrei fare una interurbana.**	vor-**ray far**-eh oona in-tair-oor-**bab**-nah
I'd like to make a reverse-charge call.	**Vorrei fare una telefonata a carico del destinatario.**	vor-**ray far**-eh oona teh-leh-fon-**ah**-tah ah **kar**-ee-koh dell dess-tee-nah-**tar**-ree-oh
I'll try again later.	**Ritelefono più tardi.**	ree-teh-**leb**-foh-noh pee-oo **tar**-dee
Can I leave a message?	**Posso lasciare un messaggio?**	**poss**-oh lash-**ah**-reh oon mess-**sab**-joh?
Hold on.	**Un attimo, per favore**	oon **ab**-tee-moh, pair fah-**vor**-eh
Could you speak up a little please?	**Può parlare più forte, per favore?**	pwoh par-**lab**-reh pee-**oo for**-teh, pair fah-**vor**-eh?
local call	**la telefonata locale**	lah teh-leh-fon-**ab**-ta loh-**kab**-leh

Shopping

How much does this cost?	**Quant'è, per favore?**	kwan-**teh** pair fah-**vor**-eh?
I would like ...	**Vorrei ...**	vor-**ray**
Do you have ...?	**Avete ...?**	ah-**veb**-teh.. ?
I'm just looking.	**Sto soltanto guardando.**	stob sol-**tan**-toh gwar-**dan**-doh
Do you take credit cards?	**Accettate carte di credito?**	ah-chet-**tab**-teh **kar**-teh dee **creb**-dee-toh?
What time do you open/close?	**A che ora apre/ chiude?**	ah keh **or**-ah **ab**-preh/kee-oo-deh?
this one	**questo**	**kweb**-stoh
that one	**quello**	**kwell**-oh
expensive	**caro**	**kar**-oh
cheap	**a buon prezzo**	ah bwon **pret**-soh
size, clothes	**la taglia**	lah **tab**-lee-ah
size, shoes	**il numero**	eel **noo**-mair-oh
white	**bianco**	bee-**ang**-koh
black	**nero**	**neb**-roh
red	**rosso**	**ross**-oh
yellow	**giallo**	**jal** loh
green	**verde**	**vair**-deh
blue	**blu**	**bloo**
brown	**marrone**	mar-**rob**-neh

Types of Shop

antique dealer	**l'antiquario**	lan-tee-**kwab**-ree-oh
bakery	**la panetteria**	lah pab-net-tair-**ree**-ah
bank	**la banca**	lah **bang**-kah
bookshop	**la libreria**	lah lee-breh-**ree**-ah
butcher's	**la macelleria**	lah mah-chell-eh-**ree**-ah
cake shop	**la pasticceria**	lah pas-tee-chair-**ee**-ah
chemist's	**la farmacia**	lah far-mah-**chee**-ah
delicatessen	**la salumeria**	lah sah loo-meh-**ree**-ah
department store	**il grande magazzino**	eel **gran**-deh mag-gad-**zee**-noh
fishmonger's	**la pescheria**	lah pess-keh-**ree**-ah
florist	**il fioraio**	eel fee-or-**eye**-oh
greengrocer	**il fruttivendolo**	eel froo-tee-**ven**-doh-loh
grocery	**alimentari**	ah-lee-men-**tah**-ree
hairdresser	**il parrucchiere**	eel par-oo-kee-**air**-eh
ice-cream parlour	**la gelateria**	lah jel-lah-tair-**ree**-ah
market	**il mercato**	eel mair-**kab**-toh
news-stand	**l'edicola**	leh-**dee**-koh-lah
post office	**l'ufficio postale**	loo-**fee**-choh pos-**tab**-leh
shoe shop	**il negozio di scarpe**	eel neh-**gob**-tsioh dee **skar**-peh
supermarket	**il supermercato**	su-pair-mair-**kab**-toh
tobacconist	**il tabaccaio**	eel tab-bak **eye** oh
travel agency	**l'agenzia di viaggi**	lah-jen-**tsee**-ah dee vee-**ad**-jee

Sightseeing

art gallery	**la pinacoteca**	lah peena-koh-**teb**-kah
bus stop	**la fermata dell'autobus**	lah fair-**mab**-tah dell **ow**-toh-booss
church	**la chiesa**	lah kee-**eb**-zah
	la basilica	lah bah-**seel**-i-kah
closed for the public holiday	**chiuso per la festa**	kee-oo-zoh pair lah **fess**-tah
garden	**il giardino**	eel jar-**dee**-no
library	**la biblioteca**	lah beeb-lee-oh-**teb**-kah
museum	**il museo**	eel moo-**zeb**-oh
railway station	**la stazione**	lah stah-tsee-**ob**-neh
tourist information	**l'ufficio turistico**	loo-**fee**-choh too-**ree**-stee-koh

Staying in a Hotel

Do you have any vacant rooms?	Avete camere libere?	ah-**veh**-teh **kab**-mair-eh **lee**-bair-eh?
double room	una camera doppia	oona **kab**-mair-ah **dob**-pee-ah
with double bed	con letto matrimoniale	kon **let**-toh mah-tree-moh-nee-**ab**-leb
twin room	una camera con due letti	oona **kab**-mair-ah kon **doo**-eh **let**-tee
single room	una camera singola	oona **kab**-mair-ah **sing**-gob-lah
room with a bath, shower	una camera con bagno, con doccia	oona **kab**-mair-ah kon **ban**-yoh, kon **dot**-chah
porter	il facchino	eel fah-**kee**-noh
key	la chiave	lah kee-**ab**-veh
I have a reservation.	Ho fatto una prenotazione.	oh **fat**-toh oona preh-nob-tah-tsee-**ob**-neh

Eating Out

Have you got a table for ...?	Avete una tavola per ... ?	ah-**veh**-teh oona **tab**-voh-lah pair ...?
I'd like to reserve a table.	Vorrei riservare una tavola.	vor-**ray** ree-sair-**vab**-reh oona **tab**-voh-lah
breakfast	colazione	koh-lah-tsee-**ob**-neh
lunch	pranzo	**pran**-tsoh
dinner	cena	**cheb**-nah
Enjoy your meal.	Buon appetito.	bwon ab-peh-**tee**-toh
The bill, please.	Il conto, per favore.	eel **kon**-toh pair fah-**vor**-eh
I am a vegetarian.	Sono vegetariano/a.	**sob**-noh veh-jeb-tar ee-**ab**-noh/nah
waitress	cameriera	kah-mair-ee-**air**-ah
waiter	cameriere	kah-mair-ee-**air**-eh
fixed price	il menù a	eel meb-**noo** ah
menu	prezzo fisso	**pret**-soh **fee**-soh
dish of the day	piatto del giorno	pee-**ab**-toh dell **jor**-no
starter	antipasto	an-tee-**pass**-toh
first course	il primo	eel **pree**-moh
main course	il secondo	eel seh-**kon**-doh
vegetables	il contorno	eel kon-**tor**-noh
dessert	il dolce	eel **doll**-cheh
cover charge	il coperto	eel koh-**pair**-toh
wine list	la lista dei vini	lah **lee**-stah day **vee**-nee
rare	al sangue	al **sang**-gweh
medium	al puntino	al poon-**tee**-noh
well done	ben cotto	ben **kot**-toh
glass	il bicchiere	eel bee-kee-**air**-eh
bottle	la bottiglia	lah bot-**teel**-yah
knife	il coltello	eel kol-**tell**-oh
fork	la forchetta	lah for-**ket**-tah
spoon	il cucchiaio	lah koo-kee-**eye**-oh

Menu Decoder

l'abbacchio	lah-**back**-kee-oh	lamb
l'aceto	lah-**cheb**-toh	vinegar
l'acqua	lah-**kwah**	water
l'acqua minerale gasata/naturale	lah-kwah mee-nair-**ab**-leb gab-**zab**-tah/ nah-too-**rab**-leh	mineral water fizzy/still
l'aglio	**labl**-yoh	garlic
al forno	al **for**-noh	baked
alla griglia	ah-lah **greel**-yah	grilled
l'anatra	**lah**-nab-trah	duck
l'aragosta	lah-rah-**goss**-tah	lobster
l'arancia	lah-**ran**-chah	orange
arrosto	ar-**ross**-toh	roast
la birra	lah **beer**-rah	beer
la bistecca	lah bee-**stek**-kah	steak
il brodo	eel **brob**-doh	broth
il burro	eel **boor**-oh	butter
il caffè	eel kah-**feb**	coffee
il carciofo	eel kar-**choff**-oh	artichoke
la carne	la **kar**-neh	meat
carne di maiale	**kar**-neh dee mab-**yab**-leh	pork
la cipolla	lah chee-**poll**-ah	onion
i fagioli	ee fab-**job**-lee	beans
il formaggio	eel for-**mad**-joh	cheese
le fragole	leh **frab**-gob-leh	strawberries
frutta fresca	**froo**-tah **fress**-kah	fresh fruit
frutti di mare	**froo**-tee dee mab-reb	seafood
i funghi	ee **foon**-gee	mushrooms
i gamberi	ee **gam**-bair-ee	prawns
il gelato	eel jel-**lab**-toh	ice cream
l'insalata	leen-sah-**lab**-tah	salad
il latte	eel **labt**-teh	milk
i legumi	ee leb-**goo**-mee	vegetables

lesso	**less**-oh	boiled
il manzo	eel **man**-tsoh	beef
la mela	lah **meb**-lah	apple
la melanzana	lah meb-lan-**tsab**-nab	aubergine
la minestra	lah mee-**ness**-trah	soup
l'olio	**loll**-yoh	oil
l'oliva	loh-**lee**-vah	olive
il pane	eel **pab**-neh	bread
il panino	eel pab-**nee**-noh	roll
le patate	leb pab-**tab**-teh	potatoes
patatine fritte	pab-tab-**teen**-eb **free**-teh	chips
il pepe	eel **peb**-peh	pepper
la pesca	lah **pess**-kab	peach
il pesce	eel **pesh**-eb	fish
il pollo	eel **poll**-oh	chicken
il pomodoro	eel pob-moh-**dor**-oh	tomato
il prosciutto cotto/crudo	eel pro-**shoo**-toh **kot**-toh/**kroo**-doh	ham cooked/cured
il riso	eel **ree**-zoh	rice
il sale	eel **sab**-leh	salt
la salsiccia	lah sal-**see**-chab	sausage
secco	**sek**-koh	dry
succo d'arancia/ di limone	**soo**-koh dah-**ran**-chab/ dee lee-**mob**-neh	orange/lemon juice
il tè	eel **teb**	tea
la tisana	lah tee-**zab**-nab	herb tea
il tonno	**ton**-noh	tuna
la torta	lah **tor**-tab	cake
l'uovo	loo-**ob**-voh	egg
l'uva	**loo**-vah	grapes
vino bianco	**vee**-noh bee-**ang**-kob	white wine
vino rosso	**vee**-noh **ross**-oh	red wine
il vitello	eel vee-**tell**-oh	veal
le vongole	leb **von**-gob-leb	baby clams
lo zucchero	lob **zoo**-kair-oh	sugar
gli zucchini	lyee dzo-**kee**-nee	courgettes
la zuppa	lah **tsoo**-pah	soup

Numbers

1	uno	**oo**-noh
2	due	**doo**-eh
3	tre	treb
4	quattro	**kwat**-roh
5	cinque	**ching**-kweh
6	sei	**say**-ee
7	sette	**set**-teh
8	otto	**ot**-toh
9	nove	**nob**-veh
10	dieci	dee-**eb**-chee
11	undici	**oon**-dee-chee
12	dodici	**dob**-dee-chee
13	tredici	**tray**-dee-chee
14	quattordici	kwat-**tor**-dee-chee
15	quindici	**kwin**-dee-chee
16	sedici	**say**-dee-chee
17	diciassette	dee-chah-**set**-teh
18	diciotto	dee-**chot**-toh
19	diciannove	dee-chah-**nob**-veh
20	venti	**ven**-tee
30	trenta	**tren**-tab
40	quaranta	kwah-**ran**-tab
50	cinquanta	ching-**kwan**-tah
60	sessanta	sess-**an**-tab
70	settanta	set-**tan**-tab
80	ottanta	ot-**tan**-tab
90	novanta	nob-**van**-tab
100	cento	**chen**-toh
1,000	mille	**mee**-leh
2,000	duemila	**doo**-eh **mee**-lab
5,000	cinquemila	**ching**-kweh **mee**-lab
1,000,000	un milione	oon meel-**yob**-neh

Time

one minute	un minuto	oon mee-**noo**-toh
one hour	un'ora	oon **or**-ah
half an hour	mezz'ora	medz-**or**-ab
a day	un giorno	oon **jor**-noh
a week	una settimana	oona set-tee-**mah**-nah
Monday	lunedì	loo-neh-**dee**
Tuesday	martedì	mar-teh-**dee**
Wednesday	mercoledì	mair-koh-leb-**dee**
Thursday	giovedì	job-veh-**dee**
Friday	venerdì	ven-air-**dee**
Saturday	sabato	**sab**-bab-toh
Sunday	domenica	doh-**meb**-nee-kab